# DATE DUE

| | | |
|---|---|---|
| | | |
| | | |
| | | |
| | | |
| | | |
| | | |
| | | |
| | | |
| | | |
| | | |
| | | |
| | | |
| | | |
| | | |
| | | |
| | | |
| | | |
| | | |

## Humanism in Business Series

The Humanistic Management Network is an international, interdisciplinary, and independent network that promotes the development of an economic system with respect for human dignity and well-being.

The Humanistic Management Network defends human dignity in face of its vulnerability. The dignity of the human being lies in its capacity to define autonomously the purpose of its existence. Since human autonomy realizes itself through social cooperation, economic relations and business activities can either foster or obstruct human life and well-being. Against the widespread objectification of human subjects into human resources, against the common instrumentalization of human beings into human capital and a mere means for profit, we uphold humanity as the ultimate end and principle of all economic activity.

In business as well as in society, respect for human dignity demands respect for human freedom. Collective decision-making, in corporations just as in governments, should henceforth be based on free and equal deliberation, participation or representation of all affected parties. Concerns of legitimacy must, in economics as in politics, precede questions of expediency.

We believe that market economies hold substantial potential for human development in general. To promote life-conducive market activities, we want to complement the quantitative metrics which have hitherto defined managerial and economic success with qualitative evaluation criteria that focus on the human dignity of every woman and every man.

As researchers, we work towards a humanistic paradigm for business and economics, trying to identify and facilitate corporate and governmental efforts for the common good.

As a think tank, we set out to disseminate intellectual tools for culturally and ecologically sustainable business practices that have the human being as their focal point.

As teachers, we strive to educate, emancipate, and enable students to contribute actively to a life-conducive economy in which human dignity is universally respected.

As practitioners, we act towards the implementation of a humanistic economy on an individual, corporate, and governmental level.

As citizens, we engage our communities in discourse about the benefits of a human-centered economy.

*Titles include:*

Claus Dierksmeier, Wolfgang Amann, Ernst von Kimakowitz, Heiko Spitzeck, and Michael Pirson (*editors*)
HUMANISTIC ETHICS IN THE AGE OF GLOBALITY

Ernst von Kimakowitz, Michael Pirson, Heiko Spitzeck, Claus Dierksmeier, and Wolfgang Amann (*editors*)
HUMANISTIC MANAGEMENT IN PRACTICE

**Humanism in Business Series**
Series Standing Order ISBN 978–0–230–24633–1

You can receive future titles in this series as they are published by placing a standing order. Please contact your bookseller or, in case of difficulty, write to us at the address below with your name and address, the title of the series and the ISBN quoted above.

Customer Servics Department, Macmillan Distribution Ltd., Houndmills, Basingstoke, Hampshire RG21 6Xs, England.

# Humanistic Ethics in the Age of Globality

Edited by

**Claus Dierksmeier**
*Professor, Department of Business Administration,*
*Stonehill College, Boston, USA*

**Wolfgang Amann**
*Director of Executive Education, Goethe Business School,*
*University of Frankfurt, Germany*

**Ernst von Kimakowitz**
*Independent Professional*

**Heiko Spitzeck**
*Professor, Fundação Dom Cabral, Brazil*

and

**Michael Pirson**
*Assistant Professor, Graduate School of Business,*
*Fordham University, New York, USA*

## palgrave
macmillan

First published 2011 by
PALGRAVE MACMILLAN

Palgrave Macmillan in the UK is an imprint of Macmillan Publishers Limited, registered in England, company number 785998, of Houndmills, Basingstoke, Hampshire RG21 6XS.

Palgrave Macmillan in the US is a division of St Martin's Press LLC, 175 Fifth Avenue, New York, NY 10010.

Palgrave Macmillan is the global academic imprint of the above companies and has companies and representatives throughout the world.

Palgrave® and Macmillan® are registered trademarks in the United States, the United Kingdom, Europe and other countries.

ISBN: 978–0–230–27327–6 hardback

This book is printed on paper suitable for recycling and made from fully managed and sustained forest sources. Logging, pulping and manufacturing processes are expected to conform to the environmental regulations of the country of origin.

A catalogue record for this book is available from the British Library.

Library of Congress Cataloging-in-Publication Data
  Humanistic ethics in the age of globality / edited by
  Claus Dierksmeier... [et al.].
    p. cm.
  Includes bibliographical references and index.
  ISBN 978–0–230–27327–6 (alk. paper)
    1. Business ethics. 2. Globalization – Moral and ethical aspects.
  3. Humanistic ethics. I. Dierksmeier, Claus.

HF5387.H8613 2011
174—dc22                                                    2011011875

10  9  8  7  6  5  4  3  2  1
20  19  18  17  16  15  14  13  12  11

Printed and bound in the United States of America

# Contents

# Acknowledgments

First and foremost, we wish to thank our authors. They have endured much: a competitive selection process and lengthy review procedures, involving all together three different rounds of feedback. We wanted to ensure that our book was not just another anthology with a motley collection of articles on the current state of globalization ethics but that, instead, the chapters in this book would form a coherent argument. While we have to leave the ultimate judgment about the success of this project to our readers, in our view, our persuasion succeeded. We are very grateful that all our authors supported our endeavor to produce a formally and materially consistent text, and promptly attended to our repeated prodding for revisions.

Also we wish to say thank you to the many supporters of the Humanistic Management Network who, through their intellectual and logistical support, not only facilitate our work and leverage our impact but also inspire us to further our efforts to promote a more humane economic and social order for all. We welcome each and every offer of support, however small, that we receive via our website or through our Facebook group. We are especially grateful to the University of Regensburg, Germany, for hosting – and to the Helga-und-Erwin-Hartl Stiftung for funding – the conference that initiated our work on this volume. We also wish to thank Laura Melkonian and Kristyn Kelley, as well as the editorial team at Palgrave Macmillan, for their great help in editing this volume. Last but certainly not least, we would like to thank our readers for accompanying us on our intellectual journey towards a more humane ethical paradigm for the world we inhabit together.

# Contributors

**Wolfgang Amann** graduated from Harvard's Institute for Management and Learning in Higher Education. He honed his research skills at the Wharton School in Philadelphia and his executive education skills at IMD in Lausanne. As a professor of strategy, he previously directed the Henley Center for Creative Destruction as well as the Henley Center of Excellence in Case Writing. He has also been Vice-Director of the Executive School at the University of St. Gallen and a visiting professor in the field of international strategy and sustainability at Hosei University in Tokyo, Tsinghua University in Beijing, the Indian Institute of Management in Bangalore, ISP St. Petersburg, Warwick Business School and Henley Business School in the UK. He now serves as the Director of Executive Education at the Goethe Business School of the University of Frankfurt, where he delivers seminars and courses on a variety of general management topics.

**Michael Buckley** is Assistant Professor of Philosophy at the City University of New York, Lehman College. His main research areas include political philosophy, ethics, and applied ethics, with a current focus on global justice and business ethics. He also serves on the board of an international nonprofit education institute, Global Majority, which promotes nonviolent conflict resolution through negotiation and mediation training. Prior to joining the faculty at Lehman College, Buckley worked as an investment and media analyst, coauthoring several books and many articles on the economics of broadcast media in the United States. His recent publications focus on the issues of justification and objectivity in political philosophy. He was awarded his Ph.D. from Emory University in 2006.

**Anthony Celano** is Professor of Philosophy at Stonehill College, Boston. He is a coeditor of Thomas Aquinas' *De divinis nominibus* for the Leonine Commission, Rome, and author of *From Priam to the Good Thief: The Significance of a Single Act in Greek Ethics and Medieval Moral Teaching,* The Etienne Gilson Series, 22, and Studies in Medieval Moral Teaching, 3 (2000), and articles on ancient and medieval moral theory. His current work includes the chapter on the thirteenth century in *The Reception of Aristotle's Nicomachean Ethics* (edited by J. Miller, forthcoming), and a study of the meaning of practical wisdom in ancient and medieval authors.

**Claus Dierksmeier** is Professor for Globalization Ethics and Economic Philosophy in the Department of Business Administration at Stonehill College, Boston. His major book publications are the following: *Der absolute Grund des Rechts: Karl Christian Friedrich Krause in Auseinandersetzung mit Fichte und Schelling* (Stuttgart-Bad Cannstatt, 2003); *Rechts- und Staatsphilosophie – Ein dogmenphilosophischer Dialog* (Gröschner, Rolf/Dierksmeier, Claus/Henkel, Michael/Wiehart, Alexander, 2000); *Das Noumenon Religion – Eine Untersuchung zur Stellung der Religion im System der praktischen Philosophie Kants* (Kant-Studien-Ergänzungshefte Nr. 133, 1998). His current research focuses on the role of freedom in business and economic theory, and on the ethics of globalization. Claus is also working as a consultant and academic adviser on questions of corporate social responsibility and serves on the Managing Board of the Humanistic Management Network.

**Richard Fincham** is Assistant Professor of Philosophy at the American University in Cairo, Egypt. He received his Ph.D. from the University of Warwick in 2004 with a dissertation on the concept of "transcendental subjectivity" within the work of Kant, Fichte, Schelling, and Schopenhauer. He was also a DAAD Stipendiat at the Ludwig-Maximilians-Universität, Munich, in 2000–01. Prior to joining AUC he taught philosophy at both the University of Greenwich and the University of Warwick. He is the author of various articles on Kant, German Idealism and German Romanticism. At present he is working on a monograph on Schelling's philosophy of nature.

**Maximilian Forschner** received his philosophical Ph.D. and Habilitation in Germany. He then became Professor of Philosophy at the Universities of Osnabrück and Erlangen-Nürnberg. His most important books are *Gesetz und Freiheit: Zum Problem der Autonomie bei Immanuel Kant* (1974); *J.-J. Rousseau* (1977); *Die stoische Ethik* (1981, 1995); *Mensch und Gesellschaft* (1989); *Über das Glück des Menschen* (1st edition 1993, 2nd edition Aufl. 1994); *Über das Handeln im Einklang mit der Natur* (1998); and *Thomas von Aquin* (2006). His research focus is on the practical philosophy of antiquity, the Middle Ages, and the enlightenment.

**Julian Friedland** is Assistant Professor at Fordham Graduate School Business in New York. Previously, he taught philosophy and business ethics for over a decade, primarily at the University of Colorado, Boulder. He is half French, obtaining his Ph.D. in philosophy at the University of Paris, where he studied the nature of meaning and value from a Wittgensteinian perspective. Since then, he has specialized in ethics, primarily as applied to business. His current research seeks to restore the ethical a priori to the field of management. He has published widely in ethics and philosophy and maintains a business ethics blog.

**Benedetta Giovanola** is Assistant Professor at the University of Macerata, Italy. She is the recipient of the Helen Potter Award (2005), awarded by the ASE (Association for Social Economics, USA) for her paper "Personhood and Human Richness. Good and Well-Being in the Capability Approach and Beyond" (*Review of Social Economy*, vol. 63, no. 2/2005). Her major publications are the following: "Re-thinking the Anthropological and Ethical Foundation of Economics and Business: Human Richness and Capabilities Enhancement" (*Journal of Business Ethics*, n. 3/2009); *Critica dell'uomo unilaterale. La ricchezza antropologica in K. Marx e F. Nietzsche* (2007), and (with F. Totaro) *Etica ed economia: il rapporto possibile* (2008). Her current research mainly focuses on the anthropological and ethical foundation of business and economics, the redefinition of the notion of economic rationality, and the relationship between development and social justice.

**Ernst von Kimakowitz** holds an M.Sc. from the London School of Economics and an award-winning Ph.D. from the University of St. Gallen, Switzerland, where he is a guest lecturer. Following several years in the strategy practice of a large management consulting firm, he now works as an independent professional, providing consulting, advisory, and executive coaching services in the corporate responsibility arena to both private and public sector clients. Ernst also serves on the Managing Board of the Humanistic Management Network.

**Ulrike Kirchengast** is a Ph.D. student at the Department of Philosophy, University of Graz, Austria. She is working on a dissertation on virtue ethics. Her academic background, apart from philosophy, includes linguistics and languages. In addition to her university studies she has obtained qualifications in economics with a focus on accountancy. Her research interests are primarily moral theory, practical ethics, and moral psychology.

**Monika Kirloskar-Steinbach** is Professor of Philosophy at the University of Konstanz, Germany. After studying in Mumbai, India, she received her Ph.D. in 2001 from the University of Konstanz with a dissertation on liberalism, secularism, and fundamentalism in India. She received her Habilitation from the same university in 2005 with a work on the ethics of immigration, in which several strands of her foci on social and political philosophy can be found. In her research she also concentrates on a philosophical analysis of problems generated by interculturality. She is currently involved in developing theories for an intercultural grounding of human rights.

**Kai Kresse**, an anthropologist, philosopher, and Africanist by training, is Vice-Director for Research at the Zentrum Moderner Orient (ZMO) in Berlin, an interdisciplinary research center on Africa, South Asia, and the Middle East. He was Lecturer in Social Anthropology at the University of St. Andrews, and Evans-Pritchard Lecturer at All Souls College, Oxford, in 2005. His research interests include African philosophy, philosophical anthropology, Islam, and the anthropological study of knowledge; his regional expertise covers East Africa and the Swahili coast. His publications include *Philosophising in Mombasa* (2007), *Struggling with History*, coedited with Edward Simpson (2007), and *Knowledge in Practice*, coedited with Trevor Marchand (2009). He is a coeditor of *Polylog: Online Journal for Intercultural Philosophy* (www.polylog.org).

**Suzan Langenberg** works as Senior Advisor in Belgium and the Netherlands. She is Founder and Director of Diversity bvba, a profit-oriented organization focused on the improvement of communicative processes in organizations. Langenberg studied history, philosophy of human sciences, and completed two contract studies in sexology and developmental psychopathology at the University of Amsterdam. In 2008 she completed her Ph.D. (Criticism as De-organization. Business Ethics and Free Speech) at Radboud University Nijmegen, Netherlands. Her main interest is the organizational position of communication and critique related to ethical business problems. She is a founding member of the Institute of Business Ethics Belgium (INBE) and founding member of Campus Gelbergen, an independent institute in Belgium that organizes courses on socially relevant topics.

**Ioanna Patsioti-Tsacpounidis** is Professor of Philosophy at the American College of Greece (ACG), where she currently serves as Department Head. She teaches philosophy courses with an emphasis on Greek philosophy, social and political philosophy, ethics, and business ethics. Before that, she taught Greek philosophy at University College London, UK, and the Open University, UK. She is a graduate of the University of Athens and UCL, London, where she earned a postgraduate diploma in Linguistics and an M.Phil. in Classics. She was awarded a Ph.D. by the Philosophy School at the University of Athens with a dissertation on Aristotle's moral epistemology. She is the author of many articles on Aristotelian philosophy and has published articles and a book on the applicability of Aristotle's ethics in the domain of business. Her current research includes the moral concepts of post-Aristotelian scholars as well as of Plato's later Academy and their relevance in business ethics and contemporary society at large.

**Michael Pirson** is Assistant Professor at Fordham Graduate School of Business in New York, as well as a research fellow and lecturer at the Harvard University. Before receiving his Ph.D., Pirson worked in international management consulting for several years. He also gained experience in the political arena while working on Hillary Clinton's Senate campaign. Michael currently serves on the board of three social enterprises, and on the Managing Board of the Humanistic Management Network.

**Heiko Spitzeck** is Professor at Fundação Dom Cabral in Brazil. His main interest is in organizational learning in terms of corporate responsibility and sustainability. His publications have appeared in numerous international journals as well as in several books published among others by Cambridge University Press. In 2010 he lectured at INSPER in Sao Paulo, Brazil. From 2008 to 2010 he was lecturer at Cranfield University's Doughty Centre for Corporate Responsibility in the UK. Between 2004 and 2006 he served as Director for oikos International, a student-driven NGO for sustainable management and economics. Spitzeck was invited to give guest lectures in Austria, Bangladesh, Brazil, Germany, Mexico, Spain, Switzerland, the United Kingdom, and the United States. He also held visiting positions at the University of California at Berkeley, Fordham University in New York as well as the University of Extremadura, Spain. Heiko was educated in Germany, Spain, and Switzerland. He received his Ph.D. from the University of St. Gallen, Switzerland.

**Ulrich Steinvorth** is Professor of Philosophy at the University of Hamburg, Germanyand and at Bilkent University Ankara, Turkey. He has taught at several universities in Germany, France, England, and the United States. He received his Ph.D. from the University of Göttingen with a thesis on Wittgenstein, and his Habilitation at the University of Mannheim with a thesis on Marx. Steinvorth has published books and articles in political philosophy, ethics, applied ethics, and metaphysics, in German, French, and English. His last book publication was *Rethinking the Western Understanding of the Self* (2009).

# Introduction

*Claus Dierksmeier, Wolfgang Amann, Ernst von Kimakowitz, Heiko Spitzeck, and Michael Pirson*

## The age of globality

Globalization was yesterday (Dasgupta and Kiely, 2006). Today we are increasingly facing a world of "globality," that is, a state of affairs where a global impact of individual actions, local business practices, and national politics is no longer the exception but has become more and more the rule (Carver and Bartelson, 2010). While numerous processes of globalization might still be stopped, and some reversed, the general trend of the developments of the last decades cannot be undone. The reach that globalization, especially economic globalization, has had in the past means that ever more people are faced with living in a state of *de facto* globality (Sklair, 1991). Whatever the future development of globalization, this emerging state of globality must be addressed, because its distinctive features require particular ways and modes of governance beyond those that characterized the era of the nation state. The search for adequate ethical norms for the state of globality has begun, and we hope our book will make a meaningful contribution to this quest.

While it is true that both global trade and cultural exchange have existed for centuries (Stearns, 2010), there are important differences between now and the past (MacGillivray, 2006). Today, an ever larger percentage of humanity is engaged in effortless global communication, building out a global imagination (around globalized brands and aesthetic idols) and a global awareness (crystallizing around certain geopolitical events and symbols). One could see in this merely the result of a hitherto unavailable level of technology. Yet this would overlook the fact that present technology is just a reflection of past economic and social incentives.

In fact, human history was not, and is not, determined by technology. Rather, the organization of any particular society may, or may not, prove conducive to the development and spread of certain technologies. Differences in how, across historical time and cultural space, humanity has chosen to organize labor and property, how to regulate business and how to conduct politics, for example, are often much more significant for the present diffusion of particular technologies and their concomitant ways of life than the mere availability of specific technological devices. For an understanding of our global life-world, therefore, the factual organization and normative orientation of societies deserve our close attention.

In today's world we observe a growing awareness – ranging from the debate over climate change to ever more areas of our life-world – that we have only one planet and that there are always more consequences to our actions than we can foresee (Beck, 1992). In short, the signature we leave on the planet today will be decipherable only in the future, while we are accountable for it already. The more, however, the range of our actions outstrips the reach of our knowledge, and the more strongly the practical effects of our practices belie our theoretical prognoses, the less we can trust the conventional way of looking "inside-out" at global affairs, accessing globalization from a purely local or national angle (McLuhan and Powers, 1989). Wherever it is the whole that has determining force, focusing solely on the parts produces not only incomplete but biased results (Hartmann, 1950). It is not incidental that the isolated query as to what globalization means to this or that regional community, has time and again proven unable to answer its own question. Suggesting that the facts and factors of globalization can be captured in theory and contained in practice from an Archimedean point somewhere on the surface of the earth, is to misunderstand that the ongoing global transformations owe their power precisely to the fact that they operate without such fixed reference points. The enormous leverage of globalized developments stems from the ubiquity of their manifestations, which renders them into a force that is both elusive and inescapable (Roniger and Waisman, 2002).

Whereas the semantics of the term "globalization" suggest viewing the ongoing processes of growing interdependencies from a perspective that begins with the parts, and ends with the whole, the idea of "globality" points to a contrasting, holistic, worldview. While in the past only a few idealistic philosophers such as Immanuel Kant (1724–1804) and Karl Christian Friedrich Krause (1781–1832) dared to propose, as a moral imperative, that we should act as if the whole world was affected by our actions, and as if the whole of humanity was to judge our conduct (Dierksmeier, 2003), it becomes apparent now that to push farther and farther away the spatial and temporal limits of the considered effects and externalities of our actions is a pragmatic necessity for socioeconomic survival. Regardless of whether the ongoing processes of globalization will slow down in the future, what will remain is this deep, fundamental shift to a mental model that encompasses the unarticulated, incalculable, and indefinite consequences of our actions just as much as those that are captured by our established accounting practices and our traditional schemes of responsibility assignment (Jonas, 1984). Globality represents the insight that we have reached a position in history where the angle of moral universalization and the pragmatic perspective of prudent circumspection render almost identical results (Elliott, 2005). Whatever governance systems we propose for the future, they must take into account the changed premises on which they rest. Political as well as economic legitimacy, less and less tied to geographical boundaries, will increasingly have to be earned in view of and in response to the interests of the whole of humanity (Brock, 2009).

On one hand, then, globality is simply a new label for the emerging *reality* of a world characterized by the planetary impact and the wholesale interconnectivity of human actions (Sirkin et al., 2008). On the other hand, globality denotes an intellectual *paradigm* that tries to address this impending state of affairs through a comprehensive, all-encompassing perspective. In the past, when the everyday life of ordinary people did not offer frequent experiences of a shared human destiny, the intellectual perspective of globality was already known and employed. Throughout the long history of philosophy, forward-looking thinkers of all centuries used a cosmopolitan frame of reference in order to address the common nature and needs of human life (Benhabib et al., 2006). In this volume, we intend to learn from such earlier attempts to conceptualize a global ethics of humanity, in order to contribute to a future ethics for business and society.

As a first step into this constructive direction, however, we need to ask how to make an inter-personally and inter-culturally valid use of ethical ideas. In the present age of globality, the multicultural premises of our social life demand academic theories that are capable of meeting *postmodern* and *relativistic challenges* to ethical rationales. How can this demand be answered? In 1948, the UN issued the *Universal Declaration of Human Rights*, based on a comprehensive consensus of peoples all over the globe on the essentials of all future human legal relations. According to its preamble, the rights it enshrines are anchored in the "recognition of the inherent dignity" of the human being. While itself not a legally binding declaration, most of its articles found equivalent articulation in the *International Covenant on Civil and Political Rights*, which since 1976 has represented a legal obligation for the signatory nations. In specific articles, the international community spells out in great detail what it deems to be both essential and universal human rights, again expressly "recognizing that these rights derive from the inherent dignity of the human person." The implicit assumption of these explicit acknowledgments is, in short, that there can be and, in fact, that there is, a global consensus about the nature of human dignity, irrespective of otherwise diverging cultural and religious backgrounds.

This codified *global* consensus on human dignity notwithstanding, its philosophical foundations have typically been constructed from the tradition of *Western* philosophy. While notions of human dignity also operate in African and Asian philosophies and religions, the Western philosophical tradition, today as well as at the time when the *Declaration of Human Rights* was formulated, stands out as the leading voice in the discourse. To some, such a degree of predominance of one cultural tradition may seem to discredit from the outset the effort of establishing globally acceptable norms. How, so the argument goes, can regional values justify universal postulates? Why should the philosophy of the West dominate the rest? Do we not thus betray in procedure what we affirm in substance: a global approach to ethics?

Such views, however, confuse the "genesis" and the "validity" of arguments. Whereas, admittedly, the past and present debate over human dignity has been heavily influenced by Western sources, this does not necessarily restrict their global validity. Rather, in appealing to human reason in general, philosophical positions from all parts of the world today aim for interpersonal plausibility across all cultural boundaries. One can reject the underlying idea that, underneath, there is *one* human reason operative in all human beings. Yet this rejection itself makes a claim for its own description of the nature of (a culturally fractured) human reason. The ensuing debate which conception of rationality – pro or contra the unity of human reason – merits our eventual approval again takes place before the court of human reason. Either party may fail to support its claims with convincing arguments, yet this can only be assessed *after* a critical examination of the theory at hand, which in turn appeals to the self-critical potentials of human rationality.

There is, in short, no way to decide the debate about the cultural relativity of rational standards other than through the universal employment of the very capacities of critical human reasoning whose universal character the relativists staunchly deny. Ethical relativists, to avoid self-contradiction, can defend their position only by refraining from claiming universal validity for their own arguments. For that reason, however, nothing compels anyone else to follow the relativistic train of thought, and we might as well continue in allegiance to more comprehensive conceptions of rationality.

In view of today's global problems, this outcome must count heavily against a relativistic perspective. Global problems, more often than not, require for their solutions global institutions and worldwide normative agreements. The burden of proof therefore lies much more with positions that reject cosmopolitan perspectives than with those who try to tackle the common problems of humankind from a single global perspective. Moreover, since only some – not all, nor even most – non-Western philosophers reject universal principles, ethical relativism also does injustice to non-Western thinkers who explicitly wish to be part of the cosmopolitan project. Thinkers in non-Western countries who argue against certain (restrictive) values of their own region and in favor of (more emancipating) global principles ought be taken seriously (Sen, 2006). Their dissenting voices can be seen as a *de facto* contradiction to the assumption that different contexts necessarily breed differing views. Sometimes, the exact same understanding of human rights, freedom, and dignity is being advanced from disparate cultural origins. We must therefore not allow ethical relativism to irresponsibly silence foreign advocates of the idea of human dignity by unthinkingly subsuming their positions under one-dimensional cultural stereotypes. Worse than the imperialistic imposition of rights that protect human dignity is surely a relativistic acquiescence in their violent denial.

Since Western philosophy has always aimed to speak to all human beings, and has done so in a continuous discourse from Plato until today, we would do better not to focus on the limited geographical and cultural confines of its origins but rather on the unlimited scope of the ideas it tries to promulgate. The answers of Western philosophers to questions about the nature and meaning of human dignity need not, of course, be worshiped uncritically as the ultimate achievements of human wisdom, but they should be seen as important stepping stones to a global debate about the dignity of human life for all inhabitants of this planet. The *procedural* character of this qualified endorsement of Western postulates about human dignity is all-important; it demands the integration of everyone in their making (Carver and Bartelson, 2010).

Such participation, in fact, serves not only as a normative touchstone but also as a pragmatic yardstick for contemporary decision-making in business and society. Both the validity and the success of complex interactions hinge ever more on the participation of all stakeholders. Discourses in the political and in the economic sphere are not, incidentally, parallel in that respect: More and better stakeholder democracy seems to be required for the improvement of organizational behavior in the public realm as well as in the domains of business (Ellerman, 1992). It is not enough to proclaim the idea of human rights and the collective destiny of humanity. It is also necessary to translate such ideas into sustainable procedures of collective action and decision-making that assure the active participation and, if that is impossible, at least the passive representation of all concerned.

We, the editors of the *Humanistic Management Network* (more on our network below) see an increasing need for intercultural cooperation on all social and societal levels, and for ethical norms to support that cooperation. In accordance with the philosophy behind the United Nations' *Global Compact*, we set out from the basic assumption that global problems demand global solutions that, more often than not, need to rest on global institutions that in turn require at least some globally shared norms in order to function. Yet while the need for global norms based on shared global problems is rarely questioned in the abstract, concrete global consensus around normative questions is rare. In consequence, absent further convergence in moral judgment, the global problems of humanity will not be tackled in a satisfactory manner and increased frictions will hamper global cooperation. In order to find a common ground of shared moral understandings between individuals as well as collectives (associations, corporations, governments, non-governmental actors) from all regions of the world and formulate valid ethical arguments with global appeal, we undertook the investigation of the moral philosophies of the past, looking for the contributions they might make to the present challenges of globality. About two years ago, we sent out a global call for papers and organized an international conference at the University of Regensburg, Germany, and have selected some of the papers presented there for this volume. What you hold in your hands is the result of the collective effort of many scholars from many countries. We cannot pretend to offer a single answer to the ethical conundrums that present themselves in the age of globality, but we do find enough consensus between the authors featured here to warrant our hope that ethical solutions to the problems of humanity can be found and furthered by way of reasoned argument.

## Learning from past actions

The past decades have proven the obvious – that simple self-interest is too narrow a basis for the kind of sustained and providential international cooperation our planet requires. In the last decades, the West has tried to globalize the rest of the world, promoting its regional values unabashedly as universals (Scruton, 2003). This "globalization project" has created more resentment than agreement, instilling a profound skepticism towards any attempt at global normative approaches (Comor, 2008). Yet, while rejecting imperialistic approaches to ethics, let us not too hastily declare all moral universalism passé. The international and intercultural cooperation that we so much need cannot, after all, succeed without at least some very basic shared understandings of the world that do not arise automatically from the mere fact that we all inhabit the same planet. Responsibility towards humanity and future generations frequently requires us to form shared understandings on how to govern the planet together, painstakingly aligning different intellectual horizons and diverging convictions. The imminent fact of "globality-without-agreement" demands that we seek the unanimity needed for worldwide cooperation; not, as before, in "identity-through-sameness" but rather in "identity-as-consonant-diversity." Whether we use "mondialization" or some other postmodern epithet to denote such processes of coming together through the convergence of many different lines of thought, is secondary (Durand, 2008). Of prime significance is that any future attempt to address global concerns steers clear from imposing a one-size-fits-all approach (Gould, 2004). Whereas globalization has, in the past, indeed often been a one-way street of cultural expansion, what globality truly demands is a multi-dimensional process of reciprocal integration, informed by the constantly changing self-understandings of the manifold cultures that comprise the human family.

Not only, nor even primarily, for lack of a united global legislative and executive, the necessary regulation of our global commons must be generated by the soft power of consensus, leading the diverse forces of business, civil society, and the public sector in joint efforts. The global governance our planet needs is premised negatively on circumspect self-restraint by all parties and persons involved, and positively on their cooperative alignment. Yet without agreement on some moral principles that would permit the formulation of elementary codes of conduct, the prospects for the collective endeavors of humanity remain dim (Kitagawa et al., 2004). While there are attempts to elaborate a global code of conduct from the consensus of world religions and faith communities with respect to central moral strictures (Küng and Kuschel, 1993), an enormous difficulty for any such endeavor arises from the fact that – with the possible exception of the Golden Rule – almost none of the traditional values offered by religions and customary ethics are wholly uncontroversial or strictly universally accepted. With every advance of globalization came a reduction in the power and effectiveness of traditional customs and religions to regulate the practices of business (Schmidt, 2006). If we are neither capable of reversing this process, nor prepared to accept that values presumed as universal should be imposed on dissenters by force, how then are we to react to the fact that conventional values no longer generate comprehensive consent and compliance?

## Learning from past thinkers

How does one arrive at a formulation of moral principles that will recommend themselves to people from all the vastly different cultural traditions the Earth has to offer? We decided to investigate inter-culturally valid arguments within the rich tradition of philosophical ethics that recommends itself through the "non-coercive coercion of the better argument" (Habermas, 1984, p. 95). What resulted from our decidedly international and broadly disseminated *Call for Papers* was, however, an anthology that comprises mostly European thinkers. While our volume does also contain examples of intercultural philosophizing in Africa and Asia (see the section NON-WESTERN AND NON-TRADITIONAL APPROACHES), we anticipate the objection that our selection still has a decidedly "Western" outlook – whatever that may mean exactly. Rejecting the view that non-Western cultures have been largely unable or unwilling to shape ethical thought-systems with sufficient clarity, consistence, or rigor to merit the appellation "philosophical," how do we explain the predominance of Western thinkers in our anthology? We think that the past political and economic domination of other cultures by the West must be factored in. In many formerly colonized regions, autochthonous traditions of philosophizing were deliberately thwarted – documents destroyed, native languages suppressed, ways and institutions of traditional education discouraged – with the result that few written records of pre-colonial philosophy survive in Africa or South America (Wallner et al., 2010), whereas in Asia and Europe written records are ample and allow us much easier access to the minds of past generations.

The predominance of European thinkers must, however, not necessarily be detrimental to a project with global aspirations. For even though the *genesis* of rationales lies, as a rule, in the particular cultural and religious background in which they are formulated, if their content proves, in fact, to be universally intelligible, this does not in any way undermine their global *validity* (Habermas, 1996). As much as it is true that human beings everywhere need agreed-upon norms in order to live and cooperate well, it may prove to be true that certain values and norms facilitate common endeavors better than others (Rescher, 1993). While the contexts and conventions as well as the laws and religions of peoples change over time and across cultures, at their center remains the single human being. To maintain this simple fact does not amount to ascribing to humanity a single and permanent nature that could simply be used as a prescriptive blueprint for ethical questions (Plessner, 1983). Neither pragmatically (in view of how human life is altered and affected by its societal setting), nor logically (the "naturalistic fallacy"), does such reasoning seem sound (Moore, 1903). On the contrary, it seems to be essential to human life to articulate itself in diverse ways and through distinct cultures, not infrequently in deliberate opposition to what is deemed the natural norm of the human form. Yet whereas the specific outlook of the many human cultures is always and everywhere in flux, what remains permanent about human life is that it takes place within and through symbolic forms (Cassirer, 1953). Culture, in brief, is part and parcel of human nature, and insofar as culture requires morals to function and all moral systems need to be buttressed as well as corrected by critical ethical thinking, the practice of reasonable ethical deliberation can very well be claimed to be a human universal.

Especially in today's rapidly changing, multicultural contexts – we hypothesized – ethical positions centering on the perceived nature and declared needs of the human being might not only offer valuable guidance, here and now, but also be able to acquire intercultural approval and importance. Our authors were therefore asked to examine their respective intellectual sources for arguments which could be used to address current concerns of humanity in the era of globality. By and large, our working hypothesis has been corroborated. While, of course, the texts of bygone eras rarely offer ready-made solutions to problems of the present, a re-reading of our intellectual traditions, inspired by these problems, nevertheless often proves fruitful. Our present troubles help us to spot the productive potentials of past cultural constellations, and seemingly superannuated intellectual frameworks can help start innovation within the very intellectual fields where contemporary reasoning stagnates.

In a way, our current state of mind operates like a lens through which some objects are seen clearly, while others appear obfuscated, or wholly out of focus. Changing the perspective by moving our intellectual focus through time and space alters the ambit of acuity and brings before our eyes the (otherwise overlooked) limits of our everyday mindset. For this reason, stepping back in time can be a way of moving forward (Lowry 1987, p. 7). Moreover, the examination of past debates and disputes benefits from the advantages of aggregated knowledge from various sources. Just as the use of slow-motion videos and multi-angle perspectives in sports photography provides insights unavailable to the athletes during their activities, the study of intellectual history allows comprehensive perspectives unseen by the actors involved. So, if we want to learn for the future, a look beyond the present, into the stores of learning offered by a long history of past trials and tribulations, recommends itself. Our research into the intellectual pedigree of present-day humanistic ethics is no exception.

## Structure of the book

We begin our portrait of the philosophical past with representatives from antiquity and the Middle Ages (in the section on PRE-MODERN THEORIES). Our authors demonstrate how metaphysical concepts of the human being as essentially oriented to moral goodness (Socrates, Plato) and to social cooperation led to early pledges for temperance and moderation in the use of worldly goods (Aristotle) as well as to demands for a cosmopolitan perspective in ethics (in the philosophy of the Stoa) and, ultimately, to a call for social justice in all economic transactions (Thomas Aquinas). From around 400 BCE until the late seventeenth century the prevailing sentiment was that individual self-interest should be curbed by and subordinated to the common good. Government was seen as a facilitator and protector of a decent way of life, and the purpose of business was defined accordingly: to provide the goods required for a civic existence aimed at social harmony.

Modern thinkers (see the section MODERN POSITIONS), however, no longer operate from a fixed conception of human nature and its inherent purposes, but have shifted their emphasis onto the freedom of each individual to remake himself in the light of his own ideas. From the premise of that freedom certain conclusions follow, such as unconditional respect for the dignity of others (Kant), regard for the sociocultural preconditions of autonomous life (Hegel), concern for the material conditions of human flourishing (Mill) and a critique of the economic forces that, if unchecked, restrict and pervert individual freedom (Marx).

Again, an overarching agreement can be discerned. The classics of modern socioeconomic thinking evaluate the success of economic enterprises and political structures within the parameter of individual and collective gains in autonomy. In contrast to various schools of thought that reduce the assessment of human welfare to the measurement of material utilities, the philosophers presented here agree that the *quantitative* dimension must itself be subjected to ultimately *qualitative* judgments in terms of human liberty. For material growth does not always signify a gain in freedom; at times, it can represent its corruption.

Hereafter (in the section on CONTEMPORARY PHILOSOPHY) we turn to authors from the present era. Philosophers of the twentieth and twenty-first century ponder enquire one can motivate people to ethical actions when their personal interests are not obviously involved (Wittgenstein), how to integrate the differing orientations of virtue (Solomon) and care for human capabilities (Sen/Nussbaum) in societal settings, where institutional power influences public opinion and impacts the ethical discourse (Habermas).

Notwithstanding the conceptual and intentional variety of these positions, a common denominator can be found. The modern interest in personal liberation continues in postmodern configurations, albeit in disguise. The interest in freedom presents itself indirectly, through a critique of the conditions that hinder the direct realization of freedom through forms of public deliberation. The philosophers whose works are discussed in this chapter are concerned with overlooked asymmetries, hidden premises, and unseen consequences of the prevailing modes of thought that, contrary to their proclaimed intentions, often impede advances towards true emancipation. Thus our authors pierce the veil of "manufactured consent" (Herman and Chomsky, 1988) which obscures the unintended realizations and the unrealized intentions of economic and political systems ostensibly oriented towards the idea of freedom; they emphasize the interests of the victims of the current state of affairs and point to the loss of human dignity endemic in societies that reduce the meaning of personal liberty to mere consumer choices.

Last but not least, we look (in the section on NON-WESTERN AND NON-TRADITIONAL APPROACHES) for parallels to the arguments found in the Western tradition in the philosophical traditions of Asia and Africa. While in part differing radically from traditional Western philosophy, even questioning its foundation on theories of rationality, these contributions show that the quest for norms with appeal and validity for all human beings is relevant to Non-Western cultures as well. With arguments that both in their general intention and frequently also in their particular form strongly resemble thought patterns common in the European tradition, the thought-systems investigated by our authors appear to aim at convergent goals: a formulation of the collective interests and values of humanity, based upon the power of dialectical reasoning and noncoercive argument. From this overlapping philosophical consensus from different times and cultures, we, the editors, finally draw our own conclusions about our initial question about the conceptual preconditions and central tenets of a humanistic ethics in the age of globality.

## About us: The Humanistic Management Network

The *Humanistic Management Network* is an international, interdisciplinary, and nonprofit network that promotes the development of an economic system in the service of human dignity and well-being. Since human autonomy realizes itself through social cooperation, economic relations and business activities can foster or obstruct human life and well-being. Against the widespread objectification of human subjects as human capital, against the instrumentalization of human beings as human resources, against the destructive exploitation of our cultural and natural environments as mere means for profit, we uphold humanity as the ultimate end and principle of all economic activities. The dignity of the human being lies, we hold, in its capacity to define autonomously the purpose of its existence. In business as well as in society, respect for human dignity demands respect for human freedom. Collective decision-making, in corporations just as in governments, should be based on free and equal deliberation, participation, or representation of all affected parties. Concerns of legitimacy must, in economics as in politics, precede questions of expediency. Thus the *Humanistic Management Network* criticizes the purely quantitative metrics which have hitherto defined managerial and economic success, promoting instead qualitative economic criteria that focus on the human dignity of every woman and every man. In short, the *Humanistic Management Network* defends human dignity in face of its socioeconomic vulnerability.

These are our main activities: *As researchers,* we work towards a humanistic paradigm for business and economics, trying to identify and facilitate corporate and governmental efforts for the common good. *As a think tank,* we set out to spread intellectual tools for culturally and ecologically sustainable business practices that have the human being as their focal point. *As teachers*, we strive to educate, emancipate, and enable students to contribute actively to a life-conducive economy in which human dignity is universally respected. *As practitioners*, we act towards the implementation of a humanistic economy on an individual, corporate, and governmental level. *As citizens*, we try to engage our communities in discourse about the benefits of a human-centered economy.

The *Humanistic Management Network* has already produced three publications in book form. The first, *Humanism in Business*, looks at how humanism can contribute to management theory and practice on a system, organizational, and personal level (Cambridge University Press, 2009). In our second volume, *Humanistic Management in Practice* (Palgrave Macmillan, 2010) we are providing case-studies on how humanistic principles can be integrated into managerial practice so that businesses can emancipate themselves from a single focus on (short-term) profit maximization, whilst remaining competitive players in a market environment. Our third book is dedicated to a humanistic reform of management education *Business Schools Under Fire – Humanistic Management Education As the Way Forward* (Palgrave Macmillan, 2011). Further volumes on related subjects will follow soon. (For more information on our work, please consult our website: www.humanetwork.org/.)

## Bibliography

Beck, U., *Risk Society: Towards a New Modernity*, (London; Newbury Park, Calif.: Sage Publications, 1992).

Benhabib, S., Waldron, J., Honig, B., Kymlicka, W., and Post, R. *Another Cosmopolitanism*, (Oxford; New York: Oxford University Press, 2006).

Brock, G., *Global Justice: A Cosmopolitan Account*, (Oxford; New York: Oxford University Press, 2009).

Carver, T. and Bartelson, J. (2010). *Globality, Democracy, and Civil Society*, (Milton Park, Abingdon, Oxon, England; New York: Routledge).

Cassirer, E., *The Philosophy of Symbolic Forms*, (New Haven: Yale University Press, 1953).

Comor, E. A., *Consumption and the Globalization Project: International Hegemony and the Annihilation of Time*, (Basingstoke England; New York: Palgrave Macmillan, 2008).

Dasgupta, S. and Kiely, R., *Globalization and After*, (New Delhi; Thousand Oaks, Calif. ; London: Sage Publications, 2006).

Dierksmeier, C., *Der absolute Grund des Rechts: Karl Christian Friedrich Krause in Auseinandersetzung mit Fichte und Schelling*, (Stuttgart-Bad Cannstatt: Frommann-Holzboog, 2003).

Durand, M.-F., *Atlas de la mondialisation: comprendre l'espace mondial contemporain*, (Paris: Sciences po, les presses, 2008).

Ellerman, D., *Property and Contract in Economics: In Case for Economic Democracy*, (Cambridge, MA: Blackwell, 1992).

Elliott, H., *Ethics for a Finite World: An Essay Concerning a Sustainable Future*, (Golden, Colo.: Fulcrum Pub, 2005).

Gould, C. C., *Globalizing Democracy and Human Rights*, (Cambridge; New York: Cambridge University Press, 2004).

Habermas, J., *Theory of Communicative Action*, (Boston: Beacon Press, 1984).

Habermas, J., *Between Facts and Norms: Contributions to a Discourse Theory of Law and Democracy*, (Cambridge, Mass.: MIT Press, 1996).

Hartmann, N., *Philosophie der Natur; Abriss der speziellen Kategorienlehre*, (Berlin,: W. de Gruyter, 1950).

Herman, E. S. and Chomsky, N., *Manufacturing Consent: The Political Economy of the Mass Media*, (New York: Pantheon Books, 1988).

Jonas, H. *The Imperative of Responsibility: In Search of an Ethics for the Technological Age*, (Chicago: University of Chicago Press, 1984).

Kitagawa, H., Mizuno, S., and Luff, P., *Searching for a Common Morality in the Global Age: The Proceedings of the International Conference on Moral Science in 2002*, (New Delhi: Lancer's Books in association with Institute of Moralogy, Kashiwa-shi, Japan, 2004).

Küng, H. and Kuschel, K.-J., *A Global Ethic: The Declaration of the Parliament of the World's Religions*, (New York: Continuum, 1993).

Lowry, S.T., *The Archeology of Economic Ideas: The Classical Greek Tradition*, (Duke University Press, Durham, 1987).

MacGillivray, A., *A Brief History of Globalization: The Untold Story of our Incredible Shrinking Planet*, (New York: Carroll & Graf, 2006).

McLuhan, M. and Powers, B. R., *The Global Village: Transformations in World Life and Media in the 21st Century*, (New York: Oxford University Press, 1989).

Moore, G. E., *Principia ethica*, (Cambridge,: At the University press, 1903).

Plessner, H., *Conditio humana*, (Frankfurt am Main: Suhrkamp, 1983).

Rescher, N., *The Validity of Values: A Normative Theory of Evaluative Rationality*, (Princeton, N.J.: Princeton University Press, 1993).

Roniger, L. and Waisman, C. H., *Globality and Multiple Modernities: Comparative North American and Latin American Perspectives*, (Brighton England; Portland, Or.: Sussex Academic Press, 2002).

Schmidt, V. H., "Multiple Modernities or Varieties of Modernity?" *Current Sociology*, 54(1) (2006): 77–97.

Scruton, R., *The West and the Rest: Globalization and the Terrorist Threat*, (Wilmington, DE: ISI Books 2003).

Sen, A., "La felicità è importante ma altre cose lo sono di più", in L. Bruni and P.L. Porta (eds), *Felicità e libertà: Economia e benessere in prospettiva relazionale* (Milano: Guerini e Associati, 2006), pp. 39–58.

Sirkin, H. L., Hemerling, J. W., and Bhattacharya, A. K., *Globality: Competing with Everyone from Everywhere for Everything*, (New York: Business Plus, 2008).

Sklair, L., *Sociology of the Global System*, (Baltimore: Johns Hopkins University Press, 1991).

Stearns, P. N., *Globalization in World History*, (London; New York: Routledge, 2010).

Wallner, F., Schmidsberger, F., and Wimmer, F. M., *Intercultural Philosophy : New Aspects and Methods*, (Frankfurt am Main; New York: Peter Lang, 2010).

# Part I
# Pre-modern Theories

# 1
# Socrates and Plato – Applying Their Humanistic Views to Modern Business

*Ioanna Patsioti-Tsacpounidis*

## 1.1 Introduction

In Athens, in the fifth century B.C., a remarkable mind placed the human being at the center of philosophical thought and posed the important question of how a person should live in order to attain happiness. Before Socrates, philosophy had mostly focused on questions about the origin and function of the cosmos. It was with Socrates that philosophy became anthropocentric and began to examine questions about human existence and well-being. His philosophical outlook was based on an introspection of oneself with a view to improving one's soul and getting closer to moral truth, but it also aimed at a more universal consideration of our existence as members of a moral community. In Socrates' thought, man takes a closer look at both the inner aspects of himself and the way he relates to fellow human beings, thus going deeper into the essence of man's social existence and establishing the basis of a humanistic philosophy. On this basis, Plato undertakes to question the moral and political foundations of his contemporary society and presents a theory of knowledge that elevates the human mind in a transcendent world, beyond the experience of the senses, where the *Forms/Ideas* (εἴδεα) as archetypes of reality reside. Having realized the need for a new humanistic drive that would channel human creativity into virtuous deeds, just like Socrates, Plato embarks on a life of philosophical contemplation that aims at awakening the soul and helping it seek what it actually possessed in its original state, but lost due to its interaction with the trivial pursuits of earthly affairs.

Both thinkers come to examine what is meant by proper ruling with a view to constructing a society based on justice, in which a person can achieve both a harmonious symbiosis with his fellow citizens and also be truly happy.

In this chapter, I examine more closely Socratic methodology and moral thought as well as the main aspects of Platonic philosophy, in an attempt to explore the humanistic aspects of their views and how these can relate to the domain of business in the age of globalization. In particular, I intend to focus on their view that nobody is willingly evil, as well as that virtue is knowledge, and examine to what extent these views can provide both a necessary and a sufficient condition for morally correct and effective decision-making in ethical management, the employer–employee and the producer–consumer relationships. I hope to show that despite some possible limitations, Socratic and Platonic moral intellectualism and humanism can promote business objectives and more successfully connect corporations to society at large.

## 1.2   The humanistic aspects of Socrates' and Plato's thought[1]

As we all know, our knowledge about Socrates' views derives mostly from his beloved student Plato, but some important information also comes from Aristotle and Xenophon. Of course, the Platonic Socrates[2] remains our main source of information, as exhibited in Plato's early, middle, and late dialogues. In fact, it is in the early dialogues that we learn about Socratic *dialectic* methodology, and about Socrates' *teleological*[3] approach to life and his concern to define what in the end constitutes true happiness, which he links to wisdom and moral excellence. In an attempt to give an answer to the question of what happiness is, he employs a dialectical method, aimed at providing the definition of a moral concept. Socratic dialectical reasoning tries to disprove the opponent's claim and leads the discussion so as to bring his interlocutor to admit the inadequacy of his definition and attempt another, eventually reaching a definition. This method may not always succeed in providing the definition of a moral concept, but at least it provides some relevant clues for a further philosophical consideration of the question. Above all, it sharpens the interlocutors' critical skills and forces them to confront their knowledge or ignorance.

For example, in the early dialogue *Euthyphro*, Socrates asks Euthyphro, a young man who is just about to sue his own father, what "piety" (το όσιον) is, and the answer he receives is that "piety is what the gods love"; this is then refuted by Socrates on the grounds that the gods disagree with each other (*Euthyphro* 5 d 7 – 8, 6 c 8 – d 3.). He thus forces

Euthyphro to give three more definitions, which are also refuted, and the whole dialogue ends in a deadlock (ἀπορία). In another early dialogue, *Laches*, Socrates tried to define "courage" (ἀνδρεία). After his interlocutor provides him with various examples of what he thought to be courageous people in terms of the way they reacted in pleasure, pain, desire, or fear, Socrates restates the question (*Laches* 191 e 9 – 12.). What Socrates requires is a definition that provides the essential, not the accidental, properties of a word that denotes an object or an idea, properties that must be, taken together, sufficient to distinguish it from any other similar class of objects or ideas (Guthrie 1971, 109–110). To that end, he responds to the interlocutor's answer providing a counterexample to the proposed definition, to show that the definition fails to provide a necessary or sufficient condition for the application of what it refers to. That is why in the *Meno* Socrates is not happy with the view that being suited to ruling over others is a necessary property for being virtuous, since it cannot apply to virtuous slaves (*Meno* 73 c 9 – d 1). Socrates wishes to come up with what constitutes the "form" (εἶδος) of something. In other words, he is not simply interested in finding out what courage is, but what it means to be truly courageous, and how this can be manifested in action in a way that enables a person to live a happy life, thus attaching a humanistic value to his methodology.

In his dialogue *Republic* Plato's own humanistic approach develops further. He builds on the Socratic position that no person would wish to act wrongly if he *really* knew the bad character of such an act. All wrongdoing is based on ignorance, on lack of knowledge of the *form* of the Good, and proper governing of a political community can only take place if the philosopher, a man of advanced ethical and intellectual rigor, becomes the ruler (520 a 7 – b 4.). Plato carries on the Socratic tradition of exploring the essence of things but elevates the concept of "form" to an "idea" by introducing the world of *Forms*, which are presented as transcendent and immaterial entities of which a sensible object can only be an image. For Plato, the most important of all the Forms, which encompasses any other, is the Form of the Good, the knowledge of which enables a person to possess an advanced ethical understanding and consequently to distinguish between right and wrong action, something which is fundamental for a happy life. The Platonic *Form of the Good* emerges from the Socratic definitions of many particular virtues or "goods" as that which is the one Virtue or one *Good-in-itself* (Slaate 2000, 90). Such knowledge is required by any prospective ruler, who should be trained by the political community itself in order to be a wise and just leader.

Plato refers to four cardinal virtues that any person, especially a ruler, should acquire: wisdom, justice, temperance, and courage. As Plato indicates: "Virtue would be a kind of health and beauty and good condition of the soul, and vice would be disease, ugliness, and weakness." (*Republic* IV, 444 e 1 – 3.) It should also be noted that all of these virtues underlie the humanistic character of Platonic moral philosophy, since they provide a human being with the strong moral endowment that is necessary for proper conduct in society.

The humanistic aspect of Plato's thought is even more evident in the case of the philosopher-ruler. In his view, the best ruler should receive a very good education from an early age, which, together with a good knowledge of mathematics and dialectics (ibid. 532 d 2 – 540 c 2.) and training in public office for some years, would enable him to run the affairs of the state as well as he can. Plato's philosopher-ruler is supposed to be a man of public service. He is not looking for a statesman who would be a demagogue or a tyrant, for these are people who are devoid of knowledge and lack an advanced ethical understanding; they are "upholders of the most monstrous idols, and themselves idols" (*Politicus* 303 b 8 – c 5.). Instead, he is looking for a ruler who has attained knowledge of the Form of the Good, that is, who possesses an advanced ethical understanding and, although he has found happiness in contemplation, is expected to leave the serenity of the philosophical life and become involved in public service. The humanistic core of the Platonic philosopher-ruler lies exactly in the fact that such a person has to go back to where he came from in order to awaken the rest of the people. In particular, in Plato's famous allegory of the sun, the line, and the cave, the philosopher-ruler is presented as the person who has managed to exit the darkness of the cave, and discern the light, which implies knowledge of the Form of the Good, and has to return to it in order to help the people "imprisoned" in the cave to set themselves free from their ignorance (*Republic* 519 e 1 – 521 a 9).[4] A ruler should not only possess an advanced understanding and be able to assert himself, but also have a virtuous disposition and act well, as indicated in the *Republic*.

The humanism of Plato's thought is also encountered in his theory of punishment as presented in his late dialogue, the *Laws*. In accordance with Socratic views, he accepts that criminal acts are essentially involuntary insofar as the wrongdoer is not aware of the harm done to his soul (*Laws* 860 d 5 – 861 a 2.). By "voluntary" Plato means what is deliberately chosen as a result of involuntary injustice to the soul (ibid. 863 e 7 – 864 a 8.). In fact, what Plato means is that the choice to commit a crime is a voluntary act, but the psychological state of injustice which leads a person to do so is involuntary. For this reason, punishment should be seen as "therapy" for the soul, not as a way of taking revenge (ibid. 862 b 4 – e 1.). The Platonic penal program is humanitarian insofar as it is intended to reform the criminal and remove moral evil from his soul; it follows a prudential approach (Mackenzie, 1981, 196–197).[5] Any theory of punishment that is based on a retributive approach would be totally rejected since it does not help the wrongdoer to understand the wrongness of the criminal act, nor does it reform him. Thus what we notice is that Plato shows respect for human dignity as well as confidence in the human will. Whether a ruler or an ordinary citizen, a person should develop the qualities of character and intellectual abilities that would enable him to know and act in a truly good manner, hence making the most of his social existence.

## 1.3   The relevance of Socrates' and Plato's humanistic ethics to modern business

Now let us examine how the humanistic ethics of both Socrates and Plato can be applied to the domain of modern business, starting with the philosophy of Socrates. The main area that this would apply to is that of ethical management, as well as the management of ethics. A manager is expected to examine everything and explore all the possibilities or options in a given situation before he comes to a clear appreciation of the issue at hand. Socrates asks: "How is one supposed to define something if one does not know what that thing is?" (*Meno* 70 b 2–4). Applied to modern business, this can mean that it is fundamental that the manager first has to understand the mission and the objectives of an organization, identify its strengths and weaknesses, acquaint himself with the workforce, and clearly define the problems it faces, before he can provide a strategic plan and start implementing it.

What follows is that in the Socratic sense, a manager should have developed the dialectical and debating skills that would help him define both the root of the corporate problems and how to resolve them. The philosophical legacy of Socrates could prove to be a necessary condition for the well-being of an organization. Whether a manager is seeking to hire the best applicant from a number of suitable candidates, or going through an assessment process of the existing employees with a view to promoting some of them, or examining current global economic conditions to decide how to act in the relevant market, or struggling to overcome a potentially destructive corporate crisis following unethical conduct, he has to possess the skills that enable him not only to argue his case effectively but, even more importantly, to have a good understanding of what should be done.

When Socrates disproves the opponent's claim, he does not do so in order to display arrogance. In fact, he never claims to possess the answers to all the moral questions he discusses with his interlocutors. He does it because he wants to find the truth, or at least to get as close to the truth as possible. And this is exactly what a manager should try to do: keep on questioning all the data available, disproving what is deficient or insufficient, and continually searching for what is better in terms of virtuous management. Also, the Socratic method aims at the essence of something, such as courage, and in so doing explains why anything that shares that essence will in fact be courageous (Woodruff, 1992, 96). Applying Socrates' philosophical insight to modern business, this can mean that an expert manager would ensure that what he imparts to his subordinates as courage is indeed always brave, noble, and fearful of injustice.[6]

In Socratic thought, a definition has a teleological character, since it must state not only the essential properties of an object, but also the "function" (ἔργον), or work, that that object must serve. As the Platonic Socrates indicates in the *Cratylus* (389 a 5 – c 9.), if a man wants to make a shuttle he must look at the "εἶδος" (form) of shuttles, and this "εἶδος" he must understand and take as his model, not in the sense of the shape of a shuttle, or merely what it *is*, but what purpose it is meant to serve (Guthrie, 1971, 121-22.). It follows from this that in order for a person to improve, he must first understand who he is. In this sense, a manager should know his own strengths and weaknesses and his own knowledge or ignorance. He should try to develop what Socrates calls self-knowledge. This is a fundamental prerequisite of a wise person, and thus of a virtuous person.

Is Socrates perhaps asking too much? Perhaps, but he definitely knows he is doing so. He knew all too well that people cannot easily overcome their desires, fight against their emotional weaknesses, or reason properly. Throughout his life he exhorted people to avoid spending too much time on and being too concerned with trivial pursuits, but rather to channel their activities towards the improvement of their souls.[7] If we extend this view to the domain of business, we see that a manager is expected to understand what the organization he serves truly is, what its essential mission is, and what goals it ought to achieve, before he introduces any business strategy. As we can see, this attaches to Socratic morality both a humanistic and a utilitarian dimension, insofar as the good has both an intrinsic and an instrumental value. A virtuous manager is a good manager exactly because of the qualities of character that he has developed and the knowledge of the good that he possesses, but at the same time because of how he invests this moral and intellectual endowment in practice. That is to say, his knowledge of the good is converted into right action. The ethical manager not only knows what the right thing is but also is aware of the utility of this knowledge in reality, which is how to serve the public good. This notion of the ethical manager incorporates a strong humanistic element.

But what would constitute the ethical manager according to both Socrates and Plato? What would be the main qualities such a person should possess in order to fulfill his purpose as well as possible? From the various Platonic dialogues we can form an understanding of what Socrates would consider a good disposition. An important quality is that of "justice" (δικαιοσύνη), which consists in this: that every part of the soul performs its proper task in harmony. So Plato would expect a manager to be just in his decision-making and use fair procedures in his assessment of employees and his treatment of customers. According to this view, such a manager should take a humanistic approach, avoiding discrimination based on people's gender, ethnicity, nationality, race, color, disability, faith, or sexual orientation.

Another important quality that the Platonic Socrates mentions is that of "temperance" (σωφροσύνη). In the dialogue *Charmides*, Socrates considers how to define temperance. Again, no satisfactory answer is provided by his interlocutors. It is made clear, however, what temperance relates to: knowledge of one's own limits, obedience to the inner laws of harmony and proportion and wise decision-making (Cf. *Charmides* 171 c 5 – 172 a 4.). Applied to modern business this can mean that a temperate manager or employee would not be arrogant towards his subordinates, colleagues, or customers, would avoid excesses in his business conduct or decisions, and would accurately discern the qualities of others. In fact, such a person would most likely never exceed prudent limits in taking a business risk at the expense of the corporation. By that I do not mean that a temperate manager would be infallible; rather, he would be wise enough to know his limits and would understand the utility of moral principles in everyday corporate conduct.

"Courage" (ανδρεία) is another quality a manager should possess. As mentioned above, in Plato's *Laches*, Socrates and his interlocutors try to define courage. It is important to note that Socrates' intellectualist conception of courage is a broad one. He does not only include the well-known Greek *topos* (τόπος) of the courageous man on the battlefield but also that of the courageous man as a member of the political community. That is, he presents courage as a civic virtue, not just a military one. It is also noteworthy that although for most people courage would be the ability or even the virtue to do the right thing in the face of death, for Socrates it is the virtue that keeps us fearful of injustice. Based on this definition of courage, I would consider civic courage – the ability, based on knowledge, to be fearful of injustice and have the strength to do the right thing in civic affairs – as highly applicable to the domain of business in general. An employer or a human resources manager, for example, should have the courage to take action when a crisis arises that seriously threatens the organization, such as a case of racial discrimination, sexual harassment, or product liability.

The virtue of courage is, however, even more applicable to the case of whistle-blowing,[8] by which term we refer to an employee's disclosure of nonpublic information regarding unethical conduct of the organization as an act of moral protest that may threaten his job. Sometimes employees experience situations that go against their moral principles, or are even brought to commit actions they deplore for fear of losing their job. This is exactly what the Socratic conception of courage refers to: to be fearless of anything but injustice. If a product is defective and can threaten people's lives, or if a government official has been secretly bribed at the expense of the organization's finances and reputation, these are acts of injustice. Of course, there is a certain controversy in the area of business ethics over whether whistle-blowing is right,[9] as some see it as an act of disloyalty to the employer. But both Socrates and Plato would have a clear position on this: one cannot remain silent and fearful when injustice occurs; one has to find the strength to fight against it, because one has a greater obligation to justice than to the organization or the public. After all, in their humanistic ethics courage is also connected to freedom, since it teaches us to exercise our freedom and stand up for what is right.

Another quality a manager or any person in the workplace should cultivate is that of honesty and truthfulness. For Socrates the whole quest for truth was connected to being honest, first and foremost, to ourselves. Telling the truth is what he does in his defense speech, thus showing real civic courage.[10] In that sense, he would not approve of any dishonest dealings in the domain of business, any deceitful advertising techniques that fool the consumer and deprive him of the right to choose, or the concealment of information vital to the well-being of employees. Socrates would not accept dishonesty, since it would be an act of injustice.

What about a manager who cannot, or perhaps should not, disclose all that he knows about an organization? Would that also be an act of deception for Socrates? How could Socrates' intellectual morality and Plato's philosopher ruler accommodate the practical demands of business should such an issue arise? The answer is not an easy one, but it can be found in Socrates' doctrine of wisdom, or his belief that virtue is knowledge. If a manager is truly wise, that is, if he possesses knowledge of the good or, in a Platonic sense, knowledge of the Form of the Good, and has cultivated these virtues, then he would never choose to do wrong knowingly. In other words, he would not conceal any information that harms the general social welfare. Also, such a person would be able to develop or even restore employee trust, as well as to motivate employees to achieve better productivity, thus promoting a cooperative spirit in the organization.[11]

In support of the humanistic aspect of Socratic and Platonic thought and their applicability in business, I should also indicate that for both of them, virtues such as courage, temperance, justice, and piety are all forms of knowledge. Each of them is a component of wisdom,[12] since virtue is knowledge. In the *Protagoras,* there is reference to the unity of virtues (*Protagoras* 329 c 6.) and in the *Laches,* as we have seen, courage is taken to be a proper part of virtue as a whole (*Laches* 190 c 8 – d 5, 199 e 6 – 7.), while in the *Euthyphro,* Socrates includes piety as a proper part of justice (*Euthyphro* 11 e 7 – 12 e 2). All these instances can be better understood if we consider the central role of wisdom among the virtues. In both Socrates' and Plato's mind, a manager cannot be just and at the same time dishonest, courageous and also impious, temperate but not magnanimous. Of course, Plato does not deny that all of these are distinct virtues, in that they are distinguished according to their objects or the parts of the soul of which they are the habits. What he wants to stress is that all these distinct virtues form a unity insofar as they manifest virtue as a whole, thus defining the essence of our moral existence. In other words, these distinct virtues when brought together reflect the knowledge of what is truly good for man and provide an excellent basis for ethical management as well as the management of ethical problems or dilemmas in business (Guthrie, 1971, 229–230).

Therefore, according to this view, a corporate executive should above all be a virtuous person, since only if this is the case would he act wisely. In fact, the most humanistic aspect of both Socrates' and Plato's thought is the view that a person cannot *knowingly* decide to do what would destroy him and all those involved along with him. In their view, a manager or the chairman of an organization who uses unethical conduct to promote corporate objectives is not truly aware of the wrongness of his approach and beliefs; he does not possess true knowledge but mere beliefs of what he thinks to be right. As Plato would suggest, such a person does not even have a vague understanding of what the *Form of Justice* refers to, for it cannot be the case that he acts so wrongly against himself, his fellow employees, the organization, and society at large.

So both Socrates and Plato would understand the dubious corporate governance of Enron and the financial manipulations that presented a fictitious growth that in the end resulted in one of the costliest bankruptcies in history, that of the seventh largest corporation in the United States,[13] as the outcome of involuntary wrongdoing. In their view, these actions were voluntary, in that the people involved knew exactly what they wanted – to make more profit for themselves – but at the same time involuntary, in that they did not really *know* what was *truly* good. Otherwise, they would not have destroyed the employees' retirement plans, which had been heavily invested in Enron's stock, they would not have caused the laying off of 5,000 employees, and they would not have led ordinary stockholders and some lenders to lose many billions, while they themselves made millions of dollars in stock options alone. Whereas for Plato's philosopher-ruler such behavior is due to lack of knowledge, or ignorance of what is right, in the eyes of others, the scheme seemed well planned and voluntarily executed in full awareness of how the law functions and how it can be manipulated. The managers took advantage of the legal loopholes in the system and used it for their own ends, regardless of whether their actions entailed any moral or social responsibility.[14] Many others in business believe that the Enron managers were aware that their behavior was fraudulent, since they took actions to avoid transparency, while cashing in short-term profits. And yet, both Socrates and Plato would insist, they did all this because they were not really *aware* of the true wrongness of their actions. If they really *knew* how disgraced they would themselves be, how destructive their actions would end up being for the organization, and how deep the public reaction against them would be, they would not have done what they did.

So, for Plato, such managers have failed to live up to the ethical standards of what the Form of the Good would entail. This view is set out mainly in the dialogue of *Protagoras*, as follows:

> If the pleasant is the good, no one who either knows or believes that there is another possible course of action, better than the one he is following, will ever continue on his present course when he might choose the better. To "act beneath yourself" is the result of pure ignorance; to "be your own master" is wisdom. [...] It must follow that no one willingly goes to meet evil or what he thinks to be evil.[15]

In that sense, if we agree with Socrates in identifying virtue with the knowledge of good and evil, it follows that virtue is sufficient for happiness, or in our case, for a successful and happy business environment. But we may still wonder how this conception of virtue is connected with the particular sorts of actions and types of character that both Socrates and Plato regard as virtuous.[16] We can still ask whether Socrates' concept of the virtuous person or Plato's philosopher-ruler can explain why the wise manager should be fearless in sorting out a management crisis that may result in the organization's bankruptcy, temper his self-indulgence and demands, and be unwilling to cheat or steal. One way to explain this behavior is the adaptive account of happiness according to which, for Socrates, a virtuous person has understood that his happiness requires him to have flexible or feasible desires, so he cultivates these desires and eliminates others, thus ensuring the satisfaction of his desires and the attainment of his happiness. So a person does not lose by being temperate, just, or courageous. However, although this argument may convince us that our happiness does not require us to profit at the expense of another person, it does not necessarily mean that we need to be concerned with others. In other words, we can still be happy if we are indifferent to other people's concerns[17] or, in the business domain, an organization can make profits not necessarily at the expense of the consumers, but without caring for their general well-being either. On this last point, I would say that Socrates' adaptive account of happiness should not be dissociated from the idea of virtue as a whole and the significance it has for the human being in the process of self-fulfillment within society. Socrates' views do involve concern for others and in no way would he hold that the idea of personal – or corporate happiness – should be devoid of a more humanistic touch.

## 1.4   Conclusion

Socrates' and Plato's humanistic legacy remains very powerful and quite applicable to business. It relates not only to the virtuous disposition a person should develop in order to do well in his business endeavors, even if it is only in the long run that that is realized. Even more, their whole philosophy is humanistic, and can be used as an excellent basis on which to define the relationship between business and society. It touches on human dignity, and for this reason is an early manifestation of what would later be called human rights. Socrates and Plato fight against injustice, and thus would be totally against any kind of preferential treatment in the workplace, an unfair game in the market, or the lack of accountability when mismanagement occurs. In that sense, their ethics include fundamental principles that provide the basis for humanistic management and corporate social responsibility. In the age of globalization, the Socratic and Platonic virtues reflect objective moral standards that highlight the universality of human nature and can help corporate people communicate with each other and with society. What is more, their views are cross-cultural, exactly because they are humanistic, and so would also be quite helpful in the domain of international business, since they would expect corporations to sustain morally responsible conduct wherever they operate. And as cosmopolitan philosophers, they would expect a corporation to be a full member of society at large, given that it consists of people who, as fully-fledged persons, are citizens of the whole world. In fact, Socrates has taught us not only that we are deficient in knowledge and how we may acquire more, but also that we are incomplete as human beings and how we can fulfill ourselves (cf. Versenyi, 1963, 123). Equally important, Plato has provided us with a model of a social structure which, however difficult to realize, is based on the most exquisite capacities and needs of the human being.

In conclusion, I would say that the moral intellectualism of both Socrates and Plato can serve the domain of business well, and provide both a necessary and a sufficient ground for proper and effective conduct. Even if it lacks a more pragmatic approach, their moral intellectualism has the force to promote the human endeavor to do well in life. The phrase "To act beneath yourself is the result of pure ignorance" echoes in our ears and calls for further action in the domain of modern business.

## Notes

1. Other writers have attempted to draw a connection between Socrates' and Plato's thought and its applicability to business, such as Kevin Morrell (383–392), who discusses the suitability of the Socratic dialogues as a tool for teaching business ethics. I agree with this position, as I also defend the significance of the Socratic methodology to business decision-making, and to Tuomo Takala (*EJBO*), who refers to Plato's myths, symbols, and metaphors as means of symbolical leading that every leader should develop in his normative agenda for the management of meaning. I agree with this insofar as in a Platonic sense a leader should be someone who seeks truth and acts accordingly in all aspects of his social life, as well as with the view that for Plato a leader must have charisma in order to be successful in his actions,

but I would question Takala's view that such charisma is something mystical that cannot be obtained by force or training. Further support for such a position is required following some textual evidence from Plato's dialogues.

2. It is sometimes claimed that the Platonic Socrates is not identical with the historical Socrates. Some people claim that we should separate them completely, while others suggest that it is through the Platonic work that we get to know the historical Socrates, that is, the person who made history, who taught Plato and many others, and influenced later philosophical thought (Vlastos, 90–91).

3. By a 'teleological' approach we mean that kind of philosophical consideration in which any action is supposed to fulfill a purpose, to accomplish an end. In such an approach there is always a "τέλος" (purpose) to attain and one has to think of the relevant means available in order to achieve this purpose.

4. Compare also: "You have received a better and more complete education than others, and you are more capable of sharing both ways of life[...] Down you must go then, each in his turn, to the habitation of the others and accustom yourselves to the observation of the obscure things there.[...] So our city will be governed by us and you with waking minds, and not, as most cities now which are inhabited and ruled darkly as in a dream by men who fight one another for shadows and wrangle for office as if that were a great good" (ibid. 520 b 6 – d 1).

5. Ibid. 59–64. Mackenzie also examines the possible objections to the humanitarian penology of Plato by reference to issues of moral psychology, as well as the supposition that such a theory of punishment may benefit the minority and not the majority; it may not serve social utility. It does, however, serve justice, and in that sense it serves humanity.

6. Cf. below for the definition of 'courage'.

7. Compare *Socrates' Defense (The Apology)* 29 d 2 – 30 b 4; Cf. *Phaedo* 80 a 1 – 84 b 6, where there is discussion about the body and soul separability issue and how important it is for the true philosopher to be totally undistracted by the temptations of the body in order to regain true knowledge and set his soul free.

8. Whistle-blowing is defined as "the voluntary release of nonpublic information, as a moral protest, by a member or former member of an organization outside the normal channels of communication to an appropriate audience about illegal and/or immoral conduct in the organization or conduct in the organization that is opposed in some significant way to the public interest." (Boatright, 90)

9. Roche takes the position that whistle-blowing is an act of disloyalty that causes disunity and creates conflict in an organization (Roche, 445), while Bok takes a more temperate position and views whistle-blowing as a way of putting the loyalty to the public that is negatively affected if the revelation is not made above that due to one's colleagues or employer (Bok, 330).

10. *Socrates' Defense* 29 d 1 b – 30 b 4, 31 a 8 – c 4, 32 b 1 – e 1 (the last reference also provides an illustrative example of Socrates' idea of civic courage).

11. Cf. Corkindale (49) who indicates that a manager's honesty and transparency can help rebuild confidence in employees, while the lack of it causes

tension and conflict, and fosters employee indifference and, ultimately, customer discontent.

12. This is also mentioned by Xenophon in his *Memorabilia* III.9.5.

13. For further information about the Enron case, see De George (211–219).

14. There has been a debate in the area of business ethics as to whether corporations should have economic goals only and try to act in accordance with the legal parameters of the country in which they operate, or whether they should also adopt some noneconomic goals in an effort to exhibit corporate social responsibility. The first view was broadly adopted by the well-known economist Milton Friedman, while the second, known as Corporate Social Responsibility (CSR), has been gaining ground since the end of the last century and the beginning of the twenty-first. Corporations are nowadays committed to greater social responsibility as manifested in their treatment of employees, conduct toward customers, and environmental concerns. They are also more careful about the impact of their business acts and practices on society (cf. Boatright, 351–361).

15. See *Protagoras* 358 b 8 – d 2. Cf. *Gorgias* 509 e 5 – 7: "no one desires to act unjustly, rather all those who act unjustly do so involuntarily".

16. Cf. Irwin (210-11), who considers whether the adaptive account of Socrates is sufficient for happiness.

17. Ibid. 214.

## Bibliography

Benson, Hugh H. (ed.), *Essays on the Philosophy of Socrates*, (Oxford: Oxford University Press, 1992).

Boatright, John R., *Ethics and the Conduct of Business*. 6th ed., (New Jersey: Pearson Education Inc, 2004).

Bok, Sisela, "Whistle-blowing and Professional Responsibilities", in Tom L. Beauchamp and Norman E. Bowie (eds) *Ethical Theory and Business*. 5th ed. (Upper Saddle River,. NJ: Prentice Hall, 1997).

Corkindale, Gill, "Commenting on a case study: What does Castlebridge risk by shifting the rest of its production offshore?" *Harvard Business Review.* (November 2007), 39–49.

De George, Richard T., *Business Ethics*. 6th ed., (Upper Saddle River, NJ: Pearson Prentice Hall, 2006).

Friedman, Milton, *Capitalism and Freedom*. (Chicago: University of Chicago Press, 1962)

Guthrie, W.C.K., *Socrates*. (Cambridge: Cambridge University Press, 1971).

Irwin, Terence H., "Socrates the Epicurean?", in Hugh H. Benson's edition, (1992), 198–219.

Mackenzie Mary Margaret, *Plato on Punishment*. (Berkeley: University of California Press, 1981).

Morrell, Kevin. "Socratic Dialogue as a Tool for Teaching Business Ethics". *Journal of Business Ethics* 53 (2004), 383–392.

Patsioti-Tsacpounidis, Ioanna. "The Relevance of an Aretaic Model in Business Ethics". *The Proceedings of the Twenty-First World Congress of Philosophy*. Vol. 1. *Ethics*. Eds. Harun Tepe and StephenVoss. Ankara: The Philosophical Society of Turkey, (2007), 175–180.

Plato. *The Collected Dialogues*. Eds. Edith Hamilton and Huntington Cairns. Bollingen Series LXXI (Princeton: Princeton University Press, 1961).

Roche, James M. "The Competitive System, to Work, to Preserve, and to Protect". *Vital. Speeches of the Day* (May 1971).

Slaate, Howard Alexander, *Plato's Dialogues and Ethics*. (New York: University Press of America, 2000).

Takala, Tuomo. "Plato and Charisma". *Electronic Journal of Business Ethics and Organizational Studies (EJBO)* Vol. 2, No. 1, (1977).

Versenyi, Laszlo, *Socratic Humanism*. (New Haven: Yale University Press, 1963).

Vlastos, Gregory, *Socrates: Ironist and Ethical Philosopher*. Transl. P. Kalligas, (Athens, 1993).

Woodruff, Paul, "Plato's Early Theory of Knowledge", in H.H. Benson's edition, (1992), 86–106.

Xenophon. *Opera Omnia*. Vol. 2. Ed. E.C. Marchant. (Oxford: Clarendon Press, 1921).

# 2
# Aristotle's Economic Ethics
*Claus Dierksmeier and Michael Pirson*

## 2.1 Introduction

Aristotle has in recent years enjoyed much attention in business and management journals (Collins, 1987; Dyck and Kleysen, 2001; Solomon, 2004; Wijnberg, 2000). Whether in relation to total quality management (Schoengrund, 1996), knowledge management (Demarest, 1997), crisis management (Darling, 1994), networking (Schonsheck, 2000), in psychological literature on well-being (Waterman, 1990), or as a general reference point for business ethics scholars (for example, Fontrodona and Mele, 2002; Gimbel, 2005; Solomon, 1992; Solomon, 2004; Wijnberg, 2000), Aristotle's philosophy enjoys enthusiastic attention in the business field. In order to understand the significance of this, it is imperative that we do not isolate the tenets of his business ethics from their wider philosophical context but, rather, explain the former by the latter. Therefore, in this chapter, we follow his arguments from their beginnings, from his theory of life (1), through his theory of the intrinsic moral (2) and the extrinsic social (3) relations of material goods, up to the point where consequences for business management today can be drawn (4). Since in Aristotle's time business organizations other than the household did not greatly matter, we will outline how his thinking about the household can be applied to modern corporations. We argue that Aristotle's conception of *chrematistike* and *oikonomia* provides a basis for answers to questions raised by the current discourse on social and financial value creation (Carroll, 1991; Carroll, 1999; McWilliams and Siegel, 2001), such as how business should view itself with regard to society, and whether social responsibility is a fundamental practice or only a functional add-on (Pava and Kraus, 1996; Scherer and Palazzo, 2007; Smith, 2003).

## 2.2 Aristotle's theory of life

Aristotle knew that if one's only goal is to make as much money as possible, a reasonably clear-cut code of conduct can easily be derived from this premise. He felt, however, that to outline a theory of such behavior was precisely what sound economic thinking was *not* about (*Pol* I, 11, 1258b, 33–34). The rules of mere money-making (*chrematistike*) he found simply too "tiresome to dwell upon (...) at greater length" (*Pol* I, 11, 1258b 34). His predominant interest, instead, was with what should rightfully be considered economics (*oikonomia*): the concern for morally adequate individual and public household management (*Pol* IX, 1, 1256b, 40–41). In other words, the very way in which Aristotle deals with economic affairs is at odds with the modern separation of economics from ethics and all other concerns of life. He therefore discusses economic and business questions as subordinate subjects within his treatise on politics, which itself is worked out in the overall framework of his ethics (Koslowski, 1993, 51–53). And Aristotle's ethics rests upon a (*teleological*) theory about life that ascribes to each living entity a certain goal (*telos*) to which it strives.

Plants, for example, need specific environments (such as soil, water, and sun) but will, given these conditions, prosper and flourish predictably in a certain way. They thereby realize their genetic program or what Aristotle calls their "final end" (*PA* I, 641b, 34–39). Human beings and organizations strive towards ends, too. However, everything human does not simply follow a predetermined path but relies greatly in its course upon human freedom and agency. Outward conditions can hamper the development of human life, of course, but failure in human affairs also stems from misguided inner direction. The possibility of affecting one's own well-being negatively, such as through turpitude and vice, is inherent in every human being and organization. For successful self-management, a (*teleological*) concept of what constitutes true well-being (as an end) and of what brings it about (as means) is therefore needed.

> In all sciences and arts the end is a good; and the greatest good and in the highest degree a good in the most authoritative of all – this is the political science of which the good is justice, in other words, the common interest. (*Pol* III, 12, 1282b, 15–19)

If economics forms part and parcel of Aristotle's political science, the proper management of economic affairs can be seen as central to his overall concerns (Dyck and Kleysen 2001, p. 562). What, then, is the contribution of the economy to the overall project of human life? What constitutes economic welfare? What ends should business organizations pursue? What are the right ways to measure economic success? To answer these questions, we need to consider what constitutes value in human life. Reflecting upon what people commonly consider as good, or as a good, makes it clear that most things are valued not absolutely but relatively. Most goods are held in esteem because they serve a certain function, because they are being employed as means to other ends and goods. Aristotle concludes,

> If, then, there is some end of the things we do, which we desire for its own sake (everything else being desired for the sake of this), and if we do not choose everything for the sake of something else (for at that rate the process would go on to infinity, so that our desire would be empty and vain), clearly this must be the good and the chief good. (*NE* I, 2, 1094a, 17–23)

What is this ultimate goal of human life? According to Aristotle, one thing is clear from the beginning, "wealth is evidently not the good we are seeking" (*NE* I, 7, 1096a, 6). The answer instead has to be gleaned from the natural faculties of the human being (*NE* I, 7, 1097b, 33). Whatever our private idiosyncrasies, certain capabilities are common to us all. In our most common faculties lie natural objectives. The quest for (goods such as) food, shelter, defense, and procreation, we share with animals. In addition, human beings seek communication, education, and cultivation (*Pol* I, 2, 1253a, 10–39). Yet even these higher goods can be declared functional; they are not necessarily sufficient in themselves, nor are they necessarily sought after universally.

Happiness, however, is universally pursued, and, moreover, is sought for its own sake. For formal reasons, it must therefore be declared the ultimate good of human life (*NE* I, 7, 1097a, 28–37). But what, materially, constitutes happiness? Aristotle's theory is not a hedonistic theory. His term for happiness (*eudaimonia*) denotes a well-ordered state of affairs. Aristotle does not extol subjective states of euphoria, received passively through the senses. Rather, *eudaimonia* describes an objective state of being, to be attained by rational activity (*NE* I, 7 1098a, 3–8). Individuals are "happy" (well-ordered) when they rationally harmonize their outer and inner world so as to live self-sufficiently (*NE* I, 7, 1097b, 15–16). Not fortune or fortunes, but a communal and virtuous lifestyle makes for happiness.

Yet striving for *eudaimonia* is not to the same as achieving it. After all, to declare happiness one's goal does not translate into a very specific program of action. So how, concretely, is happiness realized? Aristotle shuns an axiomatic answer, since he disagrees with the (Platonic) assumption that one could "deduce" morality from principles (Koslowski, 1993, p. 26). Rather, one must work from experience and develop an understanding of different customs and mores (*NE* VI, 8, 1142a, 13) so as to learn, gradually and habitually, to employ wise judgment in the management of one's affairs. The good life can neither be defined nor attained in abstraction from the communities we live in (Wijnberg, 2000, p. 334). We need the example of real people (*phronimoi*) who excel in judgment and wisdom. By observing how they master life we gain the requisite normative orientation and by imitating them we develop our own character (*NE* VI, 4, 1140a, 24; VI, 13, 1145a, 13).

## 2.3   Intrinsic and moral relations to material goods

According to Aristotle, it is only by working out a shared understanding of what constitutes a good and dignified life that we can, as a society, form an adequate notion of the necessities of life, and hence what we should demand from the economy (Solomon 2004, p. 1027). Most of our pursuits require the intelligent use of resources and benefit from social cooperation. Humans come together in cooperative units, such as households and city-states (today we would add "corporations" to the list), in order to organize common efforts and to manage shared interests. For

> Man is by nature a political animal. And therefore, men, even when they do not require one another's help, desire to live together; (although) they are also brought together by their common interests in proportion as they severally attain to any measure of well-being. This is certainly the chief end, both of individuals and of states. (*Pol* III, 6, 1278b, 18–24)

For Aristotle the function of economics (*oikonomia*) is to demonstrate how to govern such public and individual households (*oikoi*) through adequate norms (*nomoi*) of conduct. It makes sense to extend this theory of individual and public household management to the management of today's corporations as well, since they too are communities in which common purposes are pursued by organized efforts (Wijnberg 2000, p. 334). Of course, the differences between a modern, shareholder-oriented corporation and ancient households means we cannot treat them exactly the same. Yet as social organizations they also have certain structural features in common that allow us to transfer some insights about the successful management of one to the other. All households and organizations, for instance, must acquire the material necessities for their pursuits. As a sub-goal, therefore, the pursuit of wealth re-enters Aristotle's theory. Hence, the "first question" in economics is "whether the art of getting wealth is the same as the art of managing a household or a part of it, or instrumental to it (...)" (*Pol* I, 8, 1256a, 3–5). Aristotle's answer is quite blunt:

> There are two sorts of wealth-getting, (...); one is a part of household management, the other is retail trade: the former necessary and honorable, while that which consists in exchange is justly censured; for it is unnatural, and a mode by which men gain from one another. (*Pol* I,10, 1258a, 38–1258b, 2)

It would, however, be wrong to stamp Aristotle as "anti-business" on the basis of such quotations (Collins 1987, p. 567). In fact, compared to many of his contemporaries, and especially in direct comparison with his teacher Plato, Aristotle comes across as quite "pro-business." Plato, it is true, aimed for unity-through-identity in the state and strove for commonality in all things. He was therefore suspicious of the exclusive nature of private property and advocated communistic lifestyles. Aristotle, however, advances a political model of unity-in-diversity, and accepts it as part of human nature to want to have secured and secluded areas of self-realization. He acknowledges and even endorses

> ... the pleasure, when a man feels a thing to be his own; for surely the love of self is a feeling implanted by nature and not given in vain, although selfishness is rightly censured; this, however, is not the mere love of self, but the love of self in excess, like the miser's love of money; for all, or almost all, men love money and other such objects in a measure. And further, there is the greatest pleasure in doing a kindness or service to friends or guests or companions, which can only be rendered when a man has private property. (*Pol* II, 5, 1263a, 40–1263b, 4)

So, for Aristotle private property is an essential "part of the household, and the art of acquiring property is a part of the art of managing the household; for no man can live well, or indeed live at all, unless he be provided with necessaries" (*Pol* I, 4, 1253b, 23–25). Whereas Plato mistrusted commercial relationships because the grammar of prices does not express the semantics of true value, and thus engages the mind to an untruthful world, Aristotle has a rather positive view of commerce and the social relationships it engenders (Schonsheck 2000, p. 905). He views trade as a relation where, at least potentially, both partners can find benefit (*NE* V, 5, 1133b15–20, IX/2, 1164b13–23). It is not from anti-commercial sentiment, consequently, that he argues against some forms of retail trade, but from a view upon what constitutes an appropriate, as opposed to an excessive, pursuit of wealth. Economic assessments have to be based on a critical evaluation of our needs; the quantity of material goods we consume must be in proportion to the specific quality of what a good life requires. Economic analysis is thus not free-standing; success in both business and economics cannot be defined by quantitative parameters alone but must operate with reference to qualitative criteria (Wijnberg, 2000, p. 333). Economics is therefore fundamentally welded to the moral and political discourse of society (Nussbaum 1990, p. 59).

For Aristotle, there can be too much or too little of nearly everything; too much or too little sunshine for a plant, too much or too little food for an animal, and indeed, too much or too little wealth for a person (*EE* III, 4, 1231b 31). For some, the idea of too much wealth may seem odd. Is not the accumulation of property tantamount to storing up freedom and well-being? Aristotle warns against these assumptions. In all realms of life, he advocates moderation and measure, defining virtue as the rational pursuit of a mean between harmful extremes. Excess, in other words, is bad in itself. What constitutes excess depends, however, on a number of factors. Aristotle illustrates the point with an oft-cited example, referring to the very high meat consumption of Milo, a well-known wrestler of his time. It may be that, given his exercise schedule and physique, an enormous amount of meat intake is "good" for Milo; for everybody else it would be bad, because it would be excessive (*NE* II, 6, 1106b, 5). Applied to the pursuit of wealth, this notion leads to the following characteristics:

> The man who is more pleased than he ought to be by all acquisition and more pained than he ought to be by all expenditure is mean; he that feels both feelings less than he ought to is prodigal. (...) And since the two former characters consist in excess and deficiency, and where there are extremes there is also a mean, and that mean is best, (...), it necessarily follows that liberality is a middle state between

prodigality and meanness as regards getting and parting with wealth. (*EE* III, 4, 1231b, 31–39)

## 2.4   Extrinsic and social relations to material goods

Wealth, then, is for Aristotle not an end in itself but a means to the good life: a subordinate end (*NE* I, 5, 1096a, 6). As a functional good, wealth "consists in using things rather than in owning them; it is really the activity – that is, the use – of property that constitutes wealth" (*Ret* I, 5,1361a, 23). Consequently, wealth is to be evaluated in terms of how it facilitates the well-ordered or happy life. Wealth cannot be maximized, all else being equal, because the pursuit of wealth changes the inner and outer conditions in which it takes place: there are opportunity costs to its quest. Other endeavors are not undertaken; other – worthier – ends might not be pursued (Lowry, 1987, p. 234). To Aristotle, these higher ends are, internally, the striving to perfect oneself, and externally, active participation in one's political community. Whether an increase in wealth is beneficial can therefore not be answered in the abstract, but always by a concrete analysis of the foregone alternative uses of one's time and energy.

A crucial question to a modern reader is, how much is enough, and how much would be too much, for the good life (Bernstein et al., 2000; Hawken et al., 2000)? Aristotle proposes the formula that everyone should "have so much property as will enable him to live not only temperately but liberally; if the two are parted, liberality will combine with luxury; temperance will be associated with toil" (*Pol* II, 6, 1265a 29–35). To achieve a balance of wealth that realizes this goal, the government has to intervene in the economy. Although Aristotle does not dwell much on the thorny technical aspects of this issue, such as questions of the just measure and proportion of taxation, he makes clear that he means to facilitate fairness in opportunity through distributing and redistributing goods to those who have the most talent to use them (*Pol* III, 12, 1282b, 35–1283a, 2).

Legislation, however, can only provide the political framework; it cannot make individuals or households "good" without their active contribution. A functioning political community also relies on self-moderation on the part of individuals and households. There are satisfaction points for each economic unit. To strive beyond those in the pursuit of wealth is evidence of a harmful desire of wanting ever more (*pleonexia*), that is, people show no moderation mostly because they lack virtue or follow a hedonistic conception of the good (*NE* V, 1, 1129b 9-1130a, 13). Since

> their desires are unlimited they also desire that the means of grati-
> fying them should be without limit. Those (...) seek the means of
> obtaining bodily pleasures; and, since the enjoyment of these appears
> to depend on property, they are absorbed in getting wealth (...). For,
> as their enjoyment is in excess, they seek an art which produces the
> excess of enjoyment; and, if they are not able to supply their pleas-
> ures by the art of getting wealth, they try other arts, using in turn
> every faculty in a manner contrary to nature. (...), some men turn
> every quality or art into a means of getting wealth; this they con-
> ceive to be the end, and to the promotion of the end they think all
> things must contribute. (*Pol* I, 9, 1257b, 31–1258a, 18)

Aristotle also had a keen sense that such limitless pursuit of riches on
the part of some impoverishes others and undermines society (*Pol* VII,
1, 1323a, 35–1323b, 10). Property, while generally private, should therefore in its use also "be in a certain sense common" (*Pol* II, 5, 1263a, 25),
he concluded, because society – as the enabler and guarantor of our
possessions – has a stake in them.

> Like the sailor, the citizen is a member of a community. Now, sailors
> have different functions, for one of them is a rower, another a pilot,
> and a third a look-out man, a fourth is described by some similar
> term; and while the precise definition of each individual's virtue
> applies exclusively to him, there is, at the same time, a common defi-
> nition applicable to them all. For they have all of them a common
> object, which is safety in navigation. Similarly, one citizen differs
> from another, but the salvation of the community is the common
> business of them all. (*Pol* III, 4, 1276b, 21–29)

Excessive riches are bad not only intrinsically but also extrinsi-
cally insofar as they contribute to the separation of the citizen from
their community (Kasser and Ahuvia, 2002; Putnam, 2000). The poor
become too destitute to participate in political functions, while the rich
have the opportunity to opt out of their communal duties. It is from
this angle that wealth in moderation seems best for all "for in that condition of life men are most ready to follow rational principle" (*Pol* IV, 11,
1295b a, 5–6). Aristotle calls on the lawgiver to moderate and mediate,
because, according to his terse statement "The equalization of property

is one of the things that tend to prevent the citizens from quarrelling" (*Pol* II, 7, 1267a, 37–38).

Interestingly, in Aristotle's thinking being too rich is just as problematic, if not more so, as being poor. To be sure, Aristotle has no illusions about poverty's inducements to vice. Yet the infractions of law caused by poverty are petty: They do not endanger society at large. Not so with the felonies of the rich. Their "ambition and avarice, almost more than any other passions, are the motives of crime" (*Pol* II, 9, 1271a, 16–17). "The fact is that the greatest crimes are caused by excess and not by necessity. Men do not become tyrants in order that they may not suffer cold; and hence great is the honor bestowed, not on him who kills a thief, but on him who kills a tyrant" (*Pol* II, 7, 1267a, 12–16).

All in all, the state should act as an enabler of personal perfection in communal interaction. Against the view voiced by some sophists in his time (and by today's libertarians), that the state should be conceived merely as an insurance against violence and fraud, Aristotle states:

> But a state exists for the sake of a good life, and not for the sake of life only: if life only were the object, (...) brute animals might form a state, but they cannot, for they have no share in happiness or in a life of free choice. Nor does a state exist for the sake of alliance and security from injustice, nor yet for the sake of exchange and mutual intercourse; (...). whereas those who care for good government take into consideration virtue and vice in states. Whence it may be further inferred that virtue must be the care of a state which is truly so called, and not merely enjoys the name. (*Pol* III, 9, 1280a, 31–1290b, 9)

Yet a state, understood in this light, cannot arise from the calculus of barter. The public covenant is more than the inflation of the logic of private contracts to the proportions of a social contract:

> a state is not a mere society, having a common place, established for the prevention of mutual crime and for the sake of exchange. These are conditions without which a state cannot exist; but all of them together do not constitute a state, which is a community of families and aggregations of families in well-being, for the sake of a perfect and self-sufficing life. (...). The end of the state is the good life (...). (*Pol* III, 9, 1280b20–1281a, 1)

## 2.5 Consequences for the philosophy of business and management

We are now at a point where we can fully understand and appreciate Aristotle's distinction, mentioned earlier, between *chrematistike* and *oikonomia*, which is central for our application of his theory to contemporary questions of business and economics. Money-making and wealth-getting (*chrematistike*) are acceptable as long as "there is a boundary fixed" (*Pol* I, 8, 1256b, 27–34) through a purpose-bound and socially embedded household-economy (*oikonomia*). Yet taken out of this context, the pursuit of wealth typically knows "no limit of the end" and acquires "riches of the spurious kind" (*Pol* I, 9, 1257b, 28). Aristotle is fully aware that the unaccustomed eye, when looking at business transactions, cannot always easily make out which is which: "natural" versus "unnatural" *chrematistike*. In Aristotle's terms; we might speak of an "embedded" as opposed to a "nonembedded" pursuit of wealth. Since from the outside we cannot always assess correctly the (moral or immoral, "natural" or "unnatural") end a given transaction serves, self-regulation becomes all the more important (Block, 1996; Davis et al., 1997; Donaldson and Davis, 1991). Legislation alone is futile when decision-makers on all other levels do not concur and rein in their *chrematistic* impulses in favor of genuinely *oikonomic* goals (*Pol* I, 9, 1257b, 31–1258a, 5).

Aristotle's distinction between these two quite opposite orientations of economic pursuits provides a very helpful tool for thinking through contemporary dilemmas in the field of business ethics, corporate social responsibility, management theory, and social entrepreneurship. This is particularly the case, in our judgment, when it comes to questions of corporate self-regulation and corporate governance. Crucial, in our eyes, is not so much Aristotle's commendation of specific business practices in household management but rather his overall condemnation of a view that privatizes the realm of economic life and severs it from moral or political concerns. Economic life, to him, is contextualized *ab ovo*. In other words, Aristotle sees the individual not as a burgher first and a citizen later, but casts him immediately as a political being. The household is therefore, to Aristotle, not an economic entity first and then a political community: He initially conceptualizes it as an integral unit of the *polis*. Likewise, we think, one should view the corporation not as a profit-machine first and then ask how such "mechanical monsters" (Solomon, 2004, p. 1033) suddenly come to have social responsibilities.

Rather, from the outset, we should view firms as corporate citizens with social responsibilities.

Aristotle's framework also allows us to lose the unproductive divide between selfish and altruistic transactions in business (Dyck and Kleysen, 2001, p. 563). By their very nature, business organizations are committed to the interest of their members while servicing the greater community that enables their activities (Solomon, 2004, pp. 1024–1028). The requirement for ethical conduct in the business field, consequently, neither entails undue self-sacrifice, nor requires ordinary men to behave like saints. It only demands that we realize what the corporation, in fact, is: a social institution, where behavior is modeled, customs are shaped, and people engage in forms of conduct with moral and political significance (Wijnberg, 2000, p. 340). To take the perspective of virtue and a philosophy of the good life in the business context is therefore "a way of understanding or (re)conceiving what management is, not as a way to pass moral judgment on it" (Dyck and Kleysen, 2001, p. 565).

Turning a profit and creating wealth, teaches Aristotle, are not the same. It is the latter that legitimizes and limits the former. From this angle, we can extend to the modern corporation the qualified approval of the pursuit of profit that Aristotle accords to all households (Collins, 1987, p. 570). For the latter a pursuit of profit is acceptable when it is not excessive, does not harm the community, and when it remains subordinated to the pursuit of goals that are *economic* and not merely *chrematistic* in nature. The same can be said for corporations.

Viewed in that light, the currently prevailing norms and laws (*nomoi*) for business are strongly influenced by chrematistic ambitions. Scholars in economics and management suggest that businesses and their managers adhere to maximization paradigms. Having one objective which can be maximized has long been hailed by system theorists and economists as the *only* viable strategy (Jensen, 2002). In Aristotle's view, such separation of the financial and the political realms signals danger. For him, business is part of society and this embedded status needs to be reflected in all strategic decision making. Thus, *oikonomic* goal-setting processes encompass ecological, social, financial, and intergenerational concerns. *Oikonomic* businesses aim at the creation of overall well-being rather than the isolated satisfaction of a special interest group. Maximization strategies are inherently flawed, according to Aristotle, because they are excess-oriented; truly *oikonomic* strategies are, by contrast, virtue-based and moderation-oriented.

Maximization of any kind precludes moderation and stands in the way of achieving the golden mean, unless the calculus of maximization is tied to the goal of *eudaimonia*. The traditional view of neoclassical economics is that if profit is pursued, the utility of everyone increases as a consequence. With utility as a surrogate for happiness, profit maximization seems causally linked to increases in happiness, theoretically. Yet, in practice, such a clear-cut causality does not exist. Already in Aristotle's times it was evident that wealth and well-being were neither causally related nor even highly correlated. It is precisely for this reason that Aristotle distinguishes between the notions of *hedonic* and *eudaimonic* happiness. The former, induced by the senses and pleasures, is short-lived, and can often be achieved through the possession of wealth. Produced by virtuous behavior, the latter aims at excellence in all its dimensions, is less immediate but longer-lived, and cannot be procured through wealth. Recent findings demonstrate that wealth and well-being are only correlated up to a certain wealth level. Easterlin (2001), for example, notes that GNP growth and growth in well-being are actually disconnected in developed societies. Layard (2005) states that beyond a certain income level, well-being is influenced mainly by social factors rather than by income. Biswas-Diener et al. (2004) find that a materialistic attitude and a focus on income have a high negative correlation with individual happiness. Having said that, it is also evident that poor people who lack basic amenities such as shelter are very unhappy. In Aristotle's words: "No man can live well, or indeed live at all, unless he be provided with necessaries" (*Pol* I, 4, 1253b, 25–26). Martin (2005) argues that once a person passes the point of being able to afford "the normal cost of everyday life," more wealth may increasingly be accompanied by less happiness, not more. And with high levels of wealth come increased complications and worries, including concerns about losing one's level of wealth.

As a result, the connection of wealth and well-being, once beyond the poverty level, is very unclear. How else, then, can the economy and business be managed to support higher levels of *eudaimonic* well-being? Many observers deplore the *chrematistic* spirit of current day businesses and call for corporations to serve society first and put profit second (Arena, 2004). Business organizations, however, often understand themselves as legally bound to maximize profit (Ballou and Weisbrod, 2003; Jackson and Nelson, 2004). By dint of prevalent governance structures they cater to shareholder interests rather than broader societal concerns.

While Aristotle obviously never laid out blueprints for modern business organizations, based on these structural insights, we can say that businesses operated in line with his *oikonomic* understanding would be embedded within the political and social fabric of the community, and they would view themselves as servicing society, rather than society serving their financial interests. Such businesses would actively pursue strategies that integrate social responsibility, not as an add-on, but as integrative part of their day-to-day operations (see Porter and Kramer, 2006). Moreover, *oikonomic* organizations would be guided by their overall contribution to societal well-being and thus aim for a balance of different imperatives. Instead of serving one special interest group alone, such as shareholders, they aim at serving all their stakeholders and society at large (Layard, 2005; Diener and Seligman, 2004). Most importantly, business, oriented with reference to Aristotle's philosophy, should also reflect the overall balance orientation in their governance structure, giving a fair representation to all pertinent stakeholders, including employees, customers, suppliers, and societal councils (Spitzeck and Hansen, 2010). In a word, businesses need to restrain their *chrematistic* endeavors by aiming towards truly *oikonomic* goals. Shareholder value creation is not an illegitimate but a subordinated concern for an *oikonomic* enterprise. From a primary and exclusive objective of business policy the *chrematistic* aims of profitability are relegated to secondary and morally integrated goals.

When looking for business that exemplify the *oikonomic* character envisioned by Aristotle, social enterprises come to mind, as they seek to be, first and foremost, socially, ethically, and environmentally responsible (Jackson and Nelson, 2004; Savitz and Weber, 2006). They straddle the usual divide between nonprofit and for-profit organizations. Like nonprofits, social enterprises can organize in pursuit of a wide range of social missions. Like for-profits, they can generate a broad range of beneficial products and services that improve quality of life for consumers, create jobs, and contribute to the economy (Strom, 2007). Social enterprises seek to bring benefit to all stakeholders, and reinvest their surpluses to advance their social purposes, thus reaffirming the public and societal function of business.

## 2.6   Conclusion

Aristotle predicted some key problems we are facing today more than two thousand years ago. With his guidance we can reorient the discourse about the role of corporations in society. In pursuit of alternatives to correct the current excessive orientation towards shareholder value that undermines our society's long-term survival, Aristotle's theory of qualitative limitations for economic endeavors helps us conceive of alternative business organizations that create healthy wealth. Aristotle's insight into what constitutes wholesome wealth can open new strategic approaches to business that open new opportunities for organizational and societal well-being. Wealth created in a sustainable fashion is conducive to the *eudaimonic* happiness of all stakeholders. Management and leadership in the twenty-first century need to learn that serving society while making financial profits is what will define success in the future. Any corporation that wants to sustain its reputation and ensure its long-term success needs to understand that. By moving from a merely chrematistic to an *oikonomic* perspective, managers can harness their powers to do good while remaining able to do well financially.

## Bibliography

Arena, C., *Cause for Success: 10 Companies That Put Profit Second and Came in First*, (Novato, CA: New World Library, 2004).

Aristotle, *Eudemian Ethics* (EE), in W. Heinemann (ed.), Aristotle in 23 Volumes, Vol. 20, translated by H. Rackham, (Cambridge, MA: Harvard University Press, 1981).

Aristotle, *Nicomachean Ethics* (NE), translated by T. Irwin, (Indianapolis, IN: Hackett, 1985).

Aristotle: 1994, *Rhetoric* (Ret), translated by W. Rhys Roberts, D.C. Stevenson (ed.), The internet classics archives. http://classics.mit.edu/, Accessed on September 18, 2008.

Aristotle, *Parts of Animals* (PA), (Oxford: Oxford University Press, 2001).

Aristotle, *Politics* (Pol), translated by Benjamin Jowett, (eBooks@Adelaide, Adelaide, 2007).

Ballou, J.P. and B.A. Weisbrod, "Managerial Rewards and the Behavior of for-profit, Governmental, and Non-profit Organizations: Evidence from the Hospital Industry", *Journal of Public Economics* 87(9-10) (2003) 1895–1920.

Bass, B.M. and B.J. Avolio, "Transformational Leadership and Organizational Culture", *International Journal of Public Administration* 17(3/4), (1994) 541–554.

Bernstein, J., C. Brocht and M. Spade- Aguilar, *How Much is Enough?: Basic Family Budgets for Working Families*, (Washington D.C.: Economic Policy Institute, 2000).

Biswas-Diener, R., E. Diener and M. Tamir, "The Psychology of Subjective Well-being", *Daedalus* 133(2) (2004) 18–25.

Block, P., *Stewardship: Choosing Service over Self-interest* (San Francisco: Berrett-Koehler Publishers, 1996).

Carroll, A.B. and A.K. Buchholtz, *Business and Society – Ethics and Stakeholder Management* (Mason, OH: South-Western, 2003).

Carroll, A.B., "The Pyramid of Corporate Social Responsibility: Toward the Moral Management of Organizational Stakeholders", *Business Horizons* 34(4) (1991) 39–48.

Carroll, A.B., "Corporate Social Responsibility – Evolution of a Definitional Construct", *Business & Society* 38(3) (1999) 268–295.

Child, J. and S.B. Rodrigues, "Repairing the Breach of Trust in Corporate Governance", *Corporate Governance* 12(2) (2004) 143–153.

Collins, D., "Aristotle and Business", *Journal of Business Ethics* (6) (1987) 567–572.

Darling, J.R., "Crisis Management in International Business", *Leadership & Organization Development Journal* 15(8) (1994) 3–8.

Davis, J.H., F.D. Schoorman and T. Donaldson, "Toward a Stewardship Theory of Management", *Academy of Management Review* 22(1), (1997) 20–47.

Demarest, M., "Understanding Knowledge Management", *Long Range Planning* 30(3) (1997) 321–322, 374–384.

Demosthenes, *I Olynthiacs, Philippics Minor Public Orations I-XVII and XX*, (Cambridge, MA: Loeb Classical Library No. 238, 1930).

Diener, E. and M.E.P. Seligman, "Beyond money: Toward and economy of well-being", *Psychological Science in the Public Interest* 5(1) (2004) 1-31.

Donaldson, L. and J.H. Davis, "Stewardship Theory or Agency Theory: CEO Governance and Shareholder Returns", *Australian Journal of Management* 16(1) (1991) 49–66.

Donaldson, T., "Editor's Comments: Taking Ethics Seriously— A Mission Now More Possible", *Academy of Management Review* 28 (3) (2003) 363–366.

Dyck, B. and R. Kleysen, "Aristotle's Virtues and Management Thought: An Empirical Exploration of an Integrative Pedagogy", *Business Ethics Quarterly* 11(4) (2001) 561–574.

Easterlin, R., "Income and Happiness: Towards a Unified Theory", *Economic Journal* 111, (July) (2001) 465–484.

Fontrodona, J. and D. Melé, "Philosophy as a Base for Management: An Aristotelian Integrative Proposal", *Philosophy of Management* (formerly *Reason in Practice*) 2(2), (2002) 3-9.

Freedman, J.L., *Happy People: What Happiness Is, Who Has It, and Why?* (New York: Harcourt Brace Jovanovich, 1978).

Freshfields, Bruckhaus and Deringer, A Legal Framework for the Integration of Environmental, Social and Governance (ESG) Issues into Institutional Investment, (New York: United Nations Environment Programme Finance Initiative (UNEP FI), 2006).

Giddens, A., *Modernity and Self – Identity: Self and Society in the Late Modern Age*, (Cambridge, Polity Press, 1991).

Gimbel, S., "Can Corporations Be Morally Responsible? Aristotle, Stakeholders and the Non-Sale of Hershey", *Philosophy of Management, (formerly Reason in Practice)* 5(3) (2005), pp. 23–30.

Hart, S., *Capitalism at the Crossroads – The Unlimited Business Opportunities in Solving the World´s Most Difficult Problems*, (Upper Saddle River, NJ: Wharton School Publishing, 2005).

Hawken, P., A. Lovins and H. Lovins:, *Natural Capitalism: Creating the Next Industrial Revolution*, (NY: Little, Brown & Co., 2000).

Hofstede, G., B. Neuijen, D.D. Ohayv and G. Sanders, "Measuring Organizational Cultures: A Qualitative and Quantitative Study across Twenty Cases" *Administrative Science Quarterly* 35(2) (1990) 286–316.

Jackson, I. and J. Nelson, *Profits with Principles- Seven Strategies for Delivering Value with Values*, (New York: Currency Doubleday, 2004).

Jensen, M.C., "Value Maximization, Stakeholder Theory and the Corporate Objective Function", *Business Ethics Quarterly* 12(2) (2002) 235–257.

Kasmir, J., *The Myth of Mondragon: Cooperatives, Politics, and Working-Class Life in a Basque Town*, (New York: State University of New York Press, 1996).

Kasser, T. and A.C. Ahuvia, "Materialistic Values and Well-being in Business Students", *European Journal of Social Psychology* 32(1) (2002) 137–146.

Koslowski, P., *Politik und Ökonomie bei Aristoteles*, (Tuebingen: Mohr, 1993).

Lane, R., "Does money buy happiness?", *The Public Interest* 113(Fall) (1993) 56–65.

Langholm, O., *Price and Value in the Aristotelian Tradition: A Study in Scholastic Sources* (Bergen: Universitetsforlaget, 1979).

Lawrence, P. and N. Nohria, *Driven: How Human Nature Shapes Our Choices* (San Francisco: Jossey-Bass, 2002).

Lawrence, P.: 2007, Being Human – A Renewed Darwinian Theory of Human Behavior, www.prlawrence.com. Accessed on June 15, 2008.

Layard, R., *Happiness - Lessons from a New Science*, (London: Penguin Press, 2005).

Lowry, S.T., *The Archeology of Economic Ideas. The Classical Greek Tradition*, (Durham: Duke University Press, 1987).

Martin, P., *Making Happy People*, (London: Fourth Estate, 2005).

McWilliams, A. and D. Siegel, "Corporate Social Responsibility: A Theory of the Firm Perspective" *Academy of Management Review*, 26(1), (2001) 117–127.

Meikle, S., *Aristotle's Economic Thought* (Oxford: Clarendon Press, 1994).

Mukherji, P.N. and C. Sengupta, *Indigeneity and Universality in Social Science: A South Asian Response*, (Thousand Oaks, CA: Sage, 2004).

Nussbaum, M., *Love's Knowledge: Essays on Philosophy and Literature* (New York and Oxford: Oxford University Press, 1990).

Pava, M.L. and J. Kraus, "The Association between Corporate Social-Responsibility and Financial Performance: The Paradox of Social Cost", *Journal of Business Ethics* 15(3) (1996) 321–357.

Porter, M. and M. Kramer, "Strategy and Society: The Link between competitive advantage and corporate social responsibility", *Harvard Business Review*, December (2006) 1–14.

Putnam, R.D., *Bowling Alone: The Collapse and Revival of American Community*, (New York: Simon & Schuster, 2000).

Savitz, A.W. and K. Weber, *The Triple Bottom Line*, (Hoboken, NJ: John Wiley & Sons, 2006).

Schein, E.H., *Organizational Culture and Leadership: A Dynamic View*, (San Francisco: Jossey-Bass, 1985).

Scherer, A.G. and G. Palazzo, "Toward a Political Conception of Corporate Social Responsibility: Business and Society seen from a Habermasian Perspective", *Academy of Management Review* 32(4) (2007) 1096–1120.

Schoengrund, C., "Aristotle and Total Quality Management", *Total Quality Management* 7(1) (1996) 79–91.

Schonsheck, J., "Business Friends: Aristotle, Kant and other Management Theorists on the Practice of Networking", *Business Ethics Quarterly* 10(4) (2000) 897–910.

Schumpeter, J., *History of Economic Analysis* (New York: Oxford University Press, 1954).

Smith, N.C., "Corporate Social Responsibility: Whether or How?", *California Management Review* 45(4) (2003) 52–76.

Solomon, R.C., *Ethics and Excellence: Co-operation and Integrity in Business*, (Oxford and New York: Oxford University Press, 1992).

Solomon, R.C., "Aristotle, Ethics and Business Organizations", *Organization Studies* 25(6) (2004) 1021–1043.

Soudek, J., "Aristotle's Theory of Exchange. An Inquiry into the Origin of the Economic Analysis", *Proceedings of the American Philosophical Society* (96) (1952) 55–59.

Spitzeck, H. and Hansen, E.G., Stakeholder Governance – How do stakeholders influence corporate decision-making?, in: Corporate Governance (2010).

Strom, S., "Businesses Try to Make Money and Save the World", *New York Times*, May 6, 2007.

Sundaram, A.K. and A.C. Inkpen, "The Corporate Objective Revisited", *Organization Science* 15(3) (2004) 350–363.

Swift, T., "Trust, Reputation and Corporate Accountability to Stakeholders", *Business Ethics: A European Review* 10(1) (2001) 15–26.

Waterman, A.S., "The Relevance of Aristotle's Conception of Eudaimonia for the Psychological Study of Happiness", *Theoretical and Philosophical Psychology* 10 (1990) 39–44.

Wijnberg, N.M., "Normative Stakeholder Theory and Aristotle: The Link Between Ethics and Politics", *Journal of Business Ethics* (25) (2000) 329–342.

# 3
# Stoic Humanism

*Maximilian Forschner*

## 3.1 The cosmopolitanism of Stoic ethics

The ethics of the Hellenistic era, above all Epicurean and Stoic ethics, are the first examples in history of fundamentally *universalistic* ethics; that is to say, they no longer presuppose the legal framework, the special tradition, or the daily experience of the Greek *polis*, and they no longer focus on virtues whose features are gleaned from the contemplation of Greek *polis*-life. Furthermore, in their ethical aims, claims, challenges, and recommendations they no longer insist on a sharp difference between Greeks and barbarians, lords and commoners, men and women, free men and slaves, rich and poor.

Stoic philosophy, within its conclusively constructed system of thought, contains a thoroughly humanistic ethics. In this respect, no other ancient philosophical school has influenced the ethical and political tradition of the Western World to such a great extent. This ethics presents the philosophical basis of the idea of the community of all men; it marks the idea of the *kosmos* as a *cosmopolis*, a political community of gods and men, held together and directed by the laws of nature as laws of divine reason, in which man can actively participate. It marks the idea of the dignity of man on the basis of his *logos*: his capacity to speak and argue, to actively relate to himself, to form his character, to control himself, to set his own goals, and to respect this capacity in other people.

It marks the idea of the moral development of the individual, beginning with a phase which *externally* resembles the life of an animal; *internally* this life is originally directed by seminal reason (*logos spermatikos*) which may lead the individual to attain the status of a wise man (*sophos*), who lives and understands himself like a "mortal god," in total accordance and harmony with nature and the divine organization and administration of the world. This idea of moral development and progress frames, in the Stoic mind, the grades and phases of human life. It also puts forward the idea of conscience as the moral self-awareness of the *prokopton*, that is, of one who loves himself as a being *on the way* towards perfect wisdom, but who also critically sees and judges himself detached from this state of desired perfection.

Let me briefly focus on two fundamental ideas of Stoic ethics, the unity of mankind and the dignity of man, both of which are grounded in the ability of man to speak and argue and thereby to participate as a reasonable and free subject directly and actively in divine reason.

The first idea, that of the unity of mankind and its ethical and juridical implications, the Stoa convincingly develops in its doctrine of *oikeiosis*. The second idea, that of the dignity of man, the Stoa directly develops in its doctrine of *logos*. Both doctrines are intimately interconnected.

## 3.2   The idea of the unity of mankind

The Greek adjective *oikeios* means belonging to one's family, a part or a friend of one's home. The transitive verb *oikeioun* means to make a person someone else's friend, the medium and passive verb *oikeiousthai* means to be or to be made someone's friend. The prominent sources for the reconstruction of the Stoic doctrine of *oikeiosis* are Cicero, *De finibus bonorum et malorum* III, 16–18; 20–21; 62–68; Diogenes Laertius, *Lives of Eminent Philosophers*, VII, 85–86 and the *Ethike Stoicheiosis* of Hierokles, an author from the second century after Christ.

The leading idea of this doctrine is that universal nature has equipped all its sentient creatures with self-love and with a cluster of instinctive impulses and rules of conduct appropriate to preserving and developing themselves and the species within the framework of the life (and of the kind of life) of their species. The Stoics argue for this thesis with empirical and metaphysical evidence and arguments.

The metaphysical arguments first concentrate on the idea that the initial impulses and teleological endeavors of living beings to preserve themselves presuppose an original relation to their own being and to their own form of existence; and this presupposes in living beings which have self-experience of life an original experience of their life as something good. Secondly, such arguments focus on the thought that it would be absurd for universal nature to have created living beings indifferent or alien or even enemies to themselves. Universal nature is perfect reason and works with perfect reason; it is in total harmony with itself. We can understand universal nature as one immense organism, the life and the periods of life of which are organized and directed by the immanent principle of divine reason. In each species and in each individual living being universal nature manifests and loves itself.

The empirical arguments focus on the idea that it is the principle of self-love, rather than other principles, that best explains all the observable facts of the phenomena of life. In short, self-love is the fundamental principle of all life and behavior. The individual's self-love is related to and restricted by natural tendencies to preserve the species, to which the individuals of a species are naturally disposed in their behavior by an inborn rule, or even a sense of unity, with all the members of their species.

This thesis is directed against the Epicureans, who considered the longing for pleasure to be the fundamental principle of life for all sentient creatures. For the Stoics the Epicurean principle does not match the facts; and moreover, it is destructive for our moral intuitions: It undermines the ideas required for friendship, for altruistic virtue, and for the bonds of political community. For the Stoics, in each creature there is a seminally inborn program for acts of preservation and development. Self-love, in their eyes, naturally works so that it is continuously directed to the current level of development.

When classifying the phenomena of life, Stoics distinguish three principles of life: those at work in plants (*physis*), in animals (*psyche*), in men (*logos*), assuming the *logos* of man to be of the same kind as the principle of life of God or the gods. The *logos* as the principle of life in man contains the program (*logos spermatikos*) for the specific and individual self-organization of life, and for acts of preservation and development. It is at work from the outset of life. In the first phases of a human life this program works without propositional insight or free assent from the new-born or young child. By learning to speak and behave in accordance with thought and spoken imperatives and rules, the *logos* of the young person develops and one gradually discovers one's own developing reason, gradually taking possession of it so as to use it in its own way and on its own behalf.

The process of discovering and appropriating one's own reason is the phase of coming of age. But using one's own reason is a precarious affair for men: Human reason is such that one can use it either rightly or wrongly; and more often than not, when men have newly come of age, they will use it wrongly. This misuse of reason depends above all on the fact that most men grow up and live under more or less perverted and perverting political, social, and educational institutions and conditions.

Through a sound course of development the young person gradually learns how to behave well by instruction and habituation, to do what is, as the Stoics put it, *kathekon*, and to give good and fitting reasons for his behavior. *Kathekon* for the Stoics is the behavior of a living entity which fits its nature and its role within a given social whole.

As good behavior becomes habitual, as he increasingly consistently provides good reasons and as he increasingly reflects on the growing order of his actions and the reasons for them, man finally discovers the very structure and essence of right reason and the overwhelming beauty of using his reason in the right way (cf. Cicero, *De finibus* III, 20 ff.). Now man has come to the point where his outlook on life has fundamentally changed and where his way of life has a new ultimate end.

In the first phases of life his self-love was naturally set to preserve and to develop his life and the ingredients that are necessary, useful and pleasing for human life, such as health, beauty, strength, friends, money, honor, and worldly success. Now he has gained a detachment from his life and its goods because he has existentially grasped and seized the fact that one can use these things in both a good and a bad way, that they are not always useful but sometimes detrimental, that one will certainly lose all of them at the end of one's life, that, therefore, as a thinking and reflecting entity, one cannot become happy if one loves these things without reservation, that, therefore, they are not of absolute value, and that the only thing of absolute value on earth is right reason and the attitudes, behaviors, and emotions necessarily implied by or connected with right reason.

His self-love is now absolutely fixed on right reason. Without restriction and reservation he now only loves his reason and the satisfying use of his reason. He is from now on substantially indifferent to life and its goods (*adiaphora*). Of course, they are not judged to be totally worthless. He estimates them as *prohegmena*, as something positive, as something preferable to its opposite. Nature has made us so as to prefer them spontaneously. As a result, he tries to get or preserve those goods, as he did in the previous phases of his life; but he no longer loves them and strives for them in an unrestricted and unreserved manner. Moreover, he possesses them knowing and accepting the fact that he certainly will lose them all. So he possesses them as if he does not possess them. This attitude, the attitude of right reason to goods that can be lost and misused, makes him free, makes him immune to all possible misfortunes and miseries of life. In this way he comes to an agreement with fate: If his endeavors to gain life's goods fail or if he loses those goods, even if the loss is ordinarily understood as a crushing one, such as the loss of one's health, life, wife, children, honor, or money. He totally accords with fate, because he loves right reason absolutely, his own right reason, which for him is an integral and active part of cosmic reason, which forms and directs and administrates all things and events.

It is by *theoria*, above all via reflection and meditation on the astonishing and elevating results of astronomy and the expedient phenomena of biology, that the Stoic wise man gains his fundamental ontological and cosmological convictions, for example, that the world is well-ordered, a *kosmos*, not a *chaos*, that all things and events are lawfully connected, that there is a divine rational principle, force and power forming, organizing, administrating, and directing the world in reasonable relations and steps in its details and on a broader scale so that, ultimately, the order of the cosmos itself is a perfect explication of right reason.

What the Stoics call *oikeiosis*, the teleological process of self-love in living and developing beings, culminating in man in an absolute love of reason, has several aspects that call for our attention.

Through the ideal of the wise man, the Stoa pleads for a independent and relaxed attitude to worldly goods, without minimizing or denying their relative value, a value founded on a pantheist ontology legitimizing natural inclinations and their objects as *prima facie* worthy of being preferred and pursued. Through the ideal of the wise man, the Stoa also pleads for a universal humanism, an attitude that respects and loves all men as members of one great family. In Stoic eyes, the process of *oikeiosis* is a process of concentration as well as of expanding circles that describe and circumscribe the objects of love. The process results, in the mature phase of human life, in absolute love of oneself as a subject of reason; and this self-love is essentially connected with an absolute love of objective reason, of the divine reason of the cosmos as well as of individual subjects in the cosmos who are reasonable or are capable of becoming reasonable. Thus, as a result of the process of *oikeiosis*, Cicero (in formulating the Stoic doctrine) is able to state that all men are of divine origin and that, therefore, they are united by a universal kinship, so that no man should feel alienated from his fellow men, and this is simply because of the fact that he is a man (*De finibus* III, 63: *Ex hoc nascitur ut etiam communis hominum inter homines naturalis sit commendatio, ut oporteat hominem ob id ipsum, quod homo sit, non alienum videri*). This is the most basic philosophical formula of Western humanism. Because all men as men immediately stem from and participate in the divine *logos*, they all are full members of a community the laws of which are constituted by right reason (cf. *Stoicorum Veterum Fragmenta*, ed. Hans von Arnim II, 528). This natural law, the law of right reason, makes each man a subject of natural rights, even those who cannot, at the time – as children, women, foreigners, or slaves – claim rights within the framework of law of a given political community (cf. Cicero, *De officiis* I, 41).

Importantly, the Stoics draw a sharp line between the idea of a wise man (which only very few, among them perhaps the historical Socrates, could ever realize) and the many who love the position of reason and try to realize it in their lives but who still have to struggle with unreasonable inclinations and who are sometimes defeated by them and thus also feel and strive and act in unreasonable ways. For these men – the Stoics call them *prokoptontes* – reason plays the role of conscience. A true conscience is possible only on the basis of the sound self-love of man as a subject of reason, a self-love which is nevertheless not sound enough as to be firmly and unshakably in accord with right reason but which can be seduced by the attraction of worldly goods or affected by the pains and grievances of worldly evils. In the case of these men, reason as it relates to right reason plays the role of a witness, admonisher, accuser, lawyer and judge with respect to their own precarious position and their own steps towards achieving perfect reason.

## 3.3   The idea of the dignity of man

Let me now briefly explain the second central idea of Stoic ethics, that of the dignity of man. The Stoics were the first philosophers to introduce and explore the concept of human dignity. They found the basis of human dignity in man's capacity to speak, to argue, to actively relate to himself, to form and control his thoughts, his endeavors, his actions and emotions, to see and judge the world not only within the limits of the narrow horizon of particular species-bound interests but from an objective perspective, to see and judge it, at least partially and tentatively, from the perspective of God.

This capacity, if actualized, makes a man a free and sovereign person, an impartial spectator and actor, indeed, for limited time, a godlike entity. In the words of Epictetus:

> Among the arts and faculties you will find none that is self-contemplative, and therefore none that is either self-approving or self-disapproving [...] What art or faculty, then, will tell (you, what to do or not to do, of those things you are able to do)? That one which contemplates both itself and everything else. And what is this? The reasoning faculty (*dynamis logike*); for this is the only one we have

inherited which will take knowledge both of itself – what it is, and of what it is capable, and how valuable a gift it is to us – and likewise of all the other faculties [...] As was fitting, therefore, the Gods have put under our control only the most excellent faculty of all and that which dominates the rest, namely, the power to make correct use of external impressions, but all the others they have not put under our control [...] What says Zeus? "Epictetus, had it been possible I should have made both this paltry body and this small estate of yours free and unhampered. But as it is – let it not escape you – this body is not your own, but only clay cunningly compounded. Yet since I could not give you this, we have given you a certain portion of ourselves, this faculty of choice and refusal, of desire and aversion, or, in a word, the faculty which makes use of external impressions; if you care for this and place all that you have therein, you shall never be thwarted, never hampered, shall not groan, shall not blame, shall not flatter any man. What then? Are these things small in your sight?" "Far be it from me!" "Are you, then, content with them?" "I pray the Gods I may be. (*Diatribai* I, 1, 1–13, Transl. by W. A. Oldfather, my modernization)

Epictetus and all the authors of the late Stoa stress that the greatness of man results from his capacity to judge himself, to control himself, and to possess himself as a reasonable subject. By cultivating this capacity, by forming himself into a person, man becomes sovereign, a sovereign whose will, in the words of Epictetus, "not even Zeus himself has power to overcome" (*Diatribai* I, 1, 23). The empire of his sovereignty is his own reason. What he has firmly in his hand are his thoughts and his intentions, and the emotions resulting from his right thoughts and intentions. Through our thoughts and intentions we make use of our impressions; and to have an opinion and an intention depends on our assent (*synkatathesis*), the very kernel of our sovereignty.

We lose our sovereignty if we are enslaved by our impressions and by the opinions and desires provoked by unproven and un-judged impressions; such impressions seduce us into caring about worldly news and goods in an unrestricted and disorganized manner.

But now, although it is in our power to care for one thing only and devote ourselves to but one, we choose rather to care for many things, and to be tied fast to many, even to our body and our estate and brother and friend and child and slave. Wherefore, being tied fast to many things, we are burdened and dragged down by them. (*Diatribai* I, 1, 14–15)

Man's dignity is based on his *logos* and the capabilities implied in and connected with it, the most important of which is freedom of the will and of thoughts, which allows man to set his own goals and aims and to be the designer and originator of his own endeavors (*technites tes hormes*)(cf. Diogenes Laertius, *Lives of Eminent Philosophers* VII, 86 f.). It was Cicero, who, in line with Stoic thinking, made (or, rather, prepared) a distinction of eminent importance for the moral and juridical views of the Western World, a distinction between the moral meaning of dignity on the one hand and its juridical meaning on the other.

The moral meaning of dignity has as its focus an attitude of life which makes a sharp distinction between animal and human life and draws a clear border around animal goals of preserving the self and the species, of avoiding pain and finding pleasure. Man is able not only to pursue these goals; he is also able to cultivate them so as to detach them from himself; he can pursue disinterested knowledge, form and materialize aesthetic ideas, construct and realize social and political institutions according to moral and juridical ideas. These possibilities include goals of human life that differ qualitatively from those of animal life and substantially raise man above the level of the animals. The more a man controls and forms himself, the more a man lives according to these ideas, the more dignity he exposes his life to. Dignity in this sense is opposed to a vulgar way of living; it certainly has grades of realization, and is evidently realized in men to very different grades and in very different ways.

The juridical meaning of dignity comes from the same source as the moral meaning. But it draws no distinction between one man and another; it is independent of the type of their character and behavior; it obliges us to respect each man as an end in himself, that is, as a person who has a fundamental inalienable right to set and pursue his own goals; it obliges us to never totally instrumentalize a man. The universal dignity of man hence does not refer to his actual reason, but only to the possibility of realizing a life according to reason; not only to the actual capacity of an individual but also to the *dignitas humanae naturae* in each human individual, whatever his actual capacities may be in practice.

It is true that this last conclusion was not reached until the rise of Christian religion, yet the way to it had been prepared by the Stoics. Again, it was above all the Stoic and Ciceronian tradition (and a small group of Christian Dissenters) that gave life to the idea of inalienable human rights in the political sphere, in the time of the European Enlightenment. For we must remember: Insofar as it concerns human life *in this world*, this idea was not truly supported by the leading Christian churches until the end of World War II.

## 3.4   Politics, wealth, and business life

For the Stoics, wealth and political power belong to the indifferent goods of life (*adiaphora*): You can use them in a good or bad manner; they can be detrimental to their possessor; they are not valuable in absolute terms; you must not strive for them in an uncontrolled way. But they are preferable to their opposites: You naturally take, keep, use, and enjoy them, if they are available to you, but in such a way as to remain internally independent of whether you possess them or not. The Stoics, unlike Aristotle, did not distinguish between or privilege certain ways of life on any theoretical basis. Aristotle had argued that a life of philosophical *theoria* and "disinterested" scientific research and contemplation was the best, and the life of a leading politician was the second best, way of life. He did not highly estimate the life of bankers, businessmen, or shopkeepers; in his eyes they focus their life only on things of instrumental value. The Stoics rejected this process of distinction and discrimination. The Stoic sage could perfectly well take on any role in life. But in practice the great figures of the Stoa abstained from politics and business. They lived the life of teachers, searchers, scholars and, occasionally, political counselors (see Plutarch, *De stoicorum repugnantiis* 2, 1033 b.e = SVF I, 27). Prominent exceptions are Seneca and Marcus Aurelius, the one a great statesman and clever businessman, the other an important emperor.

The Stoics in theory did not privilege any particular way of making a living. Kleanthes, the second head of the school, supposedly earned his living as a porter and wrestler during his studies. In practice most of them lived by private means, and they commonly lived a very modest and independent life. But we also have evidence testifying that some received support from protectors or took money for their teaching or received fees for their books. Seneca was very rich: according to modern standards, a multi-millionaire. He was blamed for preaching asceticism and living in luxury. In his essay *De vita beata*, he tried to refute the charge and explain the Stoic doctrine. The Stoics, according to Seneca, care unconditionally about the strength and health of their minds. They also care about the commodities of life, but in a restrained manner. They readily resign themselves to inevitable circumstances, if they are harsh and painful. They also are prepared to enjoy riches but without becoming their slave. The wise man, Seneca holds, does not take himself to be unworthy of wealth; the Stoic doctrine does not commit one to asceticism and poverty. You may enjoy your riches if you are their lawful owner, but without pride and knowing quite well that wealth as such is an indifferent thing and can easily be lost.

> The sage [...] does not love wealth, but he prefers it to another standard of living; he does not take it into his soul, but into his house; nor does he repudiate it, when he has it, but keeps it" (21, 4 transl. Th. Fuhrer). "I do not say that wealth is a good; if it would be a good, it would make men good; now because you find bad men who are rich you cannot say that wealth is a good [...]; but I do say that it is worth having and useful and brings great advantages in life. (24, 5)

What matters is the strength of the soul that keeps you independent of wealth *and* poverty; the sage is happy in either position. But wealth, if honestly acquired, is a *materia* suitable for displaying the virtues of liberality, generosity, and magnanimity with regard to the right persons, the right institutions, and the right time. On the other hand, wealth is also a *materia* especially suitable for displaying the virtues of temperance and modesty with regard to one's own desires, otherwise prone to avarice, covetousness, and the love of pleasures (cf. 25, 5–7). For this reason the sage does not reject wealth but wants to have more of the *materia* to assist his virtue (*nec respuit possessas sed continet et maiorem virtuti suae materiam sumministrari vult* 21, 4). "It is a mark of a weak character not to be able to bear wealth" (*Epistula ad Lucilium* 5, 6).

Seneca writes in the tradition of Cicero's *De officiis*, in which the Stoic (especially the *Panaetian*) doctrine of virtues, above all that of *liberalitas*, *magnificentia* and *temperantia* are translated into the context of the Roman republican élite. "You have to try to acquire funds," Cicero writes, "by means that are free of turpitude; but you have to preserve and equally to increase them by means of carefulness and economy (*diligentia et parsimonia*)" (*De off.* II, 86). Panaitios, Cicero presumes, did not write on ethical questions about the treatment of wealth, because in his eyes the answers were plain and evident. Cicero himself recommends the reading of the *Oikonomikos* of Xenophon, a book which deals with the maxims of a wealthy landowner to direct the people, tasks, and labor on his estate decently and successfully. But he also adds that you must inform yourself of the honest methods for acquiring, preserving, and increasing your funds in order to be able to live an honest *and* fruitful life. To explain and teach these methods should be not so much the job of philosophers but of experienced businessmen (*De off.* II, 87).

In Stoic eyes only the sage is able to bear wealth as well as the loss of wealth in the right way. But wisdom is an ideal that is very difficult to realize, if it can be realized at all. It requires hard processes of education and exercise. Most followers of Stoicism, and Seneca says this also of himself, are not wise, but only continuously progressing and fighting on the way to wisdom: "I am not a sage [...] I will not be one [...]. It is enough for me, if I discard daily a part of my weaknesses and can achieve control over my mistakes" (*De vita beata* 17, 3).

## Bibliography

Maximilian Forschner, Oikeiosis. Die stoische Theorie der Selbstaneignung, in: Barbara Neymeyr, Jochen Schmidt, Bernhard Zimmermann (Hrsg.), Stoizismus in der europäischen Philosophie, Literatur, Kunst und Politik. Band 1, (Berlin-New York, 2008) 169–192.

Maximilian Forschner, *Stoische Oikeiosislehre und mittelalterliche Theorie des Gewissens*, in: Jan Szaif und/and Mathias Lutz-Bachmann (eds.), *Was ist das für den Menschen Gute? Menschliche Natur und Güterlehre – What Is Good for a Human Being? Numan Nature and Values*, (Berlin-New York, 2004) 126–150.

Maximilian Forschner, *Theoria and Stoic Virtue. Zeno's Legacy in Cicero, Tusculanae Disputationes V*, in: Theodore Scaltsas and Andrew S. Mason (eds), *Zeno of Citium and his Legacy: The Philosophy of Zeno*, (Larnaca, 2002) 259–290.

Maximilian Forschner, Le Portique et le Concept de Personne, in: Gilbert Romeyer Dherbey (Dir.) et Jean-Baptiste Gourinat (ed.), Les Stoïciens, Paris 2005, 293–317.

Maximilian Forschner, Über die stoische Begründung des Guten und Wertvollen, in: Methexis XVII (2004), 55–69.

Therese Fuhrer, "The Philosopher as Multi-Millionaire: Seneca on Double Standards", in: *Double Standards in the Ancient and Medieval World*, ed. Karla Pollmann, (Göttingen, 2000) 201–219.

Peter Scholz, Der Philosoph und die Politik. Die Ausbildung der philosophischen Lebensform und die Entwicklung des Verhältnisses von Philosophie und Politik im 4. und 3. Jh. v. Chr., (Stuttgart, 1998).

# 4
# Thomas Aquinas on Business and the Fulfillment of Human Needs

*Claus Dierksmeier and Anthony Celano*

In the history of Western thought, Thomas Aquinas is certainly the most influential medieval thinker. His stance on moral questions generally and his views on socio-economic justice in particular provided normative orientation to subsequent Christian thinkers, and they still influence Catholic social teaching, as exemplified in the social encyclicals of the Church. For instance, the latest papal letter, *Caritas in Veritate*, which addresses the moral challenges to business in the age of globalization, draws heavily upon the moral arguments of Thomas Aquinas. In this chapter, we wish to make Thomas's stance on the ethics of business intelligible to a readership neither steeped in medieval studies, nor familiar with specifically Christian views on morality. We first explain how Thomas's theory could be of relevance to a non-Christian audience through its appeal to the "natural light of reason" (1). Then we outline how his ideas on virtue and justice inform his theory of government and frame his discussion of social and economic justice (2). Finally, we address the principles of his economic thinking (3) and their application to the world of business (4).

## 4.1   From natural reason to natural law

Thomas Aquinas (1224–1274) wrote widely on questions of ethics, and derived his moral arguments throughout from a conception of the "natural law" (*lex naturale*) of the human being, which itself rests on a philosophical conception of the essential traits of human nature. A modern reader may be surprised by the confidence Thomas displays in his unquestioning acceptance of such universal and not infrequently counterfactual standards for the legitimacy of moral conduct. How could he believe so firmly that his audience would share his basic assumptions about both the content and the validity of the strictures of his conception of the natural law? What supports Thomas's confidence in the universal legitimacy of the natural law doctrine is his philosophical conviction that through sound thinking the order of life is recognizable, at least in its most fundamental principles. Thomas holds that the "natural light" of reason (*lumen naturale*) ultimately leads to truth (*S. th* I-II, 109, 1 ad 2; II-II, 8, 1 c; 15. 1 c; 171. 2 c & 4 ob. 3; etc.). God has endowed the human being with rational capacities sufficient for earthly life; they may be supervened, but are not contradicted or annihilated by "supernatural" (*lumen supernaturale*), that is, revelation-based, knowledge (*S. th*. I-II, 109, 1 ad 2). In emphasizing the capacity of human reason to reach truth unaided by theology, Thomas addresses the rational powers of every human being, everywhere and always (*SCG* 1, 2). Of course, not everything can be known through the workings of natural reason alone; in matters of faith and salvation the powers of rationality are inadequate (*Sent*. III, d. 1, q. 1, a. 2–3). Yet the basic tenets of theoretical philosophy can be known solely by reason, and the same holds for the fundamentals of moral reasoning (*S. th*. I-II 94, 2). For, according to Thomas, God instilled into all things "their respective inclinations to their proper acts and ends," so that by their natural law (*lex naturalis*) and inclinations all created beings are oriented towards their respective, proper good (*S. th*. I-II, 91, 2).

Thomas accepts the basic premises of Aristotle's teleological metaphysics and supplements them with another, theological, foundation for the intrinsic ends of entities. In the resulting scheme of created nature, which reveals its creator through a graduated hierarchy of beings, human life receives an elevated status. Human intellect becomes aware of the order that governs life in recognizing the natural laws of both human and sub-human life. Human reason can (potentially, if not always in practice) understand how natural laws orient all beings towards their good, which, when realized, perfects them (*De Ver.* q. 21, a. 1). Unlike animals, human beings cannot rely solely on natural instincts to achieve their good (*S. th*. I, 5, 1). As beings acting based upon rational conceptions about the world, humans need to represent to themselves the goals (as objectives) they are to pursue; they need to make explicit the implicit law that governs their lives, by spelling out as human law what they deem to be the natural law of their existence.

Thomas teaches that each person knows in their heart of hearts that "good is to be done and pursued, and evil is to be avoided" (*S. th*. I-II, 94, 2); awareness of this fundamental principle (*synderesis*) can never be expunged; as an indestructible core of sustained righteousness (*perpetuae rectitudinis*) it resides forever in everyone (*Sent.* II, d. 24, q. 3, a. 3 ad 3: Stammkötter, 2001; Celano, 2007). This fundamental moral principle notwithstanding, people do not always agree on moral questions. So what accounts for ethical disagreements? The variety of ethically charged customs and conventions often reflects the divergent contingencies of circumstance of moral practice (*S. th.* I-II 94, 4). Virtuous behavior can, and at times must, vary according to context; an insight, which is, obviously, of immediate relevance for regional ethics in general and for its culture-specific application in particular. Yet when and how may circumstances change the ethical case in point, and how far does reason offer guidance, even in changing environments?

Thomas acknowledges certain general precepts about virtue (*S. th.* II-II, 44, 2, 1), and holds in fact that "all acts of virtue are prescribed by the natural law" (*S. th.* I-II, 94, 3). Hence, if the essence of the latter is intelligible to human reason, so should be the nature of the former. Virtue pursues the good, while the natural law teaches what the basic goods of human life are. Observing the most fundamental human inclinations and reconstructing them as the natural ends of human existence, Aquinas lists the following as the basic goods of human life:

> in man there is first of all an inclination to good in accordance with the nature which he has in common with all substances: inasmuch as every substance seeks the preservation of its own existence, according to its nature. According to this inclination whatever is a means of preserving human life, and prevents its termination, belongs to the natural law. Secondly, there is in man an inclination to things that pertain to him more specially, according to that nature which he has in common with other animals: and in virtue of this inclination, those things are said to belong to the natural law, [...], such as sexual intercourse, education of offspring and so forth. Thirdly, there is in man an inclination to good, according to the nature of reason, which is proper to him: as man has a natural inclination to know the truth about God, and to live in society: and in this respect, whatever pertains to this inclination belongs to the natural law; for instance, to shun ignorance, to avoid offending those among whom one has to live, and other such things regarding the above inclination. (*S. th.* I-II 94, 2)

The general principle "to do good and to avoid evil" becomes more specific when applied to these natural goods, that is, in the command to promote (and to abstain from hindering) their realization. Some precepts of natural law can thereby be derived conceptually, while others need further contextualization and reflection.

> Some things are therefore derived from the general principles of the natural law, by way of conclusions, such as "one must not kill" may be derived as a certain conclusion from the principle that "one should do harm to no one." Some are derived by way of determination, as the law of nature holds that the one who does wrong should be punished; but that one is punished in such a manner is a determination of the law of nature. (*S. th.* I-II 95, 2)

Consequently, not only the generic principle to pursue the good and to shun evil, but also certain specific precepts of natural law that follow directly from it can be affirmed as valid across times and cultures. While contextual differentiation with regard to the specificities of regional customs (*S. th.* I-II 95, 3) and temporal affairs (*S. th.* I-II 96, 1) is accepted by Thomas, ethical diversity also has clear limits. In his view, the fundamental imperative to advance the natural goods of human life delivers a substantial context-invariant body of ethical norms, binding all humans at all times and in all places; it provides a global ethical yardstick, if you will, according to which regional customs can be measured; again, a position with direct consequences for today's debates around the intercultural nature of business ethics and corporate responsibility (CR).

In defending the universal intelligibility of the fundamentals of natural law, Thomas also promotes the universality of ethics in another, quite crucial aspect: Virtue as the pursuit of the good is based upon an adequate rational conception of morality. Since the latter always remains within the reach of every human being and because "the natural law, in the abstract, can in no wise be blotted out from men's hearts" (*S. th.* I-II 94, 6), it follows that no human being is ever wholly without (potential) virtue and an innate awareness of the good. Even those who commit atrocious sins cannot thereby divest themselves of their rational nature, or their potential to redirect their lives to the good (*S. th.* I-II 85, 2). The fundamental dignity of each person as a human being remains untarnished by their personal conduct, but their moral worth does, of course, change according to their actual actions and convictions. This is, as it were, the philosophical translation of the theological formulation that all humans are children of God. Each human being is therefore always – in business transactions as in all other aspects of life – to be treated with respect for his dignity (Melé, 2009a).

## 4.2    Government, virtue, and justice

While philosophers can determine the essential structure of the human law (*lex humana*) by inference from the eternal law (*lex aeterna*; *S. th.* I-II 93), most ordinary people do not have the time, the talent, or sufficient education, thinks Thomas, to engage in such principled ratiocination (*SCG* I, 1, 4). For their benefit the Bible presents divine law (the *lex divina*) in pictorial language, teaching all how to *live well*. While in principle the diligent deliberations of the wise (*per diligentem inquisitionem sapientum*) also produce the requisite results, the biblical code of conduct, especially the Decalogue, offers a shortcut to moral wisdom (*S. th.* I-II, 95, 2): Where the teleology of natural reason points implicitly and tentatively, the theology of supernatural revelation guides explicitly and directly (Jordan, 1994). Yet because of the universal way to earthly truth and the self-evident position of natural moral reasoning with respect to all worldly relationships, Thomas's ethics ultimately makes and defends the claim that it is valid for each human being, irrespective of religious convictions. The theological framework in which Thomas sets out his political and socio-economic theories does not therefore undermine the relative autonomy of the political sphere or its independent secular validity.

Different countries, obviously, have to deal with different circumstances and will therefore construct divergent social norms and legal codes (*S. th.* I-II 96, 5). For this reason, each political community must formulate and promulgate its own laws (*ius civile*). Yet there are strictures of natural law that apply to all peoples around the globe (*ius gentium*) because of their shared humanity (*S. th.* I-II 95, 4). Thomas distinguishes the two types of law roughly along the lines of the difference between necessary and sufficient conditions. Laws that are fundamental for social coordination and collaboration in general, especially with regard to economic transactions (*iustae emptiones, venditiones*) Thomas designates as *ius gentium*, whereas norms to optimize communal life in moral terms (*ad bonum commune civitatis*) fall under the domain of *ius civile* (*S. th.* I-II 95, 4). Thus, through the *ius gentium*, the normative orientation of natural law extends to the socio-economic realm. If, for instance, the former is oriented to social justice, the latter must be governed so as to realize this objective.

Although Thomas regards the specific ways and means of wealth allocation and management as alterable social constructs, he does affirm that the overall direction of the economic sphere must still be guided by the overarching end of natural law: the common weal. As a result, fundamental mandates of socio-economic justice permeate all commercial life: All human law should direct human acts in accordance with the order of justice (*S. th.* I-II, 91, 5) which, importantly, comprises an orientation towards the common good (*S. th.* I-II, 92, 1). Hence, beyond the demands of commutative and distributive justice, Thomas's concept of justice is committed to a wider notion of social justice, which has far-reaching consequences: In the connection between law and justice, and especially in establishing the precepts of justice as a duty to everyone (*indifferenter omnibus debitum*: ST II-II, q. 122 a. 6), one can find the beginnings of a concept of universal human rights (Finnis, 2008). Within the present-day discourse on business ethics, the socio-economic dimensions of Thomas's concept of natural law can be reformulated as the common socio-economic rights of humanity that demand unconditional respect everywhere on the globe.

Moreover, beyond the legal dimension of social justice, natural law is also linked with his theory of *virtue*. Unlike other virtues, such as temperance and wisdom, which "perfect a human being only in those affairs that are appropriate to himself" (*S. th.* II-II, 57, 1) and thus may be developed into habits by the agent acting alone, Thomas says that "what is particular to justice among other virtues is that it orders a human being in those affairs which concern another" (ibid.). Justice requires an equitable treatment of the other (*S. th.* II-II, 57, 1) according to some universally recognizable standards of fairness (*S. th.* II-II, 57, 1 ad 2). It is important for Thomas that justice, as "a habit according to which one renders with a constant and perpetual will what is right to anyone" (*S. th.* II-II 58, 1), is not limited to the legal realm, but demands that *all* actions by individual and collective agents be characterized by that spirit of fair treatment. Obviously, this postulate has great repercussions to the conception of corporate social responsibility, since it always *allows* and on occasion – for instance, following state failure – *requires* corporations to act as subsidiary facilitators of justice.

In addition, while a present day moralist might lay most stress on the benefits of a just act upon the recipient, Thomas also stresses the positive effects upon the just agent. Human virtue not only renders the act good, but also makes the human being good. This is especially true for justice, since justice, as rendering to another that which is truly his (*S. th.* II-II, 58, 11), is more than an external operation on behalf of the pertinent needs of another person. For, in acting justly, the agent restores an otherwise unbalanced equality of proportion, with the effect that he also legitimates his own position in society. *Justice justifies*, as it rectifies the agent's relation to the world. Herein, too, lies an important lesson for business leaders, who seek public acceptance for their firms through moral legitimacy (Koehn, 1995).

## 4.3   Economic and business ethics

In line with early Christian skepticism about the value of material possessions (Mt. 13, 44–46, Apg. 4, 32–37, 1. Tim. 6, 17 f.) and his own conviction of the ultimate superiority of spiritual goods (*S. th.* II-II 118 ad 5), Thomas reiterates Aristotle's position that wealth is not an end in itself, but merely an instrument (*SCG* III, 30, 2). Thomas regards neither wealth as (always and necessarily) a good, nor poverty as (always and necessarily) an evil. It depends upon the role poverty and wealth play in human life. If riches make a person anxious or immoral, then, he thinks, it is surely better that poverty free that person from these afflictions. One should, however, not go so far as to view poverty as a good in itself; it, too, is only of instrumental value and praiseworthy "only in so far as it liberates [one] from those things by which a human being is prevented from intending spiritual things [...]. And this is common to all external things that they are good to the extent that they lead to virtue, but not in themselves" (*SCG* III, 133, 4). Although Thomas supports possessions in keeping with the social position of individuals (*suam conditionem, S. th.* II-II 118, 1), he warns that whenever "the practice of virtue is hindered by them, they are not to be numbered among goods, but among evils" (*SCG* III, 133, 1). Thomas's repeated emphasis on the merely *functional* nature of possessions is of central importance for his overall socio-economic philosophy, since it inspires concepts of property and profit that, in contradistinction to modern notions (such as libertarian), are merely conveying *relative*, never *absolute*, entitlements. For Thomas's overarching socio-economic argument is that goods whose value is contingent cannot express human nature; we do not have an *unconditional* human right to their possession as such. In other words, material wealth is in agreement with the natural rights of human nature when regulated by human laws so as to promote individual virtue and the common good. Any form of wealth acquisition and business in particular is thus legitimate only through its wider social purpose.

For Thomas, it is appropriate that the lower life forms serve the higher ones, and also that the human being uses the natural wealth of the earth (*S. th.* I-II, 66, 1). For in the hierarchy of being, the more self-guided and independent an entity, the higher the ontological rank it commands (SCG IV, 11, 1–5). A stewardship of man over nature and the human appropriation of mundane objects are thus justified in his view. Yet the use of the earth and its goods has been given to humanity in common (*S. th.* II-II, 66, 1). A form of property that excludes the use by others, in other words, "private" property (from *privare* = to deprive), does *prima facie* not fall within the purview of that stewardship, and thus always requires justification. Since private property is *not* an institution of natural law, it cannot be defended *absolutely* (*S. th.* II-II 57, 3). Rather, as a social construct, its justification is relative to its function: to realize certain benign services in, and for, a given community. In legitimizing private ownership against a standard of initial equality, Thomas simultaneously regulates and limits the acceptable forms and manifestations of private property through the very societal functions that justify the institution of private property as a whole.

> First because every man is more careful to procure what is for himself alone than that which is common to many or to all: since each one would shirk the labor and leave to another that which concerns the community, as happens where there is a great number of servants. Secondly, because human affairs are conducted in more orderly fashion if each man is charged with taking care of some particular thing himself, whereas there would be confusion if everyone had to look after any one thing indeterminately. Thirdly, because a more peaceful state is ensured to man if each one is contented with his own. Hence it is to be observed that quarrels arise more frequently where there is no division of the things possessed. (*S. th.* II-II 66, 2)

Far from giving unconditional support for the privatization of earthly goods, this conditional justification *qualifies* and *limits* the individual's right to exclusive property. Thomas argues accordingly that one should "possess external things, not as one's own, but as common, so that one is ready to share them with others in their need" (*S. th.* II-II 66, 2). While not demanding "that all things should be possessed in common and that nothing should be possessed as one's own," this passage does mean that "because the division of possessions is not according to the natural law, but rather arose from human agreement which pertains to positive law" (*S. th.* II-II, 66, 2 ad 1), society can and should define the proper (quantitative and qualitative) boundaries of private possessions. There is, in short, no right to individual or corporate enrichment at the cost of the common good.

A glance at Thomas's theory of almsgiving underlines this point. Thomas views almsgiving as not merely an ethical counsel but rather as a strict moral precept (*S. th.* II-II 32, 5), since it is "necessary to virtue, namely, in so far as it is demanded by right reason." For moral reason demands, Thomas explains, that any surplus we own beyond what we need for the maintenance of ourselves and those in our charge, we are to give to the needy. Moreover, while "it is not possible for one individual to relieve the needs of all," we are bound to relieve all "those who could not be assisted if we not did assist them" (ibid.), and there is no reason why this precept for all "those who have riches" (SCG III, 135) should not also hold for corporations.

From a moral perspective, therefore, *all* our possessions are generally constrained by "the right of all persons to subsist upon the bounty of the earth" (Ryan, 1942, p. 245). Since the law accepts, however, the presence of many evils and the absence of numerous goods on behalf of the higher good of human freedom which cannot otherwise be sustained (*S. th.* I-II, 96, 2), the moral precept of almsgiving does not directly translate into legal strictures of massive income redistribution. Yet at the same time Thomas explicitly denies what is the central tenet of today's neoliberal doctrines: that legal provisions for the institution of private property can be used against the right of those in need. "Inferior things," he reiterates, "are ordered to assist those in need. Therefore the obligation to assist those in need by such things is not prevented by the division and appropriation of things which proceed from human law. And so things which some have in abundance should be used according to natural law to assist the poor" (*S. th.* II-II 66, 7). Human law, bound by the principle of justice for its legitimacy (*S. th.* I-II 95, 2), must not accept the superabundance of some in the face of the need of others (Schumacher, 1949).

In his comments on commercial relations, Thomas generally adopts and builds upon Aristotle's distinction between *oikonomia* and *chrematistike* (Dierksmeier and Pirson, 2009). While *oikonomia* represents the pursuit of certain material goods to supply a given household, *chrematistike* denotes profit-seeking. *Oikonomia* is internally oriented towards determinate *qualitative* satisfaction levels (and is thus always quantitatively limited); *chrematistike*, however, operates on the merely *quantitative* logic of "more over less." As long as *chrematistic* endeavors are still governed by the needs of *oikonomia*, they are also, if only externally, limited by the latter; unless other social goods are sacrificed in their pursuit, one can, if one must, legitimately engage in *chrematistic* businesses. However, the – internally as well as externally unlimited – pursuit of profit for profit's sake is altogether different. This boundless and, in the eyes of Aristotle, "unnatural" form of *chrematistike* meets with disapproval: It upsets the just order of means (material, pecuniary) and ends (spiritual, contemplative), turns the gain of one in the loss of another, and increases inequality in society to the detriment of both the poor (who are increasingly burdened) and the rich (who, absorbed in the pursuit of lesser goods, are ever more distracted from the true values of life).

Like all medieval authors, Thomas accepts Aristotle's criticism of greed, but Thomas provides a more neutral assessment of commercial exchange than "the Philosopher," who had admitted trade only as a necessary evil. In Thomas, exchange relationships, while often leading *subjectively* to a "certain debasement" of the tradesperson (*S. th.* II-II, 77, 4), are viewed *objectively* as societal transactions without intrinsic demerits: Their moral value is – like that of private wealth – wholly functional. Whether commercial transactions are condemned or commended depends solely on what they accomplish for society. When they benefit all involved parties and achieve a better allocation of goods overall, they gain Thomas's approval (ibid.). Later Catholic social teaching developed this notion further in the direction of a "preferential option for the poor" (Twomey, 2005).

Merchants, for example, are allowed to seek not only surplus returns for their labor, costs, and risks (that is, as reimbursement for their transport and insurance outlays), but also moderate gains resulting from the fluctuations of general market prices and particular customer demand (ibid.). The reason behind this view is that for Thomas the "just price" that is to be observed in trade is not a *quantitative* fixture but a regulative idea of a *qualitative* nature: It eliminates excessive pricing in order to prevent the exploitation of dependencies and need, and so forth, without demanding static prices fixed to an unalterable economic equilibrium (*S. th.* II-II, 77, 1).

For the later development of the feudal and mercantile economies into the capitalistic system, this slight deviation from Aristotle is of highest importance, as are the *quaestiones* 77 and 78 in Thomas's *Secundae Secunda* that have produced vastly diverging modern interpretations. On the surface, Thomas seems simply to follow the many biblical injunctions against usury (Exod. 22, 25, Levit., 25, 37, Deut. 15, 6; 23, 19, Ps. 14, 5., Lk. 6, 34), and to reiterate Aristotle's charge against the "sterile" nature of monetary transactions in favor of the "fruitful" dimensions of commodity production and exchange. On second inspection, however, we see that Thomas's approach is more subtle. On the one hand, he does value labor over exchange and, in turn, commodity exchange over monetary investment, when it comes to assessing the ethicality of revenue claims. In short, the healthy preference of "sweat equity" over capital returns that generally characterizes medieval philosophy also permeates Thomas's deliberations (*Contra impugnantes*, VI, ad 12). On the other hand, that does not mean Thomas would grant a legitimate role in generating income only to labor, and never to capital.

While Thomas censures money lending as "usury" with many of the same arguments we find in Aristotle and the Bible (*S. th.* II-II 78, 1) and also opposes the notion of interest as a legitimate reimbursement for opportunity costs (*Recompensationem [ ... ] in hoc quod de pecunia non lucratur, S. th.* II-II 78, 2, ad 1), it would nevertheless be wrong to conclude that Thomas rejected all income without labor and would therefore have dismissed outright as illegitimate today's capitalistic economy (cf. Orel, 1930). For Thomas does allow for gains from rent and also from investments (*per modum societatis*) in commercial enterprises (*S. th.* II-II 78, 2). Why these exceptions in favor of capital-based income? In either form, the invested money has served a socially productive function, for example, building up real estate in the former, outfitting a merchant voyage in the latter, that is, the money has been used as productive capital, realizing social utilities that, without the expected profit, would probably have remain unrealized. This is where the crucial difference lies.

That money lending against interest was so staunchly rejected by Thomas must be seen before the backdrop of a medieval economy where private surplus funds were not yet identified as social capital and so often remained idle or were used for ostentatious consumption (Epstein, 2009). Lending money more often than not meant, on the part of the lender, merely rejecting the morally dubious pleasures of the wastrel or the miser. Those who asked for pay to forego either option met, consequently, with moral indignation. An altogether different plane is entered once we change the model and view money as capital. Money can, after all, no longer function as a permanent measure of value when, as capital, it is itself monetarized and traded. In a thoroughly capitalized economy, money, too, carries a price, so every outlay implies not only vague opportunity costs but real costs to the lender. While probably beyond the imagination of Thomas, it is not beyond the possibilities of his ethics to deal with such a state of affairs. With regard to the contemporary economy, Thomas might well have accepted income from capital investment, as long as it was gained in a way conducive to the welfare of all stakeholders in the transaction (a condition that, sadly, is not usually met).

In sum, Thomas writes an economic ethics that does not necessarily tie income to labor, but rather to the social utility of the revenue-generating activity or entitlement. Therein lies an important regulative ideal of all business transactions (one that though observed in Thomas's day, is neglected in ours): Profits are legitimate only to the extent that they respect the qualitative confines that protect the welfare of all stakeholders. While his position cannot always directly be applied to today's business world, the principles underlying his thought may very well serve as guideposts on a way to a more humane and balanced economy. Specifically, his use of a counterfactual value theory (which limits the quantitative pursuit of profit by qualitative concerns for human well-being and establishes a hierarchy of life-promoting goods that business is to procure) renders his theory most pertinent for our time. For Thomas directs economic activity to its ultimate social purpose, a parameter which, all historical and cultural vicissitudes notwithstanding, can and should be of lasting significance to the business world.

## 4.4   Practical applications

Thomas, of course, wrote his ethics with an eye to the business practices of his days. Insofar as the latter have changed, the former may have to be adapted to meet the altered realities of the present. Yet more often than not our contemporary situation is sufficiently similar to the customs of his time as to allow for a direct transfer of ethical judgments. For example, the following moral dilemma of a grain merchant – often discussed from the days of Cicero to those of Thomas as a "case study" on the ethical demands of honorable conduct in business – has not lost any of its pertinence over the centuries. Here is the case in the words of Cicero (*De off.* III, 12, 50ff; in the translation of W. Miller, 1913):

> (...) suppose, for example, a time of dearth and famine at Rhodes, with provisions at fabulous prices; and suppose that an honest man has imported a large cargo of grain from Alexandria and that to his certain knowledge also several other importers have set sail from Alexandria, and that on the voyage he has sighted their vessels laden with grain and bound for Rhodes; is he to report the fact to the Rhodians or is he to keep his own counsel and sell his own stock at the highest market price?

To Cicero, the case of the grain merchant is comparable to a house vendor who fails to declare serious flaws in what he is selling; that is,

Cicero identifies two dimensions of commercial activity that Thomas Aquinas takes pains to distinguish: the commission of harmful, and the omission of beneficial, actions. Against this view, Thomas holds that while it "is always unlawful to give anyone an occasion of danger or loss," one is not always required to "give another the help or advice which would be of some advantage; but only in certain fixed cases, for instance when someone is subject to him, or when he is the only one who can assist him" (*S. th.* II-II, 77, 3). For Thomas the example of the house vendor and the grain merchant are not analogous because in the one case positive harm is being done by the concealment of facts, but not in the other.

> The seller, who offers a thing for sale, gives the buyer an occasion for loss or danger by offering him something defective, if from the defect the buyer could suffer loss or danger: loss, if because of the defect of such kind the thing for sale is worth less, and the seller does not subtract anything from the price because of the defect; danger, if because of this defect the use of the thing is impeded or made harmful, for example if someone sold to another a lame horse as a fast one, or sold a decrepit house as a stable one, or rotten or harmful food as nourishing. If then such defects are hidden, and the seller does not disclose them, the sale will be illicit and deceitful, and the seller is obliged to compensate for the loss. (ibid.)

In the instance of the grain merchant, however, "the goods are expected to be of less value at a future time, because of the arrival of other merchants, which was not foreseen by the buyers. And so the seller, since he sells his goods at the price actually offered to him, does not seem to act contrary to justice by not declaring what is going to happen" (ibid., ad 4.).

Whereas Cicero operates from a single concept of morality, extending across all types of human relationships and interactions, and does not ascribe to the realm of business an ethical orientation of its own (in which, because of context and custom, different standards of behavior may legitimately apply), Thomas uses the customary distinction between duties of justice and precepts of virtue precisely in order to establish one such regional realm of *business* ethics. While exempting the buyer from a *legal* obligation to reveal information whose concealment is not harmful but whose disclosure would render benefit to the customer, Thomas delegates the decision to business *ethics* proper. He declares it would be "exceedingly virtuous" (ibid.) on the part of the merchant were he to go beyond the strict demands of justice by inform-ing his customers or even by voluntarily lowering his prices. One does not need much imagination to see that there are many contemporary applications in business ethics of this general idea (such as proactive customer information and honest stakeholder dialogue).

Thomas makes thus an important step towards a modern-day concep-tion of business ethics as a dimension of responsible conduct beyond what the law requires (Melé, 2009b). In fact, today more than ever, such supererogatory (virtuous) commitments of business are essential. While, in the recent past, nation states could – to some extent – rein in the negative externalities produced through national economies, today's globalized economy is not under such political supervision. The actions of corporations are not curbed by a global government, and we can-not expect, in the foreseeable future, a system of decentralized global governance that would feature the requisite global executive powers to enforce normative mandates for business. For this reason alone, the eth-ics of, and within, business can no longer be entrusted solely to the law (Solomon, 1994). In an era in which voluntary moral action on the part of business becomes ever more important and in which institutional solutions to various "corporate prisoner's dilemmas" and to the various downward spirals of global competition ("race to the bottom") have to rely increasingly on corporate coalitions of the willing, the emphasis on any forward-looking business ethics must lie on the corporate will to do good. It is not by accident that the debate over the concept and the implications of corporate social responsibility has gained force in steady proportion with the ongoing globalization of business. Virtue, in short, is a timely subject for business.

The current intellectual quest for a responsible treatment of the accountability gaps in the global economy presents a background against which the advantages of Thomas's position become markedly visible. Demonstrating that virtuous actions reflect positively upon the agent, his ethics counsels business to regard spending on compli-ance with ethical standards beyond what the law requires as reasonable investment in corporate health and longevity. With an eye to justice as a relational virtue, corporate conduct can be managed in a way that integrates corporate and societal interests to the benefit of all con-cerned. To do so, is, moreover, not only virtuous but also highly politic since all business is embedded socially and depends upon the goodwill of society (Sison, 2003). Without denying the need for cultural diver-sification in the ethics of business, Thomas meets the common need of humanity to establish its collective endeavors with a corresponding consensus of shared normative understandings; an accomplishment that is, probably, of even greater significance today than it was in his time. For as Thomas's ethics intended to express the eternal structural laws of human reason and insofar as it achieved its timeless goal, it will prove both timely and relevant in the constantly changing contexts of our era.

## Bibliography

Bourke, V. J., Foundations of Justice. *Proceedings of the American Catholic Philosophical Association*: 36 (1962) 19–28.

Brown, O. J., *Natural Rectitude and Divine Law in Aquinas*, (Toronto: Pontifical Institute of Medieval Studies, 1981).

Carl, M., "Law, *Virtue*, and Happiness in Aquinas's Moral Theory". *The Thomist* 61(3) (1997) 425–447.

Celano, A., *Phronesis*, Prudence and Moral Goodness in the Thirteenth Century Commentaries on the *Nicomachean Ethics*, *Mediaevalia Philosophica Polonorum*. 36 (2007) 5–27.

Celano, A., "The Concept of Worldly Beatitude in the Writings of Thomas Aquinas". *Journal of the History of Philosophy* 25 (1987) 215–226; reprinted in *Great Political Thinkers*, edd. J. Dunn & I. Harris, v. VII. (Cheltenham: Edward Elgar Publishing Limited, 1994).

Cortright, S. A. and N. Michael, *Rethinking the Purpose of Business: Interdisciplinary Essays from the Catholic Social Tradition*, (Notre Dame, IN: University of Notre Dame Press, 2002).

Crowe, M., *The Changing Profile of the Natural Law*, (The Hague: Nijhoff Publishers, 1977).

Dierksmeier, C. and Pirson, M., "Oikonomia versus Chrematistike. Aristotle on Wealth and Well-Being", *Journal of Business Ethics*, 88(3) (2009) 417–430.

Epstein, Steven A., *An Economic and Social History of Later Medieval Europe, 1000–1500*, (Cambridge: Cambridge University Press, 2009).

Finnis, John, "Aquinas' Moral, Political, and Legal Philosophy", *The Stanford Encyclopedia of Philosophy (Fall 2008 Edition)*, Edward N. Zalta (Ed.), URL=<http://plato.stanford.edu/archives/fall2008/entries/aquinas-moral-political/>.

Henle, R. J., "A Catholic View of Human Rights: A Thomistic Reflection". In A. S. Rosenbaum (ed.), *The Philosophy of Human Rights*. (Santa Barbara, CA: Greenwood Press, 1980), 87–94.

Jordan, M. (1994), "The Pars moralis of the Summa theologiae as Scientia and as Ars." In Scientia und ars in Hoch- und Spätmittelalter, ed. Ingrid Craemer-Ruegenberg and Andreas Speer, pp. 468–481. Miscellanea Mediaevalia 22. Berlin and New York: Walter de Gruyter.

Keys, M. M., "Aquinas's Two Pedagogies: A Reconsideration of the Relation between Law and Moral Virtue". *American Journal of Political Science*. 45(3) (2001) 519–531.

Koehn, D., "A Role for Virtue Ethics in the Analysis of Business Practice", *Business Ethics Quarterly*, 5(3) (1995) 533–539.

Maritain, J., *The Person and the Common Good.* (New York, NY: University of Notre Dame Press, 1947).

Melé, D., "Integrating Personalism Into Virtue-Based Business Ethics: The Personalist and the Common Good Principles", *Journal of Business Ethics* (2009a) 88: 227–244.

Melé, D., *Business Ethics in Action: Seeking Human Excellence in Organizations.* (New York: Palgrave Macmillan, 2009b).

Peterson, J., "The Interdependence of Intellectual and Moral Virtue in Aquinas". *The Thomist.* 61(3) (1997) 449–454.

Ross, J. F., "Justice Is Reasonableness: Aquinas on Human Law and Morality". *The Monist.* 58 (1) (1974) 86–103.

Ryan, J., "The Economic Philosophy of St. Thomas". In R. E. Brennan (ed.), *Essays in Thomism.* (New York, NY: Sheed and Ward, 1942), 239–260.

Schumacher, L., *The Philosophy of the Equitable Distribution of Wealth. A Study in Economic Philosophy,* (Washington: Catholic University of America Press, 1949).

Sison, A. G., *The Moral Capital of Leaders: Why Virtue Matters,* (Cheltenham, UK, Northampton, MA: Edward Elgar Publishing Limited, 2003).

Sison, A. G., *Corporate Governance and Ethics: An Aristotelian Perspective,* (Cheltenham, U.K., Northampton, Mass: Edward Elgar Publishing Limited, 2008).

Solomon, C.R., *The New Word of Business: Ethics and Free Enterprise in the Global 1990s.* (Lanham: Roman & Littjefield, 1994).

Stammkötter, F.-B., "Die Entwicklung der Bestimmung der *Prudentia* in der Ethik des Albertus Magnus". In W. Senner (Ed.), *Albertus Magnus zum Gedenken nach 800 Jahren: Neue Zugänge, Aspekte und Perspektiven,* (Berlin: Akademie Verlag, 2001).

Stump, E. S., "Aquinas on Justice". *American Catholic Philosophical Quarterly.* Supplement 71 (1997) 61–78.

Twomey, G. S.,. The "preferential option for the poor" in Catholic social thought from John XXIII to John Paul II, (Lewiston, N.Y., Edwin Mellen Press, 2005).

# Part II
# Modern Positions

# 5
# Kant's Humanist Ethics

*Claus Dierksmeier*

In this chapter we investigate how Kant's philosophy contributes universalistic arguments in favor of a humanistic ethics. Kant moved the *idea of freedom* to the center of his philosophy, arguing that from a reflection on the nature of human freedom a self-critical assessment of its morally appropriate use could be gleaned. Therein, that is, in construing his ethics from (subjective) self-reflection rather than from presumed (objective) values, and in construing norms of interpersonal validity from the individual perspective ("bottom-up") rather than from ("top-down") references to prearranged ethical or metaphysical orders, lies Kant's innovation in ethics theory.

For Kant, our knowledge of human nature does not *precede* the search for moral truth but *results from* our quest for a life of integrity. His is a *procedural humanism*, a philosophy whose humanistic ethics arises from the ways and procedures by which persons seek the good. Thus Kant steered clear both of the Scylla of moral relativism and of the Charybdis of a "one-size-fits-all" ethics, which threaten all *materialistic* approaches to ethical theory. Recognizing that context affects content, Kant decided instead in favor of a *formal* approach to ethics, universalistic in procedures and structures but open to differentiation as to the regional and temporal specificities of its application. This is what makes his ethics relevant beyond the historical settings and confines of his works. After introducing into the context the anthropological basis and methodology of Kant's ethics (in sections 1–3), we discuss its moral and legal dimensions (4), his theory of politics (5), and the applicability of his ethics to contemporary business (6).

## 5.1 Kant and the enlightenment

Immanuel Kant (1724–1804) figures prominently in any anthology on ethics, so important are, as even his most pronounced critics concede, his contributions to moral theory. His works on the foundations of ethical theory, the *Critique of Practical Reason* (1787), and his treatises on legal and moral philosophy in the *Metaphysics of Morals* (1797–1798), are both considered as milestones in the history of moral reasoning. Although Kant's *Groundwork of the Metaphysics of Morals* (1785) is his most read text, familiar to almost any ethics student anywhere in the world, it is on the aforementioned works that Kant's ethics truly rests. The *Critique of Practical Reason* and the *Metaphysics of Morals* together form a unified architecture that combines the foundations of the former with the edifice of the latter. In these works, Kant conceptualizes an ethical theory that centers on the idea of humanity, defends the unconditional dignity of the human being, and proposes a procedural humanistic ethics with a claim to universal validity. How did he arrive at these positions?

Kant is often identified as an Enlightenment thinker. At first sight, this appears correct. Like Hobbes, Locke, and Rousseau, Kant was dedicated to "man's emergence from his self-imposed immaturity" (AA VIII, 35[1]) through rationality, and spoke out in favor of religious tolerance, civic freedom, and the rule of law. With these positions, Kant certainly appears to be a poster child of Enlightenment thinking. If we take a closer look, however, important differences emerge between him and other thinkers of his era, which show that his conception of emancipation was more radical (Losonsky, 2001). Kant differs from his contemporaries, or so I shall argue, because his ethics is rooted in a deeper understanding of what it means to be human. This becomes clear by way of comparison with central exponents of the Enlightenment's political theory, namely the foremost champions of "social contract theories." Thomas Hobbes (1588–1679), John Locke (1632–1704), and Jean-Jacques Rousseau (1712–1778) were working within the following paradigm: They set out with initial assumptions about the nature of the human being (which in Hobbes is drawn in negative, in Locke in positive, and in Rousseau in morally neutral terms). From these assumptions, they derive a description of a (hypothetical) situation, in which no positive law sanctions the behavior of those human beings. In this imaginary "state of nature," men lack, for example, protection against violence and fraud. A change of conditions, the argument continues, is in everyone's interest; so, based upon a (hypothetical) contract, a societal state is constructed, in which publicly sanctioned laws safeguard everyone's formerly unprotected "natural rights." With those natural rights as both purpose and measure of the law, the "nature of man" from which they derive – their anthropology – becomes the yardstick for all public legislation. To Kant, this is a methodologically ill-advised approach (Kersting, 1984). This is because the ultimate conclusion about what may be considered adequate norms in the societal state is, in these models, heavily influenced by their various assumptions about the preceding "state of nature." The anthropology of Hobbes presumes human beings to be in latent conflict, which, once anticipated, provides ample incentives for preemptive aggression. This leads to a situation in which everyone views everyone else as a potential enemy, and treats them accordingly, making Hobbes' state of nature is, in fact, so unattractive that life under almost *any governance*, even the most authoritarian and inequitable, appears preferable. It is not surprising, then, that the scope of natural rights defended in Hobbes' state is remarkably narrow. Locke disagrees. Even in the "state of nature," his much more congenial human subjects recognize and, most of the time, safeguard certain basic rights. Society is thus preferred only insofar as it achieves a *more comprehensive* protection of human rights. Rousseau's anthropology ultimately leads to yet another depiction of man in the natural state and, consequently, to a third description of the societal state. According to him, natural man sets out, morally neutral, from a parsimonious but autonomous existence governed by sparse natural needs. Through socialization, that is, by the institution of private property which exacerbates natural inequality into social inequity, human life is corrupted and individuals are increasingly dominated by the alienating power of money, artificial wants, and unnatural desires. So, people need government, Rousseau argues, in order to restore to them the qualities of natural freedom, while maintaining the advantages of civilization. In short, all turns on which anthropology you start with. How, then, does Kant compare? What are the main tenets of his anthropology? How does he arrive at conclusions about how to live in society?

## 5.2   Human nature and ethics

At first glance, Kant, too, seems to operate from a well-defined anthropology. Among his well-known statements are that man must always be treated according to his inherent dignity (AA IV, 436); that no human being shall be obliged merely to serve the purposes of others (AA IV, 433); that it is the distinguishing token of humanity to outshine everything else that has extrinsic value (a price) by its possession of intrinsic value (AA IV, 435). Furthermore, one formulation of his categorical imperative invokes the concept of humanity as a normative leitmotif of practice (AA IV, 429); nor can his taxonomy of moral duties be properly reconstructed without the clear demarcation of human and nonhuman life that underlies it. So, assumptions about the nature of man are clearly at the core of Kant's system, and also seem to function as a stepping stone to the specific postulates of his moral theory. Yet whereas the former holds true, the latter is not quite correct.

While in pre-Kantian philosophies the standard scheme of argumentation begins with a general anthropology and then, through intermediary steps, ends with specific moral prescriptions, Kant turns this sequence on its head. He derives his anthropology in large part from what he early carved out as a theory of normatively correct action. In this counter-intuitive shift lie the novelty and strength of Kant's humanistic ethics (Wood, 2003a). To understand this move away from traditional foundation models for ethics, we must briefly step back from ethics altogether, and look at the entirety of Kant's philosophical compositions. Kant is renowned for his "transcendental" idealism, his thoroughgoing "criticism," and the "Copernican turn" that he brought to philosophy (Höffe, 2002). All these tags refer to a change in philosophical methodology. Whereas his predecessors dealt right away with the problems they were concerned about, Kant introduced a hitherto unheard-of pause into the workings of philosophical reflection. He suggested that before engaging our respective problems we should question whether (and under what conditions) it is possible for us to know anything at all about them. If our mind is the cardinal tool of philosophy, then should we not first get to know the features of this tool, before employing it too readily on philosophical topics? What if, he suggested, many of the problems and antinomies that philosophers run into are caused not by the objects we deal with but by mistaken workmanship on our part? When, for instance, a given tool is inappropriate for a certain task, then try what we will, our efforts will not meet with success. Hence an exploration of the structures of our mind ought to precede any examination of the structures of the world. What goes for *theoretical* endeavors holds in *practical* philosophy – ethics – as well. We need to ask, suggests Kant, what do we bring to the table in every moral debate; what do we insert into each ethical question; what do we carry into every normative dispute? Can we, for example, identify the structures of moral judgment that inform all our decisions and all our moral assessments? What can we know about them? It is with these questions that Kant's foray into ethics begins (Guyer, 2003).

From the universal nature of reason, Kant thinks, there must follow certain structures of moral deliberation that each and every human being will have (potential) access to. Yet, typically, moral judgments look like the very opposite of something derived from universal rationality. What seems right in this context, proves wrong in another; what is apparently good for one person, turns out to be bad for the next; what was once held in esteem, is ridiculed in a later era. Is not morality, rather, constituted by particularity and specificity? Can we really claim that there is something common that applies to all humans, all over the world, and at all times? Kant's answer is in the affirmative. He does, however, qualify this response, limiting it to the *formal* components of moral judgments. In other words, Kant is quick to admit that every moral action is contextualized because it has a *material* side to it. No two contexts are exactly alike, nor are, therefore, the material components of two different moral actions. Despite this, what makes them normatively comparable is their formal content (Schönecker, 2006). For example, to be a responsible teacher may demand different (*material*) instruction methods, varying from pupil to pupil, while (and precisely because) the (*formal*) duty to promote with disinterested fairness the learning of each holds true for all. Each action takes on a certain form that, once it has been laid bare by human reason, can inform ethical assessment in such a manner as to allow interpersonal accord in morals. Apart from all the variations that gender, age, nationality, religion, and such like introduce into the arena of human behavior, Kant thinks he has found a point of departure for moral theory that is acceptable to all, giving his ethics universal scope.

Let us present an example to bring out what Kant had in mind. Assume you are sitting on the train, and you'd love to talk to someone, but, first, you have the good sense to ask yourself whether it would be OK to involve your neighbor in a chat: They might, after all, just prefer a quiet journey. Obviously, this is a case where the "Golden Rule" produces an odd result: By this venerable norm, you are told to do to others what you would like them to do to you, and not to do to them what you wouldn't like them to do to you. OK, then, you think, I hate silence and would love to talk and be talked to, so here we go! Such a situation is of the kind where applying Kant's somewhat cumbersome *categorical imperative* makes a real difference. It advises, "Act so that the maxim of thy will can always at the same time hold good as a principle of universal legislation" (AA V, 31). The emphasis is on "the maxim," or, as Kant also calls it, the "subjective principle" of the morals behind the action. Kant does not invite you to generalize from the specific type of action (talking on the train), or even its underlying behavioral pattern (starting conversations in public settings), but instead to analyze the subjective moral principle lying beneath both. This maxim, however, already involves a generalized description of the moral nature of your action (imposing your communication preferences onto others). Now, clearly, you would not want *such* a maxim to be universalized; it would put the state of your communicative universe wholly at the discretion of others. So, the universalization-test works irrespective of your personal preferences, social situation, and the like. It regards specific individuals as persons-in-general, and only from this angle does it imply moral obligations. The *categorical imperative* appeals to you to treat all human beings and their interests on an equal footing.

## 5.3   Kant's ethical methodology

Our deliberations about the difference between the "Golden Rule" and the *categorical imperative* showed that apart from the *material* side of every action – which may be very context-dependent and highly situation-specific – it always has a *formal* component, too, which proves amenable to rational assessment independent of context and situation (Lukow, 2003). Yet why should we follow the call to act according to universalizable maxims? Why would Kant think that this strategy has an appeal to everyone, regardless of who they are, and where or how they live? How can he assume that everyone would feel a commitment to this particular stricture? Before we try to answer this question, let us read a short fictional narrative that Kant provides us with. He invents a story about a man who, on account of the allegedly overwhelming force of natural desires, tries to argue himself out of the sort of moral commitments the *categorical imperative* implies.

> Suppose someone asserts of his lustful appetite that, when the desired object and the opportunity are present, it is quite irresistible. [Ask him] – if a gallows were erected before the house where he finds this opportunity, in order that he should be hanged thereon immediately after the gratification of his lust, whether he could not then control his passion; we need not be long in doubt what he would reply. Ask him, however, if his sovereign ordered him, on pain of the same immediate execution, to bear false witness against an honorable man, whom the prince might wish to destroy under a plausible pretext, would he consider it possible in that case to overcome his love of life, however great it may be. He would perhaps not venture to affirm whether he would do so or not, but he must unhesitatingly admit that it is possible to do so. He judges, therefore, that he can do a certain thing because he is conscious that he ought, and

he recognizes that he is free – a fact which but for the moral law he would never have known (AA V, 30).

What does Kant teach here? First and most clearly, that on pain of death the man in our story can free himself of whatever otherwise might drive him to immoral conduct. Yet, Kant admits, this does not prove enough; such a notion of freedom might not suffice in order to attach the notion of moral responsibility to it. For what if the man abandoned one desire in order to serve another, stronger, one, such as his lust for life? Then he might not have acted freely but driven by natural forces. Yet, oddly, as soon as the man is faced with a maxim that cannot be universalized (sacrificing an innocent man to save his skin), the power of freedom unmistakably comes to the fore, showing that "human nature is capable of [...] an elevation above every motive that nature can oppose to it" (ibid.). We cannot deduce where this capacity comes from, but there is no denying our awareness of it. This *unconditional* capacity to freedom that we might overlook in the day-to-day affairs of life demonstrates itself in the call of the moral law. According to Kant, it is not the case that we are first free and then, later, deign to adorn our freedom with moral obligations but, on the contrary, it is our moral commitments that make us free (AA V, 4, Fn.). Had the man in our example not realized the call of duty, he might have had neither reason nor motive to withstand the pressure of the king. Through the moral law, however, he became aware of his freedom.

Kant establishes his theory of human nature upon this complex and self-referential idea of moral freedom. His is not a *direct and descriptive* anthropology, so Kant does not collect and compare empirical data on how humans behaved throughout the ages. He proceeds rather *indirectly and normatively*. Indirectly, through the normative nature of our freedom we learn that the essence of being human is not only to be free but also, at the same time, to be morally bound. The internal moral law – not an observation of external phenomena – tells us who we are, by informing us who we ought to be. And this may well be the only absolutely certain knowledge we ever gain about ourselves: We may have deceptive self-images and succumb to flawed views of the world around us, but within us resides inexorable knowledge that we are meant and able to become what we ought to be. We are beings set free to achieve the moral goals that awaken our sense of freedom.

Because we are free to be moral, we are free to choose between different options. Otherwise, in a given situation, like a machine, we would simply follow the strongest drive that impelled us. The moral command to act against our natural inclination introduces into our lives the ability to step beyond all predetermined limits and thus to transcend all behavioralist stimulus-response calculus. It is here that Kant differs so crucially from his predecessors (Fleischacker, 1999). He does not simply presuppose a certain notion of freedom in order to get his moral and social theory off the ground. Instead, he demonstrates to his readers that such freedom is a fact of *their* consciousness. Kant's idea of freedom does not formulate an arbitrary axiom that we could just as well exchange by another. He begins with a premise to which we cannot but agree. All other attributes of the human being may be contentious; our freedom is not. Moral freedom, Kant demonstrates, constitutes our conscious self-awareness and hence our entire human existence.

## 5.4   Moral and legal ethics

From the preceding discussion, several important conclusions can be drawn. If freedom is what defines the human being, then respect for human life entails respect for the self-referential nature of human freedom. Freedom, however, is personal; we cannot live freely vicariously or by proxy. The act of decision-making is part and parcel of our personal individuation. The choices we make define us. Each human being, therefore, has to answer the call of the moral law in person. The inevitable subjectivity of our choices, however, does not render them arbitrary. As the awareness of our liberty comes in the form of the normative calling to honor the idea of human freedom, we perceive freedom as the burden to make the right choices. In our decisions, we are to act with responsibility to and as representatives of humanity. In Kant's famous words: "So act as to treat humanity, whether in your own person or in that of any other, in every case as an end, never as means only" (AA IV, 429).

Obviously, there is a higher moral value to some choices than to others, and people differ in their moral worth according to the life they choose. Yet our dignity as human beings rests neither in our single choices (be they moral or not), nor in our resulting (good or bad) character, but in the fact that these choices are *ours*. The respect we owe the human being attaches unconditionally to our capacity for autonomy; it is not conditional upon particular choices (Garcia, 2002). Hence we need to respect the dignity of human life even in those who constantly make bad choices (Wood, 2003b). This notion inspires the split between the *moral* and the *legal* realm within Kant's ethics, in which, again, Kant inverts the logic of traditional thinking. Before Kant many philosophers used a single ethical theory when formulating both moral and legal rules of conduct. Legal norms were often simply seen as moral commands whose importance was so elevated that their realization justified the use of coercion and forceful sanctions. The problem with such theories, where the difference between the moral and the legal realm is only *quantitative* (in the degree of importance) and not *qualitative* (in content), is clear: Those who disagree with the underlying moral system are forced to live in a way that goes against their beliefs.

Kant, in contrast, strictly separated the inward-oriented theory of morals, which is concerned with proper ethical conviction and purposes, from the outward realm of actions that affect other people. Coercion, he decided, should never be used to enforce inner morality. Legal ethics must therefore rest upon an independent principle, valid on its own grounds. Accepting the fact that ethical convictions do vary, those who live together in a finite world must learn how to coordinate the outward dimensions of individual freedom so that the moral autonomy of each becomes possible. How can this be achieved? Instead of deducing concrete commands of morality from a canon of predetermined values, Kant's *formal* approach to ethics lets the material strictures of his theory result from adequate, that is, all-inclusive, choice-procedures. What is required to assure the freedom of all becomes a norm for the behavior of each. Since the free action of some can cancel out the free action of others, we must, infers Kant, legally align our external actions through the following basic norm: "Act externally in such a manner that the free exercise of thy will may be able to coexist with the freedom of all others, according to a universal law. (AA VI, 231). Whatever material content our actions may advance, their form must be such as to allow equal freedom for all others. Coercion is justified only to enforce rules that translate this legal imperative into sanctioned law. All other ethical purposes, society must achieve based upon the free will of the citizens.

## 5.5   Kant's theory of politics

Kant theory of public decision-making was one of the first to translate the idea of political self-government into procedural terms (Saner, 1973; Arendt, 1982). Since the people themselves are the keenest guardians of their own rights, Kant thinks, "we can call the following proposition the transcendental formula of public law: All actions relating to the right of other men are unjust if their maxim is not consistent with publicity (Publizität)" (AA VIII, 381). His rationale is straightforward: "A maxim which I cannot divulge without defeating my own purpose must be kept secret if it is to succeed; and if I cannot publicly avow it without inevitably exciting universal opposition to my project, the necessary and universal opposition which can be foreseen a priori is due only to the injustice with which the maxim threatens everyone" (AA VIII, 381). Yet not every proposition that passes the test of publicity is for that reason alone a wise political maxim. If we want to govern well, we also need "another affirmative and transcendental principle of public law," to separate the wheat from the chaff, as it were. Kant suggests the following formula: "All maxims which *stand in need* of publicity, in order not to fail (to reach) their end, agree with politics and right combined" (AA VIII, 386; emphasis in original). Kant's rationale for this proposal has an interesting ring to it.

> For if they can attain their end only through publicity, they must accord with the public's universal end, happiness; and the proper task of politics is, to promote this, i.e., to make the public satisfied with its condition. If, however, this end is attainable only by means of publicity, i.e., by removing all distrust in the maxims of politics, the latter must conform to the rights of the public, for only in this is the union of the goals of all possible. (AA VIII, 368)

So only through participatory forms of government do we get governance in the best interest of the polity and the citizenry. Yet since a *direct involvement* of all citizens in each decision is neither always feasible nor desirable, political systems must be organized so as *indirectly* to achieve the adequate *representation* of comprehensive interests. Politicians must anticipate what, despite the diversity of human interests and the plurality of values, are common concerns (Beiner and Nedelsky, 2001). In his *Critique of Judgment*, Kant describes such encompassing thinking as operating under the regulative idea of the shared perspective of humankind (AA V, 293). Devising policies *as if* judging affairs from the angle of all involved, the facilitator of social processes stands a higher chance of approval and support (AA V, 294). Successful politics is more than weaving threads of empirical interests into the legal fabric of politics. Rather, it rests on the ability to take on the perspectives of each involved group and individual, formulating integrative visions that can harmonize their respective aims. As the ethical *leitmotif* of such politics serves a state of affairs in which the collectively organized freedom of all would "result, by ethical laws both inspired and restricted, as the cause of universal happiness; such that the rational beings themselves, guided by said principles, produce at the same time sustained prosperity for themselves and all others" (AA III, 525). Kant advocates, as it were, a *stakeholder model of democracy*: What concerns all should be accomplished by the – at best active and at least representative – participation of all. This model of representative deliberation applies, moreover, wherever people organize themselves to serve their common concerns. It is therefore a model that may also be of use to the administration of business organizations and to the management of their stakeholder relations.

## 5.6 Contemporary business ethics

Economic relations are social relations and as such they co-determine the societal role of individuals. Kant, however, believed that with coercive law on one side and voluntary moral commitments on the other, the realm of ethics was exhausted. He overlooked the fact that between societal law and individual morality there is a realm of institutional ethicality, arising from the complexities of organized agency in the semi-autonomous sphere of persons acting collectively. Collaborative associations, such as firms, follow a rationality of their own and tend to build their own ethical culture as well. Of course, insofar as such organizations fall under the law, their internal and external relations are bound to realize the tenets of Kant's legal philosophy (Ballet and Jolivet, 2003). Yet there remains to corporate actors considerable scope for discretion that is not legally prescribed, nor always adequately addressed by the strictures of individual morality alone. Organizational rationales, peer-pressure, systemic incentives, and market forces – all of which are endemic to corporate life and typical of the ethical pressures of the business world – require ethical reflection *sui generis*. Kant overlooked the need for an institutional ethics. In order to carry over to the economic sphere, his moral philosophy must hence be adapted to the specifics of the realm of collaborative organizations (Soares, 2003). This is feasible, since Kant did give us moral guidance about what is of paramount importance to life in business as well as in general. It is no accident that many business ethics and management textbooks quote the following passage:

> [...] everything has either a price or dignity. Whatever has a price can be replaced by something else which is equivalent; whatever, on the other hand, is above all price, and therefore admits of no equivalent, has dignity. Whatever has reference to the general inclinations and wants of mankind has a market value; whatever, without presupposing a want, corresponds to a certain taste, that is to a satisfaction in

the mere purposeless play of our faculties, has a fancy value; but that which constitutes the condition under which alone anything can be an end in itself, this has not merely a relative worth, i.e., value, but an intrinsic worth, that is, dignity. Now morality is the condition under which alone a rational being can be an end in himself, since by this alone is it possible that he should be a legislating member in the kingdom of ends. Thus morality, and humanity as capable of it, is that which alone has dignity. [...] (AA IV, 433)

Several scholars (for example, Bowie, 2002) have undertaken the step of translating Kant's position for the corporate world in light of the overarching idea of human dignity expressed here. They typically advocate a *procedural turn* (similar to that taken by Kant's moral and political philosophy), away from material objectives and towards more formal recommendations. Likewise, the argument goes, Kant's philosophy can provide orientation for corporate decisions not so much in terms of their content but in questions of process and method. A very simple and effective way to respect persons as ends in themselves is to involve them *directly* in the decisions that concern them. Thus, for instance, the tenets of stakeholder theory are being reconstructed upon Kantian premises, demanding that all those who hold a stake in the dealings of a firm, should have a say – or at least be fairly represented – in its decision-making process (Evan and Freeman, 1988). As a form of *indirect* representation of one's stakeholders, one could think of translating Kant's appeal to the judicious use of the publicity criterion into the "*New York Times* Test." Numerous business ethics textbooks recommend as a quick test for the ethicality of an action to consider whether you would wish to see what you are about to do published on the front page of the *New York Times*. If not, reconsider your course of action.

Kant's idea of human dignity has also affected current debates in human resources literature. Renowned authors, such as Amartya Sen, reject the conventional parlance of "human capital" in favor of the term "human capabilities" (Sen, 1999), in order to give emphasis to the Kantian idea that humans are far above everything that carries a price. In the Kantian perspective, human beings are neither mere resources (labor suppliers), assets (productivity generators) or liabilities (cost factors). The entire notion of "human resource management" must hence be rejected as ethically fraught from a Kantian perspective. Human beings must not be *secondary* factors in economic decision-making, because they are the *primary* objective of business, a philosophical truism that ought to be reflected in corporate behavior across the board:

in how organizations recruit and treat their employees, in how business in general deals with its customers, and in how firms treat the public (Greenwood, 2002; Maclagan, 2003).

Humans are what our economy ought to be about first and foremost. It is only human beings alone, to repeat, who determine goals. Our economy, in the Kantian view, is merely a technical system for the realization of those goals. The econometric dimension of business, that is, its quantitative measurement, must therefore be understood only as a subordinate function to assess progress towards our qualitative goals. Too often, however, this simple fact – that business is to serve humanity, and not vice versa – is forgotten and quantitative goals are set above qualitative concerns. Hence it is well within the spirit of Kant's ethics to call for a reorganization of the entire business world according to humanistic principles (structuring macro-economic policies towards the well-being of people, organizing micro-economic processes with a constant view to the dignity of each person in the supply chain, and re-arranging the meso-structures of stakeholder relationships from the angle of universal representation). In fact, the procedural involvement of the interests of all affected persons into corporate decision-making as well as economic outcome-assessments promises to be the very approach needed to realign business and society. In our increasingly globalized world, we need an ethics that, while allowing for regional specificity, neither loses comprehensive reach, nor lacks the universalistic strength of the unconditional demand for the priority of human dignity in and over all affairs. Kant's theory allows the formulation of such an ethics.

## Note

1. Kant's works are quoted (in my translation) according to the *Akademieausgabe der Preußischen bzw. Deutschen Akademie der Wissenschaften zu Berlin* (AA, volume, page).

## Bibliography

Arendt, Hannah, *Lectures on Kant's Political Philosophy*, (Chicago: Chicago UP, 1982).
Ballet, J., and P. Jolivet, "On Kantian Economics", in: *Social Science Information sur les Sciences Sociales* 42, 2/2003, (2003) pp. 185–208.
Bartuschat, W. 1999, Zur kantischen Begründung der Trias ,Freiheit, Gleichheit, Selbständigkeit' innerhalb der Rechtslehre, in: Landwehr, G. (ed.), 1999, ,Freiheit, Gleichheit, Selbständigkeit' innerhalb der Rechtsphilosophie Kants für die Gerechtigkeit in der modernen Gesellschaft, Hamburg, pp. 11–25.

Beiner, Ronald and William James Booth (eds), *Kant and Political Philosophy: The Contemporary Legacy*, (New Haven: Yale UP, 1993).

Bowie, Norman E. 2002, *A Kantian Approach to Business Ethics*, in: Frederick, Robert E. (ed.), *A Companion to Business Ethics*, (Cambridge: Blackwell, 2002).

Dierksmeier, C., Kant on "Selbständigkeit", in: *Nederlandse Tijdschrift voor Rechtsfilosofie & Rechtstheorie, Journal for Legal Philosophy and Jurisprudence*, 1/2002 (2002) 49–63.

Dierksmeier, C., Die Wirtschaftsphilosophie des "Krausismo", in: *Deutsche Zeitschrift für Philosophie, 4/2003*, (2003) 571–581.

Dierksmeier, C., John Rawls und Kants langer Schatten, in: Zeitschrift für Politikwissenschaft, Journal of Political Science, 4/2004, (2004) 1297–1322.

Dierksmeier, C., Über die Wirtschaftstheorie in Fichtes Rechtslehre von 1812, in: *Fichte-Studien 29/2006* (2006) 13–29.

Dierksmeier, C., Qualitative oder quantitative Freiheit?, in: *Rechtsphilosophische Hefte* XII/2007 (2007) 107–119.

Dodson, Kevin E., "Kant's Socialism: A Philosophical Reconstruction", in *Theory and Practice* 29, 4/2003 (2003) 525–538.

Evan, William M. and Edward Freeman, "A Stakeholder theory of the Modern Corporation: Kantian Capitalism", in: Beauchamp, Tom L. and Bowie, Norman E. (eds), *Ethical Theories of Business*, 3rd edition, (Englewood Cliffs, 1998), 97–106.

Fleischacker, Samuel,, A Third *Concept of Liberty, Judgment and Freedom in Kant and Adam Smith*. (Princeton: Princeton UP, 1999).

Flikschuh, Katrin, *Kant and Modern Political Philosophy*, (New York: Cambridge UP, 2000).

Garcia, Ernesto V., "The Social Nature of Kantian Dignity", in Hughes, Cheryl (ed.), *Social Philosophy Today, Race, Social Identity, and Human Dignity 16*, (Bowling Green, OH: Philosophy Documentation Center, 2002).

Greenwood, Michelle R., Ethics and HRM: "A Review and Conceptual Analysis", in: *Journal of Business Ethics* 36, 3/2002 (2002) 261–278.

Guyer, Paul, "Kant on the Theory and Practice of Autonomy", in: *Social Philosophy and Policy* 20, 2/2003, (2003) 70–98.

Guyer, Paul, *Kant's System of Nature and Freedom*, (Oxford: Oxford UP, 2005).

Hansson, S. O., "Kant and the revolutionary slogan ,Liberté, Egalité, Fraternité", in: *Archiv für Geschichte der Philosophie* 76, (1994) 333–339.

Höffe, Otfried, Migotti, Mark (trans.), *Categorical Principles of Law*, (State College: Pennsylvania State UP, 2002).

Höffe, Otfried, Newton, Alexandra (trans.), *Kant's Cosmopolitan Theory of Law and Peace*, (New York: Cambridge UP, 2006).

Kaufman, Alexander, *Welfare in the Kantian State*, (New York: Oxford UP, 1999).

Kersting, Wolfgang, *Wohlgeordnete Freiheit*, (Berlin: Walter de Gruyter, 1984).

Kleingeld, Pauline, *Fortschritt und Vernunft: Zur Geschichtsphilosophie Kants*, (Wuerzburg: Koenigshausen & Neumann, 1995).

Kneller, Jane and Sidney, Axinn (eds), *Autonomy and Community: Readings in Contemporary Kantian Social Philosophy*, (Albany: SUNY Press, 1998).

Landwehr, G. (ed.), *Freiheit, Gleichheit, Selbständigkeit' innerhalb der Rechtsphilosophie Kants für die Gerechtigkeit in der modernen Gesellschaft*, (Hamburg: Vandenhoeck & Ruprecht, 1999).

Losonsky, Michael, *Enlightenment and Action from Descartes to Kant: Passionate Thought*, (New York: Cambridge UP, 2001).

Lukow, Pawel, Maxims, "Moral Responsiveness, and Judgment", in *Kant-Studien* 94 (2003) 405–425.

Maclagan, Patrick, "Self-Actualization as a Moral Concept and the Implications for Motivation in Organizations: A Kantian Argument", in: *Business Ethics: A European Review 12*, 4/2003, (2003) 334–342.

Riley, Patrick, *Kant's Political Philosophy*, (Lanham: Rowman & Littlefield, 1983).

Rosen, Allen, *Kant's Theory of Justice*, (Ithaca: Cornell UP, 1993).

Saner, Hans, Ashton, E. B. (trans.), *Kant's Political Thought: Its Origins and Development*, (Chicago: University of Chicago Press, 1973).

Schild, W., *Freiheit – Gleichheit – 'Selbständigkeit' (Kant): Strukturmomente der Freiheit*, in: Schwartländer, J. (ed.), *Menchenrechte und Demokratie*, (Kehl am Rhein, 1981) 135–176.

Schönecker, Dieter, "How is a Categorical Imperative Possible? Kant's Deduction of the Moral law in 'Groundwork III'", in: Horn, Christoph and Schönecker, Dieter (eds), *Kant's "Groundwork for the Metaphysics of Morals", New Interpretations*, (Berlin: Walter de Gruyter, 2006) 302–324.

Sen, Amartya, *Development as Freedom*, (New York: Anchor Books, 1999).

Shell, Susan Meld, *The Rights of Reason: A Study of Kant's Philosophy and Politics*, (Toronto: University of Toronto Press, 1980).

Soares, C., "Corporate Versus Individual Moral Responsibility", in *Journal of Business Ethics 46*, 2/2003 (2003) 143–150.

Stroud, S., "Defending Kant's Ethics in Light of the Modern Business Organization" *Teaching Ethics* 2(2) (2002) 29–40.

Timmons, Mark (ed.), *Kant's Metaphysics of Morals: Interpretive Essays*. (Oxford: Oxford UP, 2002).

van der Linden, Harry, *Kantian Ethics and Socialism*, (Indianapolis: Hackett, 1988).

Williams, Howard (ed.), *Essays on Kant's Political Philosophy*, (Chicago: University of Chicago Press, 1992).

Williams, Howard, *Kant's Political Philosophy*, (New York: St. Martin's Press, 1983).

Wood, Allen W., "Kant and the Problem of Human Nature", in: Jacobs, Brian and Kain, Patrick (eds), *Essays on Kant's Anthropology*, (Cambridge: Cambridge UP, 2003a) 38–59.

Wood, Allen W., "Kantianism, Moral Worth and Human Welfare, Review of Human Welfare and Moral Worth", in: *Philosophical Quarterly 53*, 213/2003 (2003b) 587–595.

# 6
# Humanistic Values in German Idealism

*Richard Fincham*

The tradition of German Idealism was one of the most fertile periods of philosophical activity in Europe. It emerged within the last decade of the eighteenth century in response to the extraordinary advance that Kant's critical philosophy seemed to promise the human sciences, and lasted well into the mid-nineteenth century. In retrospect, it could be perceived to mark the ultimate development and flourishing of the ideals of the European Enlightenment. Inspired by the earlier revolution within the empirical sciences and Kant's promise of a similar revolution within the metaphysical sciences, the German Idealists were motivated by unfailing optimism about the power of human reason to resolve not only *theoretical* questions concerning the nature of the cosmos and the human being's place within it, but also all *practical* questions concerning our ethical obligations. Intimately related to the German Idealist's belief in the power of reason was their similarly fundamental belief in the reality of human freedom. Whereas earlier Enlightenment thinkers had worried that consistent ratiocination would reduce human beings to the status of mere "cogs" within the vast mechanism of nature, for the German Idealists the power of reason revealed that we possess an autonomous status, whereby our rational nature can resist the efficacy of the biologically and environmentally determined inclinations to which other forms of life seem universally subject. In this regard, for the German Idealists, the human being possesses a dignity and value over and above all other beings within the world. They were committed to the development of a new, largely secular, world order, in which, in the practical sphere, our ethical obligations are legislated by human reason alone, and not, as in the past, enforced by illegitimate and corrupt religious and political authorities. The German Idealists therefore understood the cultivation of reason and the increasing realization

94

of freedom as a process of freeing humanity from superstition and oppression.[1]

This essay is divided into two parts. Part I contains a historically orientated interpretation of two early nineteenth-century texts: Friedrich Immanuel Niethammer's *The Dispute between Philanthropinism and Humanism in the Educational Theory of our Time* of 1808, which introduced the term "humanism" (*Humanismus*) into the German philosophical tradition; and G. W. F. Hegel's *Elements of the Philosophy of Right* of 1821, which is undoubtedly the most significant and influential work of socio-political philosophy within the German Idealist tradition. This section argues that the concept of "humanism" employed by Niethammer is applicable to the ideals espoused by Hegel's socio-political philosophy (even if Hegel himself did not explicitly employ the term within this context) and enables us to declare that Hegel espouses humanistic values. Part II discusses the contemporary relevance of these humanistic values. Drawing upon the recent work of economist Wilfried Ver Eecke, it argues that the free market economy must be subject to a degree of regulation by just and representative governments in order to ensure than the humanistic values prescribed by Hegel are respected.

## 6.1 Humanistic values in Hegel's socio-political philosophy

This section is divided into three parts. It begins (part A) by comparing Niethammer and Hegel's responses to the emergence of capitalism out of feudalism in the early nineteenth century and shows how Niethammer introduces the term "humanism" to describe a cultural tendency potentially at odds with this economic order. Second (B), it shows how both Niethammer and Hegel argue that the human being should reconcile himself with this economic order insofar as it provides an opportunity for the manifestation of his essential freedom. Third (C), it shows how Hegel essentially agrees with Niethammer that "man" is a union of "humanity" (*Humanität*) and "animality" (*Animalität*) and, insofar as he believes that the needs of the latter should not encroach upon the former, could thus be said to espouse humanistic values.

### 6.1.1 The economic order in early nineteenth-century Europe and the emergence of the concept of humanism

Niethammer"s *The Dispute between Philanthropinism and Humanism in the Educational Theory of our Time* attempted to resolve a pernicious "dispute" concerning the fundamental aims of education, and advocated reform of Germany's educational institutions. Analysis of this dispute, however, takes Niethammer's discussion out of the narrow confines of educational theory *per se* and leads him to reflect upon the nature of human life within post-Enlightenment society. It is in this context that the term "humanism" attains a twofold meaning within Niethammer's text: First (1) it is derived from the term *Humanioren* to denote the classical pedagogical practice of making the study of ancient languages and literature the foundation of education[2]; second (2) the term is employed to refer to a cultural tendency – exemplified by German Idealism – that recognizes the essential autonomy and dignity of man, and which is, in its orientation, potentially opposed to the economic conditions of post-Enlightenment society.

For Niethammer, the Enlightenment acquired its most tangible manifestation in Germany through the modernization of the newly united Prussian state during the reign of Friedrich the Great. Friedrich's reforms transformed Prussia into an industrialized capitalist society and influenced similar reforms across the whole of Germany. For Niethammer, however, the consequences of this transformation were far from overwhelmingly positive. The emphasis placed upon practicality, utility, profitability, and material production not only complicated human life through the threat of hardship and poverty, it also threatened to tarnish the whole of German culture. In addition to various "unmistakable advances," therefore, Niethammer declares that there was, at that time, "*under the name of Enlightenment*, a regress of true culture."[3] He thus describes how the necessity of effectively functioning within the socio-economic conditions of post-Enlightenment society gives rise to a regressive cultural tendency which

> places the whole happiness of a nation in the quantity of material production, the whole value of the individual in the acquisition of mechanical competence, seeks all Enlightenment in the emptiness of ignominious superstition, and limits all spiritual activity to this emptying.[4]

Superstition and unquestioning obedience to religious authority were certainly shaken by the Enlightenment, but what Niethammer is specifically describing is a cultural tendency which rids the world of irrational and unfounded religious beliefs without advocating a rationally grounded replacement, with the result that the whole purpose of human life becomes viewed as successful participation within the free market economy. Niethammer thus describes how this tendency leads to "a true de-spiritualization [*Entgeisterung*] of the nation." This regressive tendency, within the sphere of pedagogy, is referred to by Niethammer as "philanthropinism." The term is used to denote the modern educational theory, the emergence of which produced the very dispute Niethammer seeks to reconcile, and is etymologically derived from the *Philanthropinen*, the name adopted in the eighteenth century by schools exemplifying this modern educational theory. Niethammer thus describes how philanthropinism confronts the reality of the post-Enlightenment economic order by advocating that schools focus upon vocational education, so as to give pupils the technical proficiency that will turn them into effective wage earners in as short a time as possible. Just as Friedrich the Great's transformation of Prussia exerted an influence throughout Germany, Niethammer says that the influence of the *Philanthropinen* likewise extended to all educational institutions.[5] Indeed, this influence led, at the beginning of the nineteenth century, to the widespread prejudice that vocational education is the only worthwhile form of education. Contrary to this prejudice, however, Niethammer is highly critical of philanthropinism. He thus describes how this bias towards vocational education "paralyses the flight of spirit [*Geistes*]" to make man "sink into vulgarity."[6]

Despite insisting upon these negative consequences, however, Niethammer is far from being a reactionary opponent of the Enlightenment. The Enlightenment has unmistakably produced some "glittering advances" insofar as the shaking of "the kingdom of superstition" and the abolition of "futile speculation" have led to a "spiritual revolution" with which the slumbering power of free-thinking has awoken.[7] This "spiritual revolution" and "awakening of free-thinking" refer to the cultural tendency – exemplified by German Idealism – which Niethammer describes as "the spirit of *humanism*." He writes:

> Another spirit [*Geist*], for which the Enlightenment only made room as a precursor, has appeared with the reawakening of genuine philosophical thinking among us, and has for the last twenty years [that is, since the decade which saw the publication of Kant's critical philosophy] seized all of the better minds among us in all branches of knowledge [...]; the ideality of the truth and the truth of the ideal, of all reason as demanded and presupposed truth, is more universally and clearly recognized.[8]

In pedagogy, this cultural tendency was demonstrated by the reluctance with which the innovations of philanthropinism were allowed to encroach upon classical pedagogy. Classical pedagogy, which focused upon the study of ancient languages in order to enable pupils "to read and study the most accomplished masterpieces of culture with the ease that the enjoyment of an artwork, and the cultivation derived from that, demands,"[9] was, when properly understood, focused upon inspiring the pupil's "concern with the spiritual subjects of the inner world,"[10] that is, with cultivating the highest, unconditionally valuable faculty of man, namely, his reason. Humanism thus focuses upon the essential autonomy and dignity of the human being emphasized by the German Idealists and uncovered by the free-thinking that the Enlightenment made possible.

The publication of Niethammer's monograph in 1808 was quickly followed by his appointment as Central School Councilor with responsibility for reorganizing the grammar schools in Bavaria. In accordance with his educational theory, Niethammer established two kinds of grammar schools, the classical *Gymnasium*, which emphasized the study of ancient languages and literatures, and the *Realgymnasium*, which focused upon practical disciplines. Within the same year, he offered the position of "Professor of Philosophical Sciences and Rector at the Nuremburg Classical Gymnasium" to Hegel, who, within the *Aegidiengymnasium*, presided over the development of the humanistic curriculum advocated by Niethammer. By 1818, however, Hegel was employed as a Philosophy Professor in Berlin, where he published, in 1821, his *Elements of the Philosophy of Right*, a handbook for use within his lectures on social and political philosophy. Hegel's reflections upon the emerging free market differ from Niethammer's in two significant respects. First, they are far more far-reaching and well informed. Niethammer, by his own admission, only considered the emerging economic order insofar as it was affecting his own native Germany,[11] whereas Hegel's reflections are based upon an appreciation of the economic conditions in other countries, especially Great Britain, and a reading of the Scottish economic philosophers, most notably, James Steuart and Adam Smith. Second, Hegel's assessment of the free market is far more positive than Niethammer's. Whilst recognizing that this economic order is by no means flawless, he argues that it represents a significant advance over that of feudalism and in fact represents the optimal economic order. For (as we shall see) Hegel argues that, as autonomous beings, the highest form of freedom and the most satisfying life that the human being can attain is a life in which he participates within a free market economy (regulated by a just and representative government). Hegel thus argues that the free market economy is an "ethical institution" that fosters and reinforces human freedom.

The most significant flaw that Hegel perceives in the free market is the manner in which it seems to inexorably produce a degree of poverty that it does not have adequate resources to deal with.[12] In pursuit of profits, employers increase the division of labor and mechanize production, which thus leads to overproduction, unemployment, and poverty. Whilst claiming that "the important question of how poverty is to be abolished is one of the most disturbing problems which agitate modern society,"[13] Hegel is, nonetheless, unable to provide a decisive solution to this problem. Charity proves ineffective insofar as "both in itself and in its operation [it] is dependent on contingency."[14] Likewise, any positive action undertaken by governments always leads to undesirable consequences. Hegel thus describes how indirectly supplying the unemployed with subsistence by giving them the opportunity to work simply exacerbates the problem insofar as overproduction causes unemployment; likewise, directly supplying the needy with subsistence by redistributive measures (for example, taxation) would "violate the principle of civil society [*bürgerlichen Gesellschaft*] and the feeling of individual independence and self-respect in its individual members."[15] Hegel thus writes that "despite an excess of wealth civil society is not rich enough, that is, its own resources are insufficient to check excessive poverty and the creation of a penurious rabble [*des Pöbels*]."[16] Hegel uses the term "rabble" (*Pöbel*) to describe what we would now term an "underclass," that is, a stratum of society that feels alienated from civil society to such an extent that it is either unable or unwilling to positively participate within the free market. He writes that:

> Poverty in itself does not make men into a rabble [*Pöbel*]; a rabble is created only when there is joined to poverty a disposition of mind, an inner indignation against the rich, against society [*Gesellschaft*], against the government, etc.[17]

Hegel therefore recognizes that not all human beings at all times will experience the free market as an institution fostering and reinforcing their freedom. While (as we shall see) Hegel clearly believes that the free market respects the optimal economic order, he nonetheless recognizes that such an economic system possesses an unfortunate flaw insofar as it is persistently in danger of alienating a minority through the very process of fostering and reinforcing the freedom of the majority.

### 6.1.2    Reconciling humanity with the economic order

Although Niethammer and Hegel disagree about the merits of the emerging free market, they nonetheless agree that human beings should reconcile themselves with these economic conditions.

Thus, while Niethammer privileges humanism insofar as it alone focuses on that autonomy which gives human beings their unique dignity,[18] he also recognizes that it would be a "logical mistake" to view the human being's autonomy as capable of an existence abstracted from that animality with which philanthropinism is concerned (to the extent that philanthropinism could also be described as "animalism"[19]). The human being, after all, must subsist within the socio-economic conditions which the world presents, and, furthermore, his essential autonomy can only attain reality within the material world with which he is confronted. Thus Niethammer criticizes the excessive subjectivism of earlier German Idealists such as J. G. Fichte, who, he claims, one-sidedly consider the human being by abstracting from his animality:

> If the philosophers of humanity isolate the spiritual nature of man through logical abstraction, and represent this logical abstraction alone as the proper essence of man, they make a logical mistake that actually induces them towards views akin to enthusiasm [*schwärmerischen Ansichten*]. But if they ground practical demands upon that logical picture, which hovering between heaven and earth nowhere possesses a true home, this even lacks purpose and meaning. If the essence of man is thought as purely isolated spirituality [*Geistigkeit*], he himself is isolated from the whole visible world and has no other connection with it, as for him the world has no other meaning than that relating to the nourishment of his animal life, which he considers as something degrading and understands as in itself a pollution from which he yearns to be free and strives to free himself [...]. Connected with this [...] is all the enthusiasm [*Schwärmerien*] and disdain and disparagement towards the earthly life, which, in the idea, could certainly be bound with a pure, devout, truly venerable mind. But, in praxis, the inappropriateness of such a mind is shown because it paralyses all powerful effects on the outer, hindering all the striving of spirit [*Geist*] to give its ideas actuality in the outer world in which alone the true activity consists, and giving the life of such a mind in its ideas and its striving towards perfection and completion, a reserve, by which it appears as the most complete egoism [*Egoismus*].[20]

Such an abstraction is a "logical mistake" insofar as our autonomy can only manifest itself as inseparably united with our animality. In contrast to the Cartesian conception of man, Niethammer thus declares that the human being's "body [...] is not merely the machine carrying the animal life, but rather, essentially invested with spirit [*Geist*], is the organ presenting his spiritual life in the outer world."[21] From this "correct" understanding of the concept of man Niethammer thus concludes that, although the humanistic concern with the human being's essential autonomy and dignity should be privileged in education as that which nurtures that which is unconditionally valuable in man, this humanistic education should not completely neglect the "animalistic" needs of those future participants in the free market (with which philanthropinism is concerned).[22]

Hegel is in complete agreement with Niethammer concerning the capacity of human beings to manifest their autonomy within the material world.[23] In reaction to the excessive subjectivism of those earlier German Idealists that Niethammer criticized for "egoism," Hegel's philosophical system conceives of the human being as an essential union of *autonomy* and *physical instantiation*.[24] Its success is praised by Charles Taylor, who sees Hegel's enduring influence as lying in the manner in which he managed to "situate subjectivity by relating it to our life as embodied and social beings, without reducing it to a function of objectified nature" by uniting "autonomy with the fullness of expressive unity with nature."[25] This reconciliation of *autonomy* and *physical instantiation* manifests itself in the *Philosophy of Right* as an attempt to prove that the institutions requisite for the full "actualization" of freedom are already in place.[26] However, Hegel does not simply assume this to be the case; he rather attempts to rigorously justify the validity of this claim. He says that "we do not begin at the highest point, i.e., with the concretely true [because] it is precisely the truth in the form of a result that we are looking for."[27]

Hegel thus refers to his use of a dialectical method. In employing such a method, Hegel begins with what he calls "the idea which people most commonly have of freedom"[28] to show that this conception of freedom is inadequate in its own terms. Within this conception of freedom, a further more complex conception is thus revealed, which, when rendered explicit, enables the previous inadequacies to be overcome. Proceeding in this manner, Hegel obtains "a series of thoughts and [...] existent shapes"[29] which all contain some inadequacies, until he finally reaches a conception of freedom which is "self-subsistent" insofar as no further inadequacies are implicit within it. It is this dialectical process that reveals that the highest possible actualization of freedom is an ethical life within the institutions of civil society and the state. In discussing this methodology, however, Hegel is keen to point out that the initial "shapes" of freedom which turn out to be inadequate, and which are thus "sublated" (*aufgehoben*) by the highest self-subsistent shape, nonetheless remain encapsulated within the highest self-subsistent shape.[30] He thus describes how our commonest idea of freedom necessarily leads to the idea that the institutions of civil society and the state provide the highest actualization of autonomy, and that the very ability of exercising this commonest idea of freedom is something that civil society and the state promote and sustain.

The commonest idea of freedom is freedom of choice. Hegel argues that this conception of freedom contains three elements. The first is "the element of pure indeterminacy" or "the unrestricted possibility of abstraction from every determinate state of mind which I may find in myself or which I may have set up in myself,"[31] that is, our potential to disentangle ourselves from the obligations placed upon us or from commitments we have made. In contrast, the second element describes "the transition from undifferentiated indeterminacy in the differentiation, determination, and positing of a determinacy as a content and object,"[32] that is, our ability to will something, our ability to commit ourselves to pursuing certain desires and inclinations. The third element describes the unity of the previously opposed elements. This unification generates a concept of "freedom [that] lies neither in indeterminacy nor in determinacy; it is both of these at once,"[33] that is, our capacity for free choice, our capacity to pursue a particular desire or inclination while at the same time recognizing that we are not irrevocably committed to it. This freedom to choose to do what we please is not as free as we may initially believe. As Hegel says, "the freedom of the will is arbitrariness" and "instead of being the will in its truth, arbitrariness is more like the will as contradiction."[34] The contradiction is generated insofar as freedom of choice is dependent upon a contingently given "content." Hegel thus concludes that, whereas "the man in the street thinks he is free if it is open to him to act as he pleases [...] his very arbitrariness implies that he is not free."[35]

Hegel therefore identifies that there must be a higher shape of freedom where our free will is not determined by something contingently given, in which "the free will...wills the free will."[36] For if freedom of choice is of value it must be subordinated to a willing of freedom as such. The human being who is committed to his own freedom is described by Hegel as a "person." The person demands that others recognize and respect his freedom and is thus the bearer of "immediate" or "abstract rights." He likewise recognizes that he should recognize and respect the freedom of other persons who are themselves bearers of such rights.[37] For example, the person has the right to appropriate "things" which are unfree and without rights, that is, he has the right to property. The person must have a right to property in order to "translate his freedom into an external sphere,"[38] that is, he must possess "the right of putting his will into any and every thing and thereby making it his"[39] in order that he can give his freedom an objective form that others are able to recognize and respect. However, Hegel identifies an inadequacy in the freedom of personhood insofar as, whilst the person may recognize that rights must be respected, it still remains contingent whether the person will respect the rights of others.

The freedom of personhood is thus sublated by the freedom of the "moral subject," who recognizes that he should respect the freedom and rights of others and is constantly wary of violating them. The moral subject thus claims the right to accept responsibility for its intentions. In his concern not to violate the rights of others, the moral subject thus demands the right to welfare, that is, the right to be able to rationally reflect upon potential actions and find satisfaction within the actions pursued. He also imputes the right to welfare to other human beings.[40] In pursuing its own rights and welfare as well as the rights and welfare of others the moral will thus pursues "the good;" the idea of the good being constituted by the unity of rights and welfare. The moral will thus conceives itself as possessing a duty to will the good, which is itself determined and legislated by its own reason. The moral will thus comes to realize that it can recognize and is bound to will only what duty itself requires. This means that, if the moral will is going to acknowledge that it is bound to promote rights and welfare, it must understand them to be required by duty itself. The dutiful moral will cannot proceed from the assumption that rights and welfare are to be valued and promoted. Rather, it must begin with the concept of duty itself – the definition of which does not include the specific duties of (a) doing right and (b) striving after welfare – so as to determine what duty specifically requires of it and whether duty requires respect for rights and welfare. The problem with the freedom of the moral subject, which Hegel clearly associates with Kantian ethics, is that reason simply tells the moral subject that it has a duty to will the good for the sake of duty, but, *contra* Kant, cannot give us any more definite guidance. The only solution is to depend upon "conscience" to decide whether a course of action is to promote the good or otherwise. But, even then, the moral subject could still be mistaken concerning what it conceives as good, with the result that such a subject is in danger of slipping into evil, namely, the evil of self-righteousness.[41]

Hegel's discussion of morality reveals that the self-legislating will of the moral subject cannot on its own adequately determine the good, with the result that it is unable to secure the rights and welfare that autonomous human beings deserve. The moral subject's conception of the good must thus be guided by ethical institutions. The freedom of the moral subject is thus sublated by the freedom of the "ethical individual," that is, a human being who recognizes that all the previously discussed shapes of freedom are respected, promoted, and sustained within institutions that already exist. The ethical individual thus recognizes that the norms that ensure that human beings possess a fully satisfying life and the full actualization of freedom cannot be decided by himself alone, but are instead best achieved by participating in ethical institutions already in place. The ethical individual thus recognizes that participation in the free market grants him the capacity to enjoy a "bourgeois freedom" in which freedom of choice, the freedom of the person, and the freedom of the moral subject are promoted and sustained. Just as I may enjoy the actualization of my freedom by participating in this economic order, so it may also be the case that my participation likewise unintentionally promotes and sustains the freedom of others, insofar as individuals participating in the free market are forced to provide benefits for others in order to obtain benefits for themselves. Hegel thus writes that:

> When men are thus dependent on one another and reciprocally related to one another in their work and the satisfaction of their needs, subjective self-seeking turns into a contribution to the satisfaction of the needs of everyone else. That is to say, by a dialectical advance, subjective self-seeking turns into the mediation of the particular through the universal, with the result that each man in earning, producing, and enjoying on his own account is *eo ipso* producing and earning for the enjoyment of everyone else.[42]

Hegel thus subscribes to Adam Smith's notion of the "invisible hand" – the notion that although in participating in the free market individuals are primarily self-seeking, the promotion of the interests of others follows as an unintended consequence. The explicit promotion of the interests of all is, for Hegel, pursued by the state, thus making the state the most developed form of ethical freedom. The state, for Hegel, is an organic unity in which government ensures that the rights and welfare of its citizens are protected, and in which citizens abide by the laws of the state insofar as they recognize them as protecting and sustaining their freedom. A successful society, for Hegel, is thus an organic whole constituted by a community of citizens whose actions work toward the continued maintenance and preservation of freedom. The legitimacy of the state is thus derived from the very concept of free will with which Hegel began. The state – just as much as the free market economy – is thus revealed to be something that the free will must will if it is to be free.

### 6.1.3   The twofold nature of "man"

We can thus see a striking parallel between the way in which the human being is conceived by Niethammer and Hegel. For Niethammer, "man" is constituted by an inexplicable and absolutely inseparable union of two elements: humanity (*Humanität*) and animality (*Animalität*). Niethammer thus writes that:

> the unconditioned in man is *reason*, and his *spiritual nature* grounds his characteristic essence; the *animal* [*das Animale*] on the other hand, which he has in common with the whole of the rest of the animal world, cannot without justification be so little included within his essence that the name *man* [*Menschheit*] describes the *humanity* [*Humanität*], merely his *spiritual nature*, with complete abstraction from the animal nature. [...] Man [*der Mensch*] is neither that spiritual nature nor that animal nature alone...; and not only *man himself* is incorrectly thought if he is thought as the one or as the other distinguished part of his essence alone, but also the one, like the other *part of his essence* is incorrectly thought if it is thought outside of its connection with the other.[43]

*Animality* makes man, just like other animals, a creature beset by various needs which require fulfillment in a necessarily self-seeking manner if his survival within the environment in which he finds himself is to be secured. *Humanity*, however, is man's essential *autonomy*, the fact that he possesses *reason* and *freedom* which differentiates him from all other animals and grants him a peculiar dignity. Thus, Niethammer proposes that the *humanity* of man should always be privileged, even though, since man's humanity cannot manifest itself in abstraction from his animality, the animalistic needs of man to preserve himself within the socio-economic conditions in which he lives should not be neglected. Hegel also gives the term "man" (*Mensch*) a quite specific definition, which parallels that of Niethammer. He thus writes that:

> At the standpoint of needs [that is, within the "system of needs," or, in other words, the free market economy]...we have before us...the composite idea which we call *man* [*das Konkretum der Vorstellung, das man Mensch nennt*]. This is the first time, and indeed properly the only time, to speak of *man* [*Menschen*] in this sense.[44]

We can therefore conjecture that Hegel's conception of the predicament of a human being living within the post-Enlightenment economic order agrees with that offered by Niethammer. For Hegel also, the human being may possess an essential autonomy that gives him a unique dignity, but this autonomy is most adequately actualized by means of successful participation within the free market. Insofar as he, like Niethammer, privileges our autonomy, however, we are justified in applying the term "humanism" (in Niethammer's second sense of the term) to Hegel's socio-political philosophy, to declare that Hegel is a *humanistic* thinker who – in prescribing the promotion and protection of human freedom – espouses *humanistic* values.

## 6.2   The contemporary relevance of Hegel's socio-political philosophy

We have seen that, for Hegel, the state is the ethical institution that represents the highest actualization of human freedom, insofar as it is an institution that consciously aims at promoting and protecting the freedom of all its citizens. Nevertheless, Hegel points out that any particular given state may fall short of this. He thus writes that "the state is no ideal work of art; it stands on earth and so in the sphere of caprice, chance, and error, and bad behavior may disfigure it in many respects."[45]

In recent years a number of thinkers, such as T. J. Lowi and Goetz Briefs, have seriously questioned the extent to which the economico-political order of modern Western societies really is promoting and protecting the interests of their individual members. In this context Wilfried Ver Eecke draws connections between the work of Lowi and Briefs, to argue that "the constitutional free market society in the latter half of the twentieth century and American capitalism in particular, have become unjust."[46] Lowi argues that in America, from the 1930s onwards, there has been an increasing tendency to substitute the public debate of legislation in Congress with a bargaining process with affected interest groups, which favors interest groups that are able to mobilize the most political pressure. This, according to Lowi, has resulted in an "unjust" economico-political order, where decisions affecting the public are not made in accordance with a just rule, but are made in a way that favors the interests of some at the expense of the interests of others.[47] Briefs makes a similar diagnosis of the economico-political order of all modern Western societies. He argues that, within such societies, the economic order has been transformed from a competitive order between individuals to a competitive order between different interest groups, which defend their own interests (often) to the detriment of society at large. Likewise, Briefs argues that interest groups have transformed Western democracies into bargaining democracies, in which the state bargains with different interest groups instead of working to promote and sustain the good of all citizens.[48]

Hegel understood very well the extent to which the state may be "disfigured" in such a way that it no longer adequately represents the interests of all citizens. Indeed, it is in order that the state adequately promotes and sustains the freedom of all citizens that Hegel – *prima facie* counterintuitively – rejects popular suffrage and general elections. In Hegel's state the legislature is composed of the representatives of different estates, with only the representatives of the business class being elected. As Hegel remarks, however, these deputies are

> representatives in an organic, rational sense only if they are representatives not of individuals or a conglomeration of them, but one of the essential spheres of society and its large scale interests.[49]

The representatives of particular branches of urban society are thus to be elected by the individuals constituting that particular branch, so the legislature will be constituted by representatives of *all* different branches of urban society. The makeup of the government is therefore not directly determined by the will of self-seeking individuals, but by "trade associations" (which Hegel calls "corporations"[50]) that possess a mediating function between the particular self-seeking individual and the universality of the state (in the same way that a bodily organ mediates between its component cells and the living animal body as a whole[51]). In support of such a system Hegel rejects "popular suffrage" insofar as "it leads inevitably to electoral indifference, since the casting of a single vote is of no significance where there is a multitude of electors"[52] – a remark which pre-empts the problem of "voter apathy"

which challenges democratic governments today.[53] Electoral indifference, Hegel goes on to argue, subverts the very purpose of general elections – which is supposedly to provide representation for the interests
of all individuals – since "election actually falls into the power of a few,
of a caucus, and so of the particular which is precisely what was to have
been neutralized."[54] As far as Hegel is concerned, therefore, the state
should secure the "equal rights of representation" of all branches of
society. The problem with a "free unrestricted election" is that it "leaves
this important consideration entirely at the mercy of chance."[55] And
the problem with modern Western democratic governments, which
Lowi and Briefs identify, is that they are unjust and do not pursue the
common good precisely insofar as they protect the interests of certain
interest groups to the detriment of those that are less well organized or
able to exert political pressure.

Hegel is adamant, therefore, that a state that promotes and sustains
the freedom of *all* citizens will not be a state that is unduly influenced
by competing interest groups within the sphere of civil society, but
rather, conversely, a state which exerts influence upon the sphere of
civil society. As we have seen, Hegel favors the capitalist free market as
the economic order best able to promote and sustain the human being's
essential freedom: He thus does not conceive of the capitalist free market as possessing unconditional value, but rather he values the capitalist free market *for* its capacity to promote and sustain human freedom.
Ver Eecke therefore attributes to Hegel the view that, insofar as they
are institutions essentially existing to promote the freedom of *all*, it
is *meritorious* for governments to *check* the effectively functioning free
market's capacity to undermine the freedom of *some* (through business
cycles, system-generated impoverishment, or exploitation). That Hegel
does indeed sanction a degree of state intervention within the free market can be seen from the following passage:

> The differing interests of producers and consumers may come into
> collision...and although a fair balance between them...may be
> brought about automatically, still their adjustment also requires a
> control which stands above both and is consciously undertaken.
> The right to the exercise of such control...depends on the fact
> that...goods in absolutely universal daily demand are offered not so
> much to an individual as such but rather to a universal purchaser,
> the public; and thus both the defence of the public's right not to be
> defrauded, and also the management of goods inspection, may lie,
> as a common concern, with a public authority. But public care and

direction are most of all necessary in the case of the larger branches of industry, because these are dependent on conditions abroad and on combinations of distant circumstances which cannot be grasped as a whole by the individuals tied to these industries for their living. [Particular interest, that is, the self-interest of particular individuals] invokes freedom of trade and commerce against control [*Regulierung*] from above; but the more blindly it sinks into self-seeking aims, the more it requires such control to bring it back to the universal.[56]

Hegel thus gives the state the role of: (1) controlling the pricing of essential consumables (to thus guard against the price fixing by oligopolies which Adam Smith described[57]); (2) monitoring the standards with which consumables are produced; and (3) regulating the global impact of certain economic activities. In his *Ethical Dimensions of the Economy*, Ver Eecke identifies eleven governmental tasks, in pursuit of which governmental intervention in the economy is necessary. These are:

1. The specification and protection of property rights (and thus the control of a justice system, police force, and army).
2. The promotion of efficiency within the free market.
3. The support and regulation of education and mental health.
4. Dealing with system-generated business cycles and their negative impact on economic growth and human well-being.
5. The creation of social welfare measures (for example, free education, free or subsidized health care, and low cost housing).
6. The creation of a system promoting and providing health care.
7. Promoting a well-functioning social contract (particularly in diverse societies).
8. Promoting transparency in the economic domain (thus preventing corruption).
9. Making wise investment decisions and strategic planning.
10. Protecting the environment.
11. Protecting cultural heritage.[58]

One could argue that, in endeavoring to provide the above, the government is endeavoring to provide "public goods;" a public good being a good that (supposedly) everyone can enjoy without anyone suffering or losing out as a consequence. Hegel reflects upon such goods within the following passage:

In the indefinite multiplication and interconnection of day-to-day needs, (a) the acquisition and exchange of the means to their satisfaction [...] and (b) the endeavors made and the transactions carried out in order to shorten the process of attainment as much as possible, give rise to factors which are a common interest, and when one man occupies himself with these his work is at the same time done for all. [...] These universal activities ... call for the oversight and care of the public authority.[59]

Like Hegel, many economists have seen a necessary role for the government in the provision of such goods. For, while there are many such goods from which society may benefit (for example, a new high-speed railway) without anyone (significantly, or, at least, not without compensation) suffering or losing out as a consequence, self-interested individuals (or individual companies) are unlikely to meet the very high costs of such projects. P. A. Samuelson proposes that the government should promote the provision of such goods in the following manner. The government should inform consumers of the potential opportunities that a proposed public good presents and ask them how much they would be willing to pay for it. If the cost of the good is lower than the total sum that consumers are willing to pay then, Samuelson argues, the government is justified in using taxation to pay for that good. Ver Eecke suggests that support and regulation of education could be treated as such a public good. He thus argues that subsidies for education and training could boost the productivity of the labor force, thereby increasing the productivity of society and increasing the future purchasing power of people's savings; everyone planning to consume on the basis of savings in the future would thus benefit from subsidies to education in the present. However, Ver Eecke also argues that subsidizing education and training by means of general taxation violates the public good argument. For this method of subsidy forces some people to pay more for a collective good than it is worth to them.[60]

This, however, does not mean that Ver Eecke believes that subsidizing educational opportunities by means of general taxation is a governmental practice that cannot be justified. It is in this context that Ver Eecke introduces – and extends the application of – Richard A. Musgrave's concept of "merit goods."[61] A merit good is a third kind of economic good that is neither a private good nor a public good, and is defined as:

a good that is so (de)meritorious that the government is justified in interfering with consumer wishes by deciding that the level of consumption is either too low (merit good) or too high (demerit good).[62]

Indeed, Ver Eecke explicitly equates seven of the eleven aforementioned governmental tasks – for which governmental intervention in the economy is necessary – as tasks that aim at the creation of such merit goods. Ver Eecke thus argues that the government's specification and enforcement of property rights "does not respect, and does not even intend to respect, the wishes of all consumers."[63] He likewise draws attention to the neo-liberal arguments that claim that governments are justified in legislating to promote the maximal efficiency of the free market, even if such legislation contradicts the wishes of citizens whose activities diminish or detract from economic efficiency.[64] He then connects the drive for maximal economic efficiency with governmental support and regulation of education and mental health, thus arguing that the promotion of the "rationality" of citizens is a precondition of their acceptance of governmental measures promoting maximal efficiency.[65] He argues that governments have a "duty to avoid the negative consequences of the business cycle, particularly those of economic recession and depression,"[66] and also that governmental provision of free medical treatment for the poor, low priced housing, and free education leads to a kind of "redistribution" for which the appellation "merit good" rather than "public good" is more appropriate.

If provision of such merit goods contradicts the wishes of – in some cases, perhaps the majority of – self-seeking consumers, what kind of arguments can be mobilized to justify such governmental interventions? It is in order to answer this question that Ver Eecke makes explicit reference to Hegel's socio-political philosophy.[67] He thus justifies governmental promotion of maximal efficiency within the free market by means of Hegel's argument that the free market is an ethical institution, which requires nurture and support, and that, more than any other economic system, is best able to help individuals attain the full actualization of freedom. Even if the free market represents the economic order best able to actualize human freedom, a society with such an economy will, Hegel suggests, potentially always contain a number of individuals alienated from its benefits insofar as unemployment and poverty are system-generated consequences of such an economy. Likewise, such a society will contain a number of individuals with mental and physical disabilities who, in their ability to competitively participate within the economic order may, *prima facie*, be disadvantaged. The free market is thus favored by Hegel because of its capacity to promote human freedom, even though such an economic order is persistently in danger of violating the freedom of some. However, if this economic order is supported as a result of its capacity to promote freedom, governments – through redistributive measures – must ensure that the impersonal demands of the free market are not allowed to significantly violate freedom, and it is for this reason that Ver Eecke believes that Hegel provides a philosophical framework through which governmental intervention in the economy in the provision of merit goods constituting social welfare measures can be justified.[68] Hegel, after all, argues that the human being requires *some* property in order to "translate his freedom into an external sphere,"[69] so that his freedom may be recognized and respected by others. Hegel can thus be seen as providing a philosophical framework justifying the modern welfare state (as well as minimum wage legislation). Indeed, with reference to Hegel, Ver Eecke concludes that "the free market philosophically implies the welfare state even though this welfare state is a violation of the free market principle."[70] The free market philosophically implies the welfare state insofar as: (a) it is an ethical institution that is promoted to the extent that it is the most effective means of securing human freedom (that is, a human being's freedom of choice, his ability to render his freedom objective through his possession of property, and his right to attain satisfaction through his actions) and so should not be permitted to significantly undermine the freedom of human beings who are unable to successfully participate within this economic order; and (b) it is an economic order that, through business cycles, division of labor, mechanization, and overproduction, inexorably leads to the unemployment, poverty, and alienation of some, whose distress needs to be alleviated if their essential freedom is not to be undermined. On the other hand, the welfare state violates the "harsh principle" of the free market – "produce, produce efficiently, and produce what others want or you will go bankrupt and/or starve to death" – insofar as it taxes successful participants in order to give less successful participants the privilege of escaping this harsh principle.[71] Indeed, Hegel himself clearly saw that state subsidies for the needy would "violate the principle of civil society"[72] and that consequently self-seeking individuals successfully participating in the sphere of civil society would come to "resent" such state interventions[73] – a "resentment" that Ver Eecke sees as "limiting" the extent of any redistributive measures proposed by the state. Nevertheless, whilst acknowledging that there is a serious question concerning the extent to which the state is justified in interfering in the free market – insofar as too much interference would subvert the very freedom that this economic order is supposed to secure – Hegel is adamant that "freedom of trade should not be such as to jeopardise the general good."[74]

## 6.3  Conclusion

We have seen that Hegel essentially agrees with Niethammer's conception of the human being as an inseparable union of humanity (*Humanität*) and animality (*Animalität*), and that, even though man's humanity can assert itself only insofar as he is given the opportunity to satisfy his animalistic needs within the socio-economic conditions in which he finds himself, the humanity of man is privileged as that which separates him from other forms of animal life and awards him a certain dignity. In prescribing ways in which the freedom essential to man's humanity is to be secured and promoted Hegel can thus be said to espouse humanistic values. Indeed, it is precisely in espousing such values that Hegel favors the free market as the economic system best able to promote human freedom, even whilst recognizing that such an economic system is not entirely flawless, inasmuch as it possesses the capacity to undermine the freedom of some. It is therefore likewise in pursuit of humanistic values that Hegel could be said to prescribe that we guard against allowing the negative system-generated consequences of the free market to significantly undermine the freedom of any and every human being. The enforcement of such values, Hegel believes, would be most adequately achieved by interventions from just and representative governments, even if, inasmuch as they threaten to subvert the very principle of the free market, the extent of such interventions have to be limited. The extent to which our governments are really just and representative and the precise extent to which they should interfere within the economy are, however, issues that remain in need of further discussion.

### Notes

1. The promise that Kant's philosophy seemed to hold for a new world order is illustrated by the following correspondence between two young men who would later be celebrated as the principal exponents of German Idealism. In 1795, G. W. F. Hegel wrote to F. W. J. Schelling that "from the Kantian system and its highest completion I expect a revolution in Germany [...]. The consequences that will result from it will astonish many a gentleman. Heads will be reeling at this summit of all philosophy by which man is being so greatly exalted. Yet why have we been so late in recognizing man's capacity for freedom, placing him in the same rank with all spirits? I believe there is no better sign of the times than this, that mankind is being presented as so worthy of respect in itself. It is proof that the aura of prestige surrounding the heads of the oppressors and gods of the earth is disappearing. The philosophers are proving the dignity of man. The peoples will

learn to feel it. Not only will they demand their rights, which have been trampled in the dust, they will take them back themselves, they will appropriate them. Religion and politics have joined hands in the *same* underhanded game. The former has taught what despotism willed: contempt for the human race, its incapacity for any good whatsoever, its incapacity to be something on its own" (Butler, Clark; Seiler, Christiane, trans. *Hegel: The Letters*. Bloomington: Indiana University Press, 1984: p. 303). A similarly devastating critique of the "immorality" of the religious and political order within Europe in the years between the fall of the Roman empire and the emergence of the Kantian system is provided in the "Third Letter" of Karl Leonhard Reinhold's *Letters on the Kantian Philosophy* (see: Reinhold, Karl Leonhard. *Letters on the Kantian Philosophy*. Cambridge: Cambridge University Press, 2005: 28–49). Reinhold's popular presentation of the ethical implications of Kant's critical philosophy was widely read in the last decades of the eighteenth century and offered a vision of the Kantian philosophy which almost certainly influenced Schelling and Hegel.

2. See: Niethammer, Friedrich. *Der Streit des Philanthropinismus und Humanismus in der Theorie des Erziehungs-Unterrichts unsrer Zeit*. Jena: Friedrich Frommann, 1808, p. 8.
3. Ibid., p. 18.
4. Ibid., p. 30–1.
5. Ibid., p. 22.
6. Ibid., p. 30.
7. Ibid., 16–17.
8. Ibid., 33–4.
9. Ibid., p. 14.
10. Ibid., p. 19.
11. Ibid., p. 10.
12. It was of course Hegel's account of this issue that had a decisive influence upon Marx.
13. Knox, T. M., trans. *Hegel's Philosophy of Right*. Oxford: Oxford University Press, 1967, §244A: 278.
14. Ibid., §242, p. 149.
15. Ibid., §245, p. 150. Hegel here, as elsewhere, uses the term *"bürgerlichen Gesellschaft"* – *civil* or *bourgeois* society – as a synonym for the emerging capitalist free market.
16. Ibid.
17. Ibid., §244A, p. 277.
18. See Niethammer, *Der Streit des Philanthropinismus und Humanismus in der Theorie des Erziehungs-Unterrichts unsrer Zeit*, p. 72.
19. Ibid., p. 8.
20. Ibid., 41–2. Niethammer's attitude towards Fichte's work always seems to have been decidedly ambivalent. For a discussion of his earlier critique of Fichte's subjective idealism see Fincham, Richard. "Refuting Fichte with 'Common Sense': Friedrich Immanuel Niethammer's Reception of the *Wissenschaftslehre 1794/5*." *Journal of the History of Philosophy* 43:3 (2005), 301–24.
21. Niethammer, *Der Streit des Philanthropinismus und Humanismus in der Theorie des Erziehungs-Unterrichts unsrer Zeit*, 33–4 and 43.

22. Ibid., p. 66.
23. Likewise, whilst himself sympathetic to Niethammer's privileging of humanism within education, Hegel also believes that educational theory should not neglect pupils' capacities to successfully participate within the socio-economic conditions with which they are confronted. He thus writes that "civil society has the right and duty of superintending and influencing education [*Erziehung*], inasmuch as education bears upon the child's capacity to become a member of society". (*Hegel's Philosophy of Right*, §239, p. 148).
24. Hegel's mature philosophical system is founded upon the principle of the absolute isomorphism between *thought* and *being*, which, in the Introduction to his *Science of Logic* of 1812 (a text which he composed whilst employed at the *Aegidiengymnasium*) is announced within the claim that "the absolute truth of being is the known Notion [*Begriff*] and the Notion as such is the absolute truth of being" (Miller, Arnold, trans. *Hegel's Science of Logic*. New York: Humanity Books 1969, p. 49) – a formulation which strikingly parallels Niethammer's earlier claim that "the spirit of *humanism*" uncovers "the ideality of the truth and the truth of the ideal" (Niethammer, *Der Streit des Philanthropinismus und Humanismus in der Theorie des Erziehungs-Unterrichts unsrer Zeit*, p. 33-4).
25. Charles. *Hegel and Modern Society*. Cambridge: Cambridge University Press, 1979, p. 167.
26. Hegel uses the term "reconciliation" (*Versöhnung*) in this context within the Preface to his *Philosophy of Right* (Knox, trans. *Hegel's Philosophy of Right*, p. 12).
27. Ibid., §32A, p. 233.
28. Ibid., §15, p. 27.
29. Ibid.,§ 32A, p. 233.
30. Ibid.
31. Ibid., §5, 21–2.
32. Ibid., §6, p. 22.
33. Ibid., §7A, p. 228.
34. Ibid., §15, p. 27.
35. Ibid., §15A, p 230.
36. Ibid., §27, p. 32.
37. Ibid., §36, p. 37.
38. Ibid., §41 p. 40.
39. Ibid., §44, p. 41.
40. Ibid., §125, 84–5.
41. Ibid., §139, 92–3.
42. Ibid., §199, 129–30.
43. Niethammer, *Der Streit des Philanthropinismus und Humanismus in der Theorie des Erziehungs-Unterrichts unsrer Zeit*, 33–4. See also ibid., p. 8.
44. Knox, trans. *Hegel's Philosophy of Right*, §190, p. 127.
45. Ibid., §258A, p. 279
46. Ver Eecke, Wilfried. *Ethical Dimensions of the Economy: Making Use of Hegel and the Concepts of Public and Merit Goods*. Berlin Heidelberg: Springer-Verlag, 2008, p. 178.
47. Ibid., 153–5.

48. Ibid., 155–8.
49. Knox, trans. *Hegel's Philosophy of Right*, §311, p. 202.
50. The "corporations" that Hegel refers to should not be confused with contemporary "business corporations." Hegel is referring to associations constituted by individuals who share a common trade or occupation, which consciously pursue the interests of all of their members. He tentatively suggests that corporations *could* significantly alleviate the problem of poverty insofar as "within the Corporation the help which poverty receives loses its accidental character and the humiliation wrongly associated with it. The wealthy perform their duties to their fellow associates." (ibid., §253, p. 154). He also observes, however, that harsh free market principles have recently led to the abolition of such corporations (see: ibid., §255A, p. 278).
51. Hegel himself describes a corporation as "a whole which is itself an organ of the entire society." (ibid., §253, p. 153).
52. Ibid., §311, p. 203.
53. Paul Diesing illustrates the contemporary problem of "voter apathy" in the United States with the following statistics: "In 1996 the Census Bureau reported that 44 percent of Americans of voting age were not registered to vote. Of the remaining 56 percent, about half vote in a presidential election, and about 33 percent vote in off-year congressional elections" (Diesing, Paul. *Hegel's Dialectical Political Economy: A Contemporary Application*. Boulder, Colorado: Westview Press, 1999, p. 134).
54. Knox, trans. *Hegel's Philosophy of Right*, §311, p. 203.
55. Ibid., p. 202.
56. Ibid., §236, p. 147.
57. Diesing. *Hegel's Dialectical Political Economy*, 56–7.
58. Ver Eecke. *Ethical Dimensions of the Economy*, 214–5.
59. Knox, trans. *Hegel's Philosophy of Right*, §235, p. 147.
60. Ver Eecke thus notes that "ideally public goods should be financed through taxation of the individuals who would benefit from the use of these goods. Furthermore, the amount of the taxation should be directly linked to the usefulness enjoyed by each consumer" (Ver Eecke. *Ethical Dimensions of the Economy*, p. 102). A great many Western governments do not finance education in this manner, however. Ver Eecke thus notes that "the local tax contribution for public elementary and secondary schools in the United States is financed for 96% by property taxes. Typically, young couples with children do not possess the largest, most expensive homes. These are sometimes owned by childless couples or couples whose children are grown. Labelling education a public good means that the government has an opportunity to help consumers achieve the fulfilment of their wishes by collecting from everyone what they want to pay for the service in return for the provision of that service. Providing education as a public good therefore requires that the government only collect what individuals feel the service is worth to them [...]. The provision of education as a public good thus requires that the government make individuals pay in proportion to their benefit. However, the actual financing method of education, violates this rule. Couples without children but with expensive homes are forced to pay more than couples with children and less expensive homes. If education can only be justified as a public good then, conceptually speaking, some people are forced to

pay more than they should, while others are allowed to pay less than they should. [...] But, the government uses its taxation power to force some people to pay more than is conceptually justified" (ibid., p. 109).

61. Ver Eecke thus writes that "the concept [of merit good] is much more broadly applicable than Musgrave himself envisioned" (ibid., p. 92).
62. Ibid., p. 238.
63. Ibid., p. 101.
64. Ibid., pp. 103–5.
65. Ibid., p. 106.
66. Ibid., p. 93.
67. Ibid., pp. 71, 91.
68. Ver Eecke points out that this Hegelian position has affinities with the "functionings and capabilities" approach developed by Sen and Nussbaum. According to this view, a just society must provide all individuals with the means to reach and develop certain important functions and capabilities, and financing this goal can only occur by some form of taxation (see: ibid., p. 86n).
69. Knox, trans. *Hegel's Philosophy of Right*, §41, p. 40.
70. Ver Eecke. *Ethical Dimensions of the Economy*, p. 88.
71. Ibid. p. 3.
72. Knox, trans. *Hegel's Philosophy of Right*, §245, p. 150.
73. See: ibid., §236, pp. 147–8.
74. Ibid., §236A, p. 276.

## Bibliography

Butler, Clark and Seiler, Christiane, trans. *Hegel: The Letters*. (Bloomington: Indiana University Press, 1984).

Diesing, Paul, *Hegel's Dialectical Political Economy: A Contemporary Application*. (Boulder, Colorado: Westview Press, 1999).

Fincham, Richard, "Refuting Fichte with 'Common Sense': Friedrich Immanuel Niethammer's Reception of the *Wissenschaftslehre 1794/5*." *Journal of the History of Philosophy* 43:3 (2005).

Knox, T. M., trans. *Hegel's Philosophy of Right*. (Oxford: Oxford University Press, 1967).

Miller, Arnold, trans. *Hegel's Science of Logic*. (New York: Humanity Books, 1969).

Niethammer, Friedrich, *Der Streit des Philanthropinismus und Humanismus in der Theorie des Erziehungs-Unterrichts unsrer Zeit*. (Jena: Friedrich Frommann, 1808).

Reinhold, Karl Leonhard, *Letters on the Kantian Philosophy*. (Cambridge: Cambridge University Press, 2005).

Taylor, Charles, *Hegel and Modern Society*. (Cambridge: Cambridge University Press, 1979).

Ver Eecke, Wilfried, *Ethical Dimensions of the Economy: Making Use of Hegel and the Concepts of Public and Merit Goods*. (Berlin Heidelberg: Springer-Verlag, 2008).

# 7
# Marx and Humanism

*Ulrich Steinvorth*

## 7.1 Theses

The economic crisis that started in 2008 has aroused new interest in Karl Marx, as he declared the recurrence of economic crises to be an inevitable property of capitalism. In the following, I attempt to examine whether this interest is well-founded. My answer is: Marx can tell us something about how to interpret modern society, but little about the kind of society that we might change the present society into. This answer may seem incompatible with Marx's famous remark that "The philosophers have only interpreted the world, in various ways; the point is to change it."[1] Doesn't Marx reject interpretations in favor of practical change? But as Marx produced theory all his life, we cannot reasonably assume this. He rejects theory that does not help to improve the world and demands theory that enables us to change the world according to our intentions. The first condition such theory must meet is that it distinguishes, amongst the confusing mass of social data, what is relevant for changes and what is irrelevant; what is basic and what is superficial; what is accidental and what is substantial. Marx did not see himself as a prophet but as a proponent of a science capable of changing society in the interest of mankind.

In principle, theorists since the time of Plato and Aristotle agree it is the task of science to distinguish the substantial from the accidental, however much they disagree on what is substantial. But today the impression prevails that the most important characteristic of modern society is that there is so much interdependence in it that we cannot distinguish the substantial and the accidental. Commentators in the media, when analyzing the present economic crisis, capitulate before confusing causes, reasons, and interdependencies that (might) have led

118

to the collapse of the financial system. Habermas, against his intention, sanctified the idea that modern society is without a substance by
choosing the catchy title *Die neue Unübersichtlichkeit*,[2] for a collection
of papers on modern society: The title literally translates as *The New
Impossibility of Seeing Clearly.*

My first thesis is that it is precisely this alleged opacity that Marx
rejects by claiming instead that modern society has a decipherable
structure that allows us to distinguish the important from the unim-
portant. My second thesis is that such a structure is provided by what I
call the "Marxian approach" rather than by Marxism. My third thesis is
that Marx developed the Marxian approach in two ways, by a reflection
on history and an analysis of commodity production, both of which
imply a moral theory. Since the third thesis implies the second and
the second the first, I can concentrate on explaining the third, by presenting Marx's approach to history and modern economy. Finally I will
consider whether the moral theory implied by the Marxian approach is
humanistic.

I have to add three warnings. First, what I call the structure of a society is a function of society that other functions and parts of society
depend on, not an unchangeable layer or element of society. Second,
what I call the Marxian approach is my artificial reconstruction of just
those elements in Marxism that I think withstand criticism. Third, I
presume that social science is in principle incapable of prediction, since
unlike physical bodies humans are influenced by predictions of their
actions. If predictions of actions are made public, they turn into recommendations or warnings.[3] Hence, social theories cannot be tested by
prediction. Though Marx made bold, falsifiable predictions (some of
which came true) and thus satisfied the Popperian criterion of scientificity, we must not take this for a proof of his scientificity but of his
falling victim, like Popper, to the physics-oriented model of social science. Its reflective property requires a conception of social science that
replaces the task of prediction with the task of clarifying the conditions
of a changing society. The Marxian approach will be an important,
though not the only, element in such a conception.

## 7.2  Marx's theory of history

The Marxian approach to history includes the following theses:[4]

*Productive powers require forms of production.* Productive powers are
 what characterizes humans. They are not tools or machines, but

capabilities by which we change the world and ourselves. They include capabilities for inventing means of production and can be efficiently used only in cooperation. Hence, individuals need social forms of organizing their capabilities. Marx calls them forms of production. Such forms have led to social differentiation, since they enable some groups to decide on the use of capacities and to become the ruling classes.

*Forms of production tend to progress.* Some individuals enjoy dominating and belonging to the ruling classes, so there will be competition for controlling the forms of production. But a group can prevail over its competitors only by organizing productive powers more efficiently, so the struggle for power entails a tendency toward more efficient forms of production. One particularly successful organizational form is *commodity production, which* aroused Marx's special interest. He considered it the vehicle of progress and modernity.

*Forms of production become fetters for capabilities.* The successful organization of productive powers leads to the discovery of new capabilities that people want to use but that require new competences for using them in cooperation. Marx presumes that capabilities are inexhaustible. If the ruling classes lack this competence they become fetters of development.

*History has been a series of class struggles.*[5] There is progress in history only if the representatives of the fettered capabilities fight for their development and succeed in replacing the old form of production by one that integrates the newly discovered capabilities.

*Today people can find a form of production that will never fetter their capabilities.* Capitalist commodity production has made possible a society of abundance "in which the free development of each is the condition for the free development of all."[6] In such a form there will still be people who decide on how capabilities are used, but everyone can participate in decisions. Abundance makes any restriction of capabilities superfluous.

The Marxian approach conceives societies as something that is constituted by, and serves, the capabilities of individuals. Although Marx is known for his remark that an individual is but "the ensemble of the social relations,"[7] the Marxian approach commits to the view that individuals do not exist for society but society exists for them. If they are the ensemble of their social relations, individuals also are the ensemble of their individual capabilities and use them in cooperation for their own sake and purposes.

Marx was not the first to describe man in this way. In his *Politics*, Aristotle, like Marx, assumes that it is because of their capabilities that humans are in need of other people. Aristotle even anticipated the idea that human associations differ and develop in the way that their capabilities differ and develop.[8] Both of them assume that the most elementary productive power is that of biological generation; it makes people come together in families. Both assume that since people have a lot of other capabilities, many of which can appear only after the more elementary ones have developed, they need more associations than just the family.[9]

Marx differs from Aristotle in conceiving the forms of organization as breeding new capabilities that require a new organization and constitute "contradictions" to the given production form. But, like Aristotle, he does not think that social contradictions and class struggles are necessary, since he expects a communist revolution to mark their final abolition. Note, however, that the Marxian approach does not imply the idea of a classless society. It is compatible with the idea that societies cannot do without classes.

Marx became Marxist by adding two theses to the Marxian approach:

*First, the economy determines the rest of society.* For the Marxian, the substance of society is constituted by (a) the use of any capability by which individuals might change the world or themselves, and (b) the form of the organization of such capabilities. For the Marxist, it is (a') the use only of *economically* productive capabilities and (b') their form of organization. Marx called (a') and (b') the *base* of society, and called the use of the other capabilities and their institutions *superstructure*: politics and justice, science and art, religion, family, and education. In traditional philosophical terminology, we might call the superstructure the "accidental" and the base the "substance". According to the Marxist, the substance is (a') and (b'), hence it is an economic function.

Marx assumed an *economic* base because his critique of commodity production suggested to him that modern history is propelled by the dynamics of commodity production (which I will explain below). But the hierarchy is dubious because politics and religion seem to have influenced the use of productive forces and their organization in earlier societies and, in science, does so today.[10] So we might favor the Marxian approach and assume that (a) and (b) are the base of society. But can we do so, given that (a) is the use of *any* capability and (b) the organizational form of any capability? Will it still be useful to distinguish between base and superstructure, or substance and accidental, if the use of any talent can belong to the base?

*Second, abundance will allow a classless society.* The Marxian expects of the productive forces growing in capitalism the rise of a form of production that will not turn into a fetter of capabilities. The Marxist also expects of them the abolition of class differences, as anyone can take up any job or profession. Until now, Marx proclaimed, man has been

> a hunter, a fisherman, a herdsman, or a critical critic, and must remain so if he does not want to lose his means of livelihood; while in communist society [...] each can become accomplished in any branch he wishes, society regulates the general production and thus makes it possible for me to do one thing today and another tomorrow, to hunt in the morning, fish in the afternoon, rear cattle in the evening, criticise after dinner, just as I have a mind, without ever becoming hunter, fisherman, herdsman or critic.[11]

If we are to take this description seriously,[12] communist society revokes or reduces the division of labor in favor of a social organization that allows everyone to develop as many talents as possible. Just as in primitive society (nearly) everyone can do anything everyone else can, apart from sex-specific activities, in a communist society everyone approaches to this original state. Marx assumed that capitalist economy already imposes on people such a tendency back to primitive times. The fluctuations of capital investment force everyone to be "fit for a variety of labors, ready to face any change of production;" the "different social functions he performs, are but so many modes of giving free scope to his own natural and acquired powers." This fitness for a variety of labors is similar to the fitness for a variety of activities required of individuals in primitive societies; though only in a sufficiently differentiated society can individuals become "fully developed."[13]

Marxism has also become known for its prediction that abundance will lead to the withering of the state as an institution for the enforcement of justice. But in this respect the Marxian approach does not necessarily differ from Marxism. True, it may seem implausible that when we live in abundance justice becomes superfluous. We imagine that even then people will vie for power or compete for the love of particularly attractive individuals, so will be capable of rights violations. But Marx is supported by Hume, who said:

> Let us suppose that nature has bestowed on the human race such profuse *abundance* of all *external* conveniences that, without any uncertainty in the event, without any care or industry on our part, every individual finds himself fully provided with whatever his most voracious appetites can want, or luxurious imagination wish or desire. His natural beauty, we shall suppose, surpasses all acquired ornaments [...] Music, poetry and contemplation form his sole business: conversation, mirth, and friendship his sole amusement. It seems evident that, in such a happy state, every other social virtue would flourish, and receive tenfold increase; but the cautious, jealous virtue of justice would never once have been dreamed of.[14]

The abundance Hume describes is the very society Marx expected. Marx also assumed that we have abundance not only of consumable goods but also of our "natural beauty" and all possible sources of satisfaction, and Hume assumed that in such conditions justice and the state are superfluous. Both of them expected there would no longer be classes and class conflicts, yet this is the crucial expectation that I think must be rejected.

If a future society of abundance could ever be one in which "music, poetry and contemplation" are people's sole business they would perhaps be right. But even if the supervision of production could be delegated to *automata*, there will be other public affairs about which there will be differences similar to class conflicts. Unless individuals are made equal by genetic or some other kind of engineering, they will choose different ways of life. Some will specialize in an art, some in a sport, some in a science, some in developing new technology, some in exploring the galaxy, some in eroticism. Rather than leading to everyone doing everything, abundance will allow everyone to pursue their own particular talents and interests unhampered. Such diversification is not the same as the contemporary division of labor, but is a division of interest groups that are similar to contemporary classes.

Classes are most often "defined by their position within social relations of production."[15] Even in a society of abundance there are different ways to use the abundant resources because not all possible uses can be realized at the same time, so different individuals will differ on how to use the resources. Whether or not we call such groups classes, they will compete for the use of resources. Such competition need not develop into war, but it is comparable to class conflicts. To solve them, states may be superfluous, but rules of justice will be necessary.

With its two Marxist additions Marx's theory gained a sharper contour and message. However, those additions are not only false, but also serve to strengthen incorrect, or at least debatable, political norms. The assumption that classes will be superfluous corresponds to the norm that they should be abolished; that individuals should not be allowed to form groups with different and competing views on how to use the resources available to a society. I think this is wrong. There should indeed be competing views about such a central question. Such competition should not, of course, turn into war, but without competition between groups that can also develop into classes, society will enjoy only the "peace of the graveyard" (*Friedhofsfrieden*).

The assumption that it is only economically productive powers that constitute the base or substance of society has the virtue of giving a clear and falsifiable significance to the idea of the substance of society. But, again, it is not only in conflict with the empirical facts but also with moral norms. It favors the view that economic activities are the most important part of human life; that labor, rather than politics or science, art or sexuality, religion or sport, is what makes humans human. In contrast, if we consider the substance of society to be any kind of activity that uses specifically human capabilities, this is a vague approach in need of clarification. But it has a better fit to both the reality of human beings and our moral ideas and intuitions.[16]

The basic idea of the Marxian approach is that societies differ according to which capabilities are used and how their use is organized, and that they develop by solving problems or "contradictions" in the organization of their use. This approach, though vaguer than the Marxist, still distinguishes between what is substantial – the use of capabilities and their organization – and what is accidental – our discussion and views about this use and our passive states and emotions. It has proved successful in social theory. To give two prominent examples, Huntington and Fukuyama explain societies and their development by what they call fundamental contradictions. Though they talk of contradictions "in human life" (Fukuyama) or of conflicts "between nations and groups of different civilizations" and "among princes" and "nations" and "ideologies" (Huntington), such conflicts can be analyzed as conflicts about the use of capabilities.[17]

## 7.3 Marx's economic theory

Marx deduced from his economic theory that the capitalist economy would soon collapse. As this did not happen his theory seems to have been falsified. What I want to show is that, first, his economic theory distinguishes between what is substantial and what is accidental in the capitalist economy and, second, this distinction is useful, if not necessary, for understanding capitalism in a way that allows its reform or abolition.[18]

Marx, in his *Capital*, started from the uncontroversial assumption that the capitalist economy is a form of commodity production, a production for a market. In the terms of his theory of history, explained above, commodity production is a form of production, a way to organize economically productive forces. He distinguishes three stages of commodity production: without money, with money, and with capital. Each stage is characterized by the same basic problem or "contradiction," as Marx calls it. He took the term "contradiction" from Hegel.[19]

Marx used the term because it allowed him to present the three stages of commodity production as successive attempts to solve a basic contradiction in commodity production. We can replace the term *contradiction* by the term *problem* or *potential conflict* without loss or change of meaning. But we need to distinguish the contradictions of commodity production from those between productive forces and the forms of their organization. These contradictions are conflicts between people who represent new, not yet organized forces and rulers who represent existing organizational forms, while the contradictions of commodity production are conflicts between two necessary goals of commodity production.

The two necessary but incongruous goals are related to *exchange value* and *use value*. The product must realize an exchange value for the producer, a value that is equivalent to his labor and the resources he spent on it. But it must also realize a use value, which is its satisfaction of some consumer demand. Like any form of production, commodity production must meet consumption interests. So commodity production must realize, on the one hand, an exchange value for the producer, or he will cease production, and on the other, a use value for the consumer.[20] Exchange value and use value, the requirements of exchange value realization on the production side and the requirements of use value satisfaction on the consumption side, establish two different aims for commodity production that may, though need not, always pull in different directions. Note that this is an abstract, not a real, concrete problem.

The difference between the two aims of commodity production cannot prevent a commodity producer from meeting a consumer who happens to demand precisely the thing the producer happens to offer. But such a meeting is rare. To live on commodity production, a society needs an easily quantifiable commodity that is accepted by all potential exchangers as an equivalent for any other commodity. Such a commodity is money. In its function as a means of exchange, money enables commodity production to break the narrow limits of moneyless exchange.

The introduction of money solves the first concrete problem of commodity production: that the specific interests of the producer and of the consumer meet only rarely. But it also imposes a second, abstract, problem on commodity production. Money becomes the only means by which producer and consumer measure the value of what they do and feel. It turns from a means of exchange into a universal measure of any good, becoming the only representation and measure of value. By its use, people misunderstand and adulterate the value of their own actions and interests. They suffer what Marx calls *alienation*.

The specific problem that equates the substance of commodity production with money is the difference between how value is measured and what value is, which is the same as the difference between exchange value and use value. Now it is no longer the problem that both values must be realized, but that both must be taken for what is valuable: the one as its representative, the other as what can be represented but often is not represented by the exchange value or money.

Again, this is an abstract problem which need not create economic difficulties, but which can also develop into a concrete problem. Since money is the only representative of value, people will prefer to hoard money instead of using it and thereby putting it into circulation, if they distrust the exchange rate between money and goods. Money will be taken out of circulation and production will collapse.

Again Marx constructs a solution to this problem. It consists of introducing an exchange that attracts money more than the simple commodity exchange. Such an exchange is that of money with labor force, plus means of production (machinery and a raw material such as cotton). Combining them to produce a commodity (such as clothing) can produce a value greater than the value spent on buying them. This is the specific exchange of industrial capitalism. Though its products may also face hoarding problems, the chance of increasing the value of one's money in the capitalist exchange is usually greater than by hoarding it. Value is now represented by industrial capital.

Production by industrial capital is the final form of commodity production. It produces both an abstract and a concrete problem for which Marx can no longer find a solution within the frame of commodity production. The abstract problem, defining the substance of capitalist economy, consists of the potential conflict of the interest in surplus production and the interest in consumption. The concrete problem appears in various forms that will result, Marx claims, in a collapse of the system.

It is crucial to see that the existence of the abstract problem is not sufficient to put an end to capitalist production. Only a real, concrete problem can do that. When Marx analyses the first two stages of commodity production, he obviously considers not the abstract but only the concrete problems to be fatal for them. This is less obviously the case in his analysis of capitalist production, for here his analysis, as well as its object, is more complex. But we have no reason to think that Marx abandons his distinction between abstract and concrete problems. The abstract problem of capitalism, the incongruity of surplus production and consumption, is a necessary but not a sufficient condition for the collapse of capitalism.

So what are the sufficient conditions? Marx agrees with Adam Smith and other economists in that capitalists need not just to make any surplus or profit but as large a profit as possible, because the smaller their profit, the greater their danger of being removed from the market by competing capitalists. This pressure leads capitalists to keep wages as low as possible and to replace workers by machines that introduce mass production. Mass production reduces the cost per unit and enables the manufacturer to ask a lower price, increasing his chances of making a profit by mass selling. But machines also reduce the wages element of production costs. It is only this part that can increase the exchange value of the profit. From this claim and the empirical fact of increasing machine production, in agreement with Smith and other economists of his time, Marx deduced that the rate of profit would tend to fall.

Now this tendency is controversial. But even if it does exist, the enormous increase in productivity has allowed capitalist firms to raise the living standards of the masses without reducing their own riches or their command over production. It does not seem plausible that from now on living standards could be raised only by replacing capitalism with communism. So Marx's claim that machine production would turn the abstract incongruity of profit and consumption interests into an insoluble problem lacks plausibility.[21]

Nevertheless, Marx's approach to capitalism is useful. If we accept Marx's claims about the abstract problems of commodity production but not those about the concrete problems, we also accept his distinction between what is substantial and what is accidental in capitalism. But it is his claims about the concrete problems that are, unfortunately, the best known. What makes his economic analysis still up to date is its claim that capitalism must meet two requirements that can pull in different directions: the universal needs of use value production and the specific needs of exchange value production. These tensions do not doom capitalism, but subject it to institutional conditions that in the end may, but need not, prove unrealizable.

For instance, exchange value production implies competition, and under real world conditions, competition entails an increase in production, as a producer has a better chance of a higher profit by increasing his production. Hence, commodity production is expansive.[22] This property explains its historical expansion in colonialism and imperialism and would entail its breakdown once it has spread throughout the world and reached the geographical limits of its expansion.[23] However, we must distinguish increasing production from overproduction. The geographic expansion of capitalism might be followed or accompanied by a qualitative expansion that uses increasing production for expanding into new fields of production,[24] such as education, the conquest of the Moon or Mars, military production, or the introduction of an unconditional basic income that would abolish the most oppressive burdens that capitalism puts on most people's lives.[25] Any such expansion is a specific form of reconciling exchange and use value production that changes society in a specific way without entailing the collapse of capitalism.

We can use Marx's economic analyses to defend capitalism as well as to reject it. In particular, as competition, not monopolies, can be expected to promote capability development, we can use Marx's analyses to strengthen market competition against the market-corrupting tendency of capitalism to favor monopolies, even though Marx condemned such a defense in his critique of Proudhon.[26] We might even use it to identify the conditions under which capitalism can escape its tendency to produce economic crises.

I conclude that Marx's analysis of commodity production allows us to distinguish what is substantial in a capitalist economy (the requirements of both exchange value and use production are met) from what is accidental (how the requirements are met). Nevertheless, how they are met can be significant, because it can create new requirements that in turn must be met. In how to meet the requirements of exchange and use value, there seems to be more leeway for producing in the interest of use value than Marx expected. But it also seems that many defenders of capitalism believe the requirements of exchange value can be subordinated to the requirements of exchange values.

## 7.4   Moral theory

What does the Marxian approach achieve that ordinary social science does not? Ordinary science did not warn us against the most important events of the last hundred years, but did the Marxian approach do better? I do not claim that it does. I claim, rather, that the Marxian approach structures society by determining a substance and its accidents. The substance is a function, the use of our capabilities, for which there are many forms, many of which are connected by development. The forms allow people in greater or lesser numbers to develop their capabilities. In modern society the form of production ties the use of our capabilities to the accumulation of exchange value. By pointing out this condition, Marx helps us understand events such as economic crises, and even world wars, as efforts to meet this condition. But such an understanding does not allow for unconditional predictions. Nor does it imply that the capitalistic production form is unacceptable; the understanding rather clarifies both its risks and chances.

The social substance, people's use of their capabilities, is a social reality that can vary in the scope of the capabilities used and the form in which the use is organized. Marx assumed the change can be predicted, but if we reject this assumption, as we must, since humans are influenced by predictions about their actions,[27] I include a normative thesis in the following set of theses that summarizes the Marxian approach:

(1) Any use of individuals' capabilities needs a social form of cooperation.
(2) Social forms are progressive or successful if they allow individuals to develop the capabilities that are known when the forms are introduced.
(3) Successful social forms allow individuals to detect new capabilities.
(4) Until the present day, successful organization forms have fettered rather than furthered the development of the capabilities whose detection they allowed.
(5) Today we can organize capabilities in a form that does not turn into their fetter but allows their unhampered development.

(6) Societies ought to organize individuals' capabilities in a form that allows the unhampered development of as many capabilities as possible.

(1) to (5) are empirical assertions that describe the social substance. (6) is a moral proposition that explains why the capabilities and organizational forms described by (1) to (5) are important.

Yet, does not accepted social science, and economics in particular, claim to give an understanding of society similar to that of the Marxian approach? True, some economists still maintain their science is as value-free and as falsifiable by prediction as physics. But it has become realized that the prediction of actions in social science influences action and cannot have the role it has in physics. It has also been accepted by quite a few economists that economic theory needs to presuppose values that are not just methodological like those in physics; rather, they are values that can be rejected by other scientists. George Shackle, for example, granting that other economists might pursue other goals, declares that his theory seeks to explain "the working of an economic system where the guiding principle is to give each individual the greatest scope for his own spontaneous use of life."[28]

Like Marx, Shackle identifies a substance of society – the working of an economic system – and assumes that it is the social substance because it serves the paramount socio-moral goal "to give each individual the greatest scope for his own spontaneous use of life." Neither substance nor moral goal is very different from those assumed by Marx. Moreover, Shackle would certainly agree with Marx that it is important to distinguish what is substantial and what is not, and that the substance, the working of an economic system, is something whose working we can change. So what is specific about the Marxian approach? There is nothing in it that established economists such as Shackle cannot accept. It is just that Marx was the first to develop an approach to economy and society that is also used today by non-Marxists. His approach is not the only one useful for social science, but one science cannot reject.

Let us finally ask what kind of morality is maintained by (6) and, more particularly, whether it is humanistic.

As to the first question, it is not a utilitarian or a need-oriented morality. It locates the principal interest of people not in happiness but in using, developing, and detecting their capabilities. This agrees with Aristotle's idea that the good life for humans consists in the development of their specific capabilities. But it deviates from Aristotle in the idea that human capabilities and their development are without limit and can go on indefinitely.

As to the question whether the Marxian moral theory is humanistic, we have to become clear about what is meant by the word. Merriam-Webster's Online Dictionary explains the term by reference to "humanitarianism" and defines this as "a philosophy that usually rejects supernaturalism and stresses an individual's dignity and worth and capacity for self-realization through reason." Similarly, the Concise Oxford Dictionary defines the word by reference to "humanism," which it defines as "a rationalistic outlook or system of thought attaching prime importance to human rather than divine or supernatural matters." According to these definitions, thesis (6) clearly expresses a humanistic morality.

Since Marx was a Marxist and not only a Marxian, let us also ask whether Marxism, if we understand it the way I have proposed, expresses a humanist morality. As a moral theory, Marxism differs from the Marxian approach in its expectation that the unhampered development of human capabilities will not only produce superabundance but also make justice, if not morality, and class divisions superfluous. In this respect Marxism follows David Hume, as we have seen. If we are ready to call Hume's moral theory humanistic, and I see no reason not to do so, we should not deny Marxism this title either.

But Marx is not only classifiable as a humanist in this general and unspecific sense. Rather, in his *Economic and Philosophic Manuscripts* of 1844, he described his ideal of a communist society and the individual in terms of a "human emancipation and rehabilitation,"[29] as a realization of "*human* nature and a new enrichment of *human* nature,"[30] "as the appropriation of the human essence."[31] He is enthusiastic in his description of

> Communism as the *positive* transcendence of *private property* [...] as the real *appropriation* of the *human* essence by and for man; [...] as the complete return of man to himself as a *social* (*i.e.*, human) being – a return accomplished consciously and embracing the entire wealth of previous humanism, and as fully developed humanism equals naturalism; it is the genuine resolution of the conflict between man and man – the true resolution of the strife between existence and essence, between objectification and self-confirmation, between freedom and necessity, between the individual and the species. Communism is the riddle of history solved, and it knows itself to be this solution.[32]

In this description Marx is a more specific sort of humanist; he implies there is a human nature from which capitalism has alienated man and that man will re-appropriate, though in a form enriched by the use of capabilities he was hindered from using in poorer and narrower conditions. Yet is this conception of communism compatible with Marx's later views, whether we understand them in the Marxist or the Marxian form? Louis Althusser has argued they are not. It belongs only to a stage of development when Marx "was dominated by Feuerbach's 'communalist' humanism."[33] But "In 1845, Marx broke radically with every theory that based history and politics on an essence of man." The break was a consequence of Marx's formation of a theory of history and politics based on radically new concepts such as the concepts of social formation, productive forces, relations of production, superstructure, ideologies, determination in the last instance by the economy, and specific determination of the other levels.

"Strictly in respect to theory," Althusser argues,

> one can and must speak openly of *Marx's theoretical anti-humanism*, and see in this *theoretical anti-humanism* the absolute (negative) precondition of the (positive) knowledge of the human world itself, and of its practical transformation.[34]

Althusser is certainly right that after 1845, Marx would no longer have described communism as he had done in 1844. Marx would have referred after 1845 to the growth of productive forces and their being fostered and fettered by the forms or relations of production and to the historical determinism that leaves no place for "the appropriation of the human essence," literally understood. But did Marx ever understand such appropriation literally?

Even if he did, Althusser and other critics of the view that Marx later stuck with his 1844 ideas overlook two points about human essence. First, the fact that man is radically dependent on and formed by his productive forces and other social relations does not exclude the possibility that he has an essence. On the contrary, it is only because man has a specifically social nature that we can be profoundly dependent on social relations. Likewise, the fact that Stone Age man and modern man are probably radically different in their behavior, thinking, and feeling does not rule out that they have the same nature of being dependent on their social relations.

It is true, though, that if human essence were defined only as man's total dependence on social relations, communism could in no sense be a re-appropriation of capabilities, nor the emancipation or enrichment, or the abolition of the alienation, of man. There cannot be emancipation or alienation unless there is an essence or nature one is emancipated or alienated from. But Marx went on using the vocabulary of emancipation and alienation after 1845.[35] It is unlikely that he did so only for propaganda purposes. So unlike Althusser, he thought that his ideas about productive forces and relations did not imply a rejection of the idea of human essence.

It is not too difficult to guess why: because the productive forces and social relations that constitute human essence are the forces and relations of people. They are not something that is imposed on people by nonhuman forces. The relations of production are imposed on the ruled classes by the ruling, but even rulers are human, and the forms of production they impose are in any case dependent on the productive forces, which are the forces of people. Hence, there can be alienation and emancipation because people can be separated from their productive forces and their sources and can appropriate them. There is human essence because people have productive powers. Although Stone Age man is very different from modern man, he still had human powers, only less developed and perhaps more appropriated. Hence, there is a human essence not only in the formal sense that there is something that influences the changes of human acting and feeling, but also in the material sense that there is something to be appropriated and emancipated.

What becomes clear in this discussion of human essence is that the productive forces that constitute human essence (as well as the substance of society) cannot plausibly be conceived as economically productive forces alone. So the Marxian approach that conceives them as productive forces in a very wide sense seems more consistent with Marx's system than the narrow sense to which they are restricted in the Marxist view.

Let us have a final look at the moral principle (6) in the Marxian approach. Is it not too dangerous to be humanistic? It demands the unhampered development of as many capabilities as possible. This may be thought unacceptable, if we think of the consequences it has for technology. Technology is a way of developing our capabilities. Should we really promote its development without restriction? If we stick to the ideas of liberty and equality, the only restrictions necessary are those designed to protect all individuals in their development of their capabilities. This is no weak restriction, but it challenges the idea that we should not do everything we can do. It implies humanism without respect for the popular idea that genetic engineering, in particular, offends human dignity and tempts us to play God.

But rather than considering this implication a vice of (6), I think it is a virtue. If we believe in liberty and equality, technological innovations should be restricted only by the condition that they must not harm or endanger anyone. This requires more control than exists today but does not set a principled limit to technology.

Let me confirm my technology-friendly interpretation of humanism with a quote from Kant that shows him to adhere to the same interpretation. Rightly considering reason the faculty by which we detect, use, and develop our capabilities, he says:

Reason in a creature is a faculty of widening the rules and purposes of the use of all its powers far beyond natural instinct; it acknowledges no limits to its projects.[36] Acknowledging no limits to the projects of reason is an idea that unites Kant, Marx, and humanistic ethics.

## Notes

1. Karl Marx, Theses on Feuerbach, Thesis XI (1845), in Marx/Engels Selected Works, vol. 1, 13–15; Progress Publishers, Moscow, 1969; trans. W. Lough.
2. Frankfurt (Suhrkamp) 1985. The English title became *The New Conservatism*.
3. This feature was known as the Thomas theorem: "the situations that men define as true, become true for them." (W.I. Thomas, *The Unadjusted Girl*, Boston 1923) It is implied in Robert Merton's notion of the self-fulfilling prophecy (Merton, "The self-fulfilling prophecy", *Antioch Review* 8, 1948, 193–210, and Merton, *Social Theory and Social Structure*, Glencoe, 1949, rev. ed. 1957). Cp. E. Nagel, *The Structure of Science*, New York 1961, but also K. Popper, *The Poverty of Historicism*, New York 1957, who discusses the character under the name of *Oedipal effect*; G. Soros, *The Alchemy of Finance*, New York 1998, and Soros, Introduction to W.H. Newton-Smith, ed., *Popper in China*, London 1992, 1–10. N.N. Taleb, *The Black Swan. The Impact of the Highly Improbable*, New York 2007, presents a more radical attack on the idea of predictability.
4. The simplest and clearest exposition of Marx's ideas is found in the *Manifesto of the Communist Party*.
5. Cp. K. Marx, Fr. Engels, *Manifesto of the Communist Party*, beginning of Chapter 1.
6. K. Marx, Fr. Engels, *Manifesto of the Communist Party*, end of Chapter 2.
7. K. Marx, *The Marx-Engels Reader*, ed. R. C. Tucker, New York (Norton) 1978, p. 145.
8. Aristotle, *Politics*, Book 1, 1256a20–58a18.
9. According to Aristotle, *Politics* Book 1, 1252 b31, they need the *polis* for the *good life*, which means, according to Aristotle (*Nicomachean Ethics* I, 1098 a7), a life of active exercise of one's specific talents. Aristotle leaves it open

whether such exercise serves the individual or the *polis*, as it does in Plato's *Republic*.

10. Of course, the hierarchy has often been criticized, and some Marxists deny that Marx followed it; for example, Ellen M. Wood, *Democracy against Capitalism*, Cambridge University Press 1995, 23ff. If they are right, it is still important to distinguish the Marxian approach from Marxism.

11. K. Marx, *The German Ideology*, transl. C. Dutt and C.P. Magill, Pt. 1, A, sec. *Private property and communism*.

12. F. Fukuyama, *The End of History and the Last Man*, New York: Free Press 1992, p. 355, says this "vision...was (not) meant seriously."

13. K. Marx, *Capital*, vol. 1, transl. Moore and Aveling; Chapter 15, sec. 9 (The Factory Acts). (MEW 23, 512).

14. David Hume, An Enquiry Concerning the Principles of Morals §145; ed. Nidditch, Oxford: Clarendon 1975, p. 183f.

15. For example, Alain Touraine, *Critique of Modernity*, Oxford (Blackwell) 1995, p. 239.

16. More particularly, it corresponds to ideas of Max Weber and Hannah Arendt. I have discussed these to some extent in my *Rethinking the Western Understanding of the Self*, Cambridge University Press, 2009.

17. F. Fukuyama, The End of History? *The National Interest*, Summer 1989, sec. III, talks of "fundamental 'contradictions' in human life that cannot be resolved in the context of modern liberalism" if we have not "reached the end of history" (as he claims we have). Samuel Huntington, The Clash of Civilizations? *Foreign Affairs* 72/3, 1993, 22–49, sec. I, explains history since the Peace of Westphalia as "the evolution of conflict in the modern world," of which "conflict between civilizations will be the latest phase." Cp. U. Steinvorth, *Huntington, Fukuyama, and Hegel*, 2009, unpublished manuscript.

18. For the following exposition of Marx's economic, cp. my publications: Marx's Analysis of Commodity Exchange, *Inquiry 19*, 1976, 99–112; Eine analytische Interpretation der Marxschen Dialektik, Meisenheim 1977; Marx's Theory of Value, *Philosophy of the Social Sciences* 7, 1977, 385–96; Böhm-Bawerks Marx-Kritik. Eine Kritik ihrer Engelsschen Voraussetzungen, *Philosophy of the Social Sciences* 7, 1977, 302–14; Modellkonstruktion und empirische Überprüfbarkeit in Marx' "Kapital," *Analyse und Kritik* 1, 1979, 164–81.

19. Hegel, Grundlinien der Philosophie des Rechts §§ 5–7, defined rational will as the "contradiction" that we are capable of both affirming and denying the possibility of an action. He presented the elements of society: family, economy (which he called civil society), and the state, as developments of this contradiction of rational will. Marx replaced rational will by commodity production and considered its contradictions the motor of modernity.

20. In his description of the opposition of exchange value and use value, Marx harks back to Aristotle's distinction between a natural and an unnatural chrematistic in Politics I 3, 1256b40–58b8.

21. Marx seems to have been clear about this point; so the role he wanted to ascribe to the fall of the profit rate is dubious. Marxists early agreed that Marx's appeal to the fall of the profit rate does not help understand the concrete conditions that put an end to capitalism. Not only the so-called

revisionists Bernstein and Kautsky judged the fall of the profit rate to be dubious; also Rosa Luxemburg and her critic Bukharin did so. N. Bucharin, Der Imperialismus und die Akkumulation des Kapitals, Wien 1926, 118, agrees with Luxemburg, Die Akkumulation des Kapitals. Antikritik, Gesammelte Werke Bd. VI, Berlin 1923, p. 411 n, that „we can still wait a good time for the decline of capitalism because of the fall of the profit, about as long as for the expiration of the sun" (translation mine, Luxemburg is quoted from Bukharin). Not accidentally Marxists fall apart about the question what the concrete conditions are that will kill capitalism.

22. This had already been pointed out by Hegel, Philosophy of Right §§ 245f.

23. So argued Rosa Luxemburg in her "Antikritik", cp. penultimate note. Bukharin ibid. (penultimate note) 115ff argued in opposition to Luxemburg that Marx did not identify capitalism's increasing production with overproduction.

24. This was argued by John A. Hobson, *Imperialism*, 1902, who influenced Luxemburg, Bukharin, and Lenin. He called "the supposed inevitability of imperial expansion as a necessary outlet for progressive industry" a "fallacy," stating "It is not industrial progress that demands the opening up of investment, but mal-distribution of consuming power which prevents the absorption of commodities and capital within the country. The over-saving which is the economic root of Imperialism is found by analysis to consist of rents, monopoly profits, and other unearned or excessive elements of income." (Univ. of Michigan Pr. 1965, 85).

25. Cp. Philippe van Parijs, *Real Freedom for All*, Oxford UP 1995; Thomas Straubhaar, *Grundeinkommen, Nachhaltigkeit für den Sozialstaat Deutschland*, HWWI Update May 2006; Philip Pettit, *A Republican Right to Basic Income?* Basic Income Studies 2, 2007, 1-8; U. Steinvorth, *Rethinking the Western Understanding of the Self*, Cambridge UP 2009, ch. 21.

26. K. Marx, *The Poverty of Philosophy*, Paris and Brussels 1847, first German publication 1885.

27. Cp. my remark on predictability in social science above, in section 1.

28. G.L.S. Shackle, *Economics for Pleasure*, Cambridge UP 1968, 240.

29. K. Marx, *The Economic and Philosophic Manuscripts of 1844*, ed. D.J. Struik, trans. M. Milligan, New York (International Publishers) 1964, p. 146.

30. Ibid., 147.

31. Ibid., 154.

32. Ibid., 135. The translation is from the *Complete Works of Marx and Engels* published by Lawrence and Wishart.

33. Louis Althusser, *For Marx*, Penguin 1969, Chapter 7: Marxism and Humanism. The chapter was first published in *Cahiers de l'I.S.E.A.*, June 1964; sec. II; the book (*Pour Marx*) in 1965 by Maspéro, Paris. Trans. Ben Brewster.

34. Ibid., sec. III

35. The *Communist Manifesto*, Chapter 2, speaks of the "emancipation of the proletariat." *Capital* 1, Chapter 15, sec. 5, Chapter 23; Chapter 24, sec. 4; Chapter 25, sec. 4, talks of alienation.

36. Kant 1963, *Second thesis*.

# 8
# John Stuart Mill and the Idea of a Stationary State Economy

*Michael Buckley*

John Stuart Mill was among the nineteenth century's greatest philosophers. Perhaps best known for his defense of moral utilitarianism and individual liberty, Mill was also a leading economic thinker of his day. His major work on economics, *Principles of Political Economy*, built upon the insights of Adam Smith, David Ricardo, and Thomas Malthus in an effort to better systematize the principles of laissez faire economics and explain its "progress in wealth." Mill also explained, like his predecessors, why laissez faire economics would eventually culminate in what was then called a "stationary state economy," a condition of economic stagnation whereby a society, having reached the physical limits of economic growth, would simply reproduce wealth by replacing worn-out goods, maintaining capital stocks, and carefully husbanding nonrenewable resources.[1] But unlike his predecessors who viewed a stationary state as a dismal condition, Mill welcomed it; for he thought it gave people a sufficient level of wealth to both free them from life's necessary but coarser toils and provide them the leisure to develop their mental and moral capacities – necessary conditions for a happier life. In this way, Mill tied his positive assessment of a stationary state to his moral defense of liberty and utility maximization.

This contrasts with contemporary views of a stationary state economy, which typically see it as a hindrance to wealth creation and thus a constraint on utility maximization. Moreover, well-functioning markets within which economies grow are seen as neutral arbiters of competing consumer choices, and therefore protective of individual liberty. As a result, contemporary economists offer a positive assessment of economic growth and market liberalization based on liberty and utility maximization, turning Mill's view on its head.

These opposing positions result from disagreement on how best to understand utility and describe markets. By retracing Mill's thought and contrasting it with similar defenses of laissez faire economics, the place and purpose of a stationary state economy can be revived for today's reader who might otherwise dismiss it as opposed to one's self-interest and irrelevant to today's issues. Mill enables us to see things otherwise. In the next section, I explain why Mill thought a stationary state rather than endless economic growth would best improve happiness. This places economic policy within a humanistic context unique to Mill. After that, I explain why Mill thought it was inaccurate to describe markets as neutral and thus protective of liberty. I close by briefly considering how Mill's assessment of a stationary state can inform contemporary debates.

## 8.1   Mill's humanism

Today, economic stagnation is viewed as a kind of social disease to be remedied quickly. Indeed, political leaders purposefully seek out ways to grow the economy, linking the idea of individual prosperity to national wealth, as Adam Smith did when he wrote, in *The Wealth of Nations*, "[b]y pursing his own interest he frequently promotes that of society more effectually than when he really intends to promote it" (Smith, 1998, p. 513). Smith's view implied a kind of providential harmony between the self-interest of society and the individual that has, since Smith's time, justified society's pursuit of economic growth through market liberalization. For if the market promotes individual prosperity, it must also promote the community's.

Defending laissez faire economics in terms of its broader social consequences was a radical idea in Smith's time. Previously, it had been thought that the pursuit of isolated self-interests would result in social conflict, not social harmony. Smith turned that idea upside-down, giving an early utilitarian justification of market economics. On a utilitarian view, policies are morally right when they promote overall happiness, morally wrong when they diminish overall happiness. If increased prosperity improves happiness, and markets increase overall prosperity, as Smith argued, then market economics is justified in virtue of the benefits it creates.

Little has changed by way of moral justification. For example, Milton Friedman defends a corporation's pursuit of profit over its pursuit of social responsibility on the grounds that profit-seeking is in fact more likely to improve overall happiness than acting in socially responsible manner (Friedman, 1970). The idea is that by producing profit, businesses must be selling products satisfying people's needs and desires. Since the satisfaction of needs and desires improves happiness, profit maximization can serve as a proxy for happiness maximization.

John Stuart Mill, a staunch defender of utilitarianism, disagreed with this logic. Mill thought that "it is only in the backward countries of the world that increased production is still an important object" (Mill, [1848] 1965, p. 755). One possible reason for this stems from his economic theory, but a more likely reason stems from his moral theory. From an economic perspective, the natural limits of arable land for food production, physical space for population growth, and additional room for capital accumulation restrict economic growth by placing physical constraints on the ability of business to employ savings productively, thus placing downward pressure on the level of profit over time. Absent counteracting forces – such as improved productivity, foreign markets, emigration, or economic busts – economies would inevitably reach a stationary state of zero growth, a condition in which economic activity is reduced to replacing worn-out goods, maintaining capital stocks, and carefully husbanding nonrenewable resources. Governments who tried to fight this outcome were foolishly working against the laws of economics.

A more likely reason for considering the pursuit of growth to be backward is based on his moral argument. Mill thought a stationary economy inevitably indicated a high level of prosperity, given its place at the end of economic development. When combined with proper distribution policies, this prosperity could free people from "the trampling, crushing, elbowing, and treading on each other's heels" characteristic of industrial life (Mill [1848] 1965, p. 754). Policies releasing people from economic toil afforded them a chance to cultivate their mental, moral, and social character, which in turn offered more happiness than did further material wealth. Societies implementing growth policies at the expense of redistributive policies effectively exchanged considerable improvements in nonmaterial pleasures for small increases in material pleasure. As such, they foolishly hindered happiness, violating Mill's humanistic aim of advancing total utility.

Mill based this moral assessment on a unique account of utilitarianism. For Mill, it was important to distinguish between higher and lower quality pleasures when calculating the total utility of a particular policy. Higher quality pleasures include "the pleasures of the intellect, of the feelings and imagination, and of the moral sentiments" (Mill [1861] 1969, p. 211). They are more valuable than lower quality pleasures associated with biological appetites and luxurious delights.

Mill's distinction between higher and lower pleasures differed from earlier accounts of utilitarianism, which viewed all pleasures equally and assessed actions according to whether they produced the greatest sum of pleasures. According to this earlier view, morally correct action can be represented as the greatest product of the straight-sum of pleasures. By contrast, Mill's position implies that morally correct actions maximize the weighted-sum of pleasures, with intellectual pleasures being assigned greater weights than physical pleasures. As a result, the two utilitarian approaches might generate different moral assessments of the same action, since the former treats all pleasures equally and the latter assigns different weights to different pleasures.

This has ramifications for economic policy, for if one considers the clothing, feeding, and sheltering of bodies to be both a necessary condition for and equally pleasurable to the education, cultivation, and broadening of experiences, then one is morally indifferent to (1) a society that generates endless amounts of consumer goods and (2) a society that creates both a sufficient amount of commodities and well-cultivated minds. Mill was not so indifferent; he thought the qualitative difference between mental and material pleasures would tip the weighted-sum in favor of the latter society, and public policy should therefore aim at both material and intellectual well-being. "Few human creatures," Mill writes, "would consent to be changed into any of the lower animals for a promise of the fullest allowance of a beast's pleasures" (Mill [1861] 1969, p. 211). By contrast, Friedman seems to base his justification on the earlier account of utilitarianism, since he thinks the satisfaction of *any* need or desire is equally good.

Mill makes the same point from the other direction. Should public policy emphasize material wealth at the expense of cultural wealth, it risks undermining a person's capacity for "nobler feelings" by shrinking the social space within which those capacities develop by either diminishing educational opportunities or exacerbating financial strains (Mill [1861] 1969, p. 213; [1859] 1977, p. 282; [1848] 1965, p. 756). Should these feelings be "killed," people will inevitably indulge their lower level pleasures. But it would be a mistake to conclude from this that people, in virtue of having indulged their material pleasures, were as happy as they could be. On the contrary, they were less happy than they would have been had they forgone some of the material consumption so as to cultivate and satisfy their higher-order pleasures. The opportunity to realize these higher-order pleasures depends upon first having attained a sufficient level of prosperity and then, upon reaching that level, implementing appropriate policies.

What were the appropriate policies? Chief among them was the redistribution of wealth through gift or inheritance tax (Mill [1848] 1965, p. 755). On Mill's view, diffusing wealth through an inheritance tax was the fairest way to ensure for all the opportunity to cultivate their higher-order pleasures.[2] This policy recommendation fit both Mill's economic and moral theory. On the economic side, he thought economic laws did not apply equally to both production and distribution, since only the production of wealth "partake[s] of the character of physical truth." Distribution is a matter of social choice. "The things once there, mankind, individually or collectively, can do with them as they like" (Mill [1848] 1965, p. 199). Society is therefore free to redistribute wealth to achieve particular social outcomes. The outcome they should achieve, according to Mill's utilitarianism, is that which maximizes the weighted-sum of material and cultural development. This means providing opportunities for people to develop their mental and moral capacities, which required a degree of leisure made possible through wealth redistribution.

Taken together, Mill's economic and utilitarian theories imply a stationary state economy should be a welcomed rather than a deprecated outcome. He recognizes in it both a high level of prosperity and the opportunity to maximize happiness through cultural, mental and moral development. A stationary state guided by proper policies would consist of "a well-paid and affluent body of laborers; no enormous fortunes, except what were earned and accumulated during a single lifetime; but a much larger body of persons than at present, not only exempt from the coarser toils, but with sufficient leisure, both physical and mental, from mechanical details, to cultivate freely the graces of life, and afford examples of them to the classes less favorable circumstanced for their growth" (Mill [1848] 1965, p. 755). It is this condition, and not one of endless economic and material growth, that offers the greatest prospect for human happiness.

## 8.2 Liberty and market economics

One might agree with Mill's analysis and still resist his argument on the grounds that utility maximization could conflict with free choice. Recall that Mill thinks utility maximization requires weights to be assigned to pleasures and policy to be divined on the basis of calculations. This removes individuals from political decisions and replaces them with bureaucratic experts, implying a paternalistic government. To take just one example, Mill thought an "indispensable" means of social improvement is "a stricter restraint on population," lest it grow too large and place downward pressure on incomes, thus impoverishing many (Mill [1848] 1965, p. 755). But how should governments restrict population growth? Mill does not describe a process, but the fact that society must make an assessment and factor it into policy decisions is a result of his economic and moral theories.[3] Any effort to set population growth rates, or to rank pleasures in general, risks falling down a slippery slope toward paternalism. For this reason, one might reject Mill's assessment and instead favor protections of freedom irrespective of consequences.

Indeed, a second important moral defense of laissez faire economics is that markets avoid paternalism by remaining neutral toward individual choices. Rather than allowing bureaucrats to assign weights and then allocate resources based on the calculations, markets can assign weights through a price-coordinated system of exchange. For example, the more pleasurable a commodity, the higher its market price; the higher its price, the more resources allocated to its production; the more resources allocated, the greater its supply. Eventually, equilibrium is established. Suppliers, as if moved by an "invisible hand," allocate resources to their most valued use, facilitating a kind of democratic process whereby people vote with their dollars and, as a consequence, rank pleasures. If education receives fewer dollars than shoes, then labor and materials are allocated to shoes rather than schools. Society does not need John Stuart Mill, or anyone else, to assign weights. Individuals freely decide through open markets. This places the decisions in the individual's hand, and avoids the paternalism of the bureaucratic expert.

This defense of markets describes them as neutral and consequently protective of individual freedom. We can again use Milton Friedman as our contemporary example. He defends capitalism by noting that it secures freedom from coercion for ordinary laborers, employers, purchasers, and sellers. For example, in a free and open marketplace employees are free from the tyranny of employers, since they can always look for other work. Likewise, employers are free from the tyranny of employees, since they can always find new help. Freedom is intrinsically linked to market economics insofar as markets provide a space within which individuals have multiple options. As a result, the preservation of market economics is at the same time the protection of individual freedom, and a fight to maintain laissez faire policies is at the same time a political battle against the specter of tyranny – a point, on Friedman's view, requiring special emphasis, since "intellectuals in particular... tend to express contempt for what they regard as material aspects of life, and to regard their own pursuit of allegedly higher values as on a different plane of significance" (Friedman, 1982, p. 8). So to the above list of freedoms ensured by the marketplace we can add the freedom of the consumer from the tyranny of the intellectual who seeks to shape the productive and distributive forces of society in a manner fitting his or her vision of the "good" society, displacing the neutrality of the marketplace with personal bias.

It is tempting to swap Mill's name for Friedman's "intellectual," and to ascribe to Mill an urge to shape distribution policy to his liking. After all, Mill thought governments rather than markets should promote mental, cultural, and social character, which implies restrictions to freedom if two further assumptions are made. First, government intervention can never promote freedom; second, markets are in fact neutral. Mill disagreed with both assumptions.

We can see why Mill disagrees with the first assumption by considering *On Liberty*, a spirited defense of liberty against all forms of tyranny, beginning with the "magistrate" and ending with the "tyranny of the prevailing opinion" (Mill [1859] 1977, p. 220). According to Mill, liberty can best be secured through legal protections – such as the individual right to free speech, association, and religious practice – and through policies promoting the effective use of these protections by, among other things, requiring education and redistributing wealth.[4] Education and income afford citizens the all-purpose means for enjoying their formally protected freedoms. Education develops rational capacities, which improve citizens' ability to rationally pursue their life plans, while income affords citizens "a fair chance of achieving by their own exertions a successful life" (Mill [1848] 1965, p. 221). In both cases, government plays a role – redistribution occurs through tax policy, and broad access to education is guaranteed by public commitments to "pay the school fees of the poorer classes of children, and defray... the entire school expenses of those who have no one else to pay for them" (Mill [1859] 1977, p. 302). Moreover, the legal protection of freedoms promotes a variety of situations and experiences within which citizens can discover their preferences and rationally choose life plans. "[D]ifferent persons... require different conditions for their spiritual development; and can no more exist healthily in the same moral, than all the variety of plants can in the same physical, atmosphere and climate" (Mill [1859] 1977, p. 270). Together, the legal protections of individual rights and the promotion of these rights through education and wealth redistribution create conditions within which individual liberty thrives.

While government can play an important role in securing liberty, Mill is careful to circumscribe its power. For example, although he supported laws requiring education, he thought a state-run educational system could undermine liberty by "moulding people to be exactly like one another," thus diminishing diversity (Mill [1859] 1977, p. 302). But Mill thought the same conforming force is equally true of commerce, and it is here that Mill challenges the second assumption – that the marketplace is in fact neutral. On Mill's view, commerce tries to shape people to buy more goods, and as such is as strong a conforming force as government. Since all conforming forces must be checked so as to preserve a variety of situations within which people can have diverse experiences, so too must commerce (Mill [1859] 1977, p. 275). So while Mill might agree with Friedman's assertion that the consumer requires protection from the intellectual, he would add that the intellectual – as well as the artist, ascetic, and environmentalist – requires protection from the consumer, or more precisely, from policies that in the name of marketplace neutrality favor consumerism over all other human endeavors. Thus, liberty requires protection from the tyranny of commerce, which seeks to commodify everything to the exclusion of other values.

## 8.3   A stationary state in a contemporary context

What are we to make of Mill's defense today? History has so far proved Mill wrong; economies have not become stagnant, and wealth redistribution is less independent of economic laws than Mill believed. Additionally, marketplace neutrality and the link between national wealth and individual prosperity remain steadfast convictions, reinforced by historical touchstones such as Smith's pin factory, which illustrated in very tangible terms the confluence between the producer and consumer's self-interest, and the oppression of Soviet-style communism, which offered a regrettable foil to Friedman's view of market neutrality. So how does Mill inform contemporary debates?

If we take Mill's idea of a stationary state seriously, by which I mean if we view it as a justifiable policy whereby wealthy states purposefully reproduce existing wealth and strategically redistribute it, then I think there are three ways it can serve us today. First, it is possible that Mill's prediction of a stationary state economy might come true, at which time Mill's reflections will help inform our assessment of the situation.

Second, Mill's moral defense helps guard against the blind pursuit of economic growth by prioritizing noncommercial values that, in some cases, are contrary and therefore assumed to be subordinate to growth policies. Finally, Mill provides a new perspective from which to address contemporary economic problems.

Regarding the first, at the outer limits of possibility remains the chance that Mill's prediction will come true. Today, some rich countries face declining populations and operate at the cutting edge of technology.[5] Together these factors place downward pressure on economic growth by limiting both the number of laborers and improvement to their productivity.[6] If populations continue to fall, and if technologies fail to deliver productive revolutions, then a stationary economy is not out of the question. If to this we add the prospect of climate change, then a stationary economy moves closer in from the outer limits of possibility.[7] Together, declining populations, the failure of technological revolutions, and environmental limits could lead to zero growth. While these were not among Mill's reasons for predicting it, his defense provides resources for dealing with such a condition should it come about. At the very least, it acknowledges existing prosperity and locates it within a broader humanistic context that, should we allow ourselves to be informed by his defense, enables us to accept zero growth and analyze the most appropriate deployment of stagnating wealth.

Second, the moral defense of a stationary state can help guard against our treating traditional moral defenses of laissez faire economics as blanket generalizations about economic activity. These traditional defenses included (a) the confluence between national and individual prosperity and (b) marketplace neutrality. The first is based on a specific account of utilitarianism that weighs all pleasures equally; the second is based on the idea that marketplace neutrality protects liberty. Mill challenges the first by providing an alternative utilitarian account that distinguishes between higher and lower pleasures. Higher pleasures can be satisfied on the condition that people enjoy sufficient leisure and wealth – necessary conditions for improving mental, moral, and social character. If policies pursue economic growth under the assumption that growth improves overall happiness, then these policies might unwittingly undermine improved happiness by exchanging these conditions – such as leisure – for small gains in material pleasure. Mill challenges the second traditional defense by exposing its narrow definition of "neutrality." This definition equates "neutrality" with "neutral toward consumer choice." But this inevitably favors commodification over other values, and thus may undermine liberty by subsuming noncommercial interests – such as preserving national parks or banning advertising in certain locations – under commercial interest at the expense of preserving noncommercial values.

I have discussed the two traditional defenses and Mill's critique of them in the preceding two sections, and simply repeat here, in the words of Mill, that utility maximization and liberty "are not only perfectly compatible with the stationary state, but, it would seem, more naturally allied with that state than with any other" (Mill [1848] 1965, p. 755).

Finally, the idea of a stationary state provides a unique perspective from which to address contemporary problems. These include extreme poverty, environmental degradation, disease, involuntary migration, and fresh water strains. Solutions to these problems may appear mutually exclusive if analyzed solely within the perspective of a growing global economy. For instance, if all states grow their economies in an effort to reduce extreme poverty, they might further degrade the environment. But policies based on a stationary state philosophy do not face this dilemma, since they forgo additional growth for the sake of other aims. This provides increased flexibility when addressing problems. For example, from a stationary state perspective, technology transfers from rich to poor countries can be seen as environmentally friendly mechanisms for reducing extreme poverty without seeming competitively unsound or market unfriendly.

Naturally, the idea of a stationary state economy by itself cannot solve these problems, but it does help us acknowledge and locate existing prosperity, and situate the pursuit of further prosperity within a larger humanistic context aiming at individual happiness and liberty. At the same time, it is not market-unfriendly; it recognizes the importance of price-coordinated systems of exchange and private property. Moreover, it is justified on grounds familiar to laissez faire economics; namely, its utilitarian consequences and the preservation of liberty. If we take the idea of a stationary state seriously we will find that the idea of economic growth must compete with it in the marketplace of ideas. If this were to happen, we will no longer blindly pursue growth policies on the assumption they improve happiness, or liberalize markets on the assumption they secure liberty. These options would be weighed against those informed by a stationary state. In this and other ways the idea of a stationary state economy is, as Mill thought, a welcomed rather than dismal prospect.

## Notes

1. Today, this condition is referred to as a "steady-state economy." See, for example, *Toward a Steady-State Economy*, ed. Herman E. Daly, W. H. Freeman and Co., 1973.

2. This was particularly true in Mill's time, given the feudal system's concentration of landed wealth. See "J. S. Mill on the Income Tax Exemption and Inheritance Taxes: The Evidence Reconsidered" Robert B. Ekelund Jr. and Douglas M. Walker, *History of Political Economy*, Winter 1996; 28: 559–581.

3. Mill does suggest people will voluntarily limit their numbers, once the consequences of ever increasing population growth makes itself known to the masses (Mill [1848] 1965, 156–157).

4. Mill also thought governments have a legitimate economic role in the financing of public goods such as lighthouses, and in the preservation of well functioning markets by ensuring contracts and protecting against fraud (Mill [1848] 1965, 800–804; p. 968).

5. Japan and Germany's population began declining after 2005, and all of Europe's population is expected to start declining after 2015. See World Population Prospects, The 2008 Revisions, United Nations, http://esa.un.org/unpp/index.asp

6. For example, Japan has both a rapidly ageing population and a technologically advanced economy; its annualized real GDP growth between 1990 and 2007 was a scant 1.5%. The IMF reports Gross Domestic Product, in constant prices (billion), at ¥565,438 and ¥443,094 for 2007 and 1990 respectively. I calculate that as a 1.5% annual growth rate. See www.imf.org/external/pubs/ft/weo/2006/01/data/dbcselm.cfm?G=2001, June 1, 2009

7. Climate change is forcing us to rethink fossil fuel-based growth – a key engine for our current prosperity. See "Climate Change 2007: Synthesis Report," www.ipcc.ch/pdf/assessment-report/ar4/syr/ar4_syr_spm.pdf., September 10, 2009

## Bibliography

Friedman, Milton, *Capitalism and Freedom*. (Chicago: The University of Chicago Press, 1982).

Friedman, Milton, "The Social Responsibility of Business is to Increase Its Profits". *New York Times Magazine*, September 13, 1970.

Mill, John Stuart, *Collected Works of John Stuart Mill*. Edited by J.M. Robson. (Toronto: University of Toronto Press, 1963–1991).

——. [1848] 1965. Principles of Political Economy. In *Collected Works*, volumes 2–3.

——. [1859] 1977. On Liberty. In *Collected Works*, volume 18.

——. [1861] 1969. Utilitarianism. In *Collected Works*, volume 10.

Smith, Adam, *An Inquiry into the Nature and Causes of the Wealth of Nations*. (Washington DC: Regnery Gateway, 1998).

# Part III
# Contemporary Philosophy

# 9
# Habermas and His Communicative Perspective

*Suzan Langenberg*

## 9.1 Introduction

*Communication* together with (building) *trust* is a crucial and indispensable ingredient of trade, of "doing" business. In his *Spirit of Law* the eighteenth-century French philosopher Montesquieu had already referred to the golden rule that no trade is possible without trust. The sociologist Anthony Giddens is a contemporary exponent of the idea that trust is an indispensable ingredient in building coherent communicative communities.[1] But is there, within business environments, any awareness of the societal and human fundamentals of communication as constantly used in creating business relationships, negotiating, all kinds of applications of information and communication technologies, letters, informal talks, meetings – in short, communication as the everyday baseline of human interactions? Little by little technical and interrelational communication seems to be becoming the core element of doing and organizing business. Analysts of the current financial and economic crisis sometimes call this a crisis in the communicative structure and culture of international society as a whole and of organizations in particular.

The organizational constructivist Karl Weick compares a business organization with an improvisation, a dynamic process that organizes itself autonomously taking different and incompatible opinions into account, and, as it does so, "producing" sense. It is an intersubjective creation of systems of opinions that are continuously negotiated, revised, and submitted in a critical dialogue. Meeting, discussing, arguing, and debating are the essential symbolic actions by which organizations stand or fall.[2] However, this communicatively driven organizational design remains without a detailed description of how communication works, or of which conditions must be met in order to see an organization this way. With certain elements from the communication theory of the German social philosopher Jürgen Habermas, we hope to supply the answers required.

In this chapter we will first present a short bibliography of Jürgen Habermas and an overview of how his theory can be situated in the procedural humanistic perspective that is the central theme of this book. Next, we will briefly pinpoint the Habermasian concepts that could be taken as humanistic, such as his *discourse ethics*, concentrated on "communication without domination" (*herrschaftsfreier Dialog*), and argumentation theory. In the subsequent paragraphs we will discuss these two frameworks in more detail. In the final section, I will apply this theory of communication to the realm of business ethics and organizational behavior.

## 9.2   Habermas and the humanistic perspective

We know Habermas primarily from his criticism of society and ideology. Habermas's observations on criticism formed the cornerstone of his historical and theoretical analysis of communicative action, which has played an important role in bridging the gap between the theory and praxis of social action and more specifically between (economic) *system* and (human) *lifeworld*.

### 9.2.1   Jürgen Habermas

The German social Philosopher Jürgen Habermas, renowned for his seminal "Theory of Communicative Action" (*Die Theorie des kommunikativen Handelns*) of 1981, has devoted his whole professional life to the historical and critical analysis of communicative action. The challenge of the collapse of German identity after World War II directed Habermas's intellectual interests towards the understanding of democracy and communicative processes. He studied with Theodor Adorno, an important figure in the *Frankfurter Schule*, which had been founded during the Weimar Republic by thirty social scientists who fought for *practical* philosophy. They were convinced that abstractly "objective" knowledge did not exist and proclaimed instead that knowledge without application is empty. The *Frankfurter Schule* is especially known for the development of a social criticism distinct from Marxism but still loyal to the idea of dialectical progress with the goal of popular emancipation. As an assistant to Adorno and later as a professor of philosophy, Habermas was associated with the *Frankfurter Schule*, with some interruptions, until his retirement in 1994. From 1971 to 1981 he was Director of the Max Planck Institute, where his research was focused on the understanding of communicative action, primarily aimed at achieving consensus on certain aspects of reality. He wanted to know how communication could lead to a certain level of social cohesion. Partly inspired by the work of Max Weber, Habermas developed a specific societal theory about its history of the development of social cohesion through communication processes.

### 9.2.2 Diagnosis

Since World War II the global economy has expanded beyond all national borders and the financial system has evolved beyond control. This phenomenon confronts us with the imperfection, incompletion, and indeterminacy of the financial, economic, and political systems that are active today. The Enlightenment – the project of the rationalization of society – is incomplete but has come to an end. Moral commitments are related to the present: They constantly change, shift, and correct this present. The economization of society continues to be further refined, in part as a "response" to forms of resistance. This systematic refinement is the consequence of an inexhaustible action dynamic. Habermas diagnoses this phenomenon as the *differentiation* of the economy as a separate system, detached from the sphere of life, while at the same time this dynamic invites reflection and indicts the dichotomy that threatens to be projected on this differentiation of western society. Business operates on the edge of this tension: It anticipates individual and group needs within the economic system that steers a complex market dynamic. This *system–lifeworld*–tension leads to reflection. The end, the goal in itself, invites the constant rethinking of its moral status, due to the infinite nature and excessive growth of an irrational desire for "more" and "progress." In business there is a tendency to avoid confrontation with and deny the "temporary borders" of existence, because this feels "threatening" and because it is impossible to provide this tension with a definitive moral judgment. The thematization of this tension leads us to an orientation on the basic normative and critical drivers that steer our global economy.[3]

### 9.2.3 Criticism

In the late Middle Ages we see the notion of critique gaining ground thanks to the rise of humanism and its criticism of the domination of Christianity, as well as factors such as the beginnings of reason, science, and discovery of new land. In the sixteenth to eighteenth centuries, the humanists were especially known for their text-critique and critique of historical sources, as is shown by the revival of the writings of Aristotle. Giovanni Pico della Mirandola (1463–94) was one of the first critical humanists who wrote about the dignity of the human being. This critique of ecclesiastical doctrines was inspired by a reinvention of Aristotle and led to a revaluation of individual experiences: The human being viewed as the center of the world took the place of the divine *logos*.

Criticism has different manifestations and had already appeared in ancient Greece. Attitude and *ethos* could be understood as a necessary self-criticism of democracy, as can frankness and speaking truth for the sake of caring for others. In certain ancient schools it was integrated into lifestyles (Socrates, Seneca). Historically, criticism manifested itself as textual criticism and through the power of critical judgment. The concept of criticism was renewed by Kant during the period of the "Enlightenment," as both an exponent of our general faculty of reason and as the personal power of judgment. During the late nineteenth century and first half of the twentieth, there was a pessimistic movement in social theory. The conviction that society must be improved ended in negation, the criticism of that which exists. The backdrop of the political tensions between socialism, communism, and national socialism in Europe in the midst of a second wave of industrial expansion drove the members of the *Frankfurter Schule* towards a negative view on the progress of society: The technologicalization and institutionalization of labor alienated the worker from his own capital: his labor.

In contrast with his predecessors Horkheimer and Adorno, Jürgen Habermas wanted to save the idea of progress.[4] According to him, criticism is only possible when a positive norm has been formulated, with which society has to comply. Instead of underlining an instrumental rationality as the only possible notion of rationality, Habermas suggests developing a positive and broadened notion of rationality: *communicative rationality*, through which the modernization of society could be accomplished. For Habermas, the concept of rationality refers to an open exchange of arguments as the most important medium for learning processes. From his perspective, rationality is not limited to the acquisition of scientific knowledge but extends to all aspects of the formation of opinions that is structured by argument. The core of rational learning processes are constituted through the critical questioning of arguments under the condition of open communication. This notion is based on a new paradigm, *intersubjectivity* as a communication model: Through language, intersubjectivity realizes itself. Language serves to enable communication in which everyone has the right to take a "yes" or "no" stance towards another's claims to validity. We use language primarily for communicative rather than cognitive purposes and thereby gain access to the world. Meanings are not fixed and can always be revised through experience.

The model[5] below describes three different world-perspectives – objective, normative (intersubjective) and expressive (subjective) – which Habermas, in his theory of communicative action, sees as resulting from the increasing rationalization of society.[6] This model emphasizes the broad spectrum over which communicative action is indispensable and also plays a decisive role in the making of judgments relating to the cognitive, normative, and expressive dimensions of our actions.

It is through communication that the rationalization of society has taken place over the past 2000 years. The contribution of Habermas lies in his broadening of the concept of rationality: The most important effect of his analysis is that we can develop an insight into the different levels of communicative action, on the one hand, and the levels of all (societal and experimental) knowledge that correspond to it, on the other.

Although the above scheme gives a clear overview, the effect of the rationalization of society is paradoxical: With the differentiation of society the origination of systems has increasingly come to dominate (*Kolonialisierung*) the lifeworld because the economic, bureaucratic, and scientific instrumentalization of knowledge has gained substantial independence. The diagnosis of Habermas is that the subjugation of the lifeworld to the supremacy of the instrumental and rational power of the systems leads to a progressive instrumentalization of culture, intersubjectivity, and human interaction.

Habermas links emancipation to the manipulability of society, two themes that he believes have always existed alongside one another in human history. From this perspective he remains an advocate of

*Table 9.1* Three different world-perspectives – objective, normative (intersubjective) and expressive (subjective)

|  | Worlds | Validity claims | Lifeworld | Culture |
|---|---|---|---|---|
| *Communicative action* | Objective | Truth | Culture | Science |
|  | Intersubjective | Normative rightness | Society | Law and morality |
|  | Subjective | Truthfulness (authenticity) | Person | Art |

the principles of enlightenment, so critical public debate is for him a requirement of a well-functioning liberal democracy. His procedural discourse-based ethical approach to the deliberative frame of this public debate determines its limits and possibilities. In the next section we will elaborate on this communicative framework.

## 9.3   The communicative approach of humanistic ethics

The communication theory of Jürgen Habermas differs from other comparative studies because he differentiates between three perspectives on the world; these are connected with three knowledge domains that in turn end up as three different validity claims: objective truth, normative rightness, and truthfulness (introduced in the previous section). In this description Habermas explicitly involves the expressive, emotional level of the speech act. Because of the uniqueness and inalienability of the emotional and experience-oriented act of knowledge acquirement, the expressive level of communicative action cannot claim universal validity. Although a level of (rational) reflexivity can be reached, it remains personally bounded because of the subjective and noninterchangeable nature of expressive claims. In theoretical and practical discourse, however, universal validity claims are the positive result of consensus-oriented discourses focused on realizing objective and normative truth.

In contrast to the use of *instrumental* rationality, Habermas develops the concept of *communicative* rationality causing emancipatory processes. This refers to a context in which people are in dialogue with one another. People who strike up a conversation are unwittingly granting one another trust in advance. They reluctantly accept that the other has good reasons for saying what he does and genuinely believes what he is saying. This frame of mind continues until it is proved wrong. In the course of the conversation, practical knowledge and skills, norms, values, and ways of life are imperceptibly used.

In the event of opposition, arguments must be marshaled, and we must also be prepared to provide our own. In this way, communicative rationality unfolds. The heart of the matter is a capacity that resides in the language itself, which invites us to address one another, to understand one another and in the case of dispute, to find common ground through argument. Habermas calls this capacity "agreement" (*Verständigung*).[7]

Reality is different from theory, though. In practice, the territory of free communication and the power of arguments is often infiltrated by the lure of money or the dictates of power. Completely open and trusting communication is rare. Nevertheless, this ideal form must always be presupposed when people address one another, even if their aim is in fact to get the better of their opponent. Even deception implies frankness.

Habermas later applied the elements elaborated in the theory of communicative action to the theme that had been central to his work from the very beginning: public openness, specifically political openness. Public debate, whether in a conference room, in newspapers and magazines, on television or on Internet forums, is indispensable for the maintenance of democracy. It is in public space that the plurality of opinions becomes manifest and where they may clash or reinforce one another in debate. Public debate is the stage on which a diversity of voices are heard, on which opinions are introduced, defended, tested, and modified.

### 9.3.1 The role of language

Like the linguistic philosophers J. L. Austin and John Searle, Habermas argues that somebody who states something thereby not only expresses judgments about natural or social reality, but also *makes an appeal* to his fellow men. Language is not just a matter of description but also makes a claim of validity. The factual and ethical rightness of what has been said is important, as people want what they say to be trusted and believed by their interlocutors. Speaking is a form of acting. According to Habermas, it is through rational examination, in particular, that people try to come to an agreement that lays the basis for social criticism. Of course, language can be also used merely strategically to reach certain goal efficiently; in fact, it may well be considered an important achievement of modern society to have perfected such a use of language. But when the strategic use of language becomes dominant, it takes on the characteristics of subordination and exclusivity.[8] Against this impending domination of language by strategic, manipulative aims, Habermas defends a free and open dialogue – real communication – through the concept of the ideal speech situation: Power has no role and participants want to reach understanding and agreement. In opposition to the *systems* of the economy and the state, Habermas stands up for the value of the daily *lifeworld* of people as responsible and united individuals.

### 9.3.2 Therapeutic and aesthetic criticism

As a part of his theory of argumentation, Habermas discusses validity claims in the theoretical, practical, and expressive domain. He makes a distinction between *discourse* (*Diskurs*) and *criticism* (*Kritik*).[9] In theoretical (obtaining the objectivity of knowledge) and practical (realizing general normative conditions for obtaining knowledge) discourse, universal validity claims are reached in an argumentative sense. However, in the domain of the judgment of the general value of expressions, Habermas uses distinctive criteria. He speaks of *aesthetic and therapeutic criticism*[10] that deviates from what theoretical and practical discourse produces in cognitive and normative general validity. In the preceding paragraph we touched on the uniqueness of expressivity in the speech act. It should be noted that expressive speech acts cannot claim universal validity because of a different use of (instrumental) rationality. In this domain of argumentative exchange, reason will be used as a reflexive medium for assigning value to evaluative and expressive utterances without claiming a universal truth. Does this mean that the effect of these nongeneralizable arguments is disqualified on organizational levels? No, because the value standard can be activated through argumentative thematization. Keulartz and Kunneman[11] suggest that the nonuniversalizability of truthfulness can be solved by introducing the *identity discourse* on the level of expressive truthfulness. Habermas radicalizes the identity-critique through what he terms the *ideal speech situation* (ISS), a device by which to criticize expressive feelings and the truthfulness of speech acts. But the social conditions for an ISS are so absolute that their realization can hardly ever be achieved. especially the assumption of nondomination (*Herrschaftsfreiheit)* in an identity discourse: How can it be measured? Is not every discourse somehow determined by power-play?

## 9.4   The communicative framework

Habermas distinguishes between two types of knowledge interests: the *objectivity of experiences* and the *validity of judgments*, where the latter cannot appeal to the first.

- Validity claims can only be achieved with the help of argumentations and counter-argumentations to test their tenability and are part of the *consensus theory of truth;*
- Objectivity of experiences is part of the theory of knowledge interests, a *constitutional theory* that examines specific angles of (communicative) rationality.

In the model below[12] we set out the knowledge-constitutive interests Habermas distinguishes[13] and the role played by the use of rationality

*Table 9.2* The communicative framework

| Cognitive interest | Type of science | Purpose | Focus | Orientation | Projected outcome |
|---|---|---|---|---|---|
| Technical | Empirical-analytic | Enhance prediction and control | Identification and manipulation of variables | Calculation | Removal of irrationality within means–ends relationships |
| Practical | Historical-hermeneutic | Improve mutual understanding | Interpretation of symbolic communication | Appreciation | Removal of misunderstanding |
| Emancipatory | Critical | Development of more rational social institutions and relations | Exposure of domination and exploitation | Transformation | Removal of relations of unnecessarily repressive domination and exploitation |

in all three knowledge domains. For our purposes we are particularly interested in the third section of this scheme, where the emancipatory effect of knowledge is oriented towards interactive relationships in which power is not exercised.

For Habermas, critical science resonates with a desire to assert the possibility of greater autonomy and responsibility in the face of institutions and practices that are felt to unnecessarily impede their contemporary expression and extension. Critical science strives to reveal how patterns of behavior and meaning are embedded in oppressive structures of domination that, potentially, are open to challenge and change.

### 9.4.1 The ideal speech situation (ISS)

In this section, we want to discuss Habermas's view on communicative intersubjectivity within the domain of his consensus theory of truth. The latter is at the core of his pragmatic approach to communicative action, aimed at the horizontal reconstruction of communicative action. With the framework of the ideal speech situation he describes the social conditions that must be fulfilled in order to radicalize the critique of objective, normative, and expressive knowledge. Participants in a discourse need equal opportunities to enter the argument and to participate, no power differences and the guarantee of truthfulness in expressions towards the other, to clarify where *systematic disturbances* in communication could appear. It is a matter of communicative symmetry. The consensus theory of truth claims the unconventional constraint of the best argument through the explanation of the formal framework of the discourse. The outcome of a discourse cannot be determined merely by logic nor empirical constraints, but through the power of the best argument.[14]

Habermas acknowledges the importance of challenging the truth of knowledge and that this argumentation has to take place between participants. The formulation of *the ideal speech situation* is also an important turning point in his consensus theory of truth. In this way, arguments are directly related to general validity claims in order to establish their truth. The ideal speech situation develops as a formal instrument that confirms a rational way of getting a real shared consensus on true, right, and truthful knowledge. The domains of aesthetic and therapeutic critique, together with the ideal speech situation, are formal instruments providing insight into the truthfulness of a speech act.

In the earlier philosophy of Habermas, he argued that an ideal speech situation is found within communication between individuals when their speech is governed by basic, but required and implied, rules. These rules of speech, Habermas suggested, are generally and tacitly accepted by both of the communicating parties, but even if they are not – perhaps if one party is lying – the ideal speech situation nevertheless remains a more broadly required principle.

His doctrine included the following: Members of the public sphere must adhere to certain rules for an *ideal speech situation* to occur. They are:

- All potential participants must have equal chances to start a discussion in a discourse within which all claims could be examined in communicative action;
- All participants must have an equal chance to participate in the discussions: Their statements, conclusions, explanations, interpretations, ideas, and suggestions must be heard, and their questions, doubts, and criticisms taken into account. Each participant has the right to express arguments for or against so that all possible criticisms show up and no unexamined prejudice remains;
- During the discussions, imbalances of power between participants must be excluded because they could hinder a frank and open dialogue where every argument and opinion has its place. Moreover, displays of power could also make certain arguments appear unchallengeable;
- All participants must express themselves truthfully: They must show honesty in the expression of their intentions and feelings in order

to exclude manipulability and strategic instead of communicative action.[15] The exclusion of all kinds of manipulative and power-driven coercion arising from communicative structures is necessary for a fair and open dialogue between equal participants.[16]

Only when these conditions are fulfilled can a critical-rational and fair debate in a discourse be realized, a discussion where all arguments can be rationally compared. This is what Habermas means by *communicative symmetry*.

### 9.4.2 Discourse ethics

With the arrival of his theory of communicative action, however, Habermas, without any explanation, stops using the concept of ISS and starts instead referring to the universal presuppositions of argumentation. He now speaks about *universal conditions of possible understanding* and *general presuppositions of communicative action*. In his discourse ethics, he incorporates presuppositions he had previously described as features of the ideal speech situation. In response to criticism, Habermas reformulated the concept of the ISS and integrated it into a *new moral system* (moral discourse and discourse ethics) that was to be derived from the presuppositions of argumentation. Since the best available argument of today can turn out to be the worst argument tomorrow, Habermas recognizes that the presuppositions of argumentation need to be tested in practice.

To avoid a *performative contradiction*,[17] the content and performance of a speech act need to be aligned. For Habermas, the veracity of statements is a central element in his communication ethics, and he also considers a statement that does not contradict the performance of the statement but its truthfulness as a *performative contradiction*. Insofar he can claim that the ISS is not just a theoretical construction, since, as a rule, participants in a debate voluntarily tend to fulfill the conditions of the ISS, driven simply by their need to be credible to others. While no empirical investigation or study could ever reveal the facticity of the ISS in pure form,[18] it still somehow seems to be operative in all discourse.

> The ideal speech situation is neither just an empirical phenomenon nor construction but in the discourse fulfilled condition of reciprocity. This condition could be – but not necessarily – counterfactual; when it is made counterfactual, it is operatively acting (working) fiction. Thus I rather speak about foreseeing or anticipating the ideal speech situation. Anticipation alone is not a guarantee that we dare

(...) establish rational consensus; at the same time the ideal speech situation is a critical standard by which actually achieved consensus can be questioned and also (verified) (...)[19]

Thus Habermas tries to capture the twofold aspect of the ISS as both a real element of discourse and, at the same time, a counterfactual standard for such discourse. The ISS-method has clarified that the application of instrumental rational reasoning can be extended to the expressive domain. Despite the weakening of this concept in his later work where he expresses its content more neutrally, the concept still retains its value. The framework is very useful for understanding the formal communication and participative structure of organizations. But the model fails when too radically applied to practice, because it is too abstract. The implementation of the formalized structure of the ISS as a social condition for the radicalization of knowledge critique is almost impossible to apply to the praxis of a pluralistic many-voiced discourse, inherent in business organizations today.

The introduction of criticism into business discourse with the ideas of Habermas may be able to clarify the paradox of the institutionalization of ethics (in order to construct a normative basis for doing business), on the one hand, and the unpredictable human *ethos*, the life-world, on the other. Habermas recasts this distinction in terms of two different types of communication: *actions*, where factual claims of validity are naively assumed, and *discourse*, which serves to justify problematic claims of the validity of opinions and norms. Voluntary participation and the orientation towards consensus are central components of discourse. In a discourse, participants subject themselves to the "unforced force of the better argument".[20]

The goal of discourse ethics is an improvement in the rationality of public discussions and political decision making. It develops procedures and institutions that enable free access to societal deliberations and the equal representation of all relevant arguments in order to ensure that moral decisions are based on the "power of the best argument" and not on manipulative power or money. Stakeholder participation[21] belongs to the method of discourse ethics and is a very well-known procedure in business environments. It places emphasis on the question of who is involved or affected by business processes and is allowed to have a say, as well as on institutional analysis. The objective that everything someone asserts can be verified as true, right, and truthful in a rational way is examined. Only in that sense will an equitable settlement (in which "the system" – the economy or the state – is not privileged over the individual) be possible. Habermas' vision of discourse ethics is procedural and thus meets an important normative standard of modernity, if by modernity we understand a project and not a static *status quo*, in which the promise of the collective self-determination of all is inextricably linked to the authentic self-realization of each.[22]

Discourse ethics can be used to gain a common understanding with internal as well as external stakeholders under the condition of the ideal speech situation. Especially when the social responsibility of an organization is at stake, no one actor can decide what is fair and which norms must be applied in the interest of all stakeholders. The starting point of discourse ethics is therefore that the realization of an impartial reconciliation of conflicts of interest refers to a discursive testing of norms and their application. By discursive testing is intended the active participation of all relevant stakeholders. With stakeholder participation in the context of the ISS, Habermas addresses the condition of an unlimited communication community where the intention of every competent speaker must be focused on realizing a level of symmetry between participants.[23]

In his book *Faktizität und Geltung*, Habermas compares the ideal communication community, an idea of the philosopher Karl-Otto Apel, and the ideal speech situation. He wants to replace this counterfactual comparing to ideal conditions by presupposed argumentations: We already have to adopt presuppositions whenever we want to reach mutual understanding. This does not involve any kind of correspondence or comparison between idea and reality. This relation between communication communities, the ISS, and discourse ethics is very interesting because of the evolution of organizations towards research and communicative communities.[24] As long as discourse ethics sticks to its rational foundation it is impossible to realize universal validity claims in relation to moral behavior. The moral validity of a norm cannot meet the condition that it can only apply with the consent of all the stakeholders involved. To a certain extent this validity remains unfounded.

### 9.4.3 Organization

Communication proves to be the Achilles' heel of organizations. It is always needed in order to organize tasks, learn and reflect, communicate results, counter criticism, resolve misunderstandings, and listen to the voices of multiple stakeholders. So how does the discourse ethics framework recommend positioning communication in organizations?

For Habermas, to ensure rationally valid argumentations, disturbances of communication must be made explicit in order to enable a critical dialogue on a cognitive, normative and expressive level. The crucial point is that for Habermas the state of idealized consensus and dialogue is an *empirical counterfactual*[25]: that people act *as if* this were a real possibility is a necessary condition for forms of collective learning. In applying discourse ethics to organizational issues, we must create the opportunity of choosing "the maxim of action which can be – either within the internal forum of reason or within the external realm of discourse – generalized, justified, and thus coordinated. Ethics must have the preferences and material goals individuals pursue, as well as the coordination of universalizable strategies on its agenda."[26] The discourse-ethical framework limits what is individually and relationally feasible and restricts reflection on motives behind the personal commitment and individual loyalty. For that reason, organizational responsibility cannot be made intelligible on every level. Universal starting points constitute the basis for generally valid behavioral expectations.

## 9.5   Applications to the business realm

What can be learned from the theory and practice of communicative action for organizations and business environments? In such environments the pressure for high-quality communication increases continuously. Decision-making processes in or between organizations frequently come to depend solely on the quality of communicative interfaces. The ISS-method proves its use insofar as it clarifies the position of participants in a business-oriented dialogue. The application of instrumental rational reasoning, however, can be broadened to the expressive domain. This insight makes it possible to involve all elements of communicative action in the judgment of organizational decision making. This complex and overall opaque process is generally perceived as a goal-oriented and reason-driven process. But the practical limits of such a strategic discourse become obvious when participating stakeholders turn away because their claims are not truly heard but rather instrumentalized for maintaining the *status quo*. Only a communicative action view respecting the basic criteria of ISS can help organizations to take the courageous step of letting stakeholders participate, including their criticism.

The way we look at an organization today is completely different from fifty years ago. Today a fixed idea of what an organization is does not exist. We see networks, thematic project groups, cooperative multidisciplinary working groups, diversified production units, innovative platforms in knowledge centers where competitors are working together, and organizational brands, but the traditional organization that could be uniquely identified through its well-defined product and production process is history. For instance, Karl Weick's (organizational psychologist) argument[27] is that organizations *are* communication: An organization exists only in the communicative act itself: "Momentarily, at least during the meeting, there appears to be an organization, and this appearance is reconstituted whenever meetings are constituted. (...) Meetings assemble and generate minorities and majorities, and in doing so, create the infrastructure that creates sense. This infrastructure varies in the frequency with which it generates good arguments, advocacy, and divergent thinking, as well as the spirit of contradiction."[28]

According to Weick, the meaning of an organization begins at the moment communication is interrupted: The interruption of the communication itself enables *sensemaking* and the reconstitution of an organization. He perceives an organization as an intersubjective creation of "systems of opinions" that have to be negotiated, reviewed, and discussed in a critical dialogue. Organizations are communicative activities and can only survive when being sensitive to communication. However, a detailed view on the functioning of communication has not yet given by Weick, nor by Habermas. The deliberative method of the ISS gives us an insight into how communication can work in practice.

Because of their need for critique and confrontation in order to survive, to become and stay creative and innovative, organizations are more vulnerable today than in the past and more receptive to environmental issues, the unforeseeable and unpredictable market, deviancy and discontinuity.[29] The construct of the ISS can help them to have a more honest, globally acceptable and trust-building impact, especially in their communication with critical external stakeholders. Critical stakeholders help to improve the quality of the arguments made. Corporations that want to do business globally need the approval of global stakeholders.

For instance, Coca-Cola, after being attacked by the media campaign "Stop Killer-Coke,"[30] started an intensive cooperation with several NGOs to collect advice on environmental and human rights issues. Through this specific stakeholder participation the confrontation with delicate, societal topics could be shared, and solutions also found in a deliberative way. Coca-Cola committed itself to start stakeholder dialogues in order to detect public dilemmas at an early stage. Another example comes from a steel factory (studied under the agreement not to release its name) with ten thousand employees, where a lot has been done to reduce hazards on the working floor. In this organization, interruptions of the production process were seen as indispensible learning points in the survival strategy of the organization. In order to deal with "interruptions" on every organizational level, this company facilitates "rule-free space." This is a "free" space within well-defined areas of responsibility where employees are at liberty to act "freely" and "responsibly," and make their own decisions in circumstances that force them to do so. According to the employees this "free" space creates many communicative moments on the shop floor, because it necessitates going into depth concerning relational trust, shared responsibility, and the capacity to frankly tell the truth.

These examples emphasize that a deliberative praxis in relation to the ISS with the effect of enlargement of the use and aim of rationality can be very useful because it visualizes the human factor in an organization, learning through rational argumentation, and makes an appeal to employees' awareness of the complexity of communication and intersubjective and interdisciplinary processes. Moreover, introducing the deliberative debate with the active participation of stakeholders as an achievable procedure attaining universally valid claims on the objective, normative, and expressive level creates an opportunity within organizations for dealing with the unpredictable, together with growing responsibility on the part of all participants.

According to Habermas, the economy is a differentiated system, detached from our life-world. Validity claims that originate from communicative action fall outside an economy taken as an autonomous, functioning system based on market mechanisms. In his dissertation, Bert van de Ven refutes this notion by making a distinction between social and systematic integration via the organization as a kind of mediating entity between system and life-world.[31] Through the principle of social integration and symbolic reproduction of the life-world, moral engagement is integrated in the capillaries of the organization and the division between *system* and *life-world* becomes blurred.

Habermas knows that the functioning of communicative rationality is fragile. Nevertheless, it is solely upon this that he pins his hopes. The gulf between rich and poor, the destruction of the environment, and the clash of cultures, demand political solutions. A supporting platform must be generated in a democratically organized public space in which citizens can exchange ideas and thrash out their differences of opinion with arguments, and arrive at the formulation of a collective will that must be the guiding force for political action.

Habermas's theoretical discourse-ethical points of departure prove very useful for understanding the communicative ethic at the interface between organization (private space) and the environment (public space), at those points where the chronic tension between private-public interest cannot be resolved through cognitively founded and universally valid claims to truth alone. We therefore specifically point to the origination of communicatively generated research communities which, in their day-to-day practices, can offer temporary solutions based on majority or minority positions. The basis of these solutions is formed by the quality of the communicative process that is determined through difference and multiple voices.

## Notes

1. Montesquieu: 1995, *De l'esprit des lois, II*, p. 609 and Giddens, Anthony: 1990, *The Consequences of Modernity*, Polity Press, Cambridge, pp. 86–7.
2. Karl Weick: 1995, *Sensemaking in Organizations*, Sage Publishers, pp. 7, 133–34.
3. Suzan Langenberg: 2010, "The Model of Critique in Business" in: Sharda S. Nandram and Margot Esther Borden (eds), *Spirituality and Business*, Springer Verlag, pp. 219–232.
4. Jürgen Habermas, 1985, *Der philosophische Diskurs der Moderne*, Suhrkamp Verlag, Frankfurt am Main, pp. 156–7.
5. Jürgen Habermas, 1981, *Theorie des kommunikativen Handelns*, Band I und II, Suhrkamp Verlag Frankfurt am Main, Band I, p. 237. A transformation of this model we can find in: Frans van Peperstraten: 2007, *Samenleving ter discussie*, uitgeverij Coutinho, Bussum, p. 277.
6. Jürgen Habermas: 1981, *Theorie des kommunikativen Handelns*, Band I und II, Suhrkamp Verlag Frankfurt am Main, Band I, pp. 130–57.
7. "Verständigung gilt als ein Prozess der Einigung unter sprach- und handlungsfähigen Subjekten" in: Jürgen Habermas, 1981, *Theorie des kommunikativen Handelns, Band 1 und II*, Suhrkamp Verlag, Frankfurt am Main, 1981, Band I, p. 386.
8. The distinction between communicative action and strategic action was drawn by Jürgen Habermas in: 1981, *Theorie des kommunikativen Handelns*, Band I und II, Suhrkamp Verlag, Frankfurt am Main, Band I, pp. 446–52.
9. Jürgen Habermas, 1981, *Theorie des kommunikativen Handelns Band 1 und II*, Suhrkamp Verlag, Frankfurt am Main, 1981, Band I, p. 70.
10. Idem, pp. 42–4.
11. Keulartz, Jozef and Harry Kunneman, *Rondom Habermas: Analyses en kritieken*, Boom, 1985, p. 106.
12. Hugh Willmot, 2003, 'Organizing Theory as Critical Science' in: Haridimos Tsoukas & Christian Knudsen, *Organization Theory*, Oxford University Press, p. 95.
13. We can find this critical analysis of knowledge creation in Jürgen Habermas, 1968, *Erkenntnis und Interesse*, Frankfurt am Main. This work was written long before his Theory of Communicative Action.

14. Jürgen Habermas, 1984, *Vorstudien und Ergänzungen zur Theorie des kommunikativen Handelns*, Suhrkamp Verlag, Frankfurt am Main, p. 161.
15. Keulartz, Jozef & Harry Kunneman, 1985, *Rondom Habermas. Analyses en kritieken*, Boom, p. 106.
16. "Reziprozität der Verhaltenserwartungen"in: Jürgen Habermas, 1982, *Vorstudien und Ergänzungen zur Theorie des kommunikativen Handelns*, Suhrkamp Verlag, Frankfurt am Main, p. 588.
17. Jürgen Habermas, 1983, *Moralbewusstsein und kommunikativen Handelns*, Suhrkamp Verlag, Frankfurt am Main, pp. 92–110.
18. We refer to the metacritical response of Habermas to the criticism of his concepts of communicative action and ideal speech situation in *Erläuterungen zur Diskursethik*, pp. 119–227. Habermas uses extended arguments to defend his conviction that with the use of reason all levels of communication can claim validity, provided there is a fundamental agreement on the consensus orientation of language. Habermas discusses this with his critics Bernard Williams, Charles Taylor, John Rawls, and Albrecht Wellmer, among others.
19. Jürgen Habermas, 1982, *Vorstudien und Ergänzungen zur Theorie des kommunikativen Handelns*, Suhrkamp Verlag, Frankfurt am Main, p. 180.
20. Jürgen Habermas, 1991, *Erläuterungen zur Diskursethik*, Frankfurt am Main, p. 123.
21. Philips, Robert: 2003, *Stakeholder Theory and Organizational Ethics*, Berrett-Koehler Publishers, Inc., San Francisco, pp. 120–34. Compare with the system analytical approach of Bowie and Werhane: 2004, *Managing Ethics*, pp. 128–9. A similar thesis can be found with Manuel Velasquez: 2002, 'Moral Reasoning', in: Norman Bowie (ed.), *The Blackwell Guide to Business Ethics*, Blackwell Publishers, Oxford, p. 113.
22. Jürgen Habermas: 1985, *Der philosophische Diskurs der Moderne*, Frankfurt am Main, p. 391.
23. Jürgen Habermas, 1983, *Moralbewusstsein und kommunikatives Handeln*, Suhrkamp Verlag, Frankfurt am Main, p. 99.
24. Jozef Keulartz, 2005, *Werken aan de grens*, Damon, pp. 28–41.
25. Jürgen Habermas, 1991, *Faktizität und Geltung*, Suhrkamp Verlag, Frankfurt am Main, pp. 18–19.
26. Peter Koslowski, 'Ethical Economy as Synthesis' in: Koslowski, Peter (ed.): 1992 *Ethics in Economics, Business and Economic Policy*, Springer Verlag, Heidelberg, p. 40.
27. Karl Weick, *Sensemaking of Organizations*, Sage publications, 1995.
28. Idem, pp. 143–44.
29. Dubbink, Wim, 'The Fragile Structure of Free-Market Society', in: *Business Ethics Quarterly*, Vol. 14, no. 1, 2004, pp. 23–46.
30. The killer-coke campaign was a reaction on the assassination of eight trade union leaders in Coca-Cola bottling plants in Colombia in 1996. The Stop Killer Coke campaign aimed to put public pressure on Coca-Cola to acknowledge its role in the killings and to persuade the company to stop collaborating with violent paramilitary organizations.
31. Bert van de Ven: 1998, *Rationaliteit en ethiek in de onderneming*, Tilburg University Press, p. 140.

# 10
## Sen and Nussbaum on Human Capabilities in Business

*Benedetta Giovanola*

## 10.1 Introduction

In recent years there have been several important critical investigations aimed at overcoming the flaws in economics and business. With regard to *economics*, different approaches and criticisms have shown that cognitive, ethical, and social limits are always present when agents (and thus economic agents too) make a choice.[1] These considerations also tie in with a sharp criticism of the standard notion of rationality and the idea of *homo oeconomicus*, as they are understood in mainstream economic theory. With regard to *business*, as well, many inquiries that were focused on the analysis of decision-making within organizations have shown that individual and collective choices are limited or enhanced by ethical, cognitive, and social elements that play a fundamental role in a company's organization and activity. In this case, the central question is whether an organization provides an environment conducive to human growth and fulfillment and whether good corporate policy can encourage and nourish individual growth, by fostering opportunities for all employees to develop their talents and potential. These concerns have been explicitly recognized by management studies and form the basis of "humanistic management" (Melé, 2003), whose inquiries tackle the issue of the relationship between business and management, on one side, and the human condition, on the other.

In general, different approaches have argued for the importance of a correct understanding of human values and human nature for the sake of both economics and business. More specifically, these inquiries highlight a broader and more fundamental meaning of rationality, which consists in the critical scrutiny of the *values* and *objectives* that underlie all behavior, and whose major function is of an *ethical-normative* kind;

they also formulate a "richer" and more complex idea of the human being (and thus of economic agents and business actors too) than the standard notion of *homo oeconomicus*. In such a way, these inquiries try to rise above the major shortcomings of economics and business, by providing them with an ethical-anthropological underpinning.

In this frame of reference, this chapter will focus on a specific approach, one that can lead to a sound ethical-anthropological foundation for economics and business, and thus foster more "humanized" models and practices: the Capability Approach (hereafter CA), as it has been developed by the Indian economist Amartya Sen and the American philosopher Martha Nussbaum.

In general, the CA can be defined as a theory of human development and quality of life, or as "a broad normative framework for the evaluation and assessment of individual well-being and social arrangements" (Robeyns, 2005, p. 94), whose core characteristic is a focus on people's *"capabilities* to do and to be" (Sen, 1987a, 1987b, 1993, 1999a), namely what people have reason to value and are effectively capable to do and to be (whereas people's effective *states* of doing and being are called *functionings*), in order to lead a "flourishing" life[2].

If applied to the more specific framework of economics and business, this approach can show that *economics and business are, and ought to be, about human values,* and should foster human fulfillment through the enhancement of valuable human capabilities. In order to support this claim, the next section pursues a critique of the standard notions of economic rationality and *homo oeconomicus*, and argues the need to go beyond them. The following section introduces Amartya Sen's trenchant criticism of these notions, and focuses on his attempt to re-establish the connection between ethics and economics: here, particular attention is paid to the concepts of agency and capability. The third section focuses on Martha Nussbaum's version of the CA approach, and discusses her attempt to provide a "middle road" between "unsatisfactory extremes," which takes the form of a particular kind of universalism, sensitive to particularism and individual differences. The fourth section dedicates specific attention to Sen and Nussbaum's anthropological reflections and aims to develop the CA's underlying anthropological model. In this framework, specific attention is paid to the notion of *anthropological richness*. The concluding section suggests that the CA's ethical-anthropological reflection can be applied to economics and business in order to argue for more "humanized" models and practices.

Finally, a methodological remark: This chapter is aimed at developing the CA's positive and constructive side, and at showing its fruitfulness as an ethical-anthropological underpinning for economics and business: As a consequence, even if the paper does not ignore differences between Sen and Nussbaum, it focuses on the distinguishing elements of the approach itself, which are common to both authors.

## 10.2 Beyond the *Homo Oeconomicus* and the standard notion of economic rationality

According to mainstream economic theory, rationality consists in maximizing one's utility function (expressed in terms of individual preferences ranked in a hierarchy) under a resource constraint. Thus, rationality concerns the relationship between preferences and choices: A *choice* is rational if it is determined by a rational set of *preferences*, and the set of preferences is defined within the contexts of *utility* theory. This means that an individual is rational if, and only if, his or her preferences can be represented by ordinal utility functions, and his or her choices maximize utility (Hausman and McPherson, 2006).

It is thus clear that economic theory does not offer any specific prescription regarding the nature, content, or value of preferences, whose rationality is assured by two purely *formal* conditions: *completeness*, according to which it is possible to express a preference or a rational indifference among all the possible alternatives; and *transitivity*, according to which, if option A is preferred to B and option B is preferred to C, then option A is also preferred to C: This means that preferences for A, B, and C are not on the same level, but are hierarchically ranked. These formal conditions have also been defined in terms of "internal consistency of choice," which is at the basis of the so-called "weak" form of rationality (Sen, 1977). But the possibility of ranking all the preferences in a hierarchic and transitive way presupposes a perfect knowledge of all the possible alternatives in order to make a rational choice, that is, a choice that maximizes utility. The requirement of perfect knowledge, together with that of self-interest maximization, leads to the so-called "strong" form of rationality (Sen, 1977), which entails serious shortcomings.

In fact, Herbert Simon (1982, 1997, 2000) has provided an excellent demonstration of the fact that our rationality, far from being unlimited, is a *bounded rationality*: Furthermore, if we shift our attention from the moment of choice to the *framing* of decisions, we find that human behavior frequently deviates from the assumption of rational choice theory, and entails a high degree of psychological complexity (Kahneman and Tversky, 1979, 1982, 2000; Slovic et al., 2002).

The formal character of the standard notion of economic rationality also entails some serious flaws. In fact, even if nothing is said about the content of preferences, the principle of "minimal benevolence" (Hausman and McPherson, 2006, p. 65) – according to which, other conditions being equal, it is morally good that people enhance their own well-being and satisfy their own preferences – rests upon a view of economic agents as utility maximizers and self-interested individuals (ibid., p. 64). Such a view leads to the *Homo Oeconomicus* model to which a great part of contemporary economic theory refers. In brief, we can say that *homo oeconomicus* is an exclusively self-interested individual, seeking to maximize self-interest and perfectly conscious of the consequences of his or her choices.

From these considerations it follows that a redefinition of the mainstream notion of economic rationality is fundamental, and also involves a reconsideration of the anthropological model proper to (neoclassical) economic theory, according to which human beings would be oriented to self-interest achievement and to the maximization of their own preference ranking (and, then, to the improvement of their well-being or utility) under resource constraints[3]. An inquiry into the ethical capabilities missing from the standard notion of economic rationality is thus needed, and requires a revision of the anthropological model underlying economics.

## 10.3   Amartya Sen on capability and agency

A trenchant criticism of mainstream economic rationality is pursued by Amartya Sen, who seeks to develop an ethical approach to economics. In this framework, he also is highly critical of the underlying "narrow view" taken of the person by economics (the *homo oeconomicus* model), according to which human beings are seen merely as the "location of their respective utilities" (Sen and Williams, 1982). Sen demonstrates that, if people behaved in the way rational choice theory prescribes, they would act like "rational fools" (Sen, 1977), whereas, in his judgment, the redefinition of (economic) *rationality* (on which the actions of economic agents rely) is strictly linked to more sophisticated assumptions about the notion of the *agent* usually assumed by economic theory as a strictly "economic agent" (that is, the *homo oeconomicus*). On the contrary, he argues, human beings are much more sophisticated than their depiction in economic theory (Sen, 1977), and human actions and decisions are driven not only by self-interest, but also by *sympathy* and *commitment*. In particular, commitment is strictly connected with a person's *moral principles* and can also diverge from personal well-being: It can modify a person's goals and her rational choice, by giving importance to other people's aims that cannot be included in the pursuit of personal interest (Sen, 2005b, p. 7).

These considerations clarify Sen's re-definition of (economic) rationality: By recognizing the importance of commitment and moral obligation, (economic) rationality can no longer be conceived as mere self-interest maximization, and the rational economic agent can no longer be conceived as a mere selfish utility-maximizer. In particular, rationality includes a critical scrutiny of *values* and *objectives* that underlie all behavior (Sen, 2002, p. 53 f.): Its major function therefore is of an *ethical-normative* kind, and is strictly connected with the capability to think and act with *wisdom*. In other words rationality, according to Sen, concerns the identification of *fundamental human values and objectives* and their concrete fulfillment through practice. Furthermore, the importance of commitment and the scrutiny of a person's values and objectives are also connected with the notion of *personal identity*, which is defined by the way a person considers herself, according to her values and objectives. Personal identity however, is strictly linked to *social identity*, a person's capability to identify herself with other persons, to consider herself in relation to others[4].

Throughout his reflections, Sen tackles both ethical and philosophical-anthropological issues at the basis of economics: In particular, both his criticism of neoclassical (utilitarian) economic theory and his redefinition of rationality have an *ethical* foundation and are grounded in the need to overcome a narrow anthropological view and show the *anthropological* complexity of human beings.

This is why Sen criticizes mainstream economics' focus on well-being and the equivalence it sees between well-being and utility: "People," Sen argues, "have aspects other than well-being. Not all their activities are aimed at maximizing well-being." In particular, "the conception of '*persons*' [...] cannot be so reduced as to attach no intrinsic importance to his *agency* role, seeing them ultimately only in terms of their well-being. There is a particular sphere in which such an agency role may be especially important, and that is the person's own *life*" (Sen, 1985, p. 186, *emphasis added*). The notion of agency, which is very important for Sen, denotes a substantive freedom to act, whose value rests upon neither results achievement, nor well-being improvement (Sen, 1987a): The value of agency consists in its capacity to express values, objectives, commitments (for example), in a way that can also deviate from the pursuit of well-being enhancement. The notion of agency directly refers to that of *capability*. In fact Sen argues that positive or substantive freedom (freedom *to* achieve something) can be defined in terms of a person's *capability* (Sen, 1999a, p. 25) or, in other words, it can be seen in the form of "individual capabilities to do things a person has reason to value" (Sen, 1999a, p. 56). In other words, the notion of "capability" directly refers to a *real opportunity* to do and to be, which best expresses the positive side of freedom (Sen, 1999a), together with a critical scrutiny that allows the selection of valuable doings and beings. To sum up, capability is the substantive freedom to achieve alternative valuable functioning combinations (Sen, 1999a, p. 79): Functionings, in their turn, are *states* of doing and being.

According to Sen, the identification of valuable or fundamental capabilities rests on each individual's evaluation (that is what *one has reason to value*). Any evaluation however is always context-dependent[5]: this is why Sen rejects any attempt to fix "a cemented list of capabilities that is seen as being absolutely complete [...] and totally fixed," since "pure theory cannot 'freeze' a list of capabilities for all societies for all time to come" (Sen, 2005a, p. 158)[6]. His idea is that the identification of fundamental capabilities, at the social level, should rest on "public reasoning," which is defined as a democratic procedure aimed at creating the space for shared evaluations (Sen, 2005a, p. 163). Moreover, a fixed and canonical list would diminish the domain of public reasoning, on which human capabilities depend (ibid., p. 163). At the same time, however, he expresses the need for an "ethical objectivity," which entails respect for individual plural evaluations and the importance of developing "views from a 'certain distance'" (ibid., p. 160 f.; 2004, p. 161)[7].

In other words, the identification of fundamental capabilities and values should rest on a democratic and dialogical procedure, which is best expressed through the exercise of public reasoning. The latter also prevents ethical relativism, just because it creates the space for shared evaluations, and respects individuals' plural conceptions at the same time. Furthermore, according to Sen, public reasoning is also at the core of both the concept and the practice of democracy: Recently, Sen has explicitly affirmed that "democracy is assessed in terms of public reasoning, which leads to an understanding of democracy as 'government by discussion.' But democracy must also be seen more generally in terms of the capacity to enrich reasoned engagement through enhancing informational availability and the feasibility of interactive discussion" (Sen, 2009, p. xii–xiii). Even if "democracy is not seen simply in terms of the setting up of some specific institutions [...], but in terms of the possibility and reach of public reasoning," the political-institutional level is of a particular (even if not exclusive) importance in creating real opportunities for public discussion and for lives one has the reason to value.

## 10.4   Beyond the universalism–particularism dichotomy: M. Nussbaum's "middle-road"

The political-institutional dimension of the CA has been extensively developed by the American philosopher Martha Nussbaum, who conceives her version of the CA as a normative underpinning for a theory of justice according to political purposes[8]. In fact, she seeks to develop a particular type of normative philosophical theory, based on a *universalist* account of central human functionings, and respect ful of human dignity. She summarizes the core of CA by defining it as "the philosophical base for fundamental constitutional princi-ples establishing a social minimum or threshold" and sees it as the object of an "overlapping consensus" (Nussbaum, 2000, pp. 5, 6). But at the same time, Nussbaum points out that the capabilities in ques-tion should be pursued for each and every person: She terms this "a *principle of each person's capability*, based on a *principle of each person as an end*" (ibid.).

Nussbaum defines her approach as a "middle road" between uni-versalistic and individualistic accounts or, in other words, between "Platonism" (based on an objective and universalistic notion of the Good) and "subjective welfarism" (based on individual preferences), which are defined as two "unsatisfactory extremes."

According to *Platonism*, actual desire and choice play no role at all in justifying something as good: In fact Platonism's main goal is "to pro-vide an argument for the objective value of the relevant state of affairs that is independent of the fact that people desire or prefer it" (ibid., p. 117). Although Platonism arises from a genuinely important concern (the concern for justice and human value), it nonetheless encounters some critical problems, especially because it seems too disdainful of the wisdom embodied in people's actual experience. In other words, it completely rejects the dimension of people's desires and choices, and totally overlooks the exercise of practical reason.

According to *subjective welfarism*, all existing preferences are on a par for political purposes, and social choice should be based on some sort of aggregation of all of them, but this is an unacceptable claim, as demon-strated by the problem of preference-deformation (ibid., p. 114). In spite of its genuine respect for people and their actual choices, subjective welfarism generates a very serious problem: It rules out the possibility of conducting a normative critique of unjust institutions.

Through her criticism of both unsatisfactory extremes, Nussbaum argues the need for a "substantive theory of justice and central goods" (Nussbaum, 2000, p. 138), that is, a substantive theory of the central capabilities (ibid., p. 139), which incorporates *substantive ethical values* (ibid., p. 135); at the same time, however, this theory ought to respect human diversity and particularity. This is why Nussbaum argues that capabilities and not functionings are the political goal that her approach seeks to promote: In fact, once human capabilities are guaranteed at a minimum threshold (in other words, once the promotion of capabilities becomes a political purpose for governments), every citizen can freely choose whether or not to convert these capabilities into functionings, in ways that vary from person to person.

On the one hand, human capabilities have a universal value, because they are grounded in the (universal) idea of human dignity: In particular, Nussbaum's approach uses the idea of a *"threshold level of each capability*, beneath which it is held that truly human functioning is not available to citizens; the social goal should be understood in terms of getting citizens above this capability threshold" (ibid., p. 6). This leads to the idea of a "basic social minimum," which can be provided by "an approach that focuses on *human capabilities*, that is, what people are actually able to do and to be – in a way informed by an intuitive idea of a life that is worthy of the dignity of the human being" (ibid., p. 5). On the other hand, even if human capabilities have a universal value, any individual can select the capabilities that are most important to him or her, as things he or she has reason to value. This is required by the importance Nussbaum assigns to "practical reason," that is, being able to form a conception of the Good and to engage in critical reflection about the planning of one's own life. The notion of practical reason clearly expresses an evaluative dimension that is central, and which recalls Sen's idea of *agency*, as well as his focus on *valued* capabilities and functionings, that is things *one has the reason to value*.

More radically than Sen, Nussbaum seeks to show that a substantive notion of the good can be compatible with the plurality of individual choices. In particular, she argues that at the level of central capabilities there is considerable convergence between an intelligently normative proceduralism and a substantive Good theory of a non-Platonist kind, sensitive to people's actual beliefs and values (ibid., p. 158). To sum up, in Nussbaum's definition, the CA is thus "strongly universalist" (ibid., p. 7), since "the capabilities in question are important for each and every citizen, in each and every nation, and each is to be treated as an end" (ibid., p. 6). But this *universalism* is of a particular type, "framed in terms of general human powers and their development" (ibid., p. 7) and "sensitive to pluralism and cultural difference" (ibid., p. 8).

## 10.5 Anthropological richness: intrapersonal relationality, inter-personal relationality, and dynamism of personhood

Both Sen and Nussbaum argue the compatibility between the reference to *universal* values (each person to be treated as an end, the idea of human dignity) and the attention to each person's *individual* particularity. These considerations lead us to a very important point about the CA's ethical-anthropological reflection. In fact, the CA attributes high importance to *human diversity*. This implies respect for difference and plurality, since each person differs from everyone else, and there is a plurality of (different) persons. However, such a respect for difference and plurality does not degrade into a form of subjectivism, nor into radical individualism. Following Aristotle, the CA assumes that there are important spheres of shared human experience (*grounding experiences*) that define fundamental capabilities, which ought to be preserved and fulfilled in a virtuous life (Nussbaum, 1993; 1995). Nevertheless, there are also differences and plurality among individuals that need to be preserved. Thus, we might argue, at the level of humanity in general, there are *universal* capabilities, but personal (and *particular*) ways of developing them. One might add that the acknowledgment of the diversity among human beings is also consistent with the CA's understanding of human flourishing as influenced by Aristotle (Giovanola 2005; 2009). In fact, according to Aristotle (1980), human beings flourish and fulfill human nature in particular ways that vary from person to person. The CA stresses this point, arguing that flourishing depends on the development of our capabilities, which are always personal.

There is also a second level of analysis that refers to the concept of a person. At this level another kind of diversity becomes evident, that is, the diversity within human beings that we might call *intrinsic diversity*. In fact, diversity is also seen in internal characteristics within every person, as shown by the notion of capability itself: People have various aspirations, desires, preferences and, above all, various capabilities. As we have noticed above, the misleading utilitarian "narrow view" of human beings consists exactly in overlooking their intrinsic pluralism and in reducing them to one function, and moreover to a merely quantitative one, that of utility maximization. Like the attention to diversity *among* individuals, the attention to human complexity and *intrinsic* diversity is also consistent with the CA's Aristotelian notion of flourishing, which depends on different life dimensions and not on just one function: This means that human beings are complex entities that are characterized by an anthropological constitutive plurality (Giovanola, 2005)[9]. The notion that best expresses the CA's focus on human beings' constitutive plurality is the notion of richness, understood in philosophical-anthropological terms, that is, the notion of *anthropological richness*.

Even if it is not explicitly used by Sen and Nussbaum, the notion of *anthropological richness* is of a central importance for the further development of some major ideas of the CA. In fact this concept enables both a better understanding of the CA's underlying anthropological model, and a clarification of its attempt to go beyond the universalism–particularism dichotomy.

For example, when Sen distinguishes between the idea of being *"well off"* and that of being *"well,"* or of having *"well-being,"* he seems to implicitly refer to such an anthropological richness. The idea of being *"well off"* conveys opulence and refers to a person's command over exterior things, whereas the idea of being *"well,"* or of having *"well-being,"* refers to something *in* a person, something that she achieves. The latter expresses a distinctively personal quality lacking in the former (Sen, 1985). We can say that in the second case, the person can flourish, whereas in the first, she can only maximize her utility and enjoy opulence. Flourishing, we could argue, requires an internal *qualitative richness*, rather than a *quantitative-economical* richness (opulence). Qualitative richness, in turn, requires the capability to select those life dimensions one has reason to value: In other words, the qualitative dimension of anthropological richness is strictly linked to the exercise of practical reason (in Nussbaum's terms) and agency (in Sen's terms). If the distinctive feature of anthropological richness is not of a quantitative, but of a qualitative kind, it is also clear that anthropological richness cannot be simply interpreted as a matter of "how much" one can do or be; it rather concerns the substantive freedom to flourish and to select *valuable* states and capabilities to do and to be, that can lead to a truly flourishing life.

The qualitative and evaluative dimension implied by the notion of anthropological richness could be developed further by extending the application of the Kantian formula of humanity as an end in itself from the interpersonal level (as Nussbaum, for example, does) to the intrapersonal level. This would not only be consistent with Kant's own formulation of the principle itself[10], but would also provide a normative criterion for the selection of valuable doings and beings than can "enrich" a person: The application of the Kantian principle at the intrapersonal level would then prescribe every single person to treat herself "never simply as a means, but always at the same time as an end," it would prevent the instrumentalization of the self and would prescribe the selection and enhancement of the life-dimensions that best express the finalistic nature of every individual. But at the same time it is important to notice that – even according to Kant – humanity is an end in itself because of its potential for freedom: Freedom, then, is the source of the unique dignity of human beings (see Kant, 1903, p. 428)[11]. The last considerations highlight a *qualitative* dimension of freedom[12], which entails a duty at the same time, since the humanity in oneself is also the source of a duty to develop one's talents or to "perfect" one's humanity. But the finalistic nature of every single individual (whose realization is both a matter of freedom and a duty) is not only individually characterized: It also expresses a common feature of humanity or, in other words, it refers to the idea of a common humanity.

These considerations shed a new light on the concept of anthropological richness. In particular, they show that the notion of human richness goes beyond the concept of well-being: In fact, it ultimately focuses not merely on each single *individual*, but also represents the *universal* feature of human essence, which is common to *every* human being. At the same time, human essence is something potential (to be realized) and it can only be fulfilled in particular ways that vary from person to person. Therefore, *anthropological richness* is at the same time universal and particular, since *every* human being expresses it – or at least should express it –through his or her *particularity* (Giovanola, 2005).

In order to further analyze the fundamental features of the notion of anthropological richness, we can look at its formulation by a thinker who, along with Aristotle, exerted great influence on the CA: Karl Marx. The Marxian influence on the CA has been explicitly acknowledged by both Sen (1980; 1985; 1987a) and Nussbaum (1988; 2000); in particular they refer to Marx's focus on positive freedom (Sen, 1987a) and to his Aristotelian understanding of human functionings (Nussbaum, 2000), which are said to be closely linked to the notion of capability (Sen, 1980; 1985a; 1999a; Nussbaum, 2000).

Marx's interpretation of the notion of (anthropological) richness is intrinsically connected with his idea of positive freedom and his understanding of human functionings, and can be grasped through a capability perspective. In fact, in his *Manuscripts*, Marx argues that instead of considering richness and poverty as political economy does, one should rather pay attention to the *"rich human being"*[13]. According to Marx, such a "rich" human being needs both *plurality of human dimensions* and *relationships with other human beings* in order to fulfill his own potential, that is, to become really *human*, and thus *social*. On the one hand, human beings should be *capable* of fulfilling, that is, free to fulfill, their own potential and to function in different ways. On the other hand, both poverty and richness should gain a "human, and therefore social meaning:" in other words, the highest richness for each human being is other human beings and that richness is felt in the form of a need (Marx, 1844, *Third Manuscript*). This means that self-realization can fully succeed only if the social and relational dimension of personhood is recognized, since every person is *intrinsically relational*. In other words, through their relational dimension, human beings can become "richer," since their relationships with others increase their identity. This recognition, far from turning into something like a communitarian identity, highlights the importance of the *interpersonal relationality* and means that interpersonal relations can change each individual's personal identity. This element is also particularly crucial in the CA, and is closely linked to the role of commitment and to the interconnection between personal identity and social identity.

These considerations introduce another very important feature expressed by the notion of anthropological richness and also implicit in the CA: the *dynamic* dimension of personhood. In fact, the CA's focus on the dimension of "being able to do and to be" shows the importance of a dynamic (and never ending) process in which people constitute their identity, and pursue human flourishing. This also means that the way we are can be changed by developing our capabilities. This is also evident from the CA's re-interpretation of the Aristotelian Greek concept of *eudaimonia*: According to the CA, in fact, human flourishing consists in a complex self-realization, but the basic idea is that there are other possibilities than the one I am realizing now: There is neither a fixed nor a firm form of the self. In this regard, the concept of anthropological richness seems the most apt expression of this openness to new possibilities of the self.

In short, the notion of *anthropological richness* is able to express the following dimensions of identity: the *intrinsic plurality* of capabilities and life dimensions, which we could define as the *intrapersonal relationality* of the self; *interpersonal relationality*, namely, the *socio-relational* dimension of the self, according to which human beings are intrinsically "relational," so that each "needs" to be in relation with others; and the *dynamic* dimension of the self, according to which identity is a dynamic notion, for human flourishing is an ongoing and never definitively defined process. This is why the notion of anthropological richness, as noted above, can serve as the ultimate foundation for the CA's concept of personhood.

## 10.6 Towards more "humanized" business and economics

These considerations have important counterparts from an ethical-anthropological perspective, even with regard to the realm of economics. In fact, whereas neoclassical economics depicts human beings as disembodied and nonembedded individualists who only have subjective preferences, the CA framework implies that there is a shared though differentiated human nature, namely, a *shared human tendency to fulfill oneself.* This also means that human beings are considered capable of acquiring capabilities and virtues that perfect them, and thus let them fulfill their humanity.

If we now attempt to apply the ethical-anthropological conception outlined above to business, the latter would undergo such substantial changes that it would depart in no small measure from its prevailing assumptions. In broad terms, the ethical-anthropological inquiry that has been developed in the previous sections can help to reconnect business theory and practice with the fostering of human values and the enhancement of human *capabilities.* The question now is whether rational economic activity in business (usually identified with the pursuit of self-interest and profit) is compatible with *ethical* activity, and whether the pursuit of efficiency is compatible with the fostering of *human fulfillment.* The analysis of these ethical issues also requires deep reflection on the vision of the human being at the basis of business, although most prevailing business theories lack an adequate *anthropological* investigation.

Filling this gap, the CA helps us to develop an *ethical-anthropological* foundation on which business can rely. However, the CA has only recently started to be applied to business: In particular, it has been used in an organizational context by Cornelius and Gagnon (1999), Cornelius et al. (2008), and Vogt (2005); more specifically, it has been used to analyze the ethical aspects of participative governance (Collier and Esteban, 1999) and to understand equality in the workplace (Cornelius, 2002; Cornelius and Gagnon, 1999, 2000, 2002, 2004).

Still, the application of the CA to business could be very fruitful in order to link business with the fostering of human values and the promotion of human capabilities. Thanks to Sen and Nussbaum's reflection, we can develop more human models for business and a more "human-ized" company strategy (Andrews, 1989), and carry out more *humanistic* management, that is "management that emphasizes the human condition and is oriented to the development of human virtue, in all its forms, to its fullest extent" (Melé, 2003, p. 79). The CA can help us to think of business as "human-based," by focusing on the constitutive elements of personhood that a more "human" business should promote.

In fact, if we apply the main features of anthropological richness to business, the latter will be intrinsically aimed at enhancing people's capabilities (intrapersonal relationality of personhood), at promoting genuine interpersonal relationships in the workplace (interpersonal relationality of personhood), at letting employees grow as a person through their practice (dynamic dimension of personhood), and finally, at contributing to the pursuit of human fulfillment and a good life (see Giovanola, 2009).

To sum up, the capability approach helps us to think of economics and business as means for human flourishing, rather than as ends in themselves. The reason lies in the CA's focus on capability enhancement and its elaboration of an ethical-anthropological underpinning for economics and business. The core of this underpinning is the notion of anthropological richness; this is what makes it possible to overcome the emphasis on self-interest and personal well-being as utility maximization, and to promote the shift from the notion of the egoistic (economic) *individual*, to the concept of *personhood*. This ultimately refers to CA's understanding of the concept of *human being* as a *normative concept*, and to its focus on the notion of a "common humanity" (Nussbaum, 1993).

According to this framework, economics and business could contribute to the pursuit of a more human development[14] for *each and every person*, by promoting the enhancement of valuable human capabilities, and the fulfillment of *each and every person's* humanity through human flourishing.

## Notes

1. On the cognitive dimension, see Kahneman and Tversky, 1979, 1982, 2000; Simon, 1982, 1997, 2000; Slovic et al., 2002; on the social dimension and the need to re-embed economics in the social context, see Hirsch, 1976; on the ethical dimension, see Sen, 1977, 1985, 1987a, 1987b, 1999a.
2. Needless to say, the notion of human flourishing (or human fulfillment), as developed by the CA, has strong Aristotelian roots (on this issue, see Giovanola, 2009). The Aristotelian notion of human flourishing or

*eudaimonia* defines the "human good" – that is, the good which is proper to the human being – and "implies the possession and the use of one's mature powers over a considerable period of time," and "the fulfillment of the natural capacities of the human species" (Cooper, 1975, p. 89, n. 1). The Aristotelian notion of human flourishing has been explicitly used and discussed by Nussbaum (1986).

3. In fact, mainstream economics is not only concerned with the issue of individual well-being, but also with the definition and measurement of social welfare, which is defined by the principle of Pareto-optimality. The latter, however, identifies optimality with efficiency (a Pareto-optimal state of affairs defines an efficient allocation of resources) and generates serious problems, of which the most serious is the impossibility of tackling equity reasons and solving the trade-off between efficiency and equity.

4. For further inquiry into Sen's concept of identity, see Sen (1999b); for an interpretation of Sen's arguments, see Davis (2003, pp. 150–166) and Giovanola (2007).

5. However, it is important to point out that Sen is also very critical of the role of context, when it inhibits human choices and a free constitution of identity (see Sen, 1999b and his discussion of adaptive preferences).

6. The difference between Sen and Nussbaum on this point is clear. In fact, the American philosopher has defined a list of fundamental human capabilities (see Nussbaum, 2000; 2006).

7. In this regard it is interesting to note that Sen, in advocating such an ethical objectivity, specifically refers to Aristotle and argues the need for an "Aristotelian ethics" based on the "fulfilment of valuable functionings and the capability to create and enjoy these functionings" (Sen, 2006, p. 52).

8. Recently Sen, too, has given increasing attention to the issue of justice, and has presented "a theory of justice," even if "in a very broad sense" (Sen, 2009, p. ix).

9. It is worth mentioning that Sen adopts the expression "constitutive plurality," although he uses it mainly as a feature of evaluation. In fact, he distinguishes a "competitive" from a "constitutive" plurality, arguing that the former relates to different views that are alternative to one another, whereas the latter describes a kind of "intrinsic diversity" internal to a certain view, embracing different, though not mutually exclusive, aspects (Sen, 1987b).

10. The Kantian formula of humanity as an end in itself prescribes: "Act in such a way that you always treat humanity, *whether in your own person or in the person of any other*, never simply as a means, but always at the same time as an end" (Kant, 1903, p. 429, italics added).

11. The connection between freedom and the idea of humanity as an end is further developed in the lectures on natural right that Kant gave in the autumn of 1784, at exactly the time he was writing the *Groundwork of the Metaphysics of Morals* (in particular, see Kant, 1974, p. 1321).

12. For an extensive study on qualitative freedom, with particular regard to Kant, see Dierksmeier (2007).

13. Marx uses the German term "Reichtum" (Marx, 1844, *Drittes Manuskript*, §2. *Privateigentum und Kommunismus*), which is usually translated as "wealth." However, since Marx intention was to give it a different meaning from the prevailing political-economic one, here I will translate it as "richness."

14. The notion of "human development" has been introduced by the *United Nations Human Development Reports*, which take the CA as their theoretical framework.

## Bibliography

Andrews, K. (ed.), *Ethics in Practice: Managing the Moral Corporation*, (Boston: Harvard Business School Press, 1989).

Aristotle, *Nichomachean Ethics*, translated by D. Ross, revised by J.L. Ackrill and J.O. Urmson, (Oxford: Oxford University Press, 1980).

Collier J. and R. Esteban, "Governance in the Participative Organisation: Freedom, Creativity and Ethics", *Journal of Business Ethics* 21(2/3) (1999) 173–188.

Cooper, J.M., *Reason and Human Good in Aristotle*, (Cambridge, Mass.: Harvard University Press, 1975)

Cornelius, N., *Building Workplace Equality: Ethics, Diversity and Inclusion*, (London: Thomson International Business Press, 2002).

Cornelius, N. and S. Gagnon, "From ethics by proxy to ethics in action: new approaches to understanding ethics and HRM", *Business Ethics: A European Review* 8(4) (1999) 225–235.

Cornelius, N. and S. Gagnon, "Re-examining workplace equality: the capabilities approach", *Human Resource Management Journal* 10(4) (2000) 68–87.

Cornelius, N. and S. Gagnon, "From equal opportunities to managing diversity to capabilities: a new theory of workplace equality?", in N. Cornelius (ed.) *Equality, Diversity and Inclusion in Work Organizations* (Thomson International Business Press, London, 2002) 13–58.

Cornelius, N. and S. Gagnon, "Still bearing the mark of Cain? Ethics and inequality measurement", *Business Ethics: A European Review* 13(1) (2004) 26–40.

Cornelius N., Todres M., Janjuha-Jivraj S., Woods A., Wallace J., "Corporate Social Responsibility and the Social Enterprise", *Journal of Business Ethics 81* (2) (2008) 355–370.

Davis, J.B, *The Theory of the Individual in Economics*, (Routledge, London, 2003).

Dierksmeier, C., "Quantitative oder qualitative Freiheit?", in P. Becchi et. al (hrsg.), *Nationen und Gerechtigkeit*, Rechtsphilosophische Hefte; Beiträge zur Rechtswissenschaft, Philosophie und Politik, Band 12, (Frankfurt a.M.-Berlin-Bern-Bruxelles-New York-Oxford-Wien: Peter Lang, 2007).

Giovanola, B., "Personhood and Human Richness. Good and Well-Being in the Capability Approach and Beyond", *Review of Social Economy* 63(2) (2005) 249–267.

Giovanola, B., "Sulla capacità di essere felici: riflessioni su ricchezza, benessere e libertà a partire dal *capability approach*", *Meridiana* 56 (2007) 83–104.

Giovanola, B., "Re-Thinking the Anthropological and Ethical Foundation of Economics and Business: Human Richness and Capabilities Enhancement", *Journal of Business Ethics*, 88 (2009) 431–444.

Hausman, D.M. and M.S. McPherson, *Economic Analysis, Moral Philosophy, and Public Policy*, 2nd edition of *Economic Analysis and Moral Philosophy*, (Cambridge – New York: Cambridge University Press 2006).

Hirsch, F., *Social Limits to Growth*, (Cambridge, Mass: Harvard University Press, 1976).

Kahneman, D. and A. Tversky: 1979, "Prospect Theory: An Analysis of Decision under Risk", *Econometrica* 47(2), 263–291.

Kahneman D., Slovic P., and A. Tversky (eds.): 1982, *Judgment Under Uncertainty: Heuristics and Biases* (Cambridge University Press, New York).

Kahneman, D. and A. Tversky (eds.), *Choices, Values and Frames* (Cambridge: Cambridge University Press, 2000).

Kant, I.: 1903, *Grundlegung zur Metaphysik der Sitten* [1785], in *Kant's gesammelte Schriften*, Abteilung I: *Werke*, Band 4 (hrsg. von der Königlich Preussischen Akademie der Wissenschaften, Berlin; subsequently ed. by de Gruyter, Berlin) [English translation by Th. Kingsmill Abbott, edited with revisions by L. Denis, *Groundwork for the metaphysics of morals*, Broadview Press, Orchard Park, NY, 2005].

Kant, I.: 1974, *Vorlesung über Moralphilosophie*, in *Kant's gesammelte Schriften*, Abteilung IV: *Vorlesungen*, Band 27 (hrsg. von der Königlich Preussischen Akademie der Wissenschaften, Berlin; subsequently ed. by de Gruyter, Berlin).

Marx, K.: 1844, "Ökonomisch-Philosophische Manüskripte aus dem Jahre 1844", in *Marx-Engels Werke* (MEW), Ergänzungsband I (Dietz Verlag, Berlin, 1968) 465–588.

Melé, D., "The Challenge of Humanistic Management", *Journal of Business Ethics* 44 (2003) 77–88.

Nussbaum, M., *The Fragility of Goodness: Luck and Ethics in Greek Tragedy and Philosophy*, (Cambridge University Press, Cambridge, 1986).

Nussbaum, M., "Nature, Function and Capability: Aristotle on Political Distribution", *Oxford Studies in Ancient Philosophy*, Supplement, (1988) 145–184.

Nussbaum, M., "Aristotelian Social Democracy", in R.B. Douglass, G. Mara, H. Richardson (eds.), *Liberalism and the Good*, (New York: Routledge, 1990), 203–252.

Nussbaum, M., "Non-Relative Virtues: an Aristotelian Approach", in M. Nussbaum and A. Sen (eds.), *The Quality of Life*, (Oxford: Clarendon Press, 1993) 242–269.

Nussbaum, M., "Aristotle on Human Nature and the Foundations of Ethics", in J.E.J. Altham, R. Harrison (eds), *World, Mind and Ethics: Essays on the Ethical Philosophy of Bernard Williams*, (Cambridge: Cambridge University Press, 1995) 86–131

Nussbaum, M., *Women and Human Development: The Capabilities Approach*, (Cambridge: Cambridge University Press, 2000).

Nussbaum, M., *Frontiers of Justice: Disability, Nationality, Species Membership*, (Cambridge, Mass.: Harvard University Press, 2006).

Nussbaum, M. and A. Sen:, "Internal Criticism and Indian Rationalist Traditions", in M. Krausz (ed.), *Relativism: Interpretation and Confrontation*, (Notre Dame, Ind.: University of Notre Dame Press, 1988).

Robeyns, I., "The Capability Approach – A Theoretical Survey", *Journal of Human Development* 6(1), (2005) 93–114.

Sen, A., "Rational Fools", *Philosophy and Public Affairs* 6, (1977) 317–344.

Sen, A., "Equality of what?", in A. Sen (ed.), *Choice, Welfare and Measurement* (Oxford: Blackwell, 1980) 353–369

Sen, A., "Well-Being, Agency, and Freedom. The Dewey Lectures 1984", *The Journal of Philosophy* 82, (1985) 169–221.

Sen, A., *On Ethics and Economics*, (Oxford: Blackwell, 1987a).

Sen, A., *The Standard of Living: The Tanner Lectures 1985*, ed.G. Hawthorn (Cambridge: Cambridge University Press, 1987b).

Sen, A., "Capability and Well-Being", in M. Nussbaum and A. Sen (eds.), *The Quality of Life* (Oxford: Clarendon Press 1993) 30–53.

Sen, A., *Development as Freedom*, (Oxford: Oxford University Press, 1999a).

Sen, A., *Reason before Identity*, (Oxford: Oxford University Press, 1999b).

Sen, A., *Rationality and Freedom*, (Cambridge, Mass.: Harvard University Press, 2002).

Sen, A., "Elements of a Theory of Human Rights", *Philosophy and Public Affairs* 32(4) (2004) 315–56.

Sen, A., "Human Rights and Capabilities", *Journal of Human Development* 6(2) (2005a) 151–66.

Sen, A., "Why Exactly is Commitment Important for Rationality?", *Economics and Philosophy* 21(1) (2005b) 5–14.

Sen, A.:, "La felicità è importante ma altre cose lo sono di più", in L. Bruni, P.L. Porta (eds), *Felicità e libertà. Economia e benessere in prospettiva relazionale* (Guerini e Associati, Milano, 2006) 39–58.

Sen A., *The Idea of Justice* (Cambridge, Mass.: Harvard University Press, 2009).

Sen, A., and B. Williams (eds), *Utilitarianism and Beyond* (Cambridge: Cambridge University Press, 1982).

Simon, H.A., *Models of Bounded Rationality*, vol. 1, 2 (Cambridge, Mass.: MIT Press, 1982).

Simon, H.A., *Models of Bounded Rationality*, vol. 3 (Cambridge, Mass.: MIT Press, 1997).

Simon, H.A., "Bounded Rationality in Social Sciences: Today and Tomorrow", *Mind & Society* 1(1) (2000) 25–41.

Slovic P., Finucane M., Peters E., and D. MacGregor:, "The Affect Heuristic", in T. Gilovich, D. Griffin, D. Kahneman (eds), *Heuristic and Biases: The Psychology of Intuitive Thought* (Cambridge – New York: Cambridge University Press, 2002) 397–420.

Vogt C. P., "Maximizing Human Potential: Capabilities Theory and the Professional Work Environment", *Journal of Business Ethics* 58, (2005) 111–123.

# 11
# Solomon on the Role of Virtue Ethics in Business

*Ulrike Kirchengast*

The aim of this chapter is to outline the main tenets of the Robert C. Solomon's modern virtue ethics. After a short explication of virtue ethics, I reconstruct the ideas of the "business-oriented" virtue theorist Robert C. Solomon and discuss how they advance a more humane understanding of the business world and how they help improve the often tense relationship between business and the rest of society.

## 11.1 Modern virtue ethics in the twentieth century

### 11.1.1 The origin of modern virtue ethics

While the term "virtue ethics" was not coined until the twentieth century, the underlying idea has been prominent in Western philosophy since the fifth century B. C.[1] The two groups of ethical theory, whose disadvantages modern virtue ethics is meant to overcome, are products of the modern era: "Deontological ethics" is any form of ethics of the Kantian type that relies heavily on the notion of duties, whereas "consequentialism" is the umbrella term[2] for theories that focus on the consequences of acts (act-utilitarianism being an example).

While in deontological and consequentialist theories the rightness/goodness of acts is the main matter of concern, virtue ethics lays its stress on the goodness of the agent: It is agent-based. For a virtue ethicist, the question is not "What shall I do?" but "How should I live?" Confining morality to the evaluation of acts is, according to virtue ethics, a vain enterprise, because it rests on an inaccurate view of what morality really is. Within the framework of virtue ethics, morality is, rather, (part of) the art of living.

The starting point of modern virtue ethics is the seminal paper "Modern Moral Philosophy" by G. E. M. Anscombe[3], which can be considered "the original call for a return to Aristotelian ethics." The first paragraph of this paper already indicates the topics that are of greatest importance for virtue ethics: Anscombe first proposes that doing moral philosophy should be put aside until we have an adequate philosophy of psychology. In accordance with this, virtue ethicists aim at an ethics which accounts for the psychological reality of mankind (it is this argument that is often turned against them by their critics, who hold that virtue ethics is actually utterly unrealistic and rests on false presuppositions about the nature of the human psyche). Secondly, Anscombe calls for the abandonment of concepts that are often considered to be the core concepts of moral philosophy, namely the concepts of moral obligation, moral duty, that is, the moral *ought*. In her eyes these are nothing but remnants of an earlier conception of ethics, based on divine law and defunct without it. Accordingly, another distinctive feature of virtue ethics is its strong opposition to the rule-centeredness of deontological ethics.

Later in the paper Anscombe suggests that it might be possible to "discard the term 'moral ought', and simply return to the ordinary 'ought'"[4], meaning that it might be better simply to ask oneself whether, for example, being just is necessary for a man to live a good life *qua* man. As she admits, "philosophically there is a huge gap, at present unfillable as far as we are concerned, which needs to be filled by an account of human nature, human action, the type of characteristic a virtue is, and above all of human 'flourishing'."[5] Trying to fill this gap, by proposing viable conceptions of human nature and flourishing, as well as finding out what makes a given character trait a virtue, has been the work of virtue ethicists ever since.

Quite notable in "Modern Moral Philosophy" is Anscombe's repeated reference to Ancient ethics, especially to Aristotle, and her emphasis on how very different it is from modern approaches. Consequently, Neo-Aristotelianism has become the most widely known version of virtue ethics; in fact, virtue ethics is sometimes even taken to be synonymous with Neo-Aristotelianism. Not all modern virtue ethicists are Neo-Aristotelians[6], and, furthermore, it is important to note that Neo-Aristotelianism must not be mistaken for a simple and uncritical recapitulation of Aristotle's philosophy. As its prominent defender Rosalind Hursthouse has stressed, Neo-Aristotelianism is a distinctively modern project, because it addresses issues Aristotle (as well as the other philosophers of antiquity) was not concerned about at all. "Indeed, one might well say that he was not concerned with providing a rational foundation for ethics; the project of trying to show how we are to get ethical judgments validated by considerations of human nature is itself a distinctively modern one."[7]

### 11.1.2 Some core concepts of virtue ethics

"A *virtue* is a good quality of character, more specifically a disposition to respond to, or acknowledge, items within its field or fields in an excellent or good enough way."[8] An agent acts virtuously only if he is properly motivated, that is, he acts for the right reasons, or in other words "for the sake of the noble." For example, a person who gave a big sum of money to a charity only because she wanted to appear in the newspaper, without any concern for the recipients, would not be regarded virtuous on this account. Michael Stocker claimed that modern ethical theories neglect or even impede a harmony between the agent's motives and reasons, values and justifications. The result of this neglect is an "ethical schizophrenia" that bars the agent from leading a good life.[9] Robert Solomon follows a similar line of argument when he argues that anybody who draws a distinction between "who I really am" and "the person I am on the job" is in bad faith and alienates himself from the possibility of happiness.[10]

Another necessary condition for the presence of virtue is that the act be accompanied by the right emotions, and a proper training of the emotions is an integral part of advancing virtue.[11] This is why young people generally cannot be virtuous in the strict sense of the term:[12] virtue is the result of habituation, that is, a process which begins with mere imitation of virtuous acts; along with the development of reason, the capacity to choose increases gradually. Virtue ethics calls for a diachronic perspective because for the evaluation *of an act* knowledge about the corresponding motives and the person's character as a whole is indispensable. Habituation not only needs time, but also the right kind of upbringing, as Aristotle most famously noted; and one needs proper role models: Virtue is a product of the community, which shows the irreconcilability of virtue ethics with any anthropological views that describe the person principally as an individual who afterwards enters– more or less voluntarily – into contractual relations. The process of acquiring virtue is comparable to acquiring a practical skill; nevertheless, "This in no way implies, it should be stressed, that virtue is going to be in all ways like a skill – clearly in some ways it is quite different."[13] The true nature of a virtue – for example whether it should best be seen as a skill or perhaps as knowledge – is a subject of discussion, but its classification as a character trait is commonly accepted. Similarly, Robert Solomon defines virtue as a beneficial character trait. The definition of a good action is derived from the goodness of the agent, as provided by Rosalind Hursthouse: An action is right exactly when it is identical to "what a virtuous agent would characteristically (acting in character) do in the circumstances."[14] In the Neo-Aristotelian version of virtue ethics, the definition reads "A virtue is a character trait a human being needs for *eudaimonia*, that is to flourish or live well."[15]

### 11.1.3   Some criticisms of virtue ethics

Of course, defining a virtue by reference to the community in which it operates has provoked quite serious criticism against virtue ethics, saying, in essence, that it would inevitably collapse into relativism and had no arguments against a pathological society that condoned the vilest practices within it and the corresponding "virtues" (Nazi society is an often-cited example). Aristotle's own community, resting on the institution of slavery and conceding full civil rights only to a minority of males, was also, in part, an evil community of this type. Solomon acknowledges this objection and seeks to refute it by resorting to the idea that "there is such a thing as the human community, and there are certain foundations to our behavior in what is called 'human nature.' It is with reference to these large parameters that one can without intellectual humility criticize fascism and human rights abuses as well as those abuses of the multinational business community that do not seem to be easily contained within the bounds of a single society."[16]

Virtue ethics presents a form of ethical naturalism: In order to know what a good human being is, one needs to know what constitutes the nature of a typical human being. While the advocacy of some kind of naturalism certainly has its appeal, it will nevertheless be confronted with the accusation of naturalistic fallacy. When trying to find some common values in "human nature," we need to be extremely cautious, or we are risk arriving at conclusions that are unacceptable from the outset. This can be seen in Aristotle, who, as is generally known, grounded his defense of slavery on an appeal to human nature. Drawing an analogy between a good human being and a good exemplar of any other species[17] runs a particularly strong risk of developing into a calamitous biologism.[18] There is, after all, a substantial difference between humans and all other animals: The range of behavioral patterns in animals is very narrow and mostly unchangeable and an animal does not have the choice of adopting a "lifestyle" different than the one established in its genes (making it quite easy to detect if a particular individual of a species is "defective"), but the nature of a human being consists precisely in the fact that it can choose from a wide variety of lifestyles.[19] "Having a choice" is just another way of saying that humans are endowed with rationality, and virtuous behavior is necessarily a result of using one's practical rationality. From the point of view of virtue ethics, rationality does not just comprise the ability to find the best means for achieving any given end, but is, rather, the ability to choose the right ends. Virtue is not the mere acquisition of values and customs found in one's society, but involves an extensive reflection upon and, if necessary, a transformation of those conventions.

To summarize: Virtue ethics, set within a broad taxonomy of ethical theories, can be seen as a third major approach alongside deontology and consequentialism, namely a nonconsequentialist teleological theory. Traditionally, moral theories were often categorized as either deontological or teleological. A deontological theory takes the concept of the right as its primary concept and defines the good in terms of the right. Teleological theories, on the other hand, take the good as primary and define the right as that which maximizes the good. Obviously, an ethics like Aristotle's does not fit properly into this scheme: Aristotelian virtue is not defined as a state that tends to promote some independently definable good; Aristotelian ethics is therefore not a consequentialist theory, but is, nevertheless, teleological.[20]

## 11.2   Robert Solomon's virtue ethics of business

### 11.2.1   Solomon's background and the origins of his business ethics

Robert C. Solomon (1942–2007) was a professor at the University of Texas at Austin who specialized in Continental Philosophy, the theory of the emotions and business ethics. According to a fellow philosopher, he was interested in philosophical questions about the meaning of life "that were not considered 'serious' if you were 'trained' in an analytic philosophy department in the 1960s and 1970s."[21] In this spirit, Solomon argues for a conception of the emotions which he calls "rational Romanticism," and his core thesis is that emotions are judgments rather than blind or irrational forces that victimize us.[22] This view seems akin to Sartre's "Sketch for a Theory of the Emotions"; Solomon's Aristotelian approach to business ethics begins with the idea that it is individual virtue and integrity that counts[23], and he repeatedly insists that the existential unity of responsibility and concern is and remains the individual.[24] It is therefore a core argument not only of Solomon but also of other virtue ethicists that it is the individual good life that counts; they do not dismiss the concept of the individual as such, but only what they perceive to be the false concept of personality promoted by "atomic individualism."[25] From the viewpoint of virtue ethics, the idea that we are, first of all, individuals, who then enter into various agreements with each other, represents a mistaken anthropology.

The emotions of care and compassion play a substantial role among Solomon's business virtues, and in this respect he admits to being influenced by the moral sentimentalists, most notably Adam Smith[26], whose "Theory of Moral Sentiments" he seems to regard more highly than his "Wealth of Nations." While he shows approval for this work too, he also directs a harsh attack at views that display Smith solely as an advocate of the free market. His cognitive account of emotions, together with his upgrading of certain emotions to the status of virtues, is a specialty of Solomon's theory, because the right emotions are usually thought of as a constitutive aspect of virtue, but not as virtues in themselves.

Our contemporary thinking about business is deeply flawed, according to Solomon, being based on a misinterpretation of Adam Smith's classic work *The Wealth of Nations* that lays too much weight on his most widely known slogans "free enterprise" and "the invisible hand," and so loses sight of what Smith really had in mind when he contended that the free pursuit of everyone's self-interest would in the end increase public prosperity.[27]

### 11.2.1.1    *The division of business ethics into three branches*

Although his fundamental uneasiness concerning the relationship between business and ethics has considerably reduced over the last decades, there are several reasons why Solomon is convinced of the necessity of a new approach to the subject. He draws a useful distinction between three branches of business ethics (on the micro-, meso-, and macro-level):[28] Business ethics on the micro-level focuses mainly on the concepts and values that define individual and role behavior. It has been substantially neglected in favor of macro-business ethics, that is, questions of public policy about government regulations and the propriety of government intervention (for example, in failing industries and affirmative action programs), and in very general business practices and programs such as pollution control, puffery and deceitfulness in advertising, and the social responsibilities of companies to the communities in which they are set.

In between the individual as the micro unit and the whole society as the macro unit there stands as an integral or meso-unit the corporation.

The corporation is best viewed as a community of people working together to accomplish a common goal, their responsibilities being at least in part defined by their roles in that community. Accordingly, Solomon's objective is an ethics for the individual in his/her corporation. It must not be forgotten, however, that every individual is not only a member of the corporation, but also a member of a larger community, and business ethics has to account for this dual citizenship. The appealing distinctiveness of Solomon's approach is his insistence on this integrating function of ethics: What he wants to avoid is the occurrence of any substantial gap between personal values within business and private life. He in no way wants to deny the importance of the aforementioned problems of public policy, but he demonstrates that a business ethics considering mainly these questions is of little use for the multitude of ordinary people working in business, who all face different problems in their daily work routines.

### 11.2.2   Becoming aware of dehumanizing myths surrounding the business world

Solomon therefore puts forward a "better way to think about business," starting with a rejection of several detrimental myths about business. What all these myths have in common is an alienating effect on the self-concept of people working in business, as well as a distorted image of business within the rest of society. Accordingly, the misguided self-image of business people leads to false beliefs about what it means to lead a good, productive life and about the requirements for being successful. Solomon denounces the "dehumanizing language" of economics because it often conceals the fact that business is, in reality, a genuinely human enterprise.[29] First of all he highlights the fact that every profession uses some self-glorifying vocabulary which is supposed to emphasize the good its members contribute to society. For example, politicians speak of "serving the state" as the ultimate purpose of their activity, lawyers point out that they "defend the rights of their clients," and so on. Interestingly, there is no such flattering self-description in the realm of business. It seems generally recognized that the only aim of businessmen and women is making as much money as they can, that is, serving their own self-interest exclusively, while self-interest here is understood in a way that Solomon does not endorse, namely in the sense of being opposed to the interests of others. The business world is often referred to as a battle, a Darwinian struggle to survive, or a jungle where everyone fights against everyone else, in short: a Hobbesian war of all against all. Hence, the corresponding virtues are warlike virtues such as ruthlessness, and courses of action are typically called "plans of attack," "battle strategies," and "campaigns." All this militaristic speech inevitably tends to confirm the self-concepts of the people involved, and it is no wonder that their actions follow accordingly. Solomon insists these are mistaken, and above all, extremely impoverished, ideas about the nature of business and also of the nature of human beings. In his view, business is a fundamentally cooperative activity, and the desire for mutual cooperation is an essential part of human nature.

Another one among the so-called "macho metaphors of business" is the "machine metaphor," which stems from the eighteenth century and, despite being slightly better than the war metaphors, has also had a considerably dehumanizing effect on business-related self-concepts. This semantic field has the advantage that it stresses the importance of cooperation within companies (after all, every employee is nothing but a cog in a big machine, which itself is a cog in an even greater machine, namely the national economy, which is again part of the global economy), but it remains a limited notion of cooperation, because one of its most weighty and threatening implications is the idea that every human being is as replaceable as a part of a machine.

Another business myth is associated with the already mentioned view that greed is good, which is based on a biased reading of the work of Adam Smith. It is often falsely assumed that people are motivated *solely* by their desire for profits. Again, Solomon contends that this is a mistaken picture of human nature. Nevertheless he admits that the belief that the justifiability or even naturalness of making money is the only motive or purpose of work is very widespread, and he calls this phenomenon "abstract greed." The phenomenon of abstract greed overshadows the fact that business is not in the first place a means to making money at any price, but a human practice that contributes to the public good as well as providing the people involved in it with meaning and satisfaction.

Of special relevance within Solomon's framework is his criticism of the "game metaphor." Speaking of business in terms of a game does have its good sides, as he concedes. The concept of a game conveys a whole range of positive associations such as enjoyment, voluntariness, thrill, challenge, and the rules of "fair play." Games are also paradigmatic practices, and in this respect can be useful to illuminate the structure of business, which is also a practice, as will be shown in the following section. But the game metaphor leaves out so many essential features of business that the idea of business it produces is, again, distorted. Solomon rightly complains "that it makes business too self-enclosed, too merely coincidentally connected with productivity, service, and prosperity."[30] Most importantly, business for most people is not something to be played voluntarily for the challenge and the excitement. Unlike in games, it is impossible to draw a line between who is in and out of business, who is the "player" and who is the "spectator." Almost everybody in a given society is somehow affected by the decisions of at least the largest corporations, as is most obvious when whole industries seem to collapse and threaten to drag down with them even the state itself. "Business becomes a game when it loses its essential aim, not just to make money but to provide essential goods and services and bring about a general and not a selfish prosperity. Business becomes a game when it takes on make-believe goals and purposes and when it pretends that it is an activity undertaken solely for its own sake."[31]

### 11.2.3 What business really is – the humane nature of business

Alluding to its etymology (busy/ness), Solomon points out that business is above all an activity, being occupied rather than making money as such. Contrary to the myths he criticizes, it is a social activity that presupposes at least two partners who share a common understanding of the basic relevant customs (how to bargain, how to pay) and – most important in the present context – it also presupposes a set of basic virtues such as honesty and trustworthiness. In other words, business is a practice, and like every practice it has its goals, rules, boundaries, and purpose. The difference between goal and purpose is shown using the example of a football game. Its goal is to carry the ball across the opponent's goal line, while it can have various purposes, such as enjoying a Sunday afternoon with one's friends, keeping in shape, or making money. Obviously the goal is inherent to the practice, whereas the purpose depends on the intention of its participants. The purpose of a practice is the reason for engaging in it. Basically Solomon maintains that dehumanizing business myths rest on false assumptions about what the purpose of business really is. An often overlooked humanistic aspect of business is that it – viewed correctly – contributes substantially to the flourishing of the people involved. A job is not only a source of income, but equally important, a source of self-esteem, contentment, and meaning for many people. Hardly anybody wants to be reduced to a set of work-related skills; people in some hard-to-define but inalienable sense insist that they be hired "for themselves" and "as a whole person" and not just as someone who can program a computer or run a company. Needless to say, a great deal of self-esteem comes from one's functional accomplishments, but "the most important feature of almost any job – and typically the most important reason why someone loves or hates what they do – is the success or failure of an individual to fit in with others, 'the people I work with.' "[32] Solomon approvingly cites Adam Smith's thesis that among the things we want most in our lives is being well-regarded by others. From this follows the fact that our self-interest is intimately tied up with the interests of others. The commonplace dichotomy of self-interest and altruism should thus be abandoned.

In order to accommodate the fundamentally humane nature of business practice, Solomon proposes that the metaphor of "corporate culture" replace the dehumanizing metaphors.[33] Although this concept is already quite dominant and is sometimes considered a mere "fad," it is useful in underlining the social nature of business. The features that make it appropriate to conceive of business as a culture are manifold: A culture is a community with a sense of togetherness, grounded on a set of established practices, and with at least a minimal shared outlook on life. Every culture possesses its rules and rituals, its particular modes of dress and behavior. Most important for the present purpose is of course the fact that every culture has its ethics, the rules that hold the society together and protect it from itself. However, a corporation is not just a culture on its own, but is itself a citizen of a larger culture, and it must therefore always be aware of the various effects it has on society as a whole. Solomon strongly resists the definition of the corporation as being nothing more than a legal entity defined in terms of obligations to its stockholders whose only "social responsibility" is to increase its profits.[34] According to his firm conviction, the corporation must be considered a morally responsible agent, and this is perhaps the most salient facet of Solomon's Aristotelian business ethics. The conception of the corporation as a culture puts an end to questions like "Where do corporate values come from?" and "How can corporations be socially responsible?"[35]

### 11.2.4   The main tenets of Solomon's Aristotelian theory

While Solomon does not agree with Aristotle on all points,[36] he shares his suspicion of purely financial thinking: "The bottom line of the Aristotelian approach to business ethics is that we have to get away from bottom-line thinking and conceive of business as an essential part of the good life."[37] Solomon defines six parameters[38] or dimensions[39] that matter for the ethics and success of business: community, excellence, membership/role identity, integrity, judgment (*phronesis*), and *holism*.

### 11.2.4.1 *Community, excellence, and membership*

The concept of community is of crucial importance in Solomon's as in any Aristotelian ethics, and it can easily be recognized that most of the other parameters cited are based upon, or rather derived from, this concept. The starting point is the idea that we are first and foremost members of organized groups, with common histories and established practices governing all aspects of our lives. Our personality can evolve only on this fundamental precondition delivered by our society, and individuality is only thinkable in the context of a greater community: It is socially constituted and socially situated. "The concept of the virtues provides the conceptual linkage between the individual and his or her society. A virtue is a pervasive trait of character that allows one to 'fit into' a particular society and to excel in it."[40]

The second and third parameters of Solomon's ethics, excellence and membership/role identity, are derived from and tightly interwoven with the basic dimension of community. His discussion of excellence (which is another common translation for the Greek word for virtue, *arête*), has two dimensions: First, it is widely acknowledged in business that it is excellence (or quality) which is the key to success: Business is supposed to be a meritocracy; yet the notion of merit is quite ambiguous. Being linked to the "business myths" Solomon so emphatically attacks, merit could equally well mean "making as much money as possible, whatever the price," in which case an overcompetitive, ruthless manager would be considered the one who has earned the greatest merits. For Solomon, on the contrary, merit and excellence, respectively, are synonyms for "doing one's best," but always within a holistic understanding of the business context that he proposes. Doing good work certainly remains a central part of business excellence in Solomon's theory, and he warns of the danger of a well-known, but sad fact: that in today's business, hard work often is not rewarded, while "schmoozing" and "going along to get along" are far more promising paths to success. A corporate climate like this not only lacks the core virtue of business – justice – it is also the ideal environment for the nurturing of vices and undermining forces such as envy and resentment.

It is noteworthy that Solomon advocates a broader range of virtues than those that are usually considered to be "moral virtues" in the strict sense, an aspect he directly adopts from Aristotle, who also includes wit and a good sense of humor in his list of the virtues. These congenial virtues contribute a lot to an overall good atmosphere at the workplace, which is important not only for productivity but also for what Solomon calls the purpose (as opposed to the mere goal) of work: living a good, flourishing life.

Solomon's request for the maintenance of a well-understood meritocracy should not be misunderstood as meaning mere incentives: Although merit deserves its reward, merit does not mean performance for reward and for no other reason. The idea of excellence is, according to Solomon, belied "by those who work 'just to make a living' and by businesses that (as so many annual reports tiresomely insist) aim solely at improving stockholder value and the bottom line. True, good products and innovative marketing do (or should) result in improving stockholder value and the bottom line, but good products and innovative marketing require their own attention, and not merely as means."[41] This thought leads on to the third dimension of Aristotelian business ethics, namely, the concept of membership or role identity. This is again intimately related to the notion of community, and essentially amounts to the idea that an employee develops his or her personal identity largely through the organizations in which he or she works.[42] Therefore it is important to choose the "right corporation," which is not the one which promises the highest income but the one that offers the best environment for a fulfilling life. Membership means also that individual duties and virtues are defined by the role an individual plays in the corporation. Certain virtues are expected from every employee who joins a company and thereby commits him or herself to loyalty towards the employer. But some virtues are role-sensitive: A human resource manager may need other virtues than an accountant.

### 11.2.4.2 Integrity, judgment, and holism

Integrity, the fourth parameter of Solomon's ethics, can be best understood as a version of the well-known doctrine of the unity of virtues. Rather than being a single virtue itself, integrity "is a complex of virtues, the virtues working together to form a coherent character, an identifiable and trustworthy personality." Integrity is not to be conflated with honesty or a simple not-giving-in (rejecting unethical orders or refusing a bribe). It often comprises active behavior as opposed to the such passive forms of resistance; the typical requirement for integrity is following the rules and practices that define the job (instead of allowing oneself to be distracted); only critical situations call for a show of integrity that is antithetical to one's assigned roles and duties. In each case, "integrity represents the integration of one's roles and responsibilities and the virtues defined by them." To this end, it is indispensable that one does not just follow the rules but makes them one's own. The possession of integrity is identical with being "true to oneself;" it amounts to a wholeness of the personality. Solomon illustrates his understanding of integrity by means of two examples of characters who lack it: the *opportunist* and the *chameleon*. He dismisses the possibility of the opportunist being in some sense true to himself because of his apparently consistent pursuit of a selfish purpose using the maxim "Do whatever it takes" and the modus operandi "Always keep your eyes open and your feet ready." To count as having integrity it is not enough to pursue any purpose by any means: The opportunist does not have respect for other people and uses them merely as his or her instruments, and this is why he or she is anything but virtuous. The chameleon is a person who does not have any purposes in life except to "fit in and do whatever seems to please other people." This example is especially remarkable as it shows quite plainly that there is no reason to suspect any excessive praise for conformism in virtue ethics. The virtuous man is not a conformist.[43] While the chameleon-like person sometimes appears to be a model of integrity, this lasts only as long as there are no disagreements among his superiors, for if this happens, his lack of principle will suddenly be revealed.

The fifth parameter on Solomon's list is the competence of practical reason which Aristotle called *phronesis*: the capacity of judgment. This is in no way a mechanical decision-procedure that simply consists in the application of general principles to particular situations; instead, it requires the ability to balance and weigh competing concerns and come to a "fair" conclusion. The development of good judgment needs correct upbringing, and, above all, enough time.[44] Judgment is relevant in the business world because one of the great arts of management is that of decision-making. Judgment is inseparably connected with the virtue Solomon specifies as the ultimate virtue of business – justice.[45] His discussion of justice shows most clearly the difficulties of judgment, and it soon becomes obvious that it is indeed impossible to find a single, all-embracing notion of justice. In a very Aristotelian manner Solomon first describes it as "the fact and perception that all members of the organization and everyone connected with it are 'getting their due'."[46] Besides being paid properly and rewarded with bonuses and promotions this requires "that one is recognized and respected for what one is, that one is not neglected or short-changed, that one is not exploited or abused." The problem with all this is the lack of any reliable procedure for the just fulfilment of requirements as simple as "equal work, equal pay." Because people are different, it is not really possible to arrive at a common standard for what exactly represents equal work. For examples, it is difficult to determine who has contributed what to team-work or whether it is the effort or the results that should count more. Should somebody who is successful in a boom be rewarded more than someone who manages to survive in a time of crisis? Justice has several dimensions, the most important being merit and equality, which are not fully reconcilable. Though the two are connected, in that equality can be defined as "of equal merit," equality is basically grounded in the idea that all human beings are the same. "Thus there is the familiar argument that everyone's needs and interests should be taken equally seriously, whatever their abilities or accomplishments."[47] It is evident that this sense of justice undermines much of what Solomon said earlier about justice in business: that everybody should be properly rewarded. Consequently it is necessary to some extent to follow Aristotle in his postulate that "equals should be treated as equals; unequals should be treated unequally." It is for right judgment to make a just decision by taking into account and weighing all dimensions relevant to the present context.

*Holism* – the sixth parameter of Solomon's theory – basically comprises a summary of his main tenets, foremost of which is the necessity of resisting the tendency to isolate our business or professional roles from the rest of our lives. "The good life may have many facets, but they are facets and not mere components, much less isolated aspects despite the tiresome emphasis on tasks, techniques and 'objectives,' that a manager's primary and ultimate concern is people."[48] The ideal of ethics, properly understood, is the integration of our roles, or at least their harmonization: Neither the personal nor the corporate should yield to the other. The notion of holism applied to corporations embraces the idea of obligations not only to stockholders, but also to stakeholders. Solomon condemns Friedman's contention that all corporate efforts to improve public life were "pure theft" and "unadulterated socialism." On the contrary, he argues, social responsibility is not just some random external obligations of corporations: "It is the very point of their existence."[49]

Finally, the concept of holism can be extended to encompass the global dimension of human society. This may appear illusory, and the global economy is far from recognizing that its ultimate purpose is to serve humanity, but Solomon's hope that overall goodness can be achieved by means of a bottom-up rather than top-down method may well be justified. "The Aristotelian approach to business ethics rather begins with the idea that it is individual virtue and integrity that counts: good corporate and social policy will follow: good corporate and social policy are both the preconditions and the result of careful cultivation and encouragement."[50]

### 11.2.4.3   A remark on "situationism"

Finally, it is worth addressing an obvious charge: that it may be impossible to maintain one's integrity when under pressure in an overwhelming situation. It is indeed difficult to imagine that many people would refuse unethical orders from their superiors, thereby risking the loss of their job. The thesis that the individual is "the victim of his situation" has been carried to extremes under the name of "situationism." Its advocates, the most famous of whom is Gilbert Harman[51], argue that character traits simply do not exist and that behavior is determined solely by the agent's situation.[52] Another line of argument endorsed by Harman is the claim that apparent observed regularities in behavior result from the fact that people tend to choose similar situations. Solomon acknowledges this, but interprets it (more realistically) in favor of his own character-based theory. But the fact that people, to a certain degree, choose their situations does not mean that an individual can resist all environmental pressure. It is therefore necessary to create a proper environment, which is, in turn, only possible with the joint efforts of many.

The fact that the environment – in our case the corporation as a whole – may well lead to an increase in bad character traits in its members can be shown by means of an example. This example shows how lack of practical judgment in management has a negative effect not only on employees but also on profitability. At present, large retail chains often steadily reduce the number of employees per shop, at the same time increasing pressure on the remaining employees to sell more than before. This is often combined with opening new stores and closing them again after a short period of time in order to have more expenses and consequently save taxes. These methods seem to produce short-term advantages, but in the longer term they have several negative effects: They severely reduce the motivation of the employees, because destructive feelings such as resentment and even anger towards the employer will probably develop. An atmosphere of uncertainty arises because people start asking themselves who will be the next to leave if the management calls for even more efficiency, so the atmosphere at work deteriorates rapidly, as mutual suspicion, fear, and envy increase. These factors may well lead to a decrease in sales, especially nowadays when most products can be purchased online: The remaining salespeople will have less time for conversations with customers and might treat them in a less friendly manner because of the constant time pressure they are exposed to. As customers often seek contact with salespeople because they hope to receive useful advice, when these expectations remain unfulfilled, even more people might resort to online shopping.

## 11.3   What can virtue ethics contribute to the creation of universally acknowledged values in the context of globalization?

Having read the above outline of Solomon's virtue ethics of business, readers may ask themselves whether his (or any virtue-oriented) approach could ever be useful within a global context. Given the increasing speed of economic as well as cultural globalization, it is necessary to find at least a common denominator in matters of ethics. This calls for a procedural approach to humanistic ethics, where shared values can be embraced by cultural traditions as diverse as African natural religions, Western monotheistic theologies, and Eastern spiritualism. While it is clear that this demand cannot reasonably cover all problems in detail, a fruitful process of dialogue is nevertheless possible, given a certain degree of openness on all sides. Virtue ethics has much to offer in order to start such a dialogue and keep it alive, because with its naturalistic idea of humans as rational beings whose natural way of life is communal, it might be of more appeal to proponents of other cultures than, for example, a moral theory grounded on an overly individualistic notion of humanity. Saying that virtue ethics "might have more appeal" to members of non-Western cultures does not mean that a single strictly defined canon of virtues should be imposed on them, but rather that its method (reasoning about the virtues that will contribute to the goodness of a human being *qua* rational animal) is one that is open to proposals differing from traditions other than Western philosophical positions. This can also be viewed in different attempts to incorporate non-Western virtue theories, such as those of Zhuang-Zi[53] or Confucius, into a broader conception of the virtues. Virtue ethics need not confine itself to looking at ancient Greek or other European virtue theories; its strength lies, among other things, in its conviction that all human beings share the same basic nature and accordingly have the same basic needs, so that a common set of values is in principle possible.

One might object to the virtue theorists' claim to know what is human goodness and *eudaimonia* that this is paternalistic, in that it restricts the range of good kinds of lives to an unacceptable degree. Even worse, the claim might be used to exclude those who do not conform to the "natural" good from moral approval, simply by imposing a single norm of what is natural and hence good, to which everybody must subscribe. This reservation may be felt by defenders of liberalism who maintain that everyone should pursue his or her own happiness. To this objection, modern virtue ethicists can again reply that it is their concern to establish not a rigid canon of virtues, but a morality that is drawn more from life than are rival theories. One might ask: Which strategy is more promising for the establishment and maintenance of an intercultural dialogue between people from different ethical backgrounds? Which principles of justice would a rational egoist consent to behind a veil of ignorance about his particular situation within society? These questions might push people to a level of abstraction that they are perhaps neither used to, nor willing to accept. It might be better to ask them about their conception of society and what it means for them to lead a good life as a human being. Undoubtedly a lot of differences will arise in this process, but that this procedure seems at least to be a better basis for mutual agreement.

In the effort of linking the concepts of virtue ethics to the problems of globalized business, one major problem seems to arise from Robert Solomon's theory: The theory seems to be too focused on individual virtue in individual companies, and one might ask oneself how a firm can succeed in being "a virtuous company" if all or many of its competitors are not virtuous and take advantage of their honesty, charity, and so forth. The claim might be that virtue is in reality not rewarding but is instead a hurdle to economic success. There are several ways to answer this charge: First, as Solomon himself claims in his writings, it is his declared aim to establish a theory of business ethics that mostly addresses ethical problems within the corporation, which he calls the molar unit as opposed to the micro unit of pure individuality and the macro unit of society as a whole. His tenet seems to be that there are different considerations to be taken into account, depending on the context, and this idea is worth considering further. Insisting upon the importance of virtues for every individual does not imply that on the broad level of international relations there is no use for norms and regulations that are based upon justice. After all, justice *is* a virtue, and a cardinal virtue at that. But the point is that ethics is not reducible to a principled theory of justice alone, nor to any other closed system. To think that we will ever reach an ethics that can address every possible dilemma would neglect the fact that human beings are often exposed to contingent circumstances they cannot influence by their rationality. Second, the process of establishing common values for international business is in dire need of people who are virtuous, or at least striving to be virtuous: The will to improve global morality is itself a manifestation of virtue. If we want corporations with higher ethical standards, we should put ethically sensitive people in executive positions.

Because virtues as traits of character are the outcome of a long process of training and personal development, it is clear that moral education will be of eminent importance within an ethics of virtue. Although this topic ranges far beyond the limits of business ethics in a narrow sense, in the context of today's globalized world the significance of good educational systems must not be neglected. One business-oriented suggestion is that ethics should be given more time in business curricula at universities. But this alone could never counteract the fact that university students are adults whose characters have already been shaped to a great extent by the education they have already received from their parents and their schools. Hence the importance of inducing ethics – or, better, philosophy in general – as an obligatory subject in schools: Young people should be encouraged to develop their critical faculties and their practical reasoning from the start, so that they become less vulnerable to the temptations of the business myths, still widespread, described above.

A strengthened focus on character formation within the whole of society should have the ultimate aim of achieving a better balanced view, first of how to lead a good life, second of the purpose of business and its proper place within society. With regard to the second of these, a notion like Solomon's which tries to give business its place within a broader conception of the good human life seems to be the best solution in the long run. The view of business not as an end in itself, but also as something conducive to the flourishing life of all stakeholders should not be lost sight of, and ideally it should be the particular duty of managers to be aware of their responsibilities, not only to their companies, but to society.

As noted before, the development of a virtuous character needs a proper upbringing with appropriate role models. This does not mean that it is only the offspring of truly virtuous parents who have the chance of leading a morally good life, but it is the case that a decent education is a great help. It is a salient feature of (most) virtue ethics that the development of a virtuous character is a never-ending process, and whether virtues or vices dominate is in fact influenced to a considerable extent by individual circumstances. In the narrower business context it should be added that people in leading positions should realize that they themselves serve as role models, and that their behavior is often imitated by those who want to climb the company hierarchy. Virtues like integrity, honesty, and awareness of one's own power are vital for people in high ranks if they are to maintain trust in the system as well as initiate processes of improvement.

A virtue ethics conception of business does not mean that a given company must always adopt public welfare as its primary aim[54]. Virtue can be needed to limit what counts as a morally legitimate mode of promoting the profits of one's corporation, and to illustrate this, a well-known example of global relevance may be considered: It is widely accepted that reducing costs is important for increasing the profits of a company. From that fact one can conclude that it is a manager's duty to keep costs as low as possible: one could also say that reducing costs is in fact a manifestation of virtue in the managerial role. However, this does mean it is necessary to transfer factories to countries with very low standards of human rights, where people can easily be exploited. Acting in this manner does not only harm people who have to work without social security, often dangerous conditions; it also harms societies in which many people lose their jobs (which leads to instability of the welfare state) and others live in constant fear of losing them. In order to solve this problem, several virtues are required on the part of many people who bear responsibilities: The managers of such international corporations have to manifest justice, benevolence, and loyalty in the right way. Fostering loyalty to one's own corporation should ideally not run contrary to the other virtues which forbid depriving others of their basic human rights. Some virtues, at first glance "old-fashioned," might be of particular relevance to global business and its improvement: First, the virtue of temperance, which is manifested in the insight that growth must not be maximized at the cost of human exploitation and the destruction of our natural habitat. Second, the virtue of humility is manifested in the acknowledgement that human life is vitally dependent on the natural world we live in, so we should not destroy the very basis for our survival in the pursuit of profits. It is hard to achieve these ends through legislative regulation alone; what is necessary is a constant effort to raise awareness and a sense of moral responsibility at all levels of society.

## 11.4 Conclusion

One of the greatest advantages of virtue ethics is its resistance to abstract conceptions of humanity that do not correspond to reality. It is not concerned with the fictional rational egoist nor the fictional utility-maximizer, but only the real person trying to be virtuous. True, in the imperative "Act as a virtuous person would typically act in the circumstances" there is also some fiction (as the truly virtuous person would in general not face the ordinary person's choices), but the virtues are certainly concepts that are more likely to be recognized as significant by most people. Virtue ethicists do acknowledge that there are not always "perfect solutions" in ethics: Outside our ethical outlook there is no independent foundation on which we could build a single correct ethical theory in one go. This ethical outlook is comparable to a boat: it can be rebuilt only from within, changing it plank by plank. This means that starting from the real human being and what is good for him is by far better than establishing fictional, abstract situations as models for ethics.

## Notes

1. See Annas, "Virtue Ethics", 515.
2. A term that was, incidentally, invented by G. E. M. Anscombe: See Mary Geach, "Introduction". In: *Human Life, Action and Ethics*, xvii.
3. See Anscombe, G. E. M. "Modern Moral Philosophy".
4. "Modern Moral Philosophy", 193.
5. Ibid.
6. See, for example, Swanton, who in her book *Virtue Ethics* explicitly rejects Neo-Aristotelian eudaimonism and rightly reminds us of the fact that virtue ethics is not a single homogenous theory but a genus comprising several approaches: "As a genus, virtue ethics should be thought of as analogous to consequentialism, as opposed to, say, hedonistic utilitarianism." (*Virtue Ethics*, 1).
7. Hursthouse, "On the Grounding of the Virtues in Human Nature", 263.
8. Swanton, *Virtue Ethics*, 19.
9. See Stocker, "The Schizophrenia of Modern Ethical Theories".
10. See Solomon, *Ethics and Excellence*, 161.
11. See Hursthouse, *On Virtue Ethics*, 113–120.
12. See Annas, "Being Virtuous and Doing the Right Thing", 7.
13. Annas, "Being Virtuous and Doing the Right Thing", 15.
14. Hursthouse, *On Virtue Ethics*, 28.
15. Ibid., 167.
16. Solomon, *Ethics and Excellence*, 206
17. See for example Foot, *Natural Goodness*.
18. See Hursthouse, "On the Grounding of the Virtues in Human Nature", 265.
19. This refers to human rationality as such rather than to external circumstances. Humans have the capacity to reflect and choose even if many are not able to fully exercise this capacity due to external circumstances.
20. See Watson, Gary. "On the Primacy of Character", 57.
21. Ciulla, Joanne B. "The Man with a Hole in his Heart", 186.
22. See Solomon, *The Passions.*, 15.

23. See Solomon, "Corporate Roles, Personal Virtues", 322.
24. See ibid., 320.
25. See Solomon, Ethics and Excellence, 74–86.
26. See Solomon, "The Moral Psychology of Business".
27. See Solomon, *Ethics and Excellence*, 85.
28. See "Corporate Roles, Personal Virtues", 319f.
29. See *Ethics and Excellence*, 22–94 and *A Better Way to think about Business*, 1–34.
30. Solomon, *Ethics and Excellence*, 31.
31. Ibid., 32.
32. See Solomon, *Ethics and Excellence*, 85–89 and *A Better Way to Think about Business*, 32.
33. See Solomon, *Ethics and Excellence*, 125–135 and *A Better Way to Think about Business*, 48–54.
34. As a example of this opinion he so deprecates he cites Friedman, "The Social Responsibility of Business is to Increase its Profits".
35. Solomon, *Ethics and Excellence*, 133.
36. See Solomon, *Ethics and Excellence*, 101–111.
37. Solomon, *A Better Way to think about Business*, xxiii.
38. See *Ethics and Excellence, 145–186*
39. See "Corporate Roles, Personal Virtues", 326–330
40. Solomon, *Ethics and Excellence*, 107.
41. Solomon, *Ethics and Excellence*, 157.
42. See ibid., 161.
43. Solomon, *Ethics and Excellence*, 191–2.
44. Solomon, *Ethics and Excellence*, 174.
45. See ibid., 231–241.
46. Ibid., 231.
47. Ibid., 234
48. Solomon, "Corporate Roles, Personal Virtues" , 331.
49. Solomon, *Ethics and Excellence*, 180.
50. Solomon, "Corporate Roles, Personal Virtues", 322.
51. See for example Harman, "Virtue Ethics meets Social Psychology".
52. See Solomon, "A Defense of Virtue Ethics in Business", 53.
53. See for example Higgins, "Negative Virtues: Zhuangzi's Wuwei".
54. See Swanton, "Role Ethics and Business Ethics", 219.

## Bibliography

Annas, Julia. "Virtue Ethics and Social Psychology". In: A Priori, Vol. 2/2003. http://www.stolaf.edu/people/huff/classes/GoodnEvil/Readings/julia_annas1.pdf, July 1, 2009
——. Virtue Ethics: What Kind of Naturalism? In: Gardiner, Stephen M., ed., *Virtue Ethics Old and New*, 11–29.
——. "Being Virtuous and Doing the Right Thing". Presidential Address to the Pacific Division meeting of the American Philosophical Association, March 2004. http://www.u.arizona.edu/~jannas/forth/rightactionvirtue.doc, July 1, 2009

Annas, Julia. "Virtue Ethics". In: Copp, David, ed., *The Oxford Handbook of Ethical Theory*, 515–536.

Anscombe, G. E. M. "Modern Moral Philosophy". In: Geach, Mary; Gormally, Luke, eds, *Human Life, Action and Ethics*, 169–194. [First published in *Philosophy* Vol. 33, No. 124/1958: 1–19].

Carr, Alfred. "Is Business Bluffing Ethical?". In: *Harvard Business Review*, Vol. 46, Issue 1/1968, 143–153.

Ciulla, Joanne B. "The Man with a Hole in his Heart: In Memory of Robert C. Solomon 1942–2007". In: *Business Ethics Quarterly*, Vol. 17, Issue 2/2007: 185–186.

Copp, David, ed., *The Oxford Handbook of Ethical Theory*. (Oxford, New York: Oxford University Press, 2006).

Crisp, Roger and Slote, Michael, eds. *Virtue Ethics*. Oxford, (New York: Oxford University Press, 1997).

Friedman, Milton. "The Social Responsibility of Business is to Increase its Profits". In: The New York Times Magazine, September 13, 1970. http://www.colorado.edu/studentgroups/libertarians/issues/friedman-soc-resp-business.html, July 1, 2009

Gardiner, Stephen M., ed., *Virtue Ethics Old and New*. (Ithaca and London: Cornell University Press, 2005).

Geach, Mary; Gormally, Luke, eds, *Human Life, Action and Ethics. Essays by G. E. M. Anscombe*. (Exeter, Charlottesville, VA: Imprint Academic, 2005).

Harman, Gilbert. "Moral Philosophy Meets Social Psychology. Virtue Ethics and the Fundamental Attribution Error". In: *Proceedings of the Aristotelian Society* 99/1999: 315–331. http://www.princeton.edu/~harman/Papers/Virtue.html, July 1, 2009

Hartman, Edwin M. "The Role of Character in Business Ethics". In: *Business Ethics Quarterly*, Vol. 8, Issue 3/1998, 547–559.

Higgins, Kathleen Marie. "Negative Virtues: Zhuangzi's Wuwei". In: Gardiner, Stephen M., ed., *Virtue Ethics Old and New*, 125–141.

Hursthouse, Rosalind. *On Virtue Ethics*. (Oxford, New York: Oxford University Press, 1999).

——. "On the Grounding of the Virtues in Human Nature. In: Szaif, Jan; Lutz-Bachmann, Matthias, eds, *Was ist das für den Menschen Gute?*, 263–275.

Solomon, Robert C. *The Passions: Emotions and the Meaning of Life*. (Indianapolis: Hackett Publishing Co., 1993). Originally published: (Garden City, N. Y.: Anchor Press/Doubleday, 1976).

——. *Ethics and Excellence: Cooperation and Integrity in Business*. (New York, Oxford: Oxford University Press, 1992).

——. "Corporate Roles, Personal Virtues: An Aristotelian Approach to Business Ethics". In: *Business Ethics Quarterly*, Vol. 2, Issue 3/1992: 317–339.

——. "The Moral Psychology of Business: Care and Compassion in the Corporation". In: *Business Ethics Quarterly*, Vol. 8, Issue 3/1998: 515–533.

——. *A Better Way to Think about Business: How Personal Integrity Leads to Corporate Success*. (New York, Oxford: Oxford University Press, 1999).

——. "Business with Virtue: Maybe next Year?". In: *Business Ethics Quarterly*, Vol. 10, Issue 1/2000: 339–341.

——. "Victims of Circumstances? A Defense of Virtue Ethics in Business". In: *Business Ethics Quarterly*, Vol. 13, Issue 1/2003: 43–62.

Statman, Daniel, ed., *Virtue Ethics: A Critical Reader*. (Washington, D. C.: Georgetown University Press, 1997).

Stocker, Michael. "The Schizophrenia of Modern Ethical Theories". Reprinted from *Journal of Philosophy*, Vol. 73/1976: 453–466. In: Crisp, Roger; Slote, Michael, eds. *Virtue Ethics*, 66–78.

Swanton, Christine. *Virtue Ethics: A Pluralistic View*. (Oxford, New York: Oxford University Press, 2003).

——. "Role Ethics and Business Ethics". In: Walker, Rebecca L.; Ivanhoe, Philip J., eds, *Working Virtue*, 207–224.

Szaif, Jan; Lutz-Bachmann, Matthias, eds, *Was ist das für den Menschen Gute? What is Good for a Human Being?* Menschliche Natur und Güterlehre. Human Nature and Human Values. (Berlin; New York: De Gruyter, 2004).

Walker, Rebecca L.; Ivanhoe, Philip J., eds, *Working Virtue: Virtue Ethics and Contemporary Moral Problems*. (Oxford, New York: Oxford University Press, 2007).

Watson, Gary. "On the Primacy of Character". In: Statman, Daniel, ed. *Virtue Ethics*, 56–81.

# 12
# Wittgenstein and the Challenge of Global Ethics
*Julian Friedland*

## 12.1 The transcendental nature of ethics and meaning

Wittgenstein took ethics extremely seriously. In fact, he took it so seriously that he gave away the bulk of his inherited family fortune to needy artists including the poets Rainer Maria Rilke and Georg Trakl, who he thought might make better use of it than himself as a salaried professor (Monk, 1990, p. 108). Paradoxically, however, he was highly critical of the academization of philosophy in general and of ethics in particular. He therefore did precious little work in ethics, traditionally conceived as an attempt to define the good and/or apply it to specific real-world contexts such as business. This is because for Wittgenstein, ethics is bound up with our natural history. It compels us by being the very lens through which we see the world (Wittgenstein, 1921, § 1, 1.1, 2.04). Hence, "man is the microcosm" (Wittgenstein, 1961, p. 84). As such, philosophy cannot itself discover and lead people to what is good (Wittgenstein, 1980, p. 3e). For we cannot, for Wittgenstein, get by means of language behind the very foundations of common sense. Thus, in one of his most famous passages, he writes:

> Disputes do not break out (among mathematicians, say) over the question whether a rule has been obeyed or not. People don't come to blows over it, for example. That is part of the framework on which the working of our language is based (for example, in giving descriptions)....If language is to be a means of communication there must be agreement not only in definitions but also (queer as this may sound) in judgments. (Wittgenstein, 1958, § 240, 242)

What grounds our ordinary common sense judgments about the good and the world in general is the very background upon which conventional language is made possible. But this does not make Wittgenstein a postmodern relativist. For as he says in the preceding dialogical remark:

> "So you are saying that human agreement decides what is true and what is false?" – It is what human beings *say* that is true and false; and they agree in the *language* they use. That is not agreement in opinions but in forms of life. (Wittgenstein, 1958, §241)

For Wittgenstein, ethics and aesthetics are part of the human form of life, which grounds our basic ability to communicate with one another. What binds us in a language is what binds us as a species, a people, a nation, a culture, or a profession; namely, collective intersubjective experiences and basic judgments of what is, for example, reasonable, desirable, dreadful, efficient, elegant, awkward, pleasing, or offensive. How, then, one might ask, do all our contextually nuanced judgments get determined? The answer is that they arise out of shared practices that have slowly, organically, evolved over time. And thus, the rules governing linguistic convention are systematically confirmed by shared backgrounds of activities, interests, and goals.

So ethics is fundamental to just about everything we do and understand. Indeed, it is a transcendental condition of our very existence. This is reinforced and made possible by our nature as social beings. Ultimately, it is the social nature of human consciousness that allows us to erect any conventional system to begin with. Hence, as Wittgenstein argues at some length, private language is logically impossible. Language is essentially conventional. If it were not, we could simply invent our own rules willy-nilly, which would not amount to language at all. Grammar compels us. And it does so by a public background of linguistic practice on which we continually rely to make sure we are applying its rules correctly. This deeper epistemological point is crucial to understanding Wittgenstein's conception of ethics and is why he was highly critical of Esperanto, a new language created for international communication and meant to bring about world peace. Although high-minded from a global ethical perspective, he found the idea deeply repellant, for it meant erecting an entire language out of thin air without any authentic organic history.

> Esperanto: The feeling of disgust we get if we utter an invented word with invented derivative syllables. The word is cold, lacking in associations, and yet it plays at being a "language." A system of purely written signs would not disgust us so much. (Wittgenstein, 1980, p. 52e)

Ethics, for Wittgenstein, has to do with that essential realm of shared experience and judgment that tends to go without saying. It is the most important part of life, for it binds us together as peoples by making sense of what and why we do just about anything and everything. And that's why he found it maddening for this essentially anthropological aspect to be routinely overlooked by most philosophers. Thanks to him, it is somewhat less ignored today, as we now owe a great deal to Wittgenstein. But, ironically, his influence is often more evident outside the halls of philosophy. Perhaps more than anything, Wittgenstein showed us how grammar became structured (much as games such as chess evolved over eons) almost biologically, to the point where it contains great wisdom about human consciousness, the conditions and limits of thought and knowledge. Take the following example from the grammar of the verb "to know":

> I know what someone else is thinking, not what I am thinking. It is correct to say "I know what you are thinking," and wrong to say "I know what I am thinking."
> (A whole cloud of philosophy condensed into a drop of grammar.)
> (Wittgenstein, 1958, p. 222e)

Wittgenstein is pointing out that to say "I know what I am thinking" goes without saying since one could never *not* know what one is actually thinking while one is thinking it. And this wisdom about knowledge is evident in the very bounds of grammatical sense. Essentially, Wittgenstein is trying to cure us of thinking, especially of theorizing, beyond the bounds of common sense. Instead of forcing our thinking into preconceived theoretical notions of what reality *must* be like, including such aspects as the good, the just, and the beautiful, he implores us to *look* at how it actually is, namely, how such concepts function in their ordinary linguistic contexts. We feel sympathy or anguish or hate, not so much because of any specific overarching theoretical definition of what the good is, but more because of a natural and cultural history that binds us together, making shared judgments and communication itself possible.

And this brings us to the particular challenge of doing philosophical ethics. If, along with Wittgenstein, we take ethics to be essentially a fundamental pre-theoretical condition of experience, then it is a purely organic human phenomenon that philosophy will (and should) have precious little ability to determine. Ethics in this sense lies transcendentally outside the realm of facts (Wittgenstein, 1980, p. 3e). So to seek to ground it in an essential definition or all-encompassing theory of what the good must logically be, would only "dirty a flower with muddy hands" (Monk, 1990, p. 54; Wittgenstein, 1965).

## 12.2 The evolution of ethical consciousness

This theoretically deflationary attitude can certainly be taken too far, as perhaps it was by Wittgenstein himself. Philosophers have indeed had a great deal of impact on public moral consciousness at pivotal historical times, such as during women's suffrage and in civil rights movements more generally. Still, it is not clear that the philosophical thinking required at such periods of social awakening is at all abstract. Indeed, it has little or nothing to do with metaethical debates about the nature of the good itself. It may well be that any great ethical leader is thus merely a product of his or her historical context. Even if that is true, it is perhaps a little disingenuous of Wittgenstein to act as if ethical philosophy were any less worthy of serious attention than the study of the nature of knowledge, epistemology. For if, as he says, a whole cloud of epistemological philosophy can be condensed into a single drop of grammar, then the same ought to be true of ethical philosophy. And philosophers and nonphilosophers can and do misuse language just as easily. Therefore, some degree of new thinking on the nature of the good and the just has surely led at times to increased clarity of vision and genuine progress.

The attributes of what one might call "a good woman," for example, have certainly changed over the last century. For women are now no longer expected to be merely subservient to men. Thus, if a person at a funeral oration this year were to say "she was a truly good woman," that would naturally imply all sorts of qualities that would have been excluded from such a statement uttered at a funeral oration a hundred years ago. The same is true of statements such as "he was a good man" or "he lived a good life." Such statements are expressions of ethical value that continually evolve (or devolve) socially over time (Wittgenstein, 1965; 1958, p. 189e). One can, for example, imagine a funeral oration for an SS soldier in Nazi Germany where the words "he was a good man," might mean something altogether different from what those same words might mean today.

On this, Wittgenstein would surely agree. But he would caution us to the dangers of erecting philosophical constructs so divorced from shared experience that they would never have a chance of compelling an ordinary person on the street. However, the ordinary person on the street does have a certain moral sensibility that has evolved over (and within) generations. As the above example shows, all sorts of behaviors and attitudes, once commonplace, may later be judged as ethically questionable by large numbers of nonphilosophers. Take bigotry in all its forms for example, or smoking. Or overeating. Or littering. Or not recycling. Or driving a large sport-utility vehicle (SUV) in New York City. Various and growing social pockets of relatively reform-minded people in effect begin to pressure others by making them feel guilty about perpetuating some irresponsible *status quo*. And they often begin this process by thinking at least somewhat philosophically about their behavior. They take the trouble of reconsidering, now and again, whether their usual habits are truly consistent with their fundamental ethical convictions. Indeed, this is how social progress occurs. We come to see that some activity and/or attitude has a negative impact and we are pressured by our conscience, and that of others around us, to change for the better. As a result, we tend to feel satisfaction and a greater sense of belonging within an ever-widening realm of human solidarity.

Ideally, by applying rational thought to action, we form good habits. Thus, new positive behaviors gradually become second nature, while bad habits are gradually stamped out. Eventually, we no longer have to think very much at all in order to embody a deeper ethical consciousness. Instead, we naturally desire and do the right thing, experiencing little or no temptation to regress into old habits. This is the ultimate goal of virtue ethics, namely, to reach complete happiness through self-actualizing activities.

Perhaps the greatest force compelling people to change their behavior on ethical grounds is the realization that their behavior is somehow causing, facilitating, or ignoring some significant harm. We look into another's suffering eyes and, in a sense, we see ourselves. This is compelling, for it is immediately experienced via our basic nature as social beings. And this is what is truly at the heart of ethics for Wittgenstein. For as he says, at various points:

> What is essential for us is, after all, spontaneous agreement, spontaneous sympathy. (1967, §667)
>
> Instinct comes first, reasoning second. (1967, §689)

So perhaps the greatest part of being ethical is simply to become conscious of the interests of those around us. And this has always been, and will ever be so. But the particular challenge of globality is specific to our age. For how can one see into another's suffering eyes when those who are made to suffer may be out of sight on the other side of the planet? Or they might be future generations (if not one's own) in any of the myriad possible worlds transformed by global ecological calamity resulting from unbridled resource depletion. When each person's actions taken in isolation have no clear or measurable negative effect on anyone in particular, everyone is much less likely to take responsibility for the collective result that billions of other people's actions, taken together, may cause.

Essentially, this is what I take to be the Wittgensteinian challenge of global ethics. While applied ethicists may at times succeed in making compelling philosophical arguments for increased personal and corporate responsibility and government regulation, these can often be rather abstract. Their theoretically based arguments do not compel us as do, say, the sad eyes of a child who is denied an education based on her race. Similarly, if one litters by carelessly discarding a plastic bag on the sidewalk, there is a clear and immediate negative consequence to that action, namely, to the beauty of the neighborhood. In such cases, negative impacts are clearly felt in concrete human terms. A mere modicum of self-reflection aided by a degree of social pressure can suffice to eventually bring even the most callous to effect a corrective behavioral change.

Unfortunately, it is not at all clear that the disparately destructive and diffuse web of actions and reactions of globality can ever be felt by another person in quite the same way. We do have high-speed global communications bringing news reports to mass audiences worldwide, and this certainly helps galvanize public concern on important issues, often at a bewildering pace. However, as new information streams in day and night on countless subjects, concerns ebb and flow in and out of public consciousness. For example, global warming is now taken much less seriously, at least in the United States, presumably in part because most Americans have not witnessed much climate change for themselves and so have tended to direct their attention to more evident and immediate concerns. In a recent poll, 48 percent say the science is exaggerated, up from only 41 percent in 2009 and 31 percent in 1997; 35 percent say the effects will either never happen (19 percent) or that they will not happen in their lifetime (16 percent) (Gallup, 2010).

Of course government regulation can step in to press consumers to behave more responsibly. In 2009, Sweden for example, introduced new dietary guidelines and labeling of grocery items according to their carbon footprints. Swedish scientists estimate that 25 percent of the emissions produced by consumers in industrialized nations is generated by the food industry. And if Sweden's new food guidelines were strictly followed, the country could cut its emissions from food production by 20 to 50 percent (Rosenthal, 2009). As a result of Swedish labeling requirements and extensive government-funded research and dissemination of the causes and impacts of global warming, consumers and business leaders are beginning to take action:

> A new generation of Swedish business leaders is stepping up to the climate challenge. Richard Bergfors, president of Max, his family's burger chain, voluntarily hired a consultant to calculate its carbon footprint; 75 percent was created by its meat.
>
> "We decided to be honest and put it all out there and say we'll do everything we can to reduce," said Mr. Bergfors, 40. In addition to putting emissions data on the menu, Max eliminated boxes from its children's meals, installed low-energy LED lights and pays for wind-generated electricity. (Rosenthal, 2009)

Consumers ordering at Max, the largest Swedish hamburger chain, now see on the menu board that a basic hamburger represents 1.7 kilograms of carbon emissions, compared to only 0.4 kilograms for a chicken sandwich. And while this has not produced a change in everyone's behavior, it does seem to be affecting the choices of some, who report beginning to feel guilty for choosing the hamburger. Since emissions counts were posted on the menu, sales of the more climate-friendly items have increased by 20 percent (Rosenthal, 2009).

Geographer Jared Diamond, following Garrett Hardin's seminal article "The Tragedy of the Commons" (1968), argues via historical evidence that most individuals will only tend to act as responsible stewards of an environmental resource if they are either forced by their governments or can each clearly see the negative effects of each of their actions on that resource (Diamond, 2005). In the latter case, as with littering, the public tends to inflict shame on the person with the irresponsible behavior. As it stands, few governments are enacting carbon emissions limits or even sweatshop labor rights standards on imports. And again, this is probably because there is precious little public support for such measures, which may increase costs, since the negative impacts of carbon emissions and labor rights abuses in the developing world remain mostly out of sight and mind to the bulk of consumers in most parts of the world. This is the practical ethical problem of global capitalism. We don't see, when shopping at, say, Wal-Mart, the poor child forced to toil in a cacao field or a factory because his parents don't earn enough to afford to send him to school.

## 12.3   The rise of corporate consciousness

Interestingly, corporations are in many ways better positioned than international government treaties to effect positive change on social and environmental issues, since they are often freer to act independently. Governments are often loath to voluntarily restrict their own industries for fear of voter retaliation. As a result, the onset of the global multinational corporation as the dominant force of economic activity may provide a crucial opportunity for meeting the new humanistic ethical challenge that globality presents.

Ethical branding and corporate consciousness are very much on the rise. For example, while the S&P 500 showed a four percent loss from 2005 to 2010, Ethisphere's list of the World's Most Ethical companies (WME) of 2010 has shown 53 percent returns. This list of 100 of the world's most ethical companies also substantially outpaced the FTSE 100 by over half as much as it did the S&P. Overall, the lesson seems to be that the WME tends to outperform the rest of the market even during times of negative growth, in this case 2008–09, in which WME losses were lower than the other two averages. Indeed, they were only at about one third of the other overage losses.

What is more, if we bring privately controlled businesses into the mix, we find that prior to the downturn in 2008, socially responsible investment assets grew by 324 percent between 1995 and 2007. That sharply outpaced growth in the wider marketplace, which only grew by 260 percent over the same period (Social Investment Forum, 2007). Even during the latest downturn, now commonly known as the Great Recession, socially responsible investment funds grew at higher rates than ever, to an estimated $2.7 trillion (Stengel, 2009). As a result, many observers are starting to refer to this market trend as the "responsibility revolution" (Hollander and Breen, 2010).

We are seeing an increase in ethical labeling, with more and more companies placing labels on their products telling customers that a percentage of proceeds from their purchase will be sent to a given non-profit such as the Nature Conservancy or Sierra Club. Shareholders in the Fortune 500 have even begun convincing the executive class of the corporations they invest in to consider corporate social responsibility as a fiduciary duty. Intel is the latest and highest profile company to do so. As a result, the company is now creating a "Board Committee on Sustainability." While this resolution had been voted down by management the previous year, Intel is now convinced that environmental, social, and governance (ESG) reporting helps preserve the longer-term interests of the company. As a result, Intel directed its outside legal counsel to "write a legal opinion specifically stating that pursuant to Delaware law, corporate responsibility and sustainability reporting based upon the committee's charter, was part of the fiduciary duty of company directors" (Kropp, 2010). This legal opinion may help form a basis for the position that such reporting is a critical factor in corporate financial performance. Ultimately, the Securities and Exchange Commission (SEC) may decide to make ESG reporting mandatory, especially given the current government trend toward increasing corporate regulation and accountability. ESG reporting represents a growing realization that corporate social responsibility (CSR) is not only the right thing to do ethically, but also provides a firm foundation for long-term stability, as this chart from Pax World Investments indicates:

## Environmental Factors

- Resource management and pollution prevention
- Reduced emission and climate impact
- Environmental reporting/disclosure

### Impact on Performance

- Avoid or minimize environmental liabilities
- Lower costs/increase profitability through energy and other efficiencies
- Reduce regulatory, litigation, and reputational risk
- Indicator of well-governed company

## Social Factors

Workplace

- Diversity
- Health and safety
- Labor–Management relations
- Human rights

Product Integrity

- Safety
- Product quality

### Impact on Performance

Workplace

- Improved productivity and morale
- Reduce turnover and absenteeism
- Openness to new ideas and innovation
- Reduce potential for litigation and reputational risk

Product Integrity

- Create brand loyalty
- Increased sales based on product safety and excellence
- Reduce potential for litigation
- Reduce reputational risk

## Governance Factors

- Executive compensation
- Broad accountability
- Shareholder rights
- Reporting and disclosure

### Impact on Performance

- Align interests of shareowners and management
- Avoid unpleasant financial surprises or "blow-ups"
- Reduce reputational risk

Although, ironically, multinational corporations (MNCs) are usually considered faceless and impersonal, we are witnessing a dramatic rise in corporate consciousness worldwide. This ethical awakening provides a unique opportunity for widespread evolution in global consumer consciousness. If, as Wittgenstein claims, ethical norms must compel us pre-theoretically to behave in specific ways, this development is certainly a case in point. We need not agree with any philosophically abstract ethical proposition to conclude that ESG reporting is in fact a good thing. Tellingly, Intel, for example, is not employing any particular definition or philosophical argument on the nature of the good, such as deontology or utility or virtue theory, to justify its new resolution. Rather, it is expressing a new global worldview, or as Wittgenstein would have said in his native German, a new *Weltbild*:

> When we first begin to *believe* anything, what we believe is not a single proposition, it is a whole system of propositions. (Light dawns gradually over the whole.)
> It is not single axioms that strike me as obvious, it is a system in which consequences and premises give one another *mutual* support. (Wittgenstein, 1972, §141–2)

In this way, Intel shareholders have come to a new global worldview on the proper place of business in society. As a result, companies embracing initiatives such as the ESG or "triple bottom line" reporting of social, environmental, and financial performance (Global Reporting Initiative) are convincingly branding themselves as socially responsible, thereby attracting like-minded investors, consumers, and suppliers. This creates a socioeconomic solidarity of vision – a global compact – between all stakeholders involved with such companies. This should come as no surprise, given the fact that humans are essentially social beings who take pleasure in shared experiences and collective enterprises. Furthermore, we in the developed world are increasingly isolated from our communities because of our extensive reliance on private automobiles, personal computers, and cell phones to interact with each other. This surely creates a greater longing for connection and belonging and gives corporations a crucial role to play in filling this new psychological void. For the power of MNCs now rivals and even exceeds the power of governments to reinforce and reshape ethical norms.

But again, while this reshaping is a kind of persuasion, it is, for Wittgenstein, more akin to a cultural or religious conversion than logical argument. In very much the same way, someone who blithely litters may gradually come to realize why littering is immoral. For example, several years ago I had the unnerving experience of witnessing a Chinese man hiking in the Grand Canyon National Park, who after finishing his can of Coke, casually tossed it over the edge of the cliff, where it landed, clearly visible, but out of reach. When he was then confronted by several Americans, he very politely replied that he did indeed appreciate the awesome beauty of the canyon very much. Obviously, this man's conception of appreciation was very different from that of the others, who tried, in a few minutes of rather vain persuasion, to explain why littering is forbidden, especially at the Grand Canyon. In order to fully understand, he would have to be given, and then reflect on, a whole host of reasons, ecological and aesthetic, or undergo public shame (or both) before he could come to see differently. At that point, he might take on a new worldview or *Weltbild*. Wittgenstein provides a similar example in the context of G. E. Moore's so-called proof of an external world:

> Men have believed they could make rain; why should not a king be brought up with a belief that the world began with him? And if Moore and this king were to meet and discuss, could Moore really prove his belief to be the right one? I do not say that Moore could not convert the king to his view, but it would be a conversion of a special kind; the king would be brought to look at the world in a different way.
>
> Remember that one is often convinced of a view by its *simplicity of symmetry*, i.e. these are what induce one to go over to this point of view. One then simply says something like: "*That's* how it must be." (Wittgenstein, 1972, §92)

This is how, say, a person or group that maintains willful ignorance of global warming might be persuaded to a different global vision. Ultimately, it takes much more than a grasp of the science. It also requires adopting a moral concern for the continuing detrimental impacts of our collective behavior on the climate—and by extension on our lives. It does not happen overnight or after simply following the logic and evidence of a single argument. Rather, it is a gradual change fostered by myriad social forces working culturally in concert.

In much this way, via ethical branding, corporations, consumers, and suppliers can begin to share in a global ethical vision of social responsibility. And like any good habit, the more consumers begin taking responsibility by shopping conscientiously, the more those habits are reinforced. Gradually, conscientiousness spreads to friends and family, creating a wider social context of elevated ethical awareness and expectation. As shoppers continue to seek deeper personal and social gratification via their consumer choices, corporations can meet this demand by finding new and convincing ways to brand themselves ethically. Fair trade labeling on coffee and cacao imports is yet another example. There is also the third-party nonprofit sweatshop auditor the Fair Labor Association (FLA), which now counts most major athletic wear MNCs among its clients. The next obvious step in this industry is a fair labor retail label. And conscientious American fast-food chains might begin following Swedish chain Max Hamburger in placing carbon footprint labels on their menus. Indeed, many chains have already begun placing caloric values on their menus. When will we see one of these companies offer an organic children's meal, for example? It is worth recalling that the first organic product to be mass-marketed in stores such as Wal-Mart was baby food. For consumers who might not yet purchase organics for themselves will often begin by purchasing it for their children. Venturing into "naturally raised" and organic options would be an excellent way for almost any fast-food giant to capture more educated and health-conscious consumers. Colorado-based chains Chipotle and Good Times, for example, are doing this already.

As consumer ethical consciousness spreads, MNCs that embrace a strong ethical mission are poised to thrive. For in the global marketplace, we are all faced with the stark choice of being part of the solution to the world's economic, social, and environmental problems, or to remain part of them. Early adopters of corporate consciousness are pressing their increasing market advantage by stepping up to this challenge. That is something we can all take heart from. And if one asks any leading CEO in corporate social responsibility "but why is it the right thing to do?" she might do best by replying, with Wittgenstein, that at this point we have exhausted the justifications. For we have reached bedrock, and our spade is turned. This is simply what we do because it is who we are (Wittgenstein, 1958, §217).

## Bibliography

Diamond, J., *Collapse: How Societies Choose or Fail to Succeed.* (Penguin: New York, 2005).
Ethisphere: World's Most Ethical Companies (2010). [Online] Available at: http://www.gallup.com/poll/126560/Americans-Global-Warming-Concerns-Continue-Drop.aspx [Accessed April 26, 2010].

Fair Labor Association (FLA). [Online] Available at: http://www.fairlabor.org [Accessed April 26, 2010].

Gallup (March 11, 2010). American's Global Warming Concerns Continue to Drop. [Online] Available at: *http://ethisphere.com/wme2010/* [Accessed April 26, 2010].

Global Reporting Initiative (GRI). [Online] Available at: . http://www.globalreporting.org [Accessed April 26, 2010].

Hardin, G., "The Tragedy of the Commons". *Science.* 162 (3859) (1968) 1243–1248.

Hollander, J. and Breen, B. *The Responsibility Revolution: How The Next Generation of Businesses Will Win.* (Jossey-Bass: San Francisco, 2010).

Kropp, R. (April 5, 2010). Intel adds Sustainability to Corporate Charter. GreenBiz. com. [Online] Available at: http://www.greenbiz.com/news/2010/04/05/intel-adds-sustainability-corporate-charter [Accessed April 26, 2010].

Monk, R., *Ludwig Wittgenstein: The Duty of Genius.* (New York: Penguin, 1990).

Pax World Investments. The Impact of ESG Criteria on Financial Performance. [Online] Available at: http://www.paxworld.com/investment-approach/the-benefits-of-esg/the-impact-of-esg-criteria-on-financial-performance/ [Accessed April 26, 2010].

Rosenthal, E. (October 22, 2009). "To Cut Global Warming, Swedes Study Their Plates". *New York Times.*

Social Investment Forum. Report on Responsible Investing Trends in the U.S. 2007. [Online] Available at: http://www.socialinvest.org/resources/research/ [Accessed April 26, 2010].

Stengel, R. (September 10, 2009). For Consumers, a Responsibility Revolution. *Time.*

Wittgenstein, L., *Tractatus Logico-philosophicus.* (New York: Harper Perennial, 1921).

Wittgenstein, L., *Philosophical Investigations.* (Oxford: Blackwell, 1958).

Wittgenstein, L., *Notebooks 1914–16.* Anscombe, G.E.M., von Wright, G.H. (1961).

Wittgenstein, L., *On Certainty.* (New York: Harper Perennial, 1972).

Wittgenstein, L., *Culture and Value.* University of Chicago Press. (eds). (Oxford: Blackwell, 1980).

Wittgenstein, L., Lecture on Ethics, *Philosophical Review,* 74 (1) (1965).

Wittgenstein, L. *Zettel.* Anscombe, G.E.M., von Wright, G.H. (eds). (Oxford: Blackwell, 1967).

# Part IV

# Non-Western and Nontraditional Approaches

# 13
# Humanistic Values in Indian and Chinese Traditions
*Monika Kirloskar-Steinbach*

## 13.1 Introduction

The main aim of this essay will be to examine humanistic values in the Indian and Chinese philosophical traditions and to argue for the need for an awareness of these positions in business ethics. From the point of view of business, one could doubt the relevance of these traditions. Indian philosophical systems are commonly thought of as preoccupied with otherworldly concerns; moreover, the feudal backdrop of ancient Chinese positions appears unsettling today. Could anything at all, one could ask, be gleaned from them, even in debates which try, for example, to develop transnational ethical norms to guide one's business conduct? In section four, I will attempt to dispel such doubts.

Any convincing inquiry about humanistic values will have to begin with an account of what it means to be a human being. First, I will use sources from the Indian philosophical tradition to try to work out such an account, focusing on what are regarded as the orthodox systems within this tradition. Using Hegel's (2001, p. 174) scathing description, one could say that these systems, with their overemphasis on spiritual liberation, try to prepare us for the death of life during life itself. This German philosopher, whose tall shadow continues to dominate intercultural debates even today, seemed to believe that due to their futile, or rather, their scant powers of reflection, proponents of orthodox systems do not philosophize but engage sporadically in bouts of fantasy. I hope to show that this is not the case. My aim will be to demonstrate that one finds an account of humanity to which we can easily relate even within the orthodox systems. Regardless of one's own cultural setting, it is easy to sympathize with their depiction of human life as fragile and weak. The same holds true for their view that fatalism is unjustified. Given human intellectual resources, human beings do have the capability of overcoming their own failings.

Using Mo Di and Mencius from the Chinese philosophical tradition, I will attempt in the following section to sketch two alternative ways of being human. In his dismissal of the whole Chinese tradition, Hegel (2001, p. 87) claimed that moral laws were established in it not with the help of inner conviction but by brute force. But even my sketchy reconstruction of Mo Di's and Mencius' intricate arguments reveals how far-fetched such a claim is.[1] I will, however, not attempt to compare the Indian and Chinese traditions with each other since the main focus of this paper lies on working out their implications for business ethics. This will be the task of section four.

Within the scope of this essay, I will not work out the wider ramifications of the positions dealt with here. But if one considers the current financial meltdown to require a search for an alternative social model, these positions indicate meaningful ways of working out such a model. As the following exploration of certain Indian metaphysical concerns and of ancient Chinese social philosophy illustrates, there is no direct relation between amassing material goods and human well-being. Although they differ in the reasons used in support of their arguments, both these traditions seem to emphasize that the individuality of a human life notwithstanding, human well-being can only be achieved within a social setting. This should not be taken to mean that members of a community should fulfill their material desires only in ways stipulated by that community. It does, however, indicate that there are good reasons for individuals themselves to try to limit the fulfillment of their material desires.

## 13.2   Indian philosophical tradition and humanity

The classical Hindu *darsanas* (worldviews) are considered to be pivotal to the development of the philosophical tradition in India. They are *Samkhya* and *Yoga* (with their interpretation of creation), *Nyaya* and *Vaisesika* (with their emphasis on categories of knowledge), the *Purvamimamsa's* Vedic science of interpretation, and finally *Uttaramimamsa* or *Vedanta* which concentrates on the fundamental principle underlying the universe. Since these philosophical systems either explicitly or implicitly do not challenge Vedic authority, they are considered to be orthodox. Their opponents are the materialistic *Carvaka*, the *Jainist*, and the *Buddhist*, systems which are considered to be heterodox. By fundamentally challenging Vedic authority and the views of the orthodox systems, these systems pushed forward the development and refinement of many orthodox views.

Against this backdrop, let us begin with the question, what is a human being? Although the various orthodox systems radically differ on various counts, all of them assume that each human being suffers and wants to overcome this painful existence. Also, it is believed that the right theory of knowledge can lay out the path to salvation and, thereby, end this suffering. Now, from a general point of view, one could argue that this assumption is plainly false for various reasons. One could, for example, point out that every satisfactory, and not one-sided, account of a human being has to consider both the highs and lows of such a life. Further, one could also put on the empiricist's hat and bring into play one's own positive experience to cast doubt on the fact that human suffering can be postulated as a universal experience. And even if one did, for the sake of the argument, accept this hypothesis, one could ask whether strategies attempting to minimize suffering are not more meaningful than the escapism involved by spiritual liberation.

In all probability, a proponent of an orthodox system would not be particularly taken aback by these doubts. She would point out that she does not categorically deny that life does not have any happier, or even lighter, moments at all. Rather, she would seek to emphasize her observation that even these moments are overlaid with suffering. The main text of the *Nyaya*, the *Nyayasutra* (IVa 54), puts the point very succinctly when it states that human beings run the risk of confusing certain kinds of pleasure with pain. The *Samkhya* system underscores another aspect of human pain. Its earliest text, *The Samkhya-karika of Isvara Krishna*, considers the objection of a fictitious opponent who states that a physician could cure bodily pain. And as for mental pains, they could be easily remedied with women, wine, and drink, and the like. But the *Samkhya* text counteracts this objection by stating "though easily available, the obvious means do not effect absolute and final removal of pain." (Radhakrishnan and Moore 1957: 426).

Furthermore, such a proponent would counter the empiricist's objection as follows: considering the fact that life is not over, it would be rather shortsighted to conclude that this streak of good luck will continue for a whole lifetime. Moreover, even if one did have the good fortune to lead such a life, worldly happiness can only be of a temporary, nonultimate nature since ultimate happiness consists in liberating oneself from the chain of life, from, for example, births and deaths. As the *Nyayasutra* (IVa 51) says, given that life is closely intertwined with pain, every new life is a continuation of this pain.

Let us suppose that this clarifies the doubts mentioned above. On the basis of the importance paid in the *darsanas* to human suffering, one could, first of all, assume the following: Philosophical inquiries can only thrive in an environment in which crucial importance is placed on an exchange of arguments. A community which highlights individual suffering is not likely to value such an exchange. In the long run, this attitude will prove to be detrimental to the pursuit of philosophical inquiries.

One could illustrate this point by contending that it is possible to liberate the self without engaging in discursive reasoning with another person. In fact, solitary strategies such as penitence, praying, fasting, and meditating could prove to be more conducive to the liberation of the soul. As Hegel (2001, p. 168) said, they could help to attain "the perfect deadening of consciousness; a point from which the transition to physical death is no great step." In other words, if an escape from this world is all that counts, there is no need to engage in argumentation, even about this escape itself. Let us call this the hostility-to-dialogue assumption.

The second assumption is closely related to the first. If a community regards spiritual liberation as the sole goal of life, it would then go on to restrict the development of the whole gamut of human capabilities. Sensual capabilities, in particular, which could be thought of as being distracting to spiritual liberation, would be discouraged. Let us call this the hostility-to-senses assumption.

### 13.2.1   The hostility-to-dialogue assumption

Let us begin to analyze this assumption by examining the views of the Vedantist Ramanuja (1017–1137 C.E.). He is an exponent of a tradition which espouses devotion (*bhakti*) to a personal God and believes that this devotion will, through a union of *Brahman* and *Atman*, lead to the union of the universal and the particular. Meditative and contemplative techniques are considered to be instrumental in this regard. So the hostility-to-dialogue assumption can be effectively tested with the help of his example. Ramanuja dismisses the views of an opponent as follows:

> This entire theory rests on a fictitious foundation of altogether hollow and vicious arguments, incapable of being stated in definite logical alternatives, and devised by men who are destitute of those particular qualities which cause individuals to be chosen by the Supreme Person revealed in the Upanishads; whose intellects are darkened by

the impression of beginningless evil; and who thus have no insight into the nature of words and sentences, into the real purport conveyed by them, and into the procedure of sound argumentation with all its methods depending on perception and the other instruments of right knowledge. The theory therefore must needs to be rejected by all those who, through texts, perception and the other means of knowledge – assisted by sound reasoning – have an insight into the true nature of things. (Thibaut, 1962: 39)

This quotation indicates that even within a tradition that does not appear to value discursive reasoning, liberation need not be interpreted as a solitary, silent endeavor. Ramanuja actively engages in such reasoning and painstakingly uses argumentative techniques to correct what he believes is an example of false reasoning.

This passage is of interest for another reason. It reveals two facets of Ramanuja's own views of a human being. In his view, a human being possesses intellectual powers that enable her to achieve right knowledge through various means, and she has the potential to gain an insight into the real nature of things. However, the hostility-to-dialogue assumption cannot be refuted on the basis of these remarks alone. One could (1) draw attention to the general framework within which philosophizing in the orthodox systems is placed, and then (2) draw implications from this for the philosophical enterprise itself.

(1) It could be argued that in the orthodox systems one philosophizes within parameters set by tradition. Ramanuja, along with exponents of the other orthodox systems, believes, for example, that reasoning cannot – and should not – surpass the limited role assigned to it. Although these systems stress the need for a logical analysis even of the arguments advanced within the Vedic tradition, one is expected not to advance any claims that contradict this tradition itself. How, one could ask, can such an attitude be conducive to dialogue?

But the claim that argumentative achievements should not overstep the boundaries set by a tradition is not totally unknown in the history of philosophy. The high esteem accorded to reasoning and argumentation often seems to go hand in hand with fear of the powers of this human faculty itself. Depending on one's perspective, human reason is thought of as being a gift or a curse. When properly carried out, it is considered to be a gift which has the power to uplift the person reasoning. Otherwise, it can become a curse which may bring about her downfall; this is often demonstrated using the example of an opponent who deliberately tries to break with tradition.

Within the fold of the Indian philosophical tradition, the heterodox *Buddhist* and *Jainist* systems are a case in point. Although they were vehemently critical of Vedic tradition themselves, they, like their ortho- dox counterparts, also attacked the materialistic *Carvaka*. The material- ist's express denial of any kind of authority led all the other systems to believe that such untrammeled reasoning could only lead to contrived fictions. Bereft of any tradition, such a person, it was thought, is bound to fall prey in her reasoning to self-praise, heresy, and self-deceit.

Now, the attempt to limit reasoning to the bounds of a given frame- work could place restraints on the range and scope of philosophical inquiries pursued. But as the Indian case shows, this circumscription does not necessarily hamper the possibility of philosophical dialogue as such. It shows that discursive reasoning can take place even within the constraints set by a tradition.

(2) One could, however, not be willing to share this optimism and draw some consequences from the philosophical setting outlined above. It could be argued that it is essential in philosophy to be able to con- tinually improve the quality of arguments proffered. If one is allowed to reason only within the limits set by tradition, there is no guarantee that such an improvement will ever take place. In all probability, the fear of untrammeled reasoning will lead one, in a discussion, to treat certain statements as infallible final truths that cannot be subjected to philosophical scrutiny. And how can the quality of arguments ever be improved if they can appeal to statements that are not open to discus- sion and analysis?

The main thrust of this charge rests on the claim that the fallibil- ity of arguments is crucial to the philosophical enterprise. But is this fallibility completely unknown to the proponents of orthodox sys- tems? In his commentary, the *Vartikka*, the *Nyaya* author Uddyotakara considers the reasons as to why pupils should also be made aware of invalid reasons. Uddyotakara believes that human beings are fallible creatures. Even if a teacher, he maintains, thinks that her reasoning is sound, it might be based on invalid, fallacious, reasons. The pupil should, on her part, be able to differentiate sound from unsound rea- soning. This is why she should also be made familiar with invalid or fallacious reasoning.[2]

It should also be pointed out that human fallibility is a constant theme in the *Vedanta* tradition. In the *Purvamimamsa*, for example, it is proposed that the infallible Vedas cannot have human authors because such authors would be fallible; a claim which, incidentally, did not remain uncontested even within the orthodox setting itself. There is, therefore, no reason to assume that the orthodox systems are incapable of supporting the quality of philosophical arguments *per se*.

## 13.2.2 The hostility-to-senses assumption

Let us now turn to the second assumption, which can be interpreted in two different ways. According to a stronger version of this claim, all kinds of sensual activity must be discouraged because they could be detrimental to the individual's spiritual liberation. On the basis of the weaker claim, one would, however, be content to state that the orthodox systems merely discourage sensual activities t are found to detract from such liberation.[3] Clearly, only the former claim, if found to hold true, would be damaging to philosophical inquiry. It would, for instance, imply that sensual activity of any kind cannot play a meaningful role in this inquiry. Consequently, sense-data cannot be of any significance in such an investigation.

But can the stronger version of this claim be sustained? All orthodox systems tend to stress the role of right knowledge in achieving spiritual liberation. Every system, however, differs on the number of fundamental means to knowledge (*pramana*) it is willing to accept and adopt, and also on what it considers to be the specific nature of such means. A means to knowledge is thought of as the specific cause of true cognition (*prama*). It helps to manifest the object and thus enables its immediate knowledge. Each means to knowledge is also said to be irreducible to any other and dependent on a unique aggregate of causal conditions.[4]

Let us take the case of the *Advaita* system, whose history can be traced back to the seventh century C.E., and which continues to be one of the most powerful philosophical systems in India today.[5] It believes in a strict nonduality and takes only the single reality of *Brahman* (the all-pervading consciousness) to be true. The empirical world is thought to possess only a practical reality. Yet, the Advaitins do not doubt that knowledge can be achieved in this world of appearances. Their analysis of direct perception is particularly interesting for our purposes.

It is believed that during direct perception the mind or inner organ (*antakarana*) approaches the object through the senses. The latter, in turn, also reach out for the object. The mind then takes on the form of the external object and is "colored" by it. The mental process is compared to an impression (*prati-mudra*) from a seal (*mudra*). For the Advaitins, therefore, sense organs are an important vehicle in the perceptual process. Yet, it has to be borne in mind that they alone are not thought to be able to process that which is perceived. They, and in fact even the mind, can only deliver the building blocks of knowledge. True cognition can only arise due to the activity of the *Atman* (the immanent Self), which in this process takes on the role of the seer.

It is evident, therefore, that in the *Advaita* case the stronger version of the hostility-to-senses assumption has to be discarded. In fact, an analysis of the other orthodox systems would reveal the same. Broadly, all of them consider sense activity to be fundamental to true cognition. It has to be noted, though, that they do not restrict direct perception to sensory perception alone. It is said to lead to knowledge of the self and its qualities, universals, essences, and relations. Nevertheless, both the assumptions considered to be detrimental to philosophical inquiry prove to be untenable.

One could, however, surmise that on account of their otherworldly leanings, the Indian positions mentioned in this section are of limited applicability to debates on business ethics. These positions, for instance, seem to leave no room for an exploration of the role of an individual in society. But one upshot of the discussion in this section is that the pursuit of material happiness cannot be unlimited. Using their argument for spiritual liberation, the orthodox positions can argue that material happiness is to be sought only within a social setting. If a search for this happiness threatens to tear the social fabric, it is to be discouraged.

Due to its very nature, this state of material happiness can only be momentary and cannot, therefore, be regarded as an end in itself. To do so would mean getting entangled by the lure of material goods, which would lead to negative social repercussions and prove to be a setback for achieving spiritual liberation. But the orthodox systems do not categorically deny the importance of the search for material happiness. If it is subjugated to the ultimate goal of spiritual liberation, they state, it is legitimate to strive for this happiness within a life well-led.

## 13.3   Chinese philosophical tradition and humanity

Let us for our purposes accept the account of a human being sketched above. In that case, the next step would be to find out how such human beings should live. The answer to this question presumes that (1) it is possible to outline a conception of such a life, and (2) such a conception does in fact describe a good life. Let us turn to two thinkers in the classical Chinese philosophical tradition who accepted both these assumptions.

### 13.3.1   Mo Di's conception of a good life

Mo Di (also Motse, Mo-Tsu, Mozi; ca. fifth century B.C.E.) would point out that a good life can only be lived within a state. So he would reformulate our question to read: how should a human being live as a member of a state?

Mo Di believes that this question can be meaningfully answered only with the help of an independent and objective standard of judgment. He points out the following discrepancy: as the wide acceptance of tools such as compasses or carpenter's squares indicates, independent standards are used when judging the quality even of pedestrian tasks. Strangely enough, no such standard is employed to judge interpersonal behavior.

But can such a universal measure be found at all? Mo Di optimistically believes that it can, but he does not locate this objective standard in human beings. Even supposedly authoritative human instances such as parents, teachers, or princes are said to be ill-suited; superhuman heaven alone can taken on this role. This is because heaven is "all-inclusive and impartial in its activities, abundant and unceasing in its blessings, and lasting and untiring in its guidance." (Mei ,1973, p. 14)

But how can something nonhuman serve as a guiding principle in interpersonal relations? And how does a person without extraordinary capabilities or capacities know what "heaven" desires? Mo Di's simple answer is that the ways of heaven can be observed by those willing to do so. He also sees no difficulty in taking heaven as a guide to human affairs. A person willing to observe heavenly ways will, in fact, discover that heaven desires the best for human beings.

> How do we know that Heaven loves the people of the World? Because it enlightens them universally. How do we know that it enlightens them universally? Because it possesses them universally. How do we know that it possesses them universally? Because it accepts sacrifices from them universally [...]. Thus I know that Heaven loves the people of the world. He who obeys the will of Heaven will regard righteousness as right. He who disobeys the will of Heaven will regard force as right. (Watson, 1967, 81–82)

Mo Di is struck by the sharp contrast between heaven's ways and contemporary life. His point of departure is a harsh and brutish state of nature in which human beings disagreed on values. In his view, they overcame this anarchy by coming together to form a hierarchically organized society which agreed on fundamental values. This mode of social organization helped them overcome the chaos, infighting, and selfishness which characterized the state of nature. However, Mo Di is convinced that the society of his day has reverted to this brutish situation it once sought to leave. A lack of objective moral standards and a social system bereft of incentives to act morally are taken to be the main features of this regress. A main cause of this social degeneration is said to be the inability of government officials in encouraging and supporting virtuous behavior and hindering immoral conduct.

Mo Di is convinced that the only antidote to these maladies consists in following the will of heaven (*t'ien chi*). Since heaven propagates universal love (*jian ai*), human beings should begin to care for each other. Behaving otherwise would mean risking heaven's retaliation; sickness, misfortune, and disaster will afflict them. Mo Di tries to clinch his argument from a human perspective by highlighting the positive consequences of universal love. The person loved, he optimistically believes, will respond to love with love. So in due course, it will lead to a mutual exchange of benefits.[6] Universal love, therefore, is the best means for mutual aid.

Now, let us put aside the broader question of whether an emotion like love could ever solve the problems at hand. Let us theoretically admit this as a possibility. Even so, one could argue that Mo Di goes too far. In theory, it is possible to find a well-defined communitarian group (such as a state) which is held together by ties of mutual love. But on a global scale such a love seems to be at best utopian, at worst completely impossible. So universal love, one could say, must be differentiated from a communal love confined to a particular social group.

Mo Di, however, would accuse us of missing the point. He would argue that there is no tangible difference between communal and universal love. Love only entails "loving others as one's self." He distinguishes two aspects of this love: its outer expression in which one tries to place the other on an equal footing, and an inner attitude which makes one supportive of the development of the other. Mo Di thus argues that universal love can be thought of as a basic attitude towards others. It can be meaningfully adopted by all and can indeed encompass the whole of mankind.

It has to be noted that Mo Di does not try to ground his conception of universal love in an overarching view of human nature. Like Confucius, he is more concerned to work out concrete ways of social and moral improvement. He therefore does not deal with the theoretical ramifications of such a life, by, for example, enumerating common features of humanity. He is satisfied in making one aware of the favorable outcomes which are likely to ensue.

In his view, partiality "gives rise to all the great harms in the world." (Watson, 1967: 39) It makes us hate and injure others. If we were to treat other states, cities, or families like our own, he says, we would not hate or damage them. Others would respond to our impartial benevolent treatment in the same manner. Peace and harmony would ensue. For Mo Di, therefore, it is unsound to restrict love only to the borders of one's own collectivity. In fact, it is imperative that it be extended to all mankind.

Although Mo Di emphatically denies that universal love is illusory, he does confess that it is difficult to put into practice. That is why he adopts a top-down strategy and argues that the ruler himself should be made to see its advantages and act according to its precepts.

> Whoever orders his people to identify themselves with their superior must love them dearly. For the people will not obey orders except when they are ordered with love and held in confidence. Lead them with wealth and honor ahead, and push them with just punishments from behind. When government is carried on like this, even though I wanted to have someone not to identify himself with me, it would be impossible. (Mei, 1973. p 77)

Further, Mo Di thinks that it is legitimate for a ruler to order his subjects to love others. Again he argues for such a decree by pointing out its positive consequences. In the past, he says, the behavioral patterns of subjects were changed according to the ruler's whims and fancies. Subjects were forced to go on a diet, wear the type of clothing specified by the crown, or even sacrifice their lives so that the ruler's fame could be increased. All these decrees were difficult to implement, and yet they were practiced. Ordaining universal love would definitely be easier to achieve than these decrees; subjects could only stand to gain from it.

Mo Di buttresses his argument by appealing to our moral imagination. His point is that universal love is brushed aside as being, for example, overtaxing and impracticable. But if we were to imagine ourselves in a difficult situation, we would immediately – and without any further doubts – entrust our near and dear ones to such a ruler. As he states laconically: "It seems to me that, on occasions like these, there are no fools in the world." (Watson, 1967, p. 42) Thus, an exercise in moral reflection would reveal an inconsistency between our beliefs and our actions. Deep within us, each of us believes that a ruler committed to universal love is desirable; yet we verbally dismiss this concept as being unfeasible.

### 13.3.2   The social-chaos assumption

Nevertheless, it is possible to criticize Mo Di using an argument inherent in his theory. One could argue that there is a palpable tension between his conception of universal love and his view of a hierarchical society. As stated above, Mo Di argues that the brutish life found in a state of nature was overcome by forming a hierarchical society. But will mutual love not disrupt this hierarchy and the social differences it implies? Will social standing and status continue to be significant in a society in which people love each other? If social hierarchy is considered to be the main feature of progress,[7] does universal love not lead to a new state of nature, inasmuch as it does away with this hierarchy? In a nutshell: If Mo Di's universal love were to be put to practice, it would lead to social chaos according to his own understanding of it. Let us call this the social-chaos assumption.

But how sound is this assumption? In an attempt to find an answer, let us return to Mo Di's heavenly guiding principle. He uses the example of heaven both to argue for certain precepts and to justify a particular social model. For example, he rejects offensive warfare of any kind as being perverse. Warfare is said to be unrighteous inasmuch as it implies killing other subjects of heaven. Since it leads to harm and injury, it is also devoid of any benefits to humans. Mo Di takes this to mean that there is no substitute for a good government. What matters solely is the quality of the treatment a ruler metes out to her subjects.[8]

As for his social model, Mo Di does not contend that members of a society have to be treated equally in every respect. Even heaven, he says, cannot be said to be wholly impartial to all human beings. It raises the wise above the masses and respects them because the former play a crucial role in promoting universal love. Heaven desires the well-being of all human beings and is aware of the close connection between human welfare and righteousness. Since the former can only be attained through the latter, it seeks out those who strive to lead a righteous life and are ready to make others aware about the importance of such a life. That is why heaven uplifts the wise, and with their succor tries to achieve its own aims.

But what makes a person wise? Mo Di thinks that high birth is inconsequential in this regard. Possession of knowledge and rhetorical skills alone cannot suffice if they are not complemented with an arduous practice of virtue. In other words: self-cultivation alone is of paramount importance. "Just as a weak trunk will have but small branches, so mere bravery without cultivation will result in dissipation. And just as a dirty source will issue in an impure stream, so unfaithful conduct will unfa-vorably affect one's fame." (Mei, 1973: 7)

One outcome of Mo Di's understanding of the wise is that mobility on the social ladder is, in principle, possible for all strata of society. All one needs for this mobility are a willingness to cultivate oneself and attempts to actually do so. But as long as only the wise help heaven to realize its desires, the key differentiation between them and the rest of society will continue to exist. Nonetheless, this is not the sole demarca-tion line in society.

Even the differentiation between the rulers and the ruled cannot be completely eliminated in the name of universal love. From the heav-enly point of view, all human beings are, on one hand, equal. Heaven desires the well-being of all of them. So the ruled, for instance, have a duty to remonstrate their rulers if the latter, for example, do not carry out their tasks properly, or if they do not promote the well-being of their subjects. On the other hand, however, rulers can be criticized only within certain limits since obedience to authority is imperative for a well-functioning state.

So the social-chaos assumption does not hold. Mo Di cannot be said to propagate a total elimination of social hierarchy. He simply under-lines the respect which is vital to well-functioning social relations. One is asked to express this respect by trying to place the other on an equal footing and, thereby, giving her due. In practice, this often means putting in an effort to improve the situation of the other.[9] Rulers, for example, are asked to enrich, honor, and respect their subjects; subordi-nates are asked to offer their services to them.[10]

Rulers should use just monetary rewards to honor the services ren-dered by their subjects; the latter should express their honor to the rulers by working well. One could interpret this point as follows: Social differentiation alone cannot be taken to be a crucial indicator of progress. Societies can only develop when they, and their members, adopt a benevolent attitude towards others. Only this benevolence can help combat the disruptive forces of egoism.

All in all, Mo Di is clear about the fact that a good life can only be led within a (human) community. However, such a bounded communal life cannot mean that we can afford to be completely indifferent to the interests of others outside our community. Jingoism cannot be justi-fied. An analysis of the consequences of such actions will reveal that partiality of any kind leads to negative social consequences. Despite the communal character of our prosaic life, Mo Di would say, we would do well to treat strangers just as we treat ourselves, and would like to be treated by them.

### 13.3.3  Mencius' conception of a good life

The Confucian Mencius (Mengzi, Meng-K'e; ca. 370–290 B.C.E.), one of Mo Di's foremost critics, would definitely not be convinced by Mo Di's interpretation of a good life. He controversially claims that the doctrine of universal love eliminates the distinction between man and beast. "If the way [of Mo] does not subside and the way of Confucius is not proclaimed, the people will be deceived by heresies and the path of morality will be blocked. When the path of morality is blocked, then we will show animals the way to devour men, and sooner or later it will come to mean men devouring men." (Lau, 1976, p. 114)

Despite Mencius' vitriolic attack, some points of intersection between him and Mo Di cannot be overlooked. Mencius also advocates benevolence, emphasizes the need for self-cultivation, takes the wise to be social role-models, and believes that heaven desires a moral life for humans. But Mencius' conception of a good life differs from that of Mo Di in many respects.

Mencius begins with the similarity between members of a species (6a7). All members of the human species are said to possess common traits such as compassion, shame, and respect, and the capacity to differentiate right from wrong (6a6, 2a6). These traits, in turn, enable the cardinal virtues of benevolence (*ren*), dutifulness (*yi*), observance of rites (*li*), wisdom (*zhi*), and faith (*hsin*), which are crucial to the relationship between father and son, between rulers and ruled, between man and woman, between young and old, and between friends. Mo Di's theory of universal love is said to be detrimental to these fundamental human relationships.

But if these virtues are inborn, why does social degeneration occur at all? Human nature, says Mencius, is like water. Just as its flow changes due to its external circumstances, so too are human beings susceptible to the circumstances they find themselves in. "That man can be made bad shows that his nature is no different from that of water in this respect." (Lau, 1976, p. 50)[11] A human being can only retain her good nature if she, like all other living beings, gets the right care and nourishment (6a8). The family is considered to be the ideal place for such care. That is why Mencius, like other Confucians, held filial piety (*xiao*) to be of the utmost importance. The love of one's parents is considered to be inborn and the purest form of love. It is the only fundamental basis of human existence and enables us to engage in other interpersonal relations. In other words, it is through filial love that we attain our humanity (4a28). Furthermore, this love is said to be in congruence with the wishes of heaven. This view leads Mencius to believe that Mo Di's doctrine of impartiality, his "love without discrimination," implies a further, second basis of human existence and, therefore, contradicts heavenly authority (3a5).

Mencius' fundamental point of difference with Mo Di is his view that universal love does not and cannot exist. He reasons that filial piety is inborn. It can, as a first step, be extended to older siblings; the respect felt towards them can then be extended towards all.[12] The natural love of parents can be extended through an intricate web of relationships to humanity at large. "A benevolent man extends his love from those he loves to those he does not love." (ibid., p. 194) Benevolence, therefore, can only be relative to the concrete relationship one has with others (7a45). Closer relationships in this web, though, have a stronger claim on oneself. Parents can indeed claim a greater love than others. It is, therefore, not only unnatural to love all to the same degree: universal love also amounts to a denial of one's parents. Universal love makes us deny the source of our humanity.

However, Mencius' underlining of filial piety is not to be understood as a vindication of self-interest. He cannot be interpreted to mean, for example, that only one's own interests and those of closer relatives should matter to us. He points out that self-interest must be given up when it becomes an obstacle to moral behavior. Nevertheless, one cannot categorically decry it. Depending on the situation, it is sometimes prudent to act in accordance with self-interest; for example, there is nothing to be gained by standing under a wall on the verge of collapse (7a2). Mencius' claim is that graded love alone will enable us to consider and fulfill the interests of all concerned in a just manner. Graded love alone leads to moral behavior.

Mencius also attributes a different role to heaven in his theory. Mo Di does not make use of a common theory of human nature. He first projects his own ideal conception of a human life onto heaven, and then, using the concept of a heavenly decree, brings this ideal conception back to earth. The two principal reasons for universal love, namely, heavenly will and positive consequences, both relate back to the human being. Nonetheless, the roots of this love are not located within this being itself.

However, Mencius, with his positive theory of human nature, does not need this line of argument. Although heaven in his view also desires human welfare, human beings are said to possess an innate, moral disposition which can be brought to the fore with the right care and nourishment. Human patterns of behavior, therefore, are not in need of fundamental external changes; a human being cannot be made good solely by the use of external force or by getting her to follow royal decrees (7b24). All that one has to do for this purpose is to begin the search within one's own self. Under the right circumstances, one cannot help but be a great human being (6a15).

However, Mencius is always aware of the frailty of human life. Without a strong commitment to our moral principles – without self-cultivation – we run the risk of giving in to adverse circumstances.

> [T]here are things a man wants more than life and there are also things he loathes more than death. This is an attitude not confined to the moral man but common to all men. The moral man simply never loses it.
>
> Here is a basketful of rice and a bowlful of soup. Getting them will mean life; not getting them will mean death. When these are given with abuse, even a wayfarer would not accept them; when these are given after being trampled upon, even a beggar would not accept them. Yet when it comes to ten thousand bushels of grain one is supposed to accept without asking if it is in accordance with the rites or if it is right to do so. What benefit are ten thousand bushels of grain to me? (Do I accept them) for the sake of beautiful houses, the enjoyment of wives and concubines, or for the sake of the gratitude my needy acquaintances will show me? What I would not accept in the first instance when it was a matter of life and death I now accept for the sake of beautiful houses; what I would not accept when it was a matter of life and death I now accept for the enjoyment of wives and concubines; what I would not accept when it was a matter of life and death I now accept for the sake of the gratitude my needy acquaintances will show me. Is there no way of putting a stop to this? This way of thinking is known as losing one's original heart. (ibid., 166–167)

For Mencius, therefore, a good life can only be led within a bounded community. In this community, a well-defined web of relationships determines the way one member deals with another. This, however, cannot be taken to mean that it is virtually impossible to extend this circle of relationships. In fact, a closer look at strangers on the boundaries of one's community would reveal many similarities in their nature and our own. So it behooves us to treat them with honor.

Both Mo Di and Mencius appeal to discursive reasoning as the basis of their claims. In fact Mencius, who openly categorizes Mo Di's views as heresy, tries to combat his opponent's views with words alone and does not resort to their suppression by force. As he himself notes, there is no alternative but to dispute such views (3b9). Also, both believe that acting virtuously means acting for the right reason. Mencius, like Mo Di, argues that there are strong arguments for treating others morally, even those outside our community. Mo Di pursues this argument by trying to outline the positive consequences of benevolent actions. For Mencius, communal ties alone enable us to perceive and treat the other as a fellow human being. Further, both would emphasize that it is not enough merely to develop a sound theory of a good life. The proof of such a theory also lies in living according to it.

## 13.4 Implications for business ethics

Today, the ease with which our philosophical predecessors attributed huge differences to members of other cultural settings is simply baffling. Indians were, for example, commonly thought of being caught up in a perennial dreamlike, irrational state and badly in need of "an externally imported world-ordering rationality." (Inden, 1990, p. 128) The Chinese were said to fare better because they at least possessed an inkling of political thought. Yet despite their long political tradition, even the Chinese, like their Indian counterparts, were considered to be notoriously lacking in individuality, dominated by custom and fatalism, and, therefore, not worthy of being considered as moral agents in their own right. Today, in all fields of philosophy this outright chauvinism is rarely supported openly. Only a few explicitly attempt to challenge the idea of equal consideration of the other, and the idea itself is rapidly gaining ground. But how does one flesh out the idea of equal consideration from the perspective of business ethics? One way would be to sketch out the concrete guidelines of conduct which would follow from such an idea. This would help managers who try to grapple with the moral and cultural diversity of their employees.

Most books on business ethics, in fact, seem to follow this line of thinking. In the transnational context, for example, individuals and corporations are asked not to do harm, promote the good, respect human rights and cultural differences, and so on (see De George, 1995, 486–487). With the help of such guidelines one tries to work out concrete ways of, for example, achieving justice, respect for life, truth-telling, avoiding child labor, and doing away with hazardous working conditions in the global corporate setting. Such books seem to be motivated by the belief that abstract and academic discussions on humanity are plainly time-consuming for managers. Instead it is thought better to present them with a handy checklist for dealing with employees/colleagues of diverse cultural backgrounds, such as members of Indian and Chinese communities. In fact, on the basis of such a view one would also expect this paper to link, at least in this concluding section, the positions of the Indian and Chinese philosophers mentioned above with their respective cultures and then work out their implications for the concrete issues that arise in the corporate setting.

There are many good reasons, however, for not proceeding in such a manner. *First*, the concept of a culture is notoriously vague and cannot be used meaningfully without further clarification. Does culture signify the artifacts produced by a particular cultural/national group? Or does it, as in its classic usage, refer to the process of individual and collective self-cultivation? Can one, moreover, without further qualifications, meaningfully talk of a single and homogenous Indian or Chinese culture, keeping in mind the sheer size and diversity of those countries?

*Second*, there is reason to believe that working out a well-meaning list of to-dos will be of limited practical use. Let us focus on one historical aspect to work out the practical import of this point. International business dealings are not a completely new phenomenon. Those engaged in such dealings in the past did not usually spend time pondering whether there were adequate grounds on which to postulate a common humanity. They were simply driven by the prospect of opening up and engaging in new and lucrative markets. Their focus on profit-making was motivated by their belief that their arduous journey into faraway lands had to pay out financially. Many of them, therefore, did not attempt to question or analyze the wider social repercussions of their business dealings. For them, any ethically informed attempt to do so would have being distracting, to say the least.

Today, if one is earnestly committed to the implementation of the idea of equal consideration such an attitude must be discarded, even in debates on business ethics. In this case, equipping a manager with a skeletal list of guidelines will be of no avail. With their help alone, a manager impute her own interpretation of such notions as refraining from harmful actions, promoting the good, and respecting the other, to the other person. It is easy to see that misunderstanding and conflicts will ensue. Such cross-cultural pitfalls, however, can be avoided if she knows what notions such as harm, the good, and respect mean for the people she is dealing with. It does not suffice, therefore, to know how to act in a particular setting. She also has to know more about the setting itself. This leads us to a further theoretical point.

In the long run, it is imperative in business ethics to work out a basis for equal consideration. To be globally applicable, this justification of equal consideration would have to be able to integrate different cultural contexts. This presupposes that one is familiar with diverse cultural contexts before (or at least while) developing such a theory. One effective way of getting acquainted with these contexts is to engage in a dialogue with the people who live in them. Such a dialogue, though, is no easy task. Especially if one is unfamiliar with a particular cultural context, it is quite likely that one will initially only perceive differences between the unfamiliar context and one's own. It would be detrimental to the development of such a theory, however, if one decided to discontinue the dialogue because the differences perceived appear to be fundamentally opposed to one's own cultural setting. To put it differently: Developing a theory of equal consideration which can integrate diverse cultural contexts presupposes a willingness to understand these contexts. Even if this process of understanding is temporarily impeded by a perception of differences, it would be rash to break off the dialogue at this point.[13]

A good case in point is the humanistic idea itself. Locating the seeds of humanism in one context alone could be of some academic interest. Yet, for our purposes, such a debate would have to be supplemented by an exploration of humanistic resources in various other (non-Western) traditions. During such an exploration, one has to be open to the possibility of initial setbacks in understanding. Depending on one's perspective, for example, many aspects of the Indian and Chinese positions expounded in this essay could be regarded as quaint and offbeat. If one does not give up at this point, however, one would proceed to discover how a case for universal humanity can be made against the backdrop of another cultural setting. Despite the particularities of such a setting, it will be hard to overlook the fact that these accounts of humanity also operate with familiar values such as human fallibility and frailty, the perfectibility of human life achieved through a honing of intellectual skills and learning, benevolence, and respect for the other. Such an exploration will also bear out the point that the idea of equal consideration can be, and has been, instantiated in different guises in diverse cultural settings.

A contextual exploration of other (intellectual) traditions could, therefore, help enrich debates in business ethics. This investigation into Indian and Chinese philosophical traditions has tried to demonstrate, first, why people should be treated according to the idea of equal consideration and, second, give substance to a contextual understanding of such an idea. Only such a contextual exploration will help a globally agile manager to see her employee, fellow colleague, or senior as an equally situated fellow human being.

## Notes

1. Since Hegel did base this statement on statistical data, its empirical dimension will not be discussed here.
2. "Because the making of mistakes is natural to man; and hence when putting forward valid reasons it often happens that he propounds reasons which (though he thinks are valid) are in reality invalid or fallacious; and when he does so he is defeated (by the pointing out of Fallacies [sic!] in his reason)." (Uddyotakara, 1999: 76–77)
3. Thus understood, the weaker claim can be interpreted to be a critique of a thorough hedonism. In fact, the orthodox systems develop various strategies to challenge this point.
4. Depending on the system concerned, direct perception (*pratyaksa*), inference (*anumana*), authority or testimony (*sabda*), comparison (*upamana*), postulation or assumption (*arthapatti*), and noncognition of a nonexistent entity (*anupalabdhi* or *abhava*) qualify as means to knowledge. In the quotation above, Ramanuja, for example, explicitly accepts texts and perception as such means.
5. The *Advaita* also belongs to the *Vedanta* system. *Vedanta* literally means "the end or the final portions of the Vedas." All the systems that are called *Vedanta* accept the older *Upanishads*, the *Bhagavad Gita*, and the *Brahmasutras* as authoritative texts.
6. Mo Di would deny that his understanding of universal love is based purely on self-interest. He thinks that if one were only concerned about one's own advantage, the other person will, in all probability, not respond with love.
7. In overcoming the state of nature, one is said to progress from chaotic anarchy to a state of affairs in which social life is ordered.
8. "If one conducts one's affairs in accordance with what is correct, acts in the name of righteousness, strives for lenience in ruling one's subjects and good faith in dealing with one's army, and thus sets an example for the armies of the other feudal lords, then one will have no enemy under heaven and bring incalculable benefit to the world." (Watson, 1967, p. 60)
9. "Now if we seek to benefit the world by taking universality as our standard, those with sharp ears and clear eyes will see and hear for others, those with sturdy limbs will work for others, and those with a knowledge of the Way will endeavor to teach others." (ibid., p. 41)
10. Heaven "desires that among men those who have strength will work for others, those who understand the Way will teach others, and those who possess wealth will share it with others. It also desires that those above will diligently attend to matters of government, and those below will diligently carry out their tasks." (ibid., p. 85)

11. " 'As far as what is genuinely in him is concerned, a man is capable of becoming good,' said Mencius. 'That is what I mean by good. As for his becoming bad, that is not the fault of his native endowment.' " (ibid., p. 163)
12. "Loving one's parents is benevolence; respecting one's elders is rightness. What is left to be done is simply the extension of these to the whole Empire." (ibid., p. 184)
13. How can one discern that one does not project one's own categories onto the other? This is part of a large debate and cannot be tackled within the scope of this paper. It suffices to say that the other parties involved in the dialogue can, and should, correct such misperceptions. Also, it is reasonable to hold that a satisfactory understanding of another context will help one locate commonalities *and* differences in it.

## Bibliography

De George, Richard, *Business Ethics*. (New Jersey: Prentice Hall, 1995).

Hegel, Georg Wilhelm Friedrich, *The Philosophy of History*, With Prefaces by Charles Hegel and the Translator John Sibree. (Ontario: Batoche Books, 2001) (http://socserv.mcmaster.ca/econ/ugcm/3ll3/hegel/history.pdf, Accessed March 30, 2009).

Inden, Ronald, *Imagining India*. (Oxford/Cambridge Mass.: Basil Blackwell, 1990).

Jha, Ganganath, *The Nyaya-Sutras of Gautama, With the Bhasya of Vatsayana and the Vartikka of Uddyotakara I, Translated into English with Notes from Vachaspati Mishra's "Nyayavarttika-Tatparyatika" Udayana's "Parishuddi" and Raguthamma's "Bhasyachandra"*. (Delhi: Motilal Banarsidass, 1999).

Lau, Din Cheuk, *Mencius, Translated with an Introduction*. (Middlesex etc.: Penguin, 1976).

Radhakrishnan, Sarvepalli and Moore, Charles (eds), *A Source Book in Indian Philosophy*. (Princeton, New Jersey: Princeton Press, 1957).

Thibaut, George, *The Vedanta-Sutras III, With the Commentary by Ramanuja*. (Delhi et al.: Motilal Banarsidass, 1962).

Watson, Burton, *Basic Writings of Mo Tzu, Hsün Tzu, and Han Fei Tzu*. (New York/London: Columbia, 1967).

Yi-Pao Mei, *The Ethical and Political Works of Motse*, Translated From the Original Chinese Text. (Westport, Connecticut: Hyperion, 1973).

# 14

## "African Humanism" and a Case Study from the Swahili Coast

*Kai Kresse*

### 14.1 Introduction

Humanism is, by its very nature, a term with transcultural and even universal appeal, as it invokes the inherent qualities supposedly possessed by all members of the human species. Yet what qualifies human beings generally as "human" or even "humane" may differ from one society or cultural framework to another. This applies within Africa as well as outside it. In this paper, I sketch out some comparative features from across the continent, using the term "African humanism" as pragmatic shorthand in which the adjective "African" points to a variety of regional and cultural contexts that qualify and determine the range of visions and versions of humanism that have been meaningful in, or for, Africa (for alternative discussions, see Macamo, 2009, Lategan, 2009). My contribution starts off by sketching out some of these visions and versions in an introductory section that also tries to convey a sense of the relevant historical backgrounds and political contexts. Touching on aspects of anticolonial and postcolonial politics, ideology, and philosophy in Africa, I proceed with a case study which is based on my own ethnographic research. This is centered on the Swahili concept of *utu*, "humanity," and the particular ways in which a Muslim poet from Kenya has presented his own interpretations of it in a didactic poem that follows classic conventions. Contextualizing and contrasting his position – which we may loosely call a "Swahili humanism" – with others, as expressed in proverbs and social debates in the Swahili context around him, I finally touch on some aspects that may be relevant to the way business practices (similarly, across Africa) are seen to be conducted properly or fairly.

Before proceeding, I would like to touch on the need for a critical discussion of the neoliberal order that African economies and societies have been pressured into, in the aftermath of the Cold War (with its peculiar opportunities and pitfalls for Africa). This is something I cannot cover adequately here, so I briefly appeal to the work of the anthropologist James Ferguson. Drawing from a broad scope of ethnographic readings, he highlights as a common basic feature across African societies that it "is not that the human world is ruled by powerful objects, but that all of the world, even the natural, bears the traces of *human agency*" (Ferguson, 2006, p. 74). This fundamental humanizing feature bears on economic as well as other social relations in Africa. This means that a common framework of moral expectations and obligations has been implicit in the ways that economic exchange and political rule work – and that rulers and subjects, politicians and people, as well as economic agents more generally, comply (at least on the surface) with the demands of this framework. However, what the "structural adjustment" programs by the IMF and World Bank have done, according to Ferguson – in a fashion that he casts as antihumanist – is to fundamentally "de-moralize" African economic relations: They took the human and social underpinnings out of the "economic" when imposing a set of objective and supposedly "scientific" rules and requirements upon African economic systems. For Ferguson, the evident failure to achieve successful economic revival through such measures points at the need to "re-moralize" African economics. In this way, the conceptual and moral concerns and assumptions still implicit in the ways that African societies work can be taken on board and brought to bear positively on the way that economics might be reshaped and revived. "African traditions of moral discourse on questions of economic process," according to Ferguson, can then be seen "as intellectual and political resources for the future" (2006: 82). These concerns should be taken on board when thinking about Africa from a business perspective as well as from one that flags up ethical concern.

## 14.2 Visions and versions of African humanism

Influential conceptualizations of "African humanism" were first coined in the political realm – what the Kenyan philosopher Oruka (1990, orig. 1978) classified as the "nationalist-ideological trend" in African philosophy. Most prominently, this was in the context of anticolonial liberation struggles by some of the leading figures of African nationalist movements in the 1950s and 1960s, who became the first generation of post-Independence rulers. Here, the relevance of the Cold War for the development of political ideologies and visions can hardly be overstated, with political and economic pressures (and offers) for capitalist or socialist orientations being applied (and considered) from the different sides. These dynamics shaped the – often forceful – efforts to create "third ways" of an "African" and therefore regionally more adequate and ethically more sound orientation in politics; this was to continue in the coming decades of African political independence, through the 1970s and 1980s. For the early phase, at least, one needs to recognize the seriousness with which ideological visions of humane, unified, egalitarian and "good" societies for the postcolonial African future were created, with a certain image of the African past in mind. These ideologies sought to go beyond the simple choice between capitalism and communism, were often critical of both, and staunch in their rejection of the imperialism, colonialism, and racism that had not only oppressed African peoples but also violated their norms and values. To reinstate the latter as national ideologies for nation-building was a major concern for the independent African states and their rulers. This involved the rhetorical use of positive key-terms that signaled a humane agenda, commonly of a one-party government that presented itself as ruling for, and with, the people: for instance, "love, hope and faith" for Kaunda's Zambia (Kaunda, 1974, p. 128), or "peace, love, and unity" later on for Moi's Kenya (Moi, 1986).

It was Kenneth Kaunda, who would become the first president of independent Zambia (formerly British Northern Rhodesia), who presented his political ideology most explicitly under the banner of "African humanism" (Kaunda, 1968, 1974). Engaged not only in Zambia's own struggle for political liberation but also in the stand-off against the racist regime of neighboring Southern Rhodesia (later Zimbabwe) where "white" minority rule over the African population continued, Kaunda flagged up a "humanist approach that is traditional and inherent in our African society" (ibid., p. 3). This approach emphasized a "man-centred society" or what he also called a "mutual aid society" (ibid., 4–5), in which there was no place for selfishness, envy, laziness, or greed. The link to socialism was strong and explicit; as Kaunda phrased it, "one cannot be a humanist without being a socialist" (1974, p. 6). Yet he rejected both communism and capitalism for their instrumental approach, which prioritized ideology over people and thus neglected their humanity. For him, the realization of African humanism relied (in theory, at least) on a "One-Party Participatory Democracy" (1974, p. 10) in which leadership was based on a consensus that was itself created through the involvement of the citizens. Nevertheless, Zambians were suffering hardship and hunger even under this "humanist" regime (see, for example, Ferguson, 2006, p 77).

Related and far better known approaches than Kaunda's include those of the three most prominent African presidents of the first generation, Julius Nyerere (Tanzania), Kwame Nkrumah (Ghana), and Leopold Sedar Senghor (Senegal), who had also been leading anti-colonial activists of their countries. The Ghanaian philosopher Wiredu (1996, p. 146) in retrospect described them as "philosopher kings", a Platonic term that captures the internal tension between their academic backgrounds, their utopian aspirations, and their (increasingly) authoritarian methods of rule once they were in power. These political thinkers-leaders-rulers presented their respective versions of an aspired political future for their countries within a liberated Africa based on the idea of strong moral "African traditions" that could show the way, and an "African personality" that could shoulder the change. This was characterized by common social values and a somewhat romanticized vision of a precolonial African past, elements seen to be underpinning, embracing, and reconnecting the continent after it had suffered colonialism.

Julius Nyerere's concept of *ujamaa* (literally "familyhood" in Swahili) alluded to the mutual responsibilities and obligations within the family as a leitmotif for the creation of a postcolonial nation-state that was built on "traditional African values." In English, this is usually called "African socialism," both by African politicians and in the Anglophone research literature (for example, Rosberg et al., 1964), but the term *ujamaa* was also invoked by less socialist-leaning statesmen, such as Kenyatta in Kenya, to push unifying nationalization policies (Kenyatta 1968). The idea of an initially nationally conceived but tentatively continental and even global "brotherhood" or "comradeship" – in Swahili, *undugu* – included and merged socialist connotations with culturalist and traditionalist ones. Modernization and social development, for Tanzania as for Africa on the whole, was envisaged as possible and desirable only along the lines of these values (see, for example, Nyerere, 1973).

Kwame Nkrumah's political ideology which aimed to rebuild Ghanaian (and African) society in the spirit of decolonization drew similarly from the idea of African traditions as social roots to create the vision of a modern African nation-state explicitly founded on a peculiar African humanism. With obvious Marxist connotations, his idea of "conscienscism" argued for the implementation of a kind of socialism which would be modern yet also "in tune with the original humanist principles underlying African society" (1978, p. 70). The goal was to satisfy the demands of an "African personality" – a term coined by

Nkrumah in particular – which was defined by those principles (ibid., p. 79).

Again along similar lines, the Senegalese poet and statesman Leopold S. Senghor (together with Aimé Césaire and others, in colonial Paris) coined a Francophone ideology of "négritude" as a common spiritual and emotive, and thus humane, social bond among Africans. Indeed, Senghor's probably most popular political book was called *Négritude et Humanisme* (1964). This was conceived of and developed in response to a dominant and oppressive rationalist mind-set of the West with its rather inhumane technocratic and colonial associations. Yet it presented not a simple relativist position but had a universal appeal (famously taken up by Jean-Paul Sartre in his introductory essay to négritude poetry, 1972). Here a fundamental African "vital force" of natural creativity, also described as a kind of "emotional rationality," was seen to provide the basis for a future humane society built upon African values, both in Africa and potentially beyond (see also Chakrabarty, 2009). This position was taken up and popularized as the stance of a political and cultural "African renaissance" movement that advocated and reflected a "new (or neo-) African culture" ranged around such a basic conception of man as *muntu* (see Jahn, 1961); I will discuss some of its problematic aspects further below.

As well as these well-known and often quoted classic examples of the early postcolonial period, we should also note the more recent presence of such a stance pushing for the political realization of African humanism in other countries. This notably became a central feature of the politics of national reconciliation and the new African renaissance in postapartheid South Africa. In different ways, the term *ubuntu*, meaning "humanity" in the Southern African Nguni group of the Bantu languages, was used as a conceptual corner-stone of a political ideology seeking to unify an internally diverse multiracial and multicultural "rainbow nation." This can be seen in Archbishop Desmond Tutu's speeches and his conceptual guidance for the Truth and Reconciliation Commission; later on and differently, in President Thabo Mbeki's call for a new "African renaissance", its impetus and driving force coming from South Africa itself (see, for example, Mbeki, 1998). The idea of an African humanism, represented in regionally specific ways of thinking and acting, had already played a certain role in the antiapartheid struggle. For instance, it was with the "quest for true humanity" that Steve Biko, the leader of the Black Consciousness Movement called for the overcoming of racist politics, anticipating "a more human face" for South Africa with freedom and equality for all its citizens (Biko, 1988: pp. 61; 114).

Such basic statements advocating political ideologies of humanism refer back to, and are rooted in, accepted social conceptions of what it means to be "human," as seen and formulated from within these societies. Thus there is a link back from political ideology to historically developed and culturally embedded assumptions of philosophical anthropology (what characterizes human beings, how humanity displays itself or is performed in actions) – or at least common and popularized versions of it. Proverbs and sayings are used as illustrations by politicians and academics from South to West Africa. That a human being is human (and humane), and a person a person, *through others*, is widely quoted in different texts and with reference to diverse regional contexts – across West and Central Africa to East and South Africa. There are also more refined theoretical elaborations upon "humanity," shaped by reflexive individuals in their respective African contexts, as elsewhere around the globe. Apart from qualified academics, this also applies to local scholars or intellectuals, educated within regional traditions of knowledge. Here, qualified fieldwork and extensive interviews with such individual "sages," by philosophers and anthropologists alike, can be illuminating (see Oruka, 1991, Presbey, 2002). This is of significance for my contribution here, as I present an illustrative case study of a theoretical discussion of "humanity" in the East African context by a Swahili poet, which takes place within a poem and uses a classic didactic genre. I will contextualize and discuss this poem and its Swahili key term *utu* (humanity, being human) with a view to related popular notions of "Swahili humanism." What applies to the Swahili example as well as the other African cases mentioned above, in terms of a common vision of being human, is the idea that social bases and contexts are imparting values to the members of the social group. Social actors are seen as fundamentally defined by, and shaping themselves in relation to, normative parameters valid within their group, provided by religious and/or cosmological frameworks that structure ritual and everyday life. For ethnographic examples for this from other African regions, we can look at, for instance, the Chemba in the Cameroonian grasslands (Fardon, 1990), the Uduk in Southern Sudan (James, 1989), or the BaKongo in Central Africa (MacGaffey, 1986). Yet while this emphasis on sociality is important to note across the continent, it does not mean that ideas and realizations of individuality should be seen as impossible or ruled out under these circumstances. Nor does it mean that intellectually disposed individuals could not develop critical notions and conceptions and present alternative interpretations to those that are commonly accepted by popular opinion within their social communities. Indeed, it was on this that Oruka directed his focus in his sage philosophy project (Oruka, 1991), which I will draw on for the following discussion of my own case study from the East African Swahili coast.

## 14.3   "Swahili humanism": an ethnographic approach and a textual case study

Before discussing a particular textual example of what could be called "Swahili humanism" – or better: a particular version and advocacy of humanism in the contemporary Swahili context – let me clarify the perspective employed here. Trained in academic philosophy and anthropology, and reasonably fluent in the Swahili language (through academic studies and travels), I pursued a doctoral research project in anthropology, on philosophical discourse on the Kenyan Swahili coast, seeking to portray and discuss selected individual Swahili thinkers in their social context (the thesis being subsequently revised and published as Kresse 2007). Since in religious terms the coastal urban communities have mostly been Muslim over the centuries – though during and after British colonial rule (1895–1963) large numbers of Christians came in from upcountry – I also engaged with the regional history of Islam, in order to better understand the background and framework within which reflections and discussions were couched. I was in contact and conversation with local intellectuals (Muslim scholars, poets, and healers), and also investigated local genres of written and oral discourse that mediated and expressed reflexive thinking and social critique: poetry, Islamic pamphlets and speeches, and everyday discussions. I based my ethnographic research on the premise that philosophy is a knowledge-oriented human activity which can be performed in many styles and idioms around the world. Thus it should also be investigated *in situ*, in the social field where it is practiced and acknowledged. For this task of writing an ethnography of philosophical discourse and practice, I developed a programmatic and general approach for an "anthropology of philosophy," exemplified by reference to Africanist literature and discussions (Kresse, 2007, 11–35) and particularly inspired by Odera Oruka's sage philosophy project (Oruka, 1991; see Graness and Kresse, 1997).

Here, I draw on an in-depth case pursued as part of my larger study, namely a poetically formulated description and discussion of "humanity" (*utu* in Swahili), composed in the 1960s by a well-known contemporary Swahili poet from Mombasa, Ahmad Nassir Juma Bhalo. During my yearlong ethnographic research in Mombasa, I spent many hours with him in person, discussing his poem and the issues covered in it. In parallel, I discussed the concept of *utu* with many other local friends and informants (who were often not highly educated or qualified). Overall, I have argued that Nassir develops and spells out an original theory of what being human and being moral means in the Swahili context (Kresse 2007: Chapter 5). This is individually shaped, drawing heavily from established social notions, beliefs, and convictions in the social world around him, but also engaging critically with these while building up his distinct interpretation of *utu*. As we will see, Ahmad Nassir conveys a universalist conceptualization of *utu*, meaning both "humanity" and "goodness" (similar to the German *Menschlichkeit*) in his poem *Utenzi wa Mtu ni Utu*. He develops his points with reference to existing social knowledge as expressed in proverbs and sayings, and he draws on established concepts and idiomatic expressions. Though his moral theory starts off from common social knowledge and uses many recognizable terms, it also goes beyond this, for instance when presenting a critique of "tribalism" (*ukabila*) in society. The poem picks up a series of sub-concepts of *utu* in a sequence of sections, covering friendship, love, humility, and other relevant key terms.

The poet uses the classic *utenzi* genre of Swahili didactic poetry as a culturally specific medium, and his verbal artistry enables him to present moral theory in an aesthetically pleasing manner. Nassir's poem contributes to a wider social discourse on morality, enriching it with his own interpretation of *utu*. As is typical for Swahili didactic poetry, it is used by the poet to remind his social peers of the existing rules and standards of proper behavior (vis-à-vis one's spouse, parents, children, and friends), which are elaborated upon and confirmed. This aspect of reminding others of the (practically relevant) things they ought to know is part of a wider moral obligation among Muslims, an obligation for which the higher educated and more knowledgeable take on a more pronounced responsibility. Derived directly from the Qur'an, this obligation is known throughout the Muslim world and is well captured in the phrase "commanding right and forbidding wrong" (see Cook, 2000). It includes the demand that everyone should keep a good caring eye on their family, friends, and neighbors so that they do not stray from the right path, and to intervene and hinder people from doing something bad. For the Swahili context, this mutual obligation of forbidding evil (*kukanyana maovu*) is very much present in the sub-text of everyday life; we may be able to see it as encapsulating something of an implicit "Islamic humanism" that underpins and informs the "Swahili humanism" I am talking about here. It involves the point of making good use of one's knowledge, of performing one's deeds according to one's knowledge, thus of having the moral obligation (toward oneself and one's peers) to put knowledge into action (see also Kresse, 2009). Let me proceed to sketch out the main conceptual features and arguments presented in the poem, and point briefly at the way that they relate to, and in turn draw from, common social knowledge in the Swahili context.

## 14.4   A Swahili poem teaching "humanity"

Ahmad Nassir's long didactic poem *Utenzi wa mtu ni utu* (The *utenzi* about "a human being is *utu*") provides basic reflection on what it means to be "human" and "good" – or on "Swahili humanism", as one of my Mombasan friends used to say, using the English term. This is done in a poem whose conceptual and aesthetic framework is determined by historical conventions of knowledge, religion, and linguistic form, and which is situated within postcolonial Mombasa. The poem was composed in 1960, when Kenya was still under colonial rule, during the month of Ramadan (a period during which Muslim intellectuals often accomplish a particular project or self-set task). At the time, Ahmad Nassir was only 24 years old (Nassir, 1978, p. 3), and for his age already incredibly well-versed in proverbs, local knowledge, and verbal artistry. Almost forty years later in my discussions with him, he emphatically confirmed (and elaborated upon) the substance of his arguments back then.

The expression *mtu ni utu* used in the title of the poem – literally: "A human being is *utu* (goodness, humanity)" – is itself a proverb, representing a kind of folk wisdom. Thus the title already indicates the complex interrelationship between individual and social knowledge that is negotiated here: Individual reflection on a common key concept is presented through reference to social conceptions of knowledge, in a form of historically established verbal art. As Ahmad Nassir says in his preface, he seeks "to explain in a pleasing and decorative way" matters that will be of benefit to the reader (ibid., p. 1). Here the poet puts himself at the service of society as a conscientious teacher of social values who uses his personal talents for the common good. The poem itself has 457 stanzas, organized in ten subsections that either highlight topical themes (such as love, friendship, and the relation between spouses) or are genre-specific conventional sections formally introducing and concluding the poem. The general patterns of the *utenzi* genre are followed: A classical rhyme scheme is kept up throughout the poem, as is the conventional order of composite parts, starting with an invocation of God and ending with a short self-description of the poet and the date of the composition. Not having sufficient space here to cover the whole poem in detail, I will limit myself to some core features of his theory of *utu*.

The section *Upendano*, mutual love (or "loving another"), is fundamentally relevant to the theory of moral goodness developed in the poem. In this part, basic conceptions of human equality, moral knowledge, freedom of action, and moral responsibility are established as parts of *utu*. Nassir sketches out an ideal kind of love (*pendo bora*; 62) that all human beings should have for one another. Marked by true mutual concern for each other, this is the precondition for human beings to live as one (*kitu kimoja*; 61). But the author admits not being able to give any real example of such love (63). Love, we could say, is thus used as a regulative principle. Rather than an empirical fact of human life it is a moral demand upon individual human beings providing practical orientation. As such, love characterizes a task that is inherent in the hypothetical statement that has just been related: If you want to live in peace with others, you have to give such love. The bottom line is: If you want the ideal world to have a chance to come about, you have to act as if you were already part of it. This conveys what could be called a circle of the moral sphere: What is aspired to in the end already has to be presupposed in the beginning; to become part of the morally good world one has to act as if one were already living in it. In such a way, through our moral imagination, we can be aware of an ideal love, and use it for our orientation when seeking to behave as moral beings.

Such love presupposes the equality of all human beings, as it is *pendo la sawa*, an egalitarian love (84). In contrast, love that is selective, we are told, "has no meaning" but causes evil (85). This shows the fundamental conception of human equality with which Nassir's elaboration of *utu* works. This does not mean that all people are the same, or that there are no differences between them. Nassir regards human beings' differences in appearance as a "tough test" to all people by God, a test which is good for them because it poses a fruitful challenge of how living together can really be achieved (117–123). The moral equality of all entails egalitarian love as a precondition, if discord, hatred, discrimination, jealousy, and quarrels are to be surmounted (70–78). Again and again, as part of *utu*, Nassir emphasizes the necessity to imagine and create an all-embracing, truly global human unity, without any *ukabila* (tribalism, ethnocentrism). He reconfirmed this point to me emphatically during interviews, stating that ethnicity (one's tribe) is nothing more than "an identity card." Accordingly, *utu* is not a concept exclusively for and by Swahili people or Swahili speakers, but for all human beings who show their *utu* as part of such a moral unity.

However, he says, it is up to us as human beings to realize our potential membership in the moral community, to decorate ourselves with *utu* (123). This underlines the moral responsibility of us individually as moral agents. We are responsible for good and bad actions (95), because as human beings "we should know good and bad" (211). Moral knowledge is the basis of responsibility. We human beings have this knowledge because God taught it to us (explicitly in the Qur'an), together with his recommendations to follow the good way. We are, however, says Nassir, not compelled by God to perform in a morally good way (if we were, we would not need any moral advice at all), but free to decide for ourselves. This appears to be why, both in the folk theories and in Nassir's poem itself, the emphasis on the actual performance of good deeds that correspond to *utu* is crucial. Performing good actions is the only way to become part of the moral community which we are assumed to be part of from the beginning: "Goodness is action" (in Swahili: *utu ni kitendo*).

A web of interrelated concepts constitutes *utu* as an exclusively human moral sphere. These concepts signify basic anthropological assumptions, qualities that are seen to be part of the human character. *Utu*, then, can be understood as a potentially universal moral concept, presented and formulated from within the Swahili framework. Displaying the basic characteristics of fundamental equality, of moral knowledge, freedom, and responsibility, the poem *Utenzi wa Mtu ni Utu* shows features we can link to classical moral theory. Such moral universalism from an African context refutes simple dismissals of all universalist positions as unjustifiable grand narratives of Eurocentric origin. With *Utenzi wa Mtu ni Utu*, we are not dealing with a mere "Swahili" version of this, but rather with an individual thinker's attempt to describe the general moral character of human nature from within the context of Swahili culture and language.

While for him, as he confirmed to me in person, *utu* is not really a religious or Islamic concept, Nassir's conceptual framework is nevertheless reliant on an Islamic conception of God for the full explication of *utu*, and in this respect he concurs with common social knowledge on *utu*. Such reliance is clear in the fundamental conception of moral knowledge, the possibility of distinction between good and bad. According to Nassir, this knowledge originates in God and has been given to human beings (via prophets, in revelations). This is taken for granted, without any further attempts at explication, such as would be expected and performed in secular moral philosophy. Here, on the whole, human beings are understood as creatures of an almighty and benevolent God. What distinguishes them from animals, namely moral knowledge and freedom of action, is linked to their creator. This points to a local philosophical anthropology, or general doctrine of human nature, which inherently includes the religious sphere.

As is also evident from the poem, Nassir insists on the principle that knowledge should be sought after and given, and must prove to be of practical value. The poet gives us a vivid illustration of this (in stanza 130):

knowledge that is not enacted
is like a person planting
a tree without any fruit
nor any leaves growing from it

*Ilimu isiyotenda*
*ni kama mtu kupanda*
*mti usio matunda*
*wala majani kumeya* (130)

To be sustained and effective in social life, however, this principle demands of people intellectual agility, and a readiness to step in when, for matters of convenience, knowledge is not confirmed, or when it is used as a superficial label of status that tries to impress without really teaching. Nassir told me about a number of related episodes in which he had been involved, each time pointing to the need for debate and communication so that knowledge can proceed to be practically meaningful; but also, to the responsibility of the knowledgeable (each according to the extent of their knowledge) to acquire knowledge through critical questioning and to apply it in practice, for the good of the community. This is a moral obligation linked to *utu*, and practicing it can mean taking the initiative and going against or beyond customs and established practices that are commonly accepted without challenge or questioning.

To conclude this section, I would like to draw attention to another popular proverb, subordinate to the main, general one providing the title for Nassir's poem, namely that human beings are qualified by their *utu* (humanity), *mtu ni utu*. This proverb, which is also quoted by Nassir in his poem, states categorically that human beings are not things (*mtu si kitu*) and must not be treated as such. This saying is commonly used in criticism of people who are seen to be developing relationships to others strategically and in pursuit of their own material gains, in an instrumental fashion. Such a purely calculating attitude in the shaping of human relationships is seen as morally improper and ultimately rejected as dehumanizing. If one treats one's human peers as things, one does not respect their *utu* (humanity); moreover, one shows that one has no *utu*. The proper moral behavior that makes us human and sees us recognized by our peers is absent when the proper basic respect to others that they deserve as human beings has not been granted. This also means one has violated one's own respectful status as moral agent and, in a way, expelled oneself from the realm of *utu*. Such dehumanizing patterns (for oneself and others) may be seen in the brutal and cruel treatment of others, but also in offensive, shameless, or arrogant behavior, including the attitude that money can buy everything and human needs, wishes, and desires are less important than anticipated material gains.

Along these lines, the saying "a human being is not a thing" (*mtu si kitu*) is also employed to voice a general social and cultural critique of the modern (or postmodern) world and its dehumanizing character, where human beings are seen to be subordinate to systems of technology, economy, and instrumental rationality and not valued in themselves. These points may be made against a "Western" attitude or paradigm of thought, which is often associated with an objectifying treatment of others. Indeed, I have often heard people who had been to Europe or the United States comment that in public social life there they sensed a lack of *utu* and they felt that people (often vulnerable, older, or poorer people) were indeed treated as things. However, this saying is equally and just as appropriately employed (by coastal Muslims in Kenya) in criticism of the postcolonial African state, the government (seen as run by Christians from upcountry), and politicians or businesspeople of regional or national importance. Again, as pointed out above, what matters in how the saying is employed in local discourse is how actions are performed, seen to be performed, and judged by others in the moral community, vis-à-vis an assumed standard of proper moral conduct.

## 14.5   Re-linking to African philosophy and ideology

Before we conclude, we should note that early writings in the wider field of African philosophy had already picked up on related terms and conceptual issues to coin a – largely hypothetical – distinct and homogenizing picture of "African thought" or "Bantu philosophy." This was problematic, as those who used such terms did so with a practical agenda in mind, even if perhaps with humanistic intentions. The Belgian missionary Placide Tempels (1945), for instance, who became known as the founding father of "ethno-philosophy," described a "dynamic philosophy of being" as the basic framework of Bantu-African thinking, in contrast to a "static" European one. Tempels initiated a basic descriptive ethno-philosophical approach (in which he over-generalized) that was later on greatly expanded and systematized by the Ruandese priest Alexis Kagame (1956, 1985) and others. However, it was condemned by other academic African philosophers such as Paulin Hountondji (1976) as being, in fact, paternalistic (serving a missionary cause) and distorting (because it used double standards as to what counted as philosophy). Yet returning to our initial characterizations from our introduction, above, we can see how ethno-philosophy could have been related, and in some ways even inspiring, to African political writers in their anticolonial and postcolonial struggles. This was precisely because of the apparent humanist undertones of a counter-vision of what African worldview is like, in contrast (and positive response) to a materialist and somewhat inhumane Western one. Thus the ideological writings of early postcolonial rulers such as Senghor, Nyerere, and Nkrumah in their advocacy of "African socialism" and "African nationalism," in different shapes and colors, can at least in part be seen in relation to this tradition (Senghor, for instance, makes explicit reference to this).

These writers, again, can be seen in proximity to the more recent strands of "ubuntuism" or *ubuntu*-philosophy that has become forceful and popular in the post-apartheid era (for example, Ramose, 1999, Broodryk, 2007) – and which has in some ways switched from being a liberating and mediating to a dominating, and sometimes dogmatic, ideology (see van Binsbergen, 2003, for a critical evaluation). *Ubuntu* has been a key term for the postapartheid government, in terms of a clearly defined political ideology of "Africanness" that has been shaping the social and political order in South Africa within a new "African Renaissance," as advocated by Thabo Mbeki and others. But we should note very clearly that, despite the linguistic closeness between *ubuntu* and *utu*, the dominant ideological use in South African political discourse works on a different level from the kind of philosophical dimensions I tried to work out for Ahmad Nassir's interpretation of *utu* above. Yet surely, philosophical and more open interpretations can be found in South Africa too, both in academic discourse and among more traditional or popular intellectuals. In parallel, we could imagine, in Kenya, an ideological take on *utu* that would be employed in political arguments, taking on more closed and dogmatic meanings, and that would therefore be more of a political instrument than a philosophical concept.

Both are possible, and indeed Kenya has witnessed the prominent political appropriation and ideological misuse of socially meaningful Swahili terms in the past. The first two presidents Jomo Kenyatta and Daniel arap Moi each employed a Swahili term to flag up their respective policies of Africanization and political unification – which can be compared to the lines of political African humanism described above (for Nyerere, Nkrumah, and Senghor). For his agenda of Africanization after independence, Kenyatta chose the Swahili term *harambee* – traditionally used as a call to "pull together" (with a rope, for example) by sailors and fishermen on the coast – to signify a call for joint efforts and mutual support among Kenyans to build up the nation (Kenyatta 1968). In this vein, *harambee* meetings were public events in which monetary contributions (to finance educational or social projects) were collected from all invited guests, under considerable social pressure. As a second example, President Moi picked up on the Swahili term *nyayo*, meaning footsteps, to legitimize his own political authority. "Footsteps" here referred to the required pathway of following the political leader, and thereby honoring the spirit and political heritage of the respected, recently deceased, Kenyatta. Moi had just taken over the presidency after his death due to his position as vice-president, lacking a proper electoral vote. Moi demanded from the people the same kind of obedience and blind following that he himself claimed to have pursued when serving Kenyatta. Thus under the mantle of his official ideology of "peace, love, and unity" that was supposed to characterize "*nyayo* philosophy," he in fact developed and pursued an authoritarian way of governing – not dissimilar to the way that Kenyatta himself had ruled (Moi, 1986, see Ngugi, 1981, p. 86).

Based on experiences in and beyond Kenya, the Kenyan philosopher Odera Oruka bitterly criticized the dogmatic misuse of power by African "supreme rulers" who used the state for their own ends. In an article called "Philosophy and Humanism in Africa," he made the case that in the (anonymous yet representative) "African Republic of Inhumanity and Death" (ARID) ,citizens could not rely on their basic rights while being prey to the arbitrary will of those in power (Oruka, 1997, 138–145). Thus Kenya is no exception to the ways in which a seemingly humanist ideology is employed in practice, in terms of rhetoric, to secure and increase an exclusive grip on power. But it is no exception either, as we saw above in the example of Ahmad Nassir's poem, to the ways that, around the world, fundamental conceptions of human beings are shaped and cast, as possible contributions to a truly global discourse of humanism.

## 14.6  Conclusion

I feel it is important to point out again features of commonality and similarity across the African continent. Not as political features, but as basic conceptual matters of semantics and social meanings at work in society, these are indeed waiting to be explored further, but critically and in much more depth. Taken seriously, this would involve a large empirical project of intra-African comparison. For my own research and presentation here, however, it has been crucial to focus on one interpretation by an individual African thinker and in an African language, to show the specificity of reflexive discourse on "humanity" and "goodness" in one particular social and cultural context (for related but different examples from West Africa, see Gyekye and Wiredu, 1992, on the Akan in Ghana, and Hallen, 2000, on the Yoruba in Nigeria; for a contemporary academic philosopher, see Eze, 2001). Emphasis on individuality and specificity within a plurality of African cultures is still important in order to correct the longstanding and continuing tendencies – in popular and academic perception outside African studies – to homogenize and lump together so-called African thought into a single category. This reflects and reinforces a diffuse and distorting image of Africa, and of African intellectual traditions as monolithic and simple – which they are not. As I have tried to illustrate here, looking at one particular regional example, African discourses on humanism are fundamentally linked to conceptions of humanity which, in each case, are embedded in particular cultural and historical settings which themselves are dynamic and in a state of flux. They are used, reshaped, and remodeled in a complex interplay between categories and genres of social knowledge and the ways in which these are elaborated upon and carried further through the creative efforts of individual thinkers (poets or others). As in other parts of the world, we are dealing with living traditions of intellectual work taking place in, and engaging with, social contexts. Depending on the individual case, the engagement may be driven by practical motives (uniting a nation, teaching a community) or by heuristic ones (seeking knowledge, analyzing a situation) and therefore, in consequence, be either more ideological in tone, as in the political versions of African humanism touched on above, or more educational, and therefore elaborating or questioning, as can be seen here.

The scope of humanism in Africa is wide and internally diverse. Yet it is possible, in conclusion, to outline some common (or at least similar) features in the wide spread of regional and historical contexts that may justify talk of "African humanism" as distinct – at least in a wider global comparison – from visions and versions of, say, South Asian, East Asian or Melanesian traditions, or indeed Western ones. As in the case of Swahili humanism examined here, these may be universally oriented as well, accounting for and exploring the meanings of "humanity" and the implications for social norms and values arising out of it, from within their own conceptual frameworks and intellectual traditions. The various notions of "African humanism" as put forward in political discourse or documented in ethnographic or historical research literature on different regions of Africa share the idea of humans as social beings who are bound to each other by mutual basic moral obligations. This idea, then, presents a basic common reference point – even if it is often used strategically or rhetorically.

From a perspective of global business and management it is very important to keep this basic reference point in mind. In South Africa and around the world, clever businesspeople have been quick and creative in picking up concepts like *ubuntu* to boost the attractiveness of their products and deals on offer, and to connect their own business practice to an image of good ethical standards or moral performance, and to "African" origins. For example, buying *Ubuntu-Cola* – and no other brand – at a student union cafeteria (as I recently did in a London university college) is probably the morally most reassuring way for students, lecturers, and others to consume fizzy drinks. As consumers, we are all likely to buy into the good "humanist" and "African" connotations as well as the "fair trade" sign. Good for business. The online community, too, has its own *ubuntu* label. Linked to the free-access, shared, and ethically recommended nonbrand Linux software, the *ubuntu* web community is linked to an online store (www.canonical.com) that offers all kind of technological accessories and gadgets, which – I would probably have to admit – I might be willing to buy from rather than from others (though, personally, I have not done so yet).

The popular "I am because we are" rhetoric, coined as an appealing African counter-dictum to the Cartesian "I think therefore I am" that paradigmatically represents Western rationalism to the outside world does represent a serious point here, despite its apparent superficiality. On the level of popular (self-)perception, it represents a common rhetoric of solidarity, or at least sociality, within African communities (and only sometimes, countries). This alludes to an emphasis on the social that is otherwise often expressed in proverbs and sayings, or other genres of verbal art, as we have seen above. And it may not be too much to say that on the common level of self-understanding for ordinary people, these expressions do matter (quite a lot), normatively, for individual social actors, and for the ways they see themselves and relate to others.

This needs to be taken into consideration in all kinds of matters when dealing and interacting with people from (and on) the African continent, whether as friends, competitors, business partners, employers, or employees. Whether this could be said to entail any more specific consequences or advice, I cannot say, but surely recognition of these factors as basic and fundamental framework conditions within which one interacts socially, and indeed as a business *partner*, with others, will matter. Acquiring a sense of the particular idioms (verbal or performative) in which these aspects are expressed and conveyed to others in respective (and differing) African contexts – whether countries, regions, or towns – could well be part of one's own social fine-tuning before, during, and after interacting with others, in order to increase the chances of successful communication and negotiation. If nothing else, knowing how to impress, charm, and appeal to people of whom one has certain hopes and expectations (material or immaterial) is likely to lead to success, as it is anywhere in the world.

If there is a more general rule about this that one could try to formulate for African contexts, perhaps it would go along these lines: You will rarely go wrong if you appeal to the sense of community (even, in fact especially, when dealing with individuals). on the negative side, you may be seen at fault if you express interest exclusively in material things and/or for material's sake. Being seen (or known) to be extremely materialist and/or self-interested in African public situations will bring no advantages, but rather lead to low esteem and bad reputation. For foreigners, especially "white" Eurasians and thus former colonizers, it would be seen as a proof that they have not understood (not yet, or still not) how things work in Africa, between people – how matters always revolve around people and social relations. This is the rhetorical reference point, at least, to which attention must be directed.

## Bibliography

Biko, S., *I write what I like*. (London: Penguin, 1988 (orig. 1978)).
Broodryk, J., *Understanding South Africa: the uBuntu way of living*. (Waterkloof: UBuntu School of Philosophy, 2007).

264   *Kai Kresse*

Chakrabarty, D. "Humanism in a global world", in J. Rüsen and H. Laass (eds), *Humanism in intercultural perspective: experiences and expectations.* (Bielefeld: Transcript, 2009) 23–36.

Cook, M., *Commanding right and forbidding wrong in Islamic Thought.* (Cambridge: Cambridge University Press, 2000).

Eze, E.Ch., *Achieving our humanity: the idea of the postracial future.* (New York: Routledge, 2001).

Fardon, R., *Between God, the dead and the wild. Chamba interpretations of religion and ritual.* (Edinburgh University Press, 1990).

Ferguson, James 2006. *Global Shadows: Africa in the neoliberal world order.* Durham and London: Duke University Press.

Graness, A. and K. Kresse (eds). *Sagacious reasoning: Henry Odera Oruka in memoriam.* (Frankfurt: Peter Lang, 1997).

Gyekye, K. and K. Wiredu., *Person and community. Ghanaian philosophical studies I.* (Washington, 1992).

Hallen, B.. *The good, the bad, and the beautiful: discourse about value in Yoruba culture.* (Bloomington: Indiana University Press, 2000).

Hountondji, P., *African philosophy: myth and reality.* (Bloomington: Indiana University Press, 1996 (orig. 1976)).

James, W., *Listening ebony.* (Oxford: University Press, 1989).

Kagame, A., *La philosophie bantu-rwandaise de l'Etre.* (Brussels, 1956).

Kagame, A., *Sprache und Sein: die Ontologie der Bantu Zentralafrikas.* (Heidelberg, 1985).

Jahn, J., *Muntu: the new African culture.* (New York: Grove Press, 1961 (orig. 1958)).

Kaunda, K., *Humanism in Zambia and a guide to its implementation. Part 1.* Lusaka: *Zambia Information Services* (1968).

Kaunda, K., *Humanism in Zambia and a guide to its implementation. Part 2.* Lusaka: Zambia Information Services (1974).

Kenyatta, J., *Suffering without bitterness: the founding of the Kenya nation.* (Nairobi: East African Publishing House, 1968).

Kresse, K., *Philosophising in Mombasa: knowledge, Islam and intellectual practice on the Swahili coast.* (Edinburgh University Press, 2007).

Kresse, K., "Knowledge and intellectual practice in a Swahili context: 'wisdom' and the social dimensions of knowledge", in *Africa: Journal of the International African Institute* vol. 79 (1) (2009) 148–67.

Lategan, B.C., "Exclusion and inclusion in the quest for a 'new' humanism: a perspective from Africa", in J. Rüsen and H. Laass (eds), *Humanism in intercultural perspective: experiences and expectations.* (Bielefeld: Transcript, 2009) 79–90.

Macamo, E., "Africa and Humanism", in J. Rüsen and H. Laass (eds), *Humanism in intercultural perspective: experiences and expectations.* (Bielefeld: Transcript, 2009) 65–77.

MacGaffey, W. *Religion and society in central Africa.* (Chicago University Press, 1986).

Mbeki, T., "On African renaissance", in *African Philosophy*, vol. 12/1, (1998) 5–10.

Moi, D. a.T., *Kenyan African nationalism. Nyayo philosophy and principles.* (Nairobi: MacMillan, 1986).

Nassir, A. *Utenzi wa Mtu ni Utu* (edited and introduced by Mohamed Kamal Khan). (Nairobi: MacMillan, 1979).

Ngugi wa Thiong'o, *Decolonizing the mind*. (Nairobi. Heinemann, 1986).

Nkrumah, K., *Conscienscism: philosophy and ideology for de-colonisation*. (London: Panaf, 1978 (orig. 1964)).

Nyerere, J., *Freedom and development: a selection from writings and speeches*. (Oxford University Press, 1973).

Oruka, H. Odera, *Trends in African philosophy*. (Nairobi, 1990 (1978)).

Oruka, H. Odera, *Sage philosophy. Indigenous thinkers and modern debate on African philosophy*. (Narobi: ACTS, 1991).

Oruka, H. Odera, "Philosophy and Humanism in Africa", in idem, *Practical Philosophy: in search of an ethical minimum*. (Nairobi: East African Educational Publishers, 1997), 138–145.

Presbey, G., "African sage philosophy and Socrates: midwifery and method", *International Philosophical Quarterly* 42/2, Issue 166, (2002) 177–92.

Ramose, M.B., *African philosophy through ubuntu*. (Harare: Mond Books, 1999).

Rosberg, C.G. and H. Friedland (eds). *African socialism*. (Stanford University Press, 1964).

Sartre, J.P., "Introduction" in *Orphee Noire*. (Paris, 1972).

Senghor, L.S., *Liberte I: Négritude et humanisme*. (Paris, 1964).

Tempels, P., *Bantu philosophy*. (Paris: Presence Africaine, 1959 (orig. 1945)).

van Binsbergen, W., "Ubuntu and the globalisation of south African thought and society", in idem, *Intercultural encounters: African and anthropological lessons towards a philosophy of interculturality*. (Muenster: Lit-Verlag, 2003) 427–57.

Wiredu, K., *Cultural universals and particulars*. (Bloomington: Indiana University Press, 1996).

# Conclusions

*Claus Dierksmeier, Wolfgang Amann, Ernst von Kimakowitz,
Heiko Spitzeck, and Michael Pirson*

Throughout this book, our authors have reconstructed and examined
ethical theories from various traditions in search of practicable models
for a contemporary humanistic ethics. They had been asked to pay special attention to the interface between business and society because of
the enormous impact that economic behavior has upon culture, politics, and the environment. Since the onset of economic globalization,
the premises for any and all ethics changed markedly. The traditional
ways (such as religious, political, or conventional) and institutions that
reinforce and sanction collective values are being rapidly transformed
by the forceful dynamics of the global economy. Against this changed
background, the perennial question about the good has to be raised
anew. In our concluding remarks, we therefore first outline the current
configurations a humanistic ethics needs to address, before highlighting the main conclusions of the studies made by our authors.

## Business and society in the age of globality

A world on the move demands a different ethics from that of a stationary social system. Ours, however, is a world in rapid motion: With
astounding speed the global production and exchange of products is
transforming the natural and cultural face of the earth. Biological systems vanish, customary rules of behavior fade, legal frameworks are
in a process of constant transformation, languages dwindle, and many
traditional religions and conventions are on the wane. In their stead,
driven by an exponential increase in information exchange, resource
consumption, and technological production, novel forms of interaction
and communication take hold. New ways of life spread quickly, through
cyberspace, from the remotest localities all around the earth. Changing

economic and social systems have created unprecedented wealth in some places, whereas elsewhere unacceptable poverty persists.

This transformation has inspired triumphalist narratives that see humanity heading towards a paradise of freedom and autonomy where all human needs are met. In contrast there are apocalyptic predictions and visions that see us facing endless war, civil strife, environmental destruction, and cultural poverty. Where are we headed, then? Are we nearing one global culture or "multiple modernities"? And what will be the future role of business in society? Will transnational corporations become an integral part of a peaceful global citizenry, and close ranks with the various nongovernmental organizations that work toward the improvement of human existence? Or will big business impede the advance toward more humane forms of life? In brief, will business foster or hinder humanistic progress?

So far the messages are mixed and ambiguous. On the one hand, business has proved enormously beneficial to society. Numerous technological innovations and breathtaking growth in material productivity have alleviated many ancient ailments and continue to emancipate ever more people from conditions of material and social deprivation. Economic growth requires, but also often drives and pays for, better health and education systems, paving the way for social development (Bhagwati, 2007). On the other hand, the increasingly competitive global environment of business has sharpened the detrimental effects asymmetrical relationships and social inequalities have on our social and environmental life-world (Pogge, 2008).

Today, even the conservative business press wonders whether the current form of economic globalization is sustainable. Until recently, economic pundits and politicians hailed the greater connectivity and the speed at which the global integration of business is occurring as a creator of progressive social development. Today this triumphalism has been replaced by serious concerns about corporate mismanagement and neglect of the social and moral repercussions of business. Once hailed as a messianic force bringing salvation to a world in turmoil and distress, the unfettered market and its corporate captains now appear responsible for nearly everything people dislike, including environmental destruction, the decay of cultural and spiritual values, and growing inequalities (Bakan, 2004).

Historically, corporations were social constructs, designed to carry out various common tasks and solve problems collectively. How, then, did they change from universal problem-solvers to global problem-makers?

And what does this transition imply for the ethical assessment of the firm and the system of "free enterprise" overall?

The world has dramatically changed since Adam Smith (1723–1790) penned the "Wealth of Nations". Economists of the eighteenth and early nineteenth centuries developed their theories in a world of business units much smaller than today's multinational companies (Galbraith, 1967). Tiny enterprises typically do not ruin their environment. Small firms rely strongly on their surroundings, so they often engage in efforts to preserve and strengthen them (Polanyi, 1957). Quantitative change, however, can trigger qualitative transformation. The de-territorialized power and the immense size of modern corporate structures and production today has radically altered the business world. Manufacturing processes that were relatively harmless in small numbers may be harmful to the environment in bulk (over-fishing and intensive agriculture, for example). The combined and connected impacts of formerly isolated forms of business, as well as the simultaneous exploitation of biological systems by several industrial users can bring those systems to their tipping point (Meadows and Club of Rome, 1972).

Commercialization also stretches and tears the cultural fabrics and moral threads of society. The concentrated assault on the public consciousness through massive advertising leads to deformations of the collective mind and of individual identity (Berger, 2010). When face-to-face encounters in the local marketplace are gradually substituted by anonymous exchanges in an increasingly virtual economy, when the individual's intrinsic and spiritual motivations are more and more crowded out by extrinsic and material incentives aimed at the mass personality, and when brands first assume, then constitute, and ultimately replace the individuality of their customers, the combined effect is a creeping commodification of personal relations and a suffocation of cultural values (Featherstone, 1991; Klein, 1999).

Yet why have corporations developed from moderately sized joint-stock companies to the anonymous behemoths of our era? One often-given answer is that our financial markets demand ever larger profits from firms. Often these extreme profits can only be squeezed out of economies of scale or quasi-monopolistic market positions, both of which encourage corporate growth to a point where it conflicts with the cultural and ecological surroundings of business. Yet, in and of itself, sheer *scale* is not the problem; size just amplifies the tendencies inherent in any business model. There are, after all, cases to the contrary, where major business growth has benign impact. The "social good" of firms like *GrameenBank* and the "environmental good" created by corporations such as *TerraCycle* increase proportionately with the growing size of their operations (von Kimakowitz et al., 2010). Social entrepreneurs show us that the tools of business can be used to deliver social and ecological benefits. Their efforts demonstrate that the interests of society and business can be aligned (Elkington and Hartigan, 2008).

The salient point is not to paint big business black or white but rather to understand how economic transactions are embedded in and expressive of human relationships. Textbook lore to the contrary, there is no "economic law" forcing corporations to engage in nothing but profit maximization. Economic laws, rightly understood, are generalizations of human behavior; they change in substance and form with the latter. Often overlooked, this cultural and political malleability of our economic life is in fact its foremost characteristic (Brodbeck, 1995). Human action and inaction can and do change "the economy" – for better or worse. Ideas, that is to say, which govern human behavior in general, also have economic impact in particular; as John Maynard Keynes famously noted,

> the ideas of economists and political philosophers both when they are right and when they are wrong, are more powerful than is commonly understood. Indeed the world is ruled by little else. Practical men, who believe themselves to be quite exempt from any intellectual influences, are usually the slaves of some defunct economist. Madmen in authority, who hear voices in the air, are distilling their frenzy from some academic scribbler of a few years back. I am sure that the power of vested interests is vastly exaggerated compared with the gradual encroachment of ideas. Not, indeed, immediately, but after a certain interval; for in the field of economic and political philosophy there are not many who are influenced by new theories after they are twenty-five or thirty years of age, so that the ideas which civil servants and politicians and even agitators apply to current events are not likely to be the newest. But, soon or late, it is ideas, not vested interests, which are dangerous for good or evil.[1]

Keynes was right; and since the staid ideas of single-minded profit maximization, proffered by the neoclassical paradigm, have worn out, we ought to form and formulate newer, better ones. In their stead, what we need is a humanistic paradigm that centers our ideas and theories about the economy on the well-being of people.

## Towards a humanistic ethics for the age of globality

Whether one is a proponent of global government or of global governance, any global alliance for the collective regulation of industries across cultural and religious divides requires certain shared understandings in order to function (Ruggie, 2008). Take sustainability policies, for example. Transnational efforts to "internalize negative externalities" require that all involved parties agree – qualitatively – on the basic evaluative parameters to be used (that is, on what constitutes harmful business practices) and concur – quantitatively – on the scope of their application (where to place the temporal and spatial parameters). The formidable contribution of humanistic ethics to these problems lies in its capacity to facilitate an overlapping normative consensus between diverging moral standards. A human-centered ethics transforms and transcends the limits of traditional (local and national) accounting metrics by representing the interests of humanity as a whole. From its cosmopolitan viewpoint, a humanistic ethics provides a perspective sufficiently wide to engender a truly comprehensive account of the socially beneficial as well as the detrimental aspects of business.

As much of our economic and social world is already globalized, ethics is also currently undergoing a process of reflective globalization (Sullivan and Kymlicka, 2007). The decline of traditional and particularistic modes of customary governance accentuates a trend towards planetary forms of accountability and post-conventional codes of conduct that function across cultural and geographical divides (Ebrahim and Weisband, 2007). To safeguard the common interests of humanity and to pave the way to a more humane future for all, a return to the methods and models of humanistic philosophy is then a natural step: In addressing its ethics to all human beings, humanism presents *eo ipso* an ethics of globality.

However, the humanistic approach cannot be reduced to one ethical system (Appiah, 2006). Neither the current nor the past diversity of humanistic thinking points us in the direction of a uniform theory. Instead, due to its employment in divergent historical and cultural constellations, the concept of "humanism" has no undisputed single meaning today. The conceptual foundations of the idea of humanism will therefore need much clarification before one can begin working towards a coherent concept of a humanistic ethics for the present age. The term "humanism" was used to denote *ethical* positions in ancient *philosophy* (encompassing positions as different as the relativism of Protagoras and the moral absolutism of Plato) as well as in Christian medieval *theology*, but also signifies certain *cultural* tendencies during the Renaissance, a revival of *both* ancient and Renaissance traditions in the philosophies of *German Idealism* as well as in successive theories (such as Humboldt's philosophy). The term humanism was, moreover, used for the revitalization of ancient education and ideals of *metaphysical* virtue by German philosophers during the 1920s and 1930s, as well as to classify *atheistic* approaches to the question of what makes a human life good (where humanistic theory overlaps with the realm of Marxist doctrines). The term also finds use as an epithet for the works of Sartre and other *existentialists* and for some *psychoanalytic* and leftist writers from the 1940s to the 1970s. Last but not least, humanism serves as an umbrella term for a number of personality-focused and/or humanitarian ethics in various non-Western traditions such as the *ubuntu* and *ulu* concepts of African philosophers (Geerk, 1998).

Despite this wide range of meanings, the term "humanism" should not be abandoned. Instead, we need to make its meaning clearer and more coherent through reconstructive arguments and philosophical discourse so as to promote the uptake of humanistic values in business and society. We have dedicated our book to this project. In a sense, we had work against the muscle memory of the academic mind. We asked our authors to forego the pleasures of the academic's favorite hobby – looking for differences – and instead to seek out and emphasize features common to their subjects. We wanted to know to what extent the economic philosophers of different periods and places agree, to find out whether a *humanistic consensus* for business ethics can be derived from their arguments.

## Lessons from antiquity and the Middle Ages

From **Socrates and Plato** (Chapter II.A) we learn that business people who seek profits alone misunderstand the intricate nature of business. As economic success depends to a large degree on human labor and ingenuity, developing an adequate understanding of human nature is not just a fanciful sport for intellectuals but also of paramount importance for the adequate and successful conduct of business, argues Ioanna Patsioti-Tsacpounidis. What is good for people in general, will also, as a rule, be good for business in particular. Socrates and Plato teach us, for instance, that *virtue* is essential for the happiness and health of our private and collective lives; because doing well and doing good coincide on a human level, virtuous conduct is also vital in the socioeconomic sphere.

Interestingly, this insight commits us to the (counterintuitive) view that individuals who seek their own benefits at the expense of others do not really "know" what they are doing. Their reckless pursuit of self-interest proves their ignorance insofar as it undermines the very human relations which foster lasting success. Corrupt actions must hence be understood as the progeny of an insufficiently enlightened intellect; a mind capable of attaching itself to patent material benefits but incapable of seeing the deeper – ethical and spiritual – needs of the human person.

Socrates and Plato thus inspire us to replace the narrow anthropology of present-day economics (which pits atomistic individuals in hedonistic pursuits against their fellows) with a richer vision of the human being, one that includes moral perspectives. Once managers begin to understand that the soundness of their personal lives depend on the soundness of their ethical views and practices, policies of humanistic management will become more common.

**Aristotle** (Chapter II.B) continues the argument against a reckless and ceaseless pursuit of wealth (*pleonexia*) by distinguishing the pursuit of material goods to supply a given household (*oikonomia*) from profit-seeking (*chrematistike*). The former is internally oriented towards determinate *qualitative* satisfaction levels; the latter, however, operates on the merely *quantitative* logic of "more over less." Aristotle argues that as long as profit-seeking endeavors are governed and limited by the needs of true *oikonomia*, they can be both legitimate and beneficial. Altogether different is, however, the *unbounded* pursuit of profit for profit's sake. This limitless, insatiable, and, in the eyes of Aristotle, "unnatural" form of business meets with his disapproval, as it upsets the proper relationship between means (material and pecuniary) and ends (political, ethical, and spiritual).

Moreover, the unbounded pursuit of wealth tends to turn the gain of one individual into the loss of another, and so enhances existing inequalities in society. More inequality, however, is to the detriment of both the poor (who, increasingly burdened, find it ever more difficult to lead a dignified life) and the rich (who, absorbed in the pursuit of lesser goods, are distracted from life's true values). Together, individuals and the political community must therefore do everything in their means in order to prevent the unbounded pursuit of wealth, lest the true end of business – human well-being – be lost because of the ravaging ways and means employed in that pursuit.

For the management of contemporary firms, certain practical guidelines for humanistic management can be concluded from these premises. Firms should operate from a value proposition that puts social over financial goods, being willing at times to forgo short-term profits in favor of making vital contributions to social welfare in the long term. That change of priorities should also be reflected in their internal policies. Their management of incentives and promotion, for example, should reward work for the full range of qualitative (e.g. social) goals of the corporation, rather than just track quantitative growth.

The **philosophy of the Stoa** (Chapter II.C) reworks the ethical themes of Socrates, Plato, and Aristotle, while giving them a more global application. Stoic philosophers were the first to promulgate a truly universalistic ethics based upon the idea of human dignity. Seeing the world not as *chaos* but as a *kosmos*, well-ordered by universal laws, they also held the human being to be part of the *cosmopolis*, a well-ordered universal community of reasonable beings. Hence their cosmopolitan approach to ethics: As rational beings, all humans possess inalienable dignity; they are all to be treated and respected as members of one extended family, united by universal humanism.

Since, in the Stoic view, the goal of human life is to become wise and live according to the dictates of reason, no human being must be so instrumentalized as to be obstructed in their achievement of that goal. Likewise, all the goods of life must be administered in such a manner as to serve the individual's maturing towards intellectual and practical wisdom. Wealth, consequently, counts as just a relative, never as an absolute good. Its value depends strictly on its function for good or bad. The pursuit of wealth is acceptable, for example, as a means to develop and display the virtues of liberality, generosity, magnanimity, temperance, and modesty as well as to procure the material means needed for a dignified existence. One must not, however, strive for wealth without restraint, as this lack of circumspection in itself would constitute an unwise practice. We should, in short, as Seneca put it, let wealth into our house, but not into our soul.

In a comprehensive sense, **Thomas Aquinas** (Chapter II.D) sums up the wisdoms of ancient philosophy and integrates them with the Christian world view. The ancient respect for human rationality resurfaces in his theory, as well as the emphasis on the ability of every human being to discern between good and evil, and, consequently, to lead a decent life in accordance with human nature. Since, in the Christian perspective, human beings receive their essence from God, the dignity and the fundamental rights that attach to the human existence are of an absolute and unconditional nature. Neither individuals, nor society as a whole, can deprive a human being of his inborn rights.

Both individually and collectively we are thus bound to help *everyone* to live with dignity, that is, in a way that appropriately recognizes and respects the divine origin of the human form. For the constitution of society and business, important consequences follow from this notion. Whatever the specific agreements and customs in any given culture and at any given time, certain principles should be common to all human arrangements, demanding absolute respect as moral universals. In other words, Thomas Aquinas formulates an ethics of globality from the perspective of a Christian universalism.

Within this normative approach, earthly goods should be administered with an eye to the benefit of all; therefore, the economy should be so regulated that wealth and its pursuit cannot impede but will instead further universal advancement towards a life in accordance with human nature. For Thomas, this means first and foremost that *social justice* must permeate every economic transaction. Parties cannot simply agree on what suits them best, but must, for their agreement to be valid, respect both the nature of the human being in general and the specific interests of all affected persons – today we might say "of all stakeholders" – in particular. The idea of social justice thus provides an implicit corrective to every transaction: public as well as private, political as well as economic.

Thomas sees the power of private property as an incentive for rewarding diligence and utility-creation and welcomes the propensity of commerce and trade to increase the overall material welfare of society. Nonetheless, his endorsement of the pursuit of individual and collective wealth remains strictly limited. Wealth must always contribute to humane relations in society, lest it be illegitimate. Thomas makes very clear that whatever people own in superabundance rightfully belongs to those who need it more. Of course, alms should be given on voluntary charitable basis. But, as long as deprivation persists, both personal and collective luxuries are also subject to redistribution by legal means.

Thomas, in sum, denies that business and private property constitute a realm where public interests can be ignored or discounted. On the contrary, it is only because business has a capacity to serve the public interest and the common good that some independence and sector-specific autonomy can be granted to economic transactions at all. To allow the persistence of business practices or allocations of wealth, however, which prove patently detrimental to society at large, would have seemed utterly absurd to Thomas.

## The teachings of the moderns

After this presentation of the economic ethics of the pre-modern centuries, our authors turn to the philosophies of the modern (Part III) and contemporary period (Part IV). The thinkers investigated so far made extensive use of metaphysical theorems in order to establish their ethics, but the modern and postmodern contributions to our book are characterized by an attempt to find a different methodological approach. Either they try to do without metaphysics completely, or they limit themselves to premises which no-one has plausible reasons for rejecting.

The philosophy of **Immanuel Kant** (Chapter III.A) represents a landmark in modern humanistic thinking. The philosophers of ancient and medieval times established their ideas of human dignity based on metaphysical notions whose principles were often outside the realm of general human experience. For instance, several tenets of Christian doctrines were supported by faith in the divine origin of creation. Kant, however, shifts the source of his metaphysical account of human nature to the shared human experience of personal autonomy. In our capacity for self-determination, Kant argues, lies the single transcendent principle that people, regardless of their divergent religious creeds and cultural affiliations, can all recognize and adhere to: the idea of a (morally) responsible freedom.

Consequently, Kant translates the old humanistic stricture – that life in society must be ordered so as to support the flourishing of human nature – into new formulas expressive of the central role he ascribes to human freedom. For Kant, to respect human dignity means always to treat other people as the free authors of their own lives; we are to refrain from objectifying others and subordinating them wholly to our own purposes; on the contrary, we are meant to support and advance everyone's autonomy. In the realm of business, for instance, it is important we know how to differentiate between *objects* that have a *relative* value, expressed in *prices*, and subjects, whose *absolute* value is symbolized in their *dignity*. Economic *transactions* are, consequently, to be regarded as first and foremost *relations* between human subjects; and this reminder is tantamount to the imperative to treat every person directly involved or indirectly affected with respect for *their* subjective purposes and ends. Economic relations in which a human being is objectified into a mere "human resource", or into mere "human capital" can never be morally justified. Instead, Kant writes: "So act as to treat humanity, whether in thine own person or in that of any other, in every case as an end withal, never as means only."

As economic resources and capital must always be used to support personal autonomy, the pursuit of profit can hence be a legitimate secondary goal of firms and individuals, but only as long as they thereby promote the primary goal of society: human emancipation and liberation. Profits are a derived goal; the primary goal is the perspective of responsible freedom. In order to realize this primary obligation of advancing human freedom it is a most natural step to involve in decisions the people that those decisions are likely to affect. Thus does Kant link individual liberty to collective freedom. For the societal realm, Kant suggests pursuing only collective endeavors that *require* "publicity (Publizität)," so as to garner sufficient public support. Such publicity, in assuring the passive representation of all and the active participation of most stakeholders, makes for enterprises that are both legitimate and effective, he surmises. Interestingly, this idea can be applied not only to the political realm but also to the ethical re-conceptualization of business. Indeed, one can find in this a philosophical reconstruction of the spirit that drives social entrepreneurs to create the very environments they need to succeed by involving their stakeholders and the public at large.

The philosophers of **German Idealism** (Chapter III.B) continued Kant's emphasis on the importance of freedom and personal autonomy for the realization of human dignity. More than Kant, though, they asked if the modern market economy was conducive to progress in the attainment of individual freedom. In his reconstruction of the socio-economic deliberations of F. I. Niethammer and G. W. F. Hegel, Robert Fincham shows how Niethammer criticized an exaggerated concentration on practicality, utility, profitability and material production on the grounds that it could introduce regressive cultural tendencies into society. When, as Niethammer put it, one seeks and finds the "whole happiness of a nation in the quantity of material production, the whole value of the individual in the acquisition of mechanical competence," then, indeed, there is little room in society for the cultivation of the spiritual values of humanism.

Just as the human body is nurtured by nature and can improve its relationship and interactions with its biological environment through improvements in the natural sciences, the human mind is nurtured by culture and advanced in its symbolic interchanges by an improved understanding of art, history, religion, and philosophy. And just as neglect of physical needs damages the human body, neglect of cultural needs ruins the development of the mind, the very source of human freedom. For true freedom, to the German Idealists, is not simply liberty of choice or freedom from outward restrictions but rather the wise self-determination. Whereas "the man in the street thinks he is free if it is open to him to act as he pleases, [...] his very arbitrariness implies that he is not free," argues Hegel. For such a person is not yet free from the inward coercion imposed by the limitations of his or her inadequate understanding and the consequent misuse of his or her capacities.

Individuals need to be educated to make a self-reflective use of their freedom and to chose wisely. Social institutions exist to help them develop a sense of self and a sense of purpose, educating individuals by involvement and interaction with their cultural and political surroundings. Interestingly, for Hegel, the *market economy* is also one such "ethical institution" that allows individuals to develop mature and responsible forms of freedom. Since the citizens of a commercial society are "reciprocally related to one another in their work and the satisfaction of their needs, subjective self-seeking turns into a contribution to the satisfaction of the needs of everyone else," and thus they become educated to recognize and respect each other's interests. Likewise, their understanding of freedom will gradually move from a *negation* of any and all societal restrictions to an *affirmation* of tried and proven forms of inter-personal co-determination.

At the same time, participation in the "system of needs," as Hegel calls the market economy, offers individuals a wide array of possibilities for living out their particular vocations and talents. Thus the market is conducive both to the development of individual freedoms and their peaceful social coordination, which is the primary moral justification of the market. In so legitimating the market economy by its contribution to the cultivation of human autonomy, Hegel at the same time limits the demands the economic sphere can make on society. Governments need to check and regulate the functioning of the free market so as to make sure that the facilitation of the freedom of many does not threaten the liberty of some.

Since the impersonal demands of the free market must never undermine the chances for anyone's personal freedom, the state has to safeguard procedures of political governance (apart from the bargaining processes of groups with vested interests) that guarantee that the freedom and dignity of all individuals is preserved, including those who are excluded from participation in the market because of system-generated imbalances. The freedom of trade and commerce (from public control) finds its limits in the autonomy it is to foster. Hence economic forces must never be allowed to overpower those other ethical institutions (family, religions, science, art, and religion, for example) which – often to a considerably higher degree than the economic "system of needs" – are engaged in the maintenance and advancement of human liberty. Public concerns must forever trump private interests, with government setting the parameters for the subsidiary self-governance of the corporate sector.

The philosophy of **Karl Marx** (Chapter III.C) is both a continuation of and a break with the preceding philosophical tradition. It continues the Hegelian approach of analyzing the intra-societal tensions ("contradictions") that in some ways foster and in others hamper the further development of human freedom. It breaks with that tradition by replacing the former idealistic interpretation of these social phenomena with a thoroughly materialistic account of history. This shift in emphasis has merits as well as demerits for the understanding of human collaboration and for the advancement of a humanistic ethics. In order to separate the wheat from the chaff, Ulrich Steinvorth picks out from Marx's theory certain desirable elements ("the *Marxian* approach") that can and should be salvaged, even though we might have good reasons to reject wholesale Marxism ("the *Marxist* approach").

At the core of the Marxian approach, which Steinvorth wants to conserve, is a focus on human capabilities and their productive use in society. He agrees with Marx's materialism insofar as he, too, assigns to the materialistic development of our productive forces a central role in the historical evolution of humanity. Unlike standard Marxist theory, however, his Marxian approach does not commit one to a narrowly *economic* reading of those productive forces. While a Marxist will interpret the dynamics of art, science, religion, politics, and philosophy as derived from economic structures, a Marxian can admit their independent and codeterminative influence on social change. The Marxian will thus stress that human development hinges crucially on how personal freedom and individual capacities are socially organized at any given time. There are better and worse ways of organizing human talent; and only a societal form that allows for an optimal utilization and integration of human capabilities will endure.

While the typical Marxist dreams of a classless society, the Marxian has no problem with a continued functional differentiation of society, with associations who develop differently according to the divergent forms their capabilities assume. Functional subgroups may take on similar organizational shapes, as do social classes, but they need not engage in a violent "class struggle" with one another. Rather, predicts

Steinvorth, societies will differ precisely (not least in their survival over time) according to how intelligently they are organized, in other words, to how far their subgroups can be brought to collaborate peacefully and productively. Whereas the Marxist views the capitalistic organization of labor as necessarily transitory since it is beset with internal "contradictions" that will eventually made the capitalistic order implode, the Marxian can imagine a productive resolution of those contradictions by an evolution of the current modes of societal organization into superior forms that are more suited to encouraging and harmonizing the free use of everyone's capabilities.

The Marxist and the Marxian agree, however, on one crucial point: that the present capitalistic form of economic production will (have to) change. Both foresee that our economy will transform from its present "alienated" form into another. Currently, human beings are alienated from their innermost nature in that they are being ordered about by money. Over time, money has changed from a mere means of value exchange and value representation into a substantial end in itself. Humanity has thus become instrumentalized by its instrument. Whereas, however, the Marxist awaits and welcomes a destructive dissolution of this state of affairs, the Marxian believes that social forms can be found that establish economic interchanges that are not marred by such alienation. The Marxian affirms, in other words, the malleability of our economic and political history through human design and collaboration. After all, the "productive forces" that drive history in both the Marxist and the Marxian understanding are but congealed social relations. Steinvorth stresses that: "They are nothing that is imposed on people by non-human forces." As our socioeconomic arrangements can be altered, the crucial question becomes how the human being can identify their essence and, in its light, work improvements in society.

Marx drew our attention to the fact that the human essence is not revealed in our biological code alone. Rather, we must also examine human nature in the economic forms in which collective human life takes place. Similarly, adds the Marxian in contrast to the traditional Marxist, we must also take into account further symbolic forms in which human life seeks and finds self-expression. The human essence is revealed not only in the material manifestations of our economic institutions but also in the mental, spiritual, aesthetic, and ethical forms in which humanity makes coordinated use of its collective capabilities. This Marxian approach to history and society is thus considerably more complex but also considerably more correct than the cruder Marxist position that surrenders the destiny of humankind solely to the inexorable force of economic drivers. In other words, from a Marxian perspective, both capitalists and Marxists get it wrong in that they understand the economy as a quasi-physical entity whose forces we might be able to compute but never alter. Instead we ought to see human freedom at the root of each and every societal institution in which our collective life is organized. If some such forms are found to be exerting alienating influences, they can be changed.

The analysis of economic forces from the point of view of their contribution to human liberty continued in the works of **John Stuart Mill** (Chapter III.D) Michael Buckley shows that Mill was already thinking about ideas still being discussed by enthusiasts for sustainability: Are there limits to growth, and, instead of testing them, should we not rather aim to achieve and maintain a "stationary economy"? Challenging his peers and predecessors, Mill argued that it is a sign of societal maturity to reach a point where the focus of economic development is no longer growth but stability, reproducing wealth by replacing worn-out goods, maintaining capital stocks and carefully husbanding nonrenewable resources. If the purpose of the economy is to set human life free for the unfettered development of its mental and moral capacities, why should it grow beyond the point where it supplies people with enough wealth to free them from life's hardships?

Freedom, for Mill, includes freedom from excess work and from conformity pressures to engage in it (such as through a culture of overconsumption). Continuous growth keeps people toiling ceaselessly, but conscious limits on the growth of economies can become economic preconditions for increased leisure and happiness. Higher and more cultivated pleasures than sheer commodity consumption require that people have sufficient time and education to engage in them. So, if our policies pursue limitless economic growth, these policies might unwittingly undermine improved societal happiness by exchanging the cultural conditions for human improvement, such as leisure, for ever smaller gains in material pleasure; thus engineering rapid progress in the wrong direction.

Mill challenges the concept of economic "value neutrality" that the proponents of growth-oriented economies typically put forward when arguing against democratic regulation. However, equating "neutrality" with "neutrality within and towards the realm of consumer choices" inevitably favors commodities over all other valuables. The liberty to indulge in noncommercial interests – such as the enjoyment of national parks, or of public spaces without advertising – is thus being thwarted by the liberties of marketers, advertisers, and other professional commodity "pushers" to serve their vested interests.

Not only because of our present interest to preserve our natural environments intact but also from a concern for the preservation of cultural and political autonomy, one ought to speak out in favor of the idea of less economic growth, at least in richer societies. Obviously, argues Buckley, the idea of the stationary economic state is not to be imposed from above but must be adopted from below in order to meet the requirements for liberty in Mill's philosophy. It is incumbent therefore on academics and other nonpartisan voices to discuss in earnest the idea of the stationary economy, lest in the contest over public opinion the vested interests and their siren song of boundless growth forever prevail.

## Contemporary insights

Moving into the twentieth century (section IV), modern philosophy becomes postmodern in the sense that it reflects increasingly on the cultural and social preconditions of the modern mindset. Whereas modern philosophers argued straightforwardly for their understandings of freedom and autonomy-based ethics, the postmodern condition reinforces sensitivity to the fact that across time and cultures, diversity, rather than uniformity, is the hallmark of philosophical reflection. This insight has an impact on present-day philosophical methodologies. Whereas modern thinkers focused mostly on the *substantive* contents of their respective ethical theories, postmodern approaches pay much more attention to *procedural* questions about how to arrive at convergent moral understandings. For instance, instead of addressing the social diversity of viewpoints on liberty from a preconceived understanding of freedom, the business of the postmodern philosopher can be described, in brief, as moving in the opposite direction, from an acknowledgment of that diversity to its possible reconciliation through an overlapping consensus of varied worldviews.

The simultaneity of manifold and often contrary moral perspectives is the very problem on which **Jürgen Habermas** concentrates (Chapter IV.A). In a society whose subsystems have become differentiated to a high degree and where, at the same time, the population is multicultural, the likelihood that a single ethical system can satisfactorily answer all pertinent questions is low. Suzan Langenberg shows how the communicative ethics of Habermas addresses this problem and how it can be applied to the interface between business and society in order to solve the chronic tensions that exist between their respective tendencies and often incompatible claims.

For communication processes marred by contested claims about relevance and truth, Habermas proposes an interesting regulative ideal. Notwithstanding disagreement on the *material* level, he holds that unanimity about the *formal* procedures on how to corroborate or falsify contested claims can be elaborated through discourse in what he terms the *ideal speech situation*. Scientific communities approximate this ideal of constructive communication, since their discourses are characterized by multiple different voices expressing dissent over a wide range of theories, while still agreeing on how to settle such disputes by the standards of good research and argumentation. Likewise, in the social and political arena, Habermas argues, we can make use of the regulative ideal of fair, unbiased, and productive discourse.

While it is unlikely that any factual communication ever fully meets all the requirements of this *ideal speech situation*, the normative power of this construct nevertheless does operate in how we communicate with one another in real life. An individual who wants to persuade others will typically aim to appear unbiased, taking opposing views under appropriate consideration, arguing by competence and reason rather than from authority and power, and so on. Making this implicitly operative ideal of fair communication explicit, the theory of the *ideal speech situation* points us to a form of stakeholder dialogue to which different parties can agree to aspire: a model of conversation undistorted by vested interests and the asymmetries of power; a dialogue, that is to say, that can raise the quality of argumentation through the participation of all and the representation of everyone concerned. Thus orientation towards the Habermasian construct of the *ideal speech situation* can help business to engage in more honest, globally acceptable and trust-building interchanges, especially when communicating with its critics.

Once, however, society does engage in an open dialogue about the appropriate norms for socioeconomic life, what ideas should guide the debate? The economist **Amartya Sen** and the philosopher **Martha Nussbaum** (Chapter IV.B) have tried to answer this question with their so-called capabilities approach. Against the narrowly materialistic anthropology that underlies neoclassical economics and depicts the economic agent as a *homo oeconomicus*, acting always and for ever as a solitary, self-interested, and perfectly rational maximizer of utility, Sen and Nussbaum pit quite a different theory; one that, in the language of Benedetta Giovanola, emphasizes the "anthropological richness" of human life.

Reality diverges from the axioms of the *homo oeconomicus* model not only through a *minus* of preference-stability, acuity of information, and rational consistency, as research on the "bounded rationality" of the human being has long emphasized, but also, Sen and Nussbaum argue, through a *plus* of ethical and sociorelational dimensions hitherto disregarded by neoclassical economics. Since the human person realizes himself in and through different relations, each characterized by commitments to values of a varied nature, a uniform and purely quantitative assessment of human aspirations as "utility maximization" fails to reflect the important qualitative distinctions people make between the different things they value. In consequence, while conventional models describe economic behavior as resulting in an algorithmic manner from a calculation of fixed, rank-ordered internal preferences in the light of changing external environs and incentives, Sen and Nussbaum stress the permanent dimension of human freedom underlying all economic agency.

The concept of economic freedom endorsed by Sen and Nussbaum, says Benedetta Giovanola, is not one of an arbitrary freedom of choice which aims for the quantitative maximization of options. On the contrary, since "the distinctive feature of anthropological richness is not of a quantitative, but of a qualitative kind, it is also clear that anthropological richness cannot be simply interpreted as a matter of 'how much' one can do or be; it rather concerns the substantive freedom to flourish and to select valuable states and capabilities." Hence economic decision-making should be democratic, not technocratic. Before making (quantitative) econometric computations we need to make a (qualitative) public evaluation of the goals desired for business and the economy. What should they be?

Since personal freedom is realized in the concrete capabilities of each of us, we will find the most appropriate use of our collective economic means in servicing the development of free capability of each person. The material preconditions of a free life can be fostered by social interaction. Consequently, argue Sen and Nussbaum, the overarching objective of a liberal socioeconomic system should be the creation of conditions that improve the capabilities of all to enjoy the freedoms they (have reason to) value. Instead of mere quantitative growth, this qualitative development of our productive forces should from now on be defined and pursued as economic success.

While Sen and Nussbaum emphasize the consequences of a qualitative orientation towards the human being in the context of *economic ethics*, **Robert Solomon's** theory of virtue ethics (Chapter IV.C) translates this same idea into the realm of *business ethics*. Ulrike Kirchengast reports how, according to Solomon, we have come to create mistaken myths and metaphors about the business world, which continue to have a dehumanizing impact on the self-perception of business people. Four such myths and metaphors Solomon finds especially at fault: the *war metaphor*, leading to business people seeing themselves as warrior-like; the *machine metaphor* that treats people as easily replaceable cogs in a machine; the *myth of abstract greed*, defining business as a mere means of making money; and the *game metaphor*, which fails to differentiate between spectators and players.

Let us unfold this message: When business people use military rhetoric involving "plans of attack," "battle strategies," and "campaigns" in order to describe their business activities, it is little wonder that such martial metaphors influence managerial behavior, marking out ruthlessness as a virtue. In a similar vein, machine metaphors, by implying that human beings are comparable to ball-bearings, lead to business concepts that discount individuality and reduce human beings to the mere function they are assigned to carry out. Likewise the business myth of abstract greed distorts our perspective on economic life. Gaining a sense of purpose and satisfaction from taking on corporate responsibility and contributing to something greater than enrichment becomes redundant when all motivations to engage in business activities are believed to rest ultimately on covetousness. Last, the game metaphor overlooks the fact that most people are not in business for the excitement. The game metaphor neglects the serious consequences business decisions have on society; foul play by business injures not only the players on the opposing side but also risks the welfare of third parties who never signed up to be part of the game.

Solomon explains, "What all these myths have in common is an alienating effect on the self-concept of people working in business as well as a contorted image of business within the rest of society." Those myths misdirect us towards false beliefs of what a good, productive life entails and how we define personal success and the role of business in society, thus putting into practice the underlying reduced theoretical understanding of the nature of business. In contrast to such reductionist mental models, Solomon defends business as "a social activity that presupposes [...] a set of some basic virtues like honesty and trustworthiness." He aims, in other words, to overcome bottom-line thinking with a theory that describes business as an essential part of a moral conception of the good life.

Solomon reaches back to the (especially Aristotelian) tradition of vir-tue ethics in order to make clear that excellence in business never just means financial success. Rather, in the notion of excellence in busi-ness the moral and the economic dimensions are fused. The paragon of a business leader whose accomplishments prove to be sustainable is someone who also excels in virtue, because virtue makes the personal relationships on which the long-term success of business depend last and thrive. Hence a much more fitting metaphor for business life is that of a "corporate culture," as the concept of *culture* emphasizes the social and socially construed nature of business. Based on shared values, com-mon practices and rituals, people belonging to any culture develop a sense of togetherness and an ethical compact: There are ground rules that hold the collective endeavor together and protect it from internal as well as external corruption. Since a corporation is never an isolated, freestanding culture but embedded in the societies in which it oper-ates, it must conceive of itself as a "citizen" of those larger cultures too. Consequently, Solomon's business ethics argues in favor of the idea of *corporate citizenship*, which depicts the corporation as an agent with codeterminative moral responsibilities for the public realm in which it operates.

For any ethics to have a practical effect, it must be rooted in our emotional understanding of our self and our world. This is the insight that Julian Friedland draws from his analysis of **Ludwig Wittgenstein** (Chapter IV.D). Wittgenstein doubts the power of pure theory to pro-pel us into action. Rather, he holds, convictions and practices result from pre-reflective sentiments and interpretations of a nontheoretical nature. To promote ethics one therefore should do more than merely give a true account of the good; one must be concerned with questions of ethical motivation.

Typically, face-to-face relations provide us with concrete experiences (such as seeing the pain or pleasure of others) which trigger emotional reactions capable of inspiring our moral agency. When, however, such concrete input is lacking, as in the frequently extremely abstract rela-tionships of global business transactions, this customary way of evok-ing moral responses proves deficient. Hence it is of utmost importance to find a functional equivalent to the density and intensity of face-to-face relationships for the realm of global interaction.

Through the interplay between the virtual personalities of multina-tional corporations, represented through their brands, on one hand, and on the other, through a growing global consciousness resulting from the diffuse communicative acts of many individuals and the concerted action of the media, such a functional equivalent can, however, be constructed. It is essential that the abstractness of ethical demands is complemented by concrete perceptions that successfully carry its message across cultures. Just as global marketing puts an individual face on the positive effects of business products and services, its negative externalities must also be captured in gripping pictures and narratives. For the success of humanistic ethics on a global scale, close attention to the aesthetic and symbolic preconditions of its worldwide perception and application, is essential, argues Friedland.

## Intercultural perspectives

So far, all the ethical positions discussed originated from thinkers anchored within the Western tradition. In a globalized world, however, a crucial question is precisely whether and how insights gained within one cultural framework also carry over to others. Given the moral and cultural diversity of their employees, today's managers encounter this problem directly. On the one hand, in any given situation, one cannot but impute one's own understanding of what it means to, for instance, promote the good, refrain from harmful actions, and respect human dignity. On the other hand, misunderstandings and conflicts frequently ensue from such imputations. Intercultural understanding is needed in order to reduce the frequency of cross-cultural pitfalls and moderate their effects. A central task for contemporary management is hence the study of cultural and ethnic differences in order to learn what notions like harm, the good, and respect mean for people from different backgrounds. The idea of a humanistic ethics for the age of globality thus requires the integration of divergent notions of decent behavior into our account of morality.

Monika Kirloskar-Steinbach argues that in the **Indian and Chinese tradition** (Chapter V.A), too, the humanistic ideal has found ample expression. Cultural diversity thus does not defeat the case for a shared global ethics. While often different from the West and internally diverse, Asian traditions agree with Western accounts of humanity in their description of human fallibility and frailty as well as the perfectibility of human life, based on an innate sense of morality, advanced through a honing of intellectual skills and learning, benevolence, and mutual respect.

Kirloskar believes that we must rid ourselves of prejudices about Asian cultures that block the path toward a productive intellectual interchange with their value systems. In the West, examples of such mental barriers are assumptions that Eastern cultures are too authoritarian and hierarchical for the development of an ethics based upon critical reasoning, or that Asiatic philosophies are far too spiritualistic to render practical advice for the material world of business. Both views, Monika Kirloskar shows, are mistaken.

While it is true that some Eastern thinkers, like many Western intellectuals, have warned against a form of untrammeled reasoning that sets out to dissolve traditional or metaphysical frameworks, they are nonetheless fierce advocates of critical intellectual scrutiny. Since all human beings, including figures of wisdom and authority, are perceived to be fallible, traditional positions must never simply be accepted as infallible final truths but always be subjected to close scrutiny. The quality of traditional as well as nontraditional arguments can, after all, only be ascertained if people learn to think for themselves and differentiate sound from unsound reasoning.

Likewise, the admittedly strong emphasis that Eastern thinkers put on the spiritual liberation of the individual does not stand in the way of a development of an ethics with tangible applications to social life. On the contrary, important sociomoral strictures result precisely from the convergence of many Asian traditions on the view that material happiness is transitory and contingent on circumstance. The human condition is seen as one that benefits from material goods but gains more from being integrated into an intact social community. Since true human well-being can only be achieved within a healthy social setting that also caters to the spiritual and moral health of individuals, one should realize material needs only in ways stipulated by that framework and never give expression to material desires in ways that threaten to tear the social fabric.

With regard to more specific postulates on how to organize human life Eastern thinkers differ just as much amongst themselves as do their Western colleagues. For instance, the Chinese philosophers Mo Tze and Meng Tze took strictly opposing views in the debate on universalism versus particularism. Whereas Mo Tze argued for universal and global love as the overarching principle of ethics, Meng Tze set great store by the specificity of close-knit personal relationships.

Mo Tze thought only a cosmic perspective (seeking moral orientation by a contemplation of the ways of "heaven") would give us the requisite intellectual breadth to overcome the pettiness of particularistic strivings so as to extend benevolence to all human beings alike. People would eventually respond to this unselfish and impartial love in kind, and a reciprocal exchange of benefits could occur from all sides, furthering the well-being of everyone. Peace and harmony can thrive, once we refrain from restricting our love only to the borders of our own communities. It is hence imperative that we extend a helping hand to all mankind.

In contrast, Meng Tze based his ethics on the intimate feeling of inborn filial piety, which can be widened slowly, gradually, and in ever-increasing circles, first to one's siblings, then to the larger family, and so on, until the feeling and practice of respect ultimately extends to all human beings. While particularistic in *genesis*, the ethics of Meng Tze is thus at the same time universalistic in its intended scope and *validity*. According to Meng Tze, all human beings "possess common traits like compassion, shame, respect, and the capacity to differentiate between right and wrong. These traits, in turn, enable cardinal virtues of benevolence (*ren*), dutifulness (*yi*), observance of rites (*li*), wisdom (*zhi*), and faith (*hsin*) which are crucial to the relationship between father and son, between rulers and ruled, between man and woman, between young and old, and between friends."

So, while Mo Tze advocates the application of the cosmopolitan principles of his ethics of love in a top-down direction, and Meng Tze defends a bottom-up approach to globality, they agree on important humanistic tenets. Both argue that each person possesses an innate, moral disposition that can be brought to the fore by the right care and nourishment. Given the frailty of human life, without a strong commitment to moral principles, and without concentrated self-cultivation, we run the risk of giving in to adverse circumstances. Virtue, and consequently the good life, can only be realized in community with others who foster our pursuit of what is just and good.

It is therefore vital that we erect a social order which is truly meritocratic. We must prefer authority based on competence over authority based on role, and give power only to those deserving respectful subordination. *Vice versa*, striving for, and attaining of virtue becomes crucial for the adequate fulfillment of management positions in business and society. The accumulation of power by persons without competence and virtue must be avoided.

A similar lesson can be learned from the various traditions of **African humanism** (Chapter V.B). While emphasis on individuality and specificity within a range of African cultures is important in order to counter any tendency to homogenize and lump so-called African thought into a single category, we can nevertheless identify features of commonality and similarity across the different versions of humanistic thinking on the African continent. Not in politics necessarily, but as basic conceptual matters of semantics and social meanings at work in and throughout African societies, certain ideas of a common humanity prevail. Different regions of Africa share, for example, the idea of humans as social beings who are bound to each other by mutual moral obligations, from which arises a common rhetoric of sociality and solidarity. Under various names – in Swahili, for example, through the concepts of *utu* (humanity, being human), *ujamaa* (familyhood), *upendano* (mutual love) and *undugu* (brotherhood, comradeship) or through the use of *ubuntu* (meaning "humanity" in the Southern African Nguni group of the Bantu languages) – the African cultures make an important contribution "to a truly global discourse of humanism," according to Kai Kresse.

Humanistic thought grew especially during colonial and postcolonial times, trying to overcome separation and build a sense of community upon relevant notions of African identity. The principal use of humanistic rhetoric was productive and constructive: In the anticolonial liberation struggles, African leaders and intellectuals invoked the universal humanistic ideals of freedom, equality, and dignity. Staunch in their rejection of imperialism, colonialism and racism that had not only oppressed African peoples but also violated their communal norms and traditional values, projections of a more humanistic past and future served as regulative ideals to nourish and foster a renewed African identity. A vision of African humanism was created in order to overcome a dehumanizing reality.

The gradual development of African humanism can be captured in the image of a hermeneutical spiral: Moral reflection begins with and draws from established social and religious notions, beliefs, and convictions, such as standards of proper behavior (vis-à-vis one's spouse, parents, children and friends). Inspired by communal practices and the widespread teachings of the Qur'an, the idea takes root that one has a moral obligation not only to stay on the right path oneself but also to prevent one's peers from failing to fulfill their ethical roles. From clear responsibilities for those on whose well-being one has influence, begins a moral discourse of a self-reflective nature which ultimately also engages critically with the very traditions it stems from. Through a gradual widening of the circles of responsibility, African thinkers built up universalistic concepts of what it means to be human and what it means to be good, ending eventually with a stern critique of tribalism, parochialism, and ethnocentrism (*ukabila*) in favor of an all-encompassing idea of human friendship and a truly global human unity.

Today, an important moral function of humanistic ideals in Africa is to reconstruct a common framework of moral expectations and obligations that defends basic moral concerns and assumptions implicit in the customs and conventions of African societies, and to assert these human-centered visions of mutual aid and solidarity against tendencies of selfishness, envy, laziness, and greed. Against a backdrop of governmental authoritarianism, the corrective power of such ideals to advance leadership based on consensus and to improve the involvement of citizens in their own governance becomes particularly important.

Rejecting overly narrow (technocratic and materialistic) understandings of human reason and social progress by a defense of various countervailing factors such as emotional rationality, communal spirituality, relational personhood, and the natural creativity of the human mind, proverbs and sayings are often used to express as well as to illustrate more comprehensive notions of human rationality and identity. Mediated both in written and oral discourse, the overarching consensus of the various humanistic traditions of Africa, Kresse suggests, lies in the important insight that a human being is and becomes human (as well as humane) *through others*. Without ethics, no functioning sociality; without sociality, no fully-developed personality; this is the general idea behind the Swahili concept of *utu* that stands for humanity *and* goodness at the same time.

True mutual and charitable concern for each other, although not always prevailing in life, is, in this perspective, much more than a mere moral demand upon individuals; it presents a formula for flourishing sociality, a orientating norm on how to live well, together with others. A purely calculating attitude, including the attitude that money can buy everything and that human needs, wishes, and desires can be subordinated to anticipated material gains, is rejected throughout African cultures. "If one treats one's human peers as things, one does not respect their *utu* (humanity); moreover, one shows that one has no *utu*," explains Kresse. In this lies an important lesson for business relationships too. If pursued only strategically, with an eye to material gains alone, such an instrumental fashion of treating others will is likely to fail to produce the desired results, as such behavior runs counter to deeply held cultural values about how to treat fellow human beings. To follow a humanistic ethics in business is thus not only a postulate of corporate responsibility but also, simply, a way to corporate health.

## An emergent "humanistic consensus"?

Importantly, this strong form of moral universalism from both Asian and African contexts refutes as too simple all wholesale dismissals of universalistic positions as unjustifiable narratives of Eurocentric origin. It demonstrates, instead, how similar humanistic viewpoints can be developed from different places across time and space. Existing cultural diversity, we learn, can be integrated into the concept of a humanistic ethics and need not conflict with it. If we abstain from identifying each part of the world with a unique, fixed, and uniform set of values, the internal diversity of the world's cultures and their variegated voices opens up before our eyes. A readiness to reconsider our own cherished beliefs in the name of the one humanity on whose behalf we are debating and discussing must translate into a willingness to welcome alterity, even, indeed especially, in the form of diverging concepts of what it means to be human. Otherness is not for us to define; the other is respected when we honor his or her self-determination. A *procedural* approach to humanistic ethics therefore seems to be the way forward; through discourse and collaborative thinking a truly integrative ethics of humanity can indeed develop. We hope that this procedural approach – represented, for example, in the way a transnational consensus about the recently proposed social responsibility standard ISO 26000 was worked out and how this standard suggests that future stakeholder conflicts be settled – will gain further support both in academe and in practice.

*The Humanistic Management Network* and the authors of this volume have undertaken a first step towards a global discourse on humanistic ethics. By revisiting the intellect of thinkers across the globe and throughout the ages, we hope that participants in this debate will have gained useful insights into the intellectual foundations of (ethical) business practices and humanistic management. The synopsis of our study shows an emergent *humanistic consensus*. Thinkers from all ages and regions agree that the institutions and forces governing both business and society can be altered by human endeavor. The seemingly impersonal powers that govern politics and the economy are but the objectified dimension of our subjective freedom. As we are responsible for the use of the latter, so we are capable of changing the former. Alienation is not inevitable. Another world, a more humane world, is possible. As the intellectual realization of our freedom for responsible action paves the way for its practical realization, our discourse on humanistic ethics in the age of globality is an attempt to contribute to the very change we wish to see in our lives. We ask our readers to remain in discussion with us, as *The Humanistic Management Network* continues its research through further book projects – all dedicated to working towards a humanistic paradigm shift in the realm of business and socioeconomic literature.

We will consider our endeavors to be truly successful only when, independently from us, the discussion is furthered and carried beyond the confines of our personal and academic networks. We wholeheartedly invite our readers to take part in this dissemination and broadening of the humanistic perspective.

## Note

1. Keynes, J. M. (1936). *The general theory of employment interest and money*, London: Macmillan and Co., 383f.

## Bibliography

Appiah, A., *Cosmopolitanism: ethics in a world of strangers*, (London: Allen Lane, 2006).

Bakan, J., *The corporation : the pathological pursuit of profit and power*, (Penguin Books, Canada, 2004).

Bhagwati, J. N., *In defense of globalization*, (Oxford; New York, Oxford University Press, 2007).

Berger, A. A., *The objects of affection: semiotics and consumer culture*, (New York: Palgrave Macmillan 2010).

Brodbeck, K.-H., *Entscheidung zur Kreativität*, (Darmstadt: Wissenschaftliche Buchgesellschaft, 1995).

Ebrahim, A., and Weisband, E., *Global accountabilities: participation, pluralism, and public ethics*, (Cambridge; New York: Cambridge University Press, 2007).

Elkington, J., and Hartigan, P., *The power of unreasonable people: how social entrepreneurs create markets that change the world*, (Boston, Mass.: Harvard Business School Press, 2008).

Featherstone, M., *Consumer culture and postmodernism*, (London; Newbury Park, Calif.: Sage Publications, 1991).

Galbraith, J. K., *The new industrial state*, (Boston: Houghton Mifflin, 1967).

Geerk, F., *2000 Jahre Humanismus: der Humanismus als historische Bewegung*, (Basel: Schwabe, 1998).

Klein, N., *No logo: taking aim at the brand bullies*, (New York: Picador, 1999).

Meadows, D. H., and Club of Rome., *The Limits to growth; a report for the Club of Rome's project on the predicament of mankind*, (New York: Universe Books, 1972).

Pogge, T. W. M., Moellendorf, D. and Horton, K. 2008. *Global responsibilities*, St. Paul, MN, Paragon House.

Polanyi, K., *The great transformation*, (Boston: Beacon Press, 1957).

Ruggie, J. G., *Embedding global markets: an enduring challenge*, (Aldershot, England; Burlington, VT: Ashgate, 2008).

Sullivan, W. M. and Kymlicka, W., *The globalization of ethics*, (Cambridge; New York: Cambridge University Press, 2007).

von Kimakowitz, E., Pirson, M., Spitzeck, H., Dierksmeier, C., and Amann, W. "Humanistic Management in Practice", H. M. Network, (ed.) *Humanism in Business*. (New York: Palgrave Macmillan, 2010).

# Index

293